"Collectively, the book's contributors illuminate the richness and complexity of the field, and they articulate why the Midwest deserves consideration anew in both scholarly research and the popular imagination."
—Elizabeth Grennan Browning, *Michigan*

"This is a valuable contribution to a reenergi
of midwestern history will need to be famil
academic and public libraries will want to a
—Robert G. Barrows, *Indiana Magazine of History*

"*Finding a New Midwestern History* provides convincing proof that the Midwest requires serious scholarly engagement. The twenty-one essays reveal a region bursting with unexplored questions about its past. . . . These essays serve as a first step by providing modes to inquire into the complex narratives that these authors illuminate. It promises to be electrifying work."
—Sara Egge, *Agricultural History*

"Reflects the laudable strengthening of midwestern academic studies in recent years and is another important contribution to midwestern studies by the University of Nebraska Press."
—*Omaha World-Herald*

"This engaging collection of essays examines midwestern history from a wide variety of perspectives, offering valuable insights into the region."
—William C. Barnett, *Annals of Iowa*

"This new edited collection stands as an important guidepost for some of the more recent trends and issues in the new midwestern history. It is a superb collection on an important topic. It is a unique contribution to the rebirth of midwestern history."
—Gregory Schneider, professor of history at Emporia State University and author of *Rock Island Requiem: The Collapse of a Mighty Fine Line*

"[The editors and contributors] have made a strong case for revisiting midwestern regionalism. . . . The book is written in clear, precise, lively, and often evocative prose."
—Michael Allen, professor of history at the University of Washington–Tacoma

"There is no single 'Midwest,' of course, but projects such as this . . . offer a much-needed alternative to disdain and cheerleading alike."
—John Wilson, *First Things*

"The editors and authors deliver a rewarding excursion into a new field. Readers interested in the Midwest will come away with a greatly enriched appreciation for the region."
—Jonathan Kasparek, kirkcenter.org

"Unexpected, intensely satisfying, and full of riches."
—Steve Donoghue, *Open Letters Review*

FINDING A NEW MIDWESTERN HISTORY

FINDING A NEW MIDWESTERN HISTORY

*Edited and with an introduction by Jon K. Lauck,
Gleaves Whitney, and Joseph Hogan*

University of Nebraska Press ❧ Lincoln

Publication of this volume was assisted by The Virginia Faulkner Fund, established in memory of Virginia Faulkner, editor in chief of the University of Nebraska Press.

Library of Congress Cataloging-in-Publication Data
Names: Lauck, Jon, 1971– editor. | Whitney, Gleaves, editor. | Hogan, Joseph, 1946– editor.
Title: Finding a new midwestern history / edited and with an introduction by Jon K. Lauck, Gleaves Whitney, and Joseph Hogan.
Description: Lincoln: University of Nebraska Press, 2018. | Includes bibliographical references and index.
Identifiers: LCCN 2017053349
ISBN 9781496201829 (cloth: alk. paper)
ISBN 9781496222350 (paperback)
ISBN 9781496208798 (epub)
ISBN 9781496208804 (mobi)
ISBN 9781496208811 (pdf)
Subjects: LCSH: Middle West—History.
Classification: LCC F351 .F46 2018 | DDC 977—dc23 LC record available at https://lccn.loc.gov/2017053349

Set in Minion Pro by E. Cuddy.

Dedicated to the Memory of
James Seaton, 1944–2017:
husband, father,
scholar, midwesterner

Contents

PART 6. THE MIDWESTERN EXPERIENCE

Illustrations

Table

Introduction

TOWARD A NEW MIDWESTERN HISTORY

Jon K. Lauck, Joseph Hogan, and Gleaves Whitney

About lunchtime on the first Saturday in May of 2015, midwesterners from Toledo to Chicago were caught off guard by the unfamiliar rumble of an earthquake underfoot.[1] Registering a modest magnitude of 4.2, the tremor caused limited damage—chimneys cracked, wall plaster splintered, cans of soup toppled from their shelves. Since such events are rare for the Upper Midwest, most commentators called the earthquake a freak occurrence. Near the epicenter of the quake, at Grand Valley State University in Grand Rapids, Michigan, historians of the American Midwest had gathered that same day at another extremely rare event—to discuss the history, culture, and geography of their region. The symbolism of these simultaneously rare occurrences was not lost on the scholars gathered in Michigan at a conference to talk about their region and its lost history.

In comparison to such regions as the South, the Far West, and New England, the Midwest and its culture—the history of its peoples and places; its literature, music, and art; the complexity and richness of its landscapes—had been neglected. And this neglect has been both scholarly and popular: historians as well as literary and art critics tend not to examine the Midwest seriously in their academic work, while the myth of the Midwest has not, in the popular imagination, ascended to the level of the proud, literary South; the cultured and storied Northeast; or the hip, innovative West Coast. The longtime regionalist and University of Nebraska historian John R. Wunder recently observed that large universities have abandoned the field of midwestern history, few scholars identify themselves as midwestern historians, research chairs in midwestern history are lacking, and graduate students are not trained in the field. Wunder argues that the "infrastructure for the study of the

Midwest is missing."[2] Too many colleges in the Midwest, some argue, tend to "shun the communities around them and to present themselves as not really Midwestern, but as scholarly outposts in flyover territory."[3] In scholarly circles at the end of the twentieth century, the Midwest had become a "lost region."[4]

What the historians gathered in Michigan in the spring of 2015 hoped to effect was, if not a seismic shift in scholarly and popular sentiment, at least a few rumbles on the cultural landscape, or to move the needle a bit on the cultural Richter scale. They hoped to give greater energy to the effort to revive midwestern history, which has of late included the creation of a new Midwestern History Association devoted to advancing the study of the Midwest similar to the scholarly associations active in other regions.[5] This effort has been bolstered by new academic journals and other outlets designed to promote the study of and writing about the Midwest.[6] At long last, it seems, substantive progress is being made toward reviving the field of midwestern history. The scholars gathered in Michigan in the spring of 2015 sought to spur and support that revival, and the chapters gathered here, which are derived from the lectures at that conference, are designed to move us toward a new and more robust field of midwestern history. With the critical leadership and assistance of the Hauenstein Center at Grand Valley State University and the Midwestern History Association, the 2015 "Finding the Lost Region" conference was held again in 2016, 2017, and 2018, and the conference became a critical generator of emerging work on the Midwest that is leading to larger projects.

The precise shape of a revived field of midwestern history has yet to be determined. This hoped-for revival is in its infancy and its results will not be fully ascertainable for another decade or more. A bit of midwestern modesty is needed during the early years of this effort, instead of the issuance of grand pronouncements about what the future will hold or what the field's precise contours will be decades hence. It should be said, however, that the intended result of this book and the broader movement is to give life to a moribund field of study, to promote a diversity of viewpoints within this field, and to generally give legitimacy to the serious study of a large region of the United States that has been neglected by scholars.

More narrowly, the purpose of this book is to disseminate the fruits of that highly unusual 2015 conference in Michigan and thereby to share the enthusiasm of the historians gathered at the prospect of a more vigorous future for midwestern studies. The topics first explored by the historians at the Michigan conference, and now here in the following chapters, are various, each representing yet another facet of midwestern history and culture worth examining more deeply. We hope they can each serve as a jumping-off point for more studies and inquiries that will enliven the study of the Midwest. We intend that they serve as the beginning of a much broader conversation, not a premature narrowing of what the field's future parameters might be.

The section "The Midwest as a Region" includes three chapters. In "The Birth of the Midwest and the Rise of Regional Theory," Michael C. Steiner examines the slow entry of the idea and location of the "Middle West" into the national consciousness during the thirty-year period between the 1880s and the 1910s. Focusing on this crucial era of emerging regional awareness, Steiner examines the role that a generation of intellectuals, artists, and public figures played at the birth of the region, acting as midwives and architects to shape not only public awareness of the Middle West but also of regionalism in general. Steiner focuses on architect Frank Lloyd Wright (1867–1959), writer Hamlin Garland (1860–1940), and historian Frederick Jackson Turner (1861–1932), all three of whom were among the first to label their native region the "Middle West" and were—along with California contemporary Josiah Royce (1855–1916)—the first Americans to develop self-conscious regional theories and aesthetic expressions. After comparing their distinctive regional concepts and their relationship to the pivotal 1893 World's Columbian Exposition in Chicago, Steiner concludes by pointing forward to deeper, more complex visions of the Midwest—drawing upon working-class, feminist, and multiracial perspectives—that would enrich midwestern regionalism across the twentieth century and into the present.

In "How Nature and Culture Shaped Early Settlement in the Midwest," James Davis examines the interplay of culture and geography in the Midwest. Davis argues that, in the Midwest, cultural desires and geographical realities heavily influenced the creation, growth, and fate of towns at falls or rapids on navigable rivers and on the inside and outside bends of navigable rivers. They also, according to Davis, influenced the creation and operation of farmsteads. Turbulent falls and rapids, water sweeping around river bends, and variations of wind, sunlight, and elevation helped shape the environment. Although many settlers had little formal education, Davis points out that they were eager to learn, and they responded intelligently to geographic forces in locating and constructing towns and farmsteads. Their knowledge and decision-making gave the Midwest the form and shape it maintains down to the present.

In the third chapter of the section, "First Cousins: The Civil War's Impact on Midwestern Identity," Nicole Etcheson explores the ways in which the Lower Midwest has shared ties—including settlement patterns, culture, and economic activities—with the Upper South. These ties, Etcheson points out, have at times included racist attitudes toward African Americans. During the Civil War, however, midwesterners asserted a Northern identity and came to accept advances in black rights such as emancipation and black male suffrage. After the Civil War, white midwesterners remained ambivalent about race: the Midwest included some segregation but not the disfranchisement and closely monitored racial lines of the South, and it included progress on civil rights alongside episodes of racial friction. Etcheson concludes that, although the Lower Midwest still shared much with the Upper South, the Civil War marked a breaking point at which the region increasingly distinguished itself as separate from the South. Etcheson's findings comport with Michael Steiner's emphasis on the emergence of a midwestern identity in the decades after the Civil War.

The second section of the book, "The Midwest's People," includes four chapters. In the first, "Native Americans and Midwestern History," Susan Gray considers an analytical challenge posed by regional accounts of Indigenous experience: the historical mobility of both the Midwest and the Native peoples who have lived, and continue to live, there. The movement of the Midwest, from the coinage of the term in the nineteenth century to the present, is directly related to the migrations of Native peoples in response to European and Euro-American colonialism. Until recently, accounts of Native Americans in the Midwest focused on the Ohio River valley and emphasized their migration from the region as a result of the federal Indian Removal Act of 1830, an interpretation dating from the late nineteenth century, a period when the Midwest became equated with the Old Northwest, whose history epitomized the national narrative predicated on the dispossession of Indigenous lands and peoples. In contrast, Gray shows that the federal policy of removal did not account for many migrations of Indigenous peoples west of the Mississippi, and she reflects on the enduring presence of the Anishinaabeg in the northern Great Lakes where removal completely failed.

In the second chapter in this section, "American and European Immigrant Groups in the Midwest by the Mid-Nineteenth Century," Gregory Rose examines the 1850 Census, investigating the distribution of birthplaces for the immigrant populations living in the five states of the Old Northwest in the mid-nineteenth century. Rose finds that settlers from different regions of the United States tended to concentrate in distinctive areas of the Old Northwest. Southern-born immigrants dominated in the southern portions of Ohio, Indiana, and Illinois; northerners from New England and New York were most prevalent in Michigan and Wisconsin and quite numerous in northern Ohio and northern Illinois. Midlanders, primarily from Pennsylvania, were most significantly present in the middle section of Ohio and westward into Illinois. Concentrations of foreign-born settlers, primarily from Germany, Ireland, and England, appeared in or near urban centers where labor was in demand, such as Cincinnati, Detroit, and Chicago. But their compatriots also formed notable rural settlements or colonies, such as the German areas at the end of Saginaw Bay in Michigan and in eastern Wisconsin or the Dutch region of west central Michigan, the place where the ground rumbled as the historians assembled in this volume discussed the future of midwestern studies. Rose concludes that, while scattered exceptions to this broad perspective existed—the African American population, for example, tended to be more southern in origin—these generalizations about population origins and distributions also held true for the 1860 Census, although by that time the percentage of United States–born immigrants to the Old Northwest was declining as the percentage of new arrivals born in foreign countries increased.

In "Civic Life in a Midwestern Community," Paula Nelson examines nineteenth- and early twentieth century midwestern communities, which relied on direct action by individuals, families, or neighborhoods to ameliorate the hardships of life. As Nelson describes, formal organizations such as churches, ladies' aid societies, or lodges worked to instill and support cultural values and personal character, provide companionship and sociability, community improvement, and uplift. Nelson describes the ways in which individuals and voluntary associations in one midwestern town provided for community needs. With the advent of economic consolidation by the end of the nineteenth century, these older forms of association, service, and community began to give way to nationally organized service clubs with different ideals.

In "Politics in the Promised Land," Jeffrey Helgeson places the history of the Great Migration of African Americans from the South to the Midwest between the 1920s and 1970s in the context of the much longer history of racial politics in the region. Helgeson begins with the fact that the Midwest was built on a vision of a white producers' republic hostile to black newcomers and that elements of racial inequality and segregation persist. At the same time, Helgeson acknowledges that the region also became a seedbed for important progress through the development of an abolitionist politics and from its own rich history of labor and civil rights struggles. From this perspective, Helgeson argues that the Great Migration did not introduce race as a problem to the Midwest. On the contrary, questions of racial inequality and exclusion were present from the beginning of the region, a point that becomes even clearer when one puts this history in the context of expropriation of Native Americans' land. Yet the region has been defined as well by the social openings, however limited, that black migrants and their descendants in the region enjoyed and then expanded as they created their own opportunities in the job markets, artistic worlds, and political arenas of a region that was much more open to black achievement than the Jim Crow South.

The section titled "The Iconic Midwest" features three chapters. In the first, "Midwestern Small Towns," John E. Miller begins by observing that, for three-quarters or so of their history, Americans largely matured and lived in the ubiquitous small towns that dotted the landscape. No section of the United States, Miller argues, has been shaped and affected so much by its small towns as the Midwest, and none has been more closely associated with them in the public mind. One must always distinguish between the symbolism and imagery that small towns project and the reality of the lives that are actually lived there, however. One should not, according to Miller, be surprised at the large degree of ambivalence that Americans exhibit in contemplating their small towns. After briefly analyzing the imagery associated with the subject, Miller goes on to discuss small towns' physical layouts, economic functions, social configurations, class divisions, and cultural manifestations. Always, time matters. Towns grew, evolved, and often declined as the decades passed by, influenced by the rise of industrialization, urbanization, bureaucratization, specialization, and professionalization. Many have been passed by and some are in survival mode, while countless others have literally become ghost towns. Miller concludes that, while broad social forces have generally determined whether small towns succeed or survive, the actions of people also still matter in the success of a midwestern small town.

According to Christopher Laingen, in "The Agrarian Midwest," during the twentieth century, the Midwest gradually and quietly transformed from a decentralized, mixed-crop-and-livestock farming area into a large-scale, cash-grain farming area, as soybeans began replacing rotation crops (wheat, oats, and hay) on the region's most productive land as well as on the more marginal lands that make up the region's periphery. The transformation, Laingen points out, has been geographically uneven and highly complex; in some areas this transformation has been completed for years, while in others it could be argued as to whether or not it has even begun. Laingen uses data from the Census of Agriculture at state and county scales from 1925 to 2012 to map changes in crops, livestock, and land use to help illustrate the dramatic changes that have and continue to occur on the Midwest's iconic rural landscape.

In the final chapter in this section, "The Role of Sports in the Midwest," David McMahon explains the prominence of sports in the American Midwest and how various forms of athletics blossomed in the region.

Drawing on his own experiences, the literature of midwestern sport, and the critical differences between the practice of sports in the Midwest in comparison to the American South and other regions, especially as it relates to race relations, McMahon opens a window on a major slice of experience for many midwesterners. In so doing, McMahon weakens an argument periodically made against the study of the Midwest.

The fifth section, "Midwestern Landscapes," features three chapters. In "The View from the River," Michael Allen examines the important role of rivers in the history of the Midwest and the creation of a unique midwestern river culture. Allen focuses on the Ohio and Upper Mississippi River valleys. Proceeding chronologically, Allen examines Mound Builder and Woodland Indian river cultures, European explorers, the military history of the river, riverboats and riverboatmen, and political debates over river improvements and the Army Corps of Engineers. Allen discusses the role of rivers as dividing lines between free and slave states, as well as the role of rivers in midwestern folklore and popular culture—folk heroes, newspaper humor, American literature, painting, and jazz, country, and rock-and-roll music, are all influences that have shaped American culture more generally but are seldom traced to the Midwest.

Jon Butler begins his chapter, "The Midwest's Spiritual Landscapes," by referencing Garrison Keillor's latest iconic image of midwestern religion—pleasant Protestants and Catholics united around lime Jell-O salad at small-town church suppers. Despite this imagery of homogeneity, according to Butler, the Midwest's religious tensions and bonds also demonstrate the region's surprising status as the nation's most religiously diverse area. Distinctive Indian cultures still clash over an invasive Christianity. Protestants imbibed anti-Catholicism, and Protestants and Catholics both imbibed antisemitism. Religion shaped community in townships, towns, and cities, especially for immigrants, whether Christians and Jews from Europe or African Americans from the American South. The region hosts major Protestant and Jewish denominational headquarters and powerful Catholic archdioceses. Its diversity, Butler points out, has long extended far beyond the familiar American Protestant–Catholic–Jewish triad, hosting America's first Islamic mosques, major late twentieth-century Hindu and Sikh populations, historic Mormon settlements, and a wealth of sects from the Amish to the Church of God of Anderson, Indiana, and Baháʼí to Guy Ballard's "I AM" movement—a region alive with spiritual possibility for as long as it has been settled.

In "The Development of Midwestern Cities," Jon Teaford explores how midwestern metropolises share a common historical trajectory that distinguishes them from cities in other regions. A distinctive regional heritage, Teaford argues, renders them a class apart. Most notably, the chief midwestern cities are all creations of the nineteenth century. The midwestern network of cities developed during the relatively short period from 1830 to 1890. The years 1890 to 1930 were, Teaford explains, a heyday for midwestern cities as they built upon their existing advantages and astounded the nation with new manifestations of their greatness. In contrast, the late twentieth century was a period of readjustment as midwestern metropolises coped with a world less favorable to their fortunes.

The fifth section, "The Midwest's Voices," includes four chapters. In "Of Murals and Mirrors," Zachary Michael Jack examines the personal histories and ideologies of three of regionalism's most deeply rooted muralists and artist-critics—Grant Wood, John Bloom, and Robert Francis White—while weaving these important legacies into a larger inquiry into the challenges facing the displaced regionalists of a digital age.

In "Midwestern Intellectuals," the late James Seaton suggests that one way to describe a "Midwest intellectual" would be a figure with midwestern ties whose ideas go against the grain of the progressive consensus dominating the media, academia, and cultural life generally on the coasts. Seaton focuses on four such figures: Christopher Lasch, Kenneth Rexroth, Russell Kirk, and Deirdre McCloskey, who were all born in the Midwest but none of whom are known primarily as midwesterners. Yet, as Seaton points out, each in their own way has ultimately challenged the coastal consensus by renewing and championing important aspects of what, for better or worse, are usually identified as "midwestern values"— traditional morality, cultural conservatism, and patriotism. We are sad to report that Professor Seaton passed away during the spring of 2017 after a heroic battle with cancer. This volume is dedicated to his memory.

In "Midwestern Musicians," James P. Leary explores how the Midwest's bedrock folk/vernacular musicians are culturally plural, polyglot, and multifaceted. They have been and continue to be rooted in the region but attentive to musical strains in contingent regions, the nation, and hearth or Old World nations. Similarly they are extensions of Anglo and African American traditions and their intersections, but also bound up with the sounds of Woodland Indians and European immigrants, especially Germanic, Irish, Scandinavian, and Slavic peoples. This chapter focuses on key historical moments, movements, and infrastructures in Chicago—a destination and crossroads at the Midwest's center—during a crucial formative period from the late nineteenth through the mid-twentieth century.

In "Midwestern Writers," David Pichaske explores the many representations of the Midwest throughout the nation's history: a frontier Other full of escape, space, adventure, and potential (Twain's *Huck Finn*, Rolvaag's *Giants in the Earth*); the quintessence of America, both small town and industrial-capitalist (Lewis's *Main Street*, Sinclair's *The Jungle*); and a perhaps nostalgic retreat from postmodernist abstraction and political chaos (Garrison Keillor's *Lake Wobegon Days*, Robert Bly's *Silence in the Snowy Fields*). While younger Midwest writers may accommodate currently popular agendas of cultural diversity, political correctness, environmentalism, and even neo-Gothicism, Pichaske suggests they should operate in the tradition of Midwest realism, being concrete and accurate, both historically and environmentally. Or, Pichaske argues, midwesterners might just forget the national audience and its notions and write to themselves in their own tradition. Pichaske concludes that while distribution is difficult these days, any number of authors and publications show that printed books can still be successfully marketed to a regional audience, adding that midwesterners might also move in the direction of online publication and distribution.

The sixth and final section, "The Midwestern Experience," features four chapters. In "The Upper Midwest as the Second Promised Land," Gleaves Whitney links the Upper Midwest to the American republic's founding generation. In popular culture, the founders' lives and achievements are embedded along the Eastern Seaboard, not the interior flyover country. Yet George Washington and other founders wrote frequently and fervently of the strategic importance of places like the Upper Mississippi Valley, the Great Lakes, and Detroit. It is no overstatement to say that the founding generation became preoccupied with the future heartland of America. In terms of the impact on the Upper Midwest's historical geography, three founders in particular would influence the future heartland. Thomas Jefferson, Alexander Hamilton, and John Adams all developed ideas for the new republic—including its western lands—that were both overlapping and competing. This chapter, which joins historical geography to intellectual history, looks into the Jeffersonian vision of establishing an agrarian republic, the Hamiltonian vision of establishing a commercial republic, and the Adamsian vision of establishing a virtuous republic. Each of these three species of republic can be identified with corresponding landscape features in the Upper Midwest. While the conventional use of these adjectives—Jeffersonian, Hamiltonian, Adamsian; agrarian, commercial, virtuous—simplifies as well as overstates the differences among the three visions, it also provides useful analytic categories to understand the development of the United States in the nineteenth century when the three visions coexisted and would make their mark on the Upper Midwest's landscapes.

Pamela Riney-Kehrberg, in "Growing Up Midwestern," examines the complicated task of describing the term "midwestern childhood." Growing up midwestern, Riney-Kehrberg explains, encompasses a whole range of historical experiences, from childhood and youth on one of the region's many family farms, to life in a high-rise housing project in Chicago, or another of the Midwest's larger cities. It encompasses life on farms and in towns of all sizes. It includes the lives of many children of middling economic origins, as well as the rich and desperately poor. Riney-Kehrberg concludes that this ought to be an area of greater research if a unified narrative of midwestern childhood and youth is to be written.

In "The Best of Babbitt," Hank Meijer illustrates how the stereotypes and contradictions of the American Midwest and the tensions inherent in what it means to be a midwesterner are nowhere better exemplified than in the unlikely odyssey of Michigander Arthur Vandenberg. Chronicling Vandenberg's career from his beginning as editor of the

Grand Rapids Herald to his rise to prominence in the U.S. Senate, Meijer carefully explores the distinctly midwestern character of his subject. Vandenberg's feuds and friendship with Sinclair Lewis and Robert Taft, his leadership in the American delegation at the founding of the United Nations, as well as on the Marshall Plan and the resolution enabling NATO, reveal, as Meijer shows, the global consequences of Vandenberg's commitment to the Midwest.

In "Of Conformity and Cosmopolitanism," J. L. Anderson asks whether people in the Midwest, given the growth of mass culture and the standardization of American life since World War II, can claim any particular traits that mark them as unique. Indeed, some midwesterners have identified conformity as one of the traits that people in the region have demonstrated throughout the period. Conformity to boosterism and market-oriented agrarian ideology has been pervasive, Anderson explains. For all their conformity, however, many middle-class midwesterners have demonstrated a significant degree of cosmopolitanism. Regardless of where they live, midwesterners simultaneously recognize the value of home as well as the wider world. Garrison Keillor's fictional Lake Wobegon has been a common cultural reference point for white, middle-class midwesterners as they articulate who they are, including both conformity and cosmopolitanism. Anderson concludes that while Keillor and others have lamented the loss of unique regional identity in the Midwest, it persists and is highlighted when midwesterners leave home.

After Anderson's lecture in Michigan in the spring of 2015, it was announced that Garrison Keillor would be retiring and, as a result, that perhaps the best-known voice of the Midwest in recent decades would soon be going silent, or at least losing its former prominence. However one may view the work of Keillor, his retirement is surely another sign that scholars should work harder to give some voice to the history of the Midwest. We hope this volume and the work of its many authors will aid the process of giving voice to a forgotten region and of reconnecting to an earlier and once strong tradition of midwestern historical and literary regionalism.[7] Based on the success of that earth-moving conference in 2015, which is the basis of this volume, and on various and related initiatives, we think that progress is being made and that, as Wisconsin's largest newspaper has opined, the "study of Midwestern history is now having a moment."[8] We hope to make it last.

Notes

1. Ralph Ellis, "Rare earthquake shakes western Michigan, registers magnitude of 4.2," CNN, May 3, 2015.
2. Jon K. Lauck, "Interview of John R. Wunder," *Great Plains Quarterly* 35, no. 3 (Summer 2015): 298.
3. Frederick E. Witzig, "The Perils and Promise of Midwestern Studies," *Studies in Midwestern History* 1, no. 2 (March 2015): 15 (quoting Richard Longworth).
4. Jon K. Lauck, *The Lost Region: Toward a Revival of Midwestern History* (Iowa City: University of Iowa Press, 2013).
5. Jennifer Schuessler, "Plowing Deeper: A New Historical Association for the Midwest," *New York Times*, October 22, 2014; Jon K. Lauck, "The Origins and Progress of the Midwestern History Association, 2013–2016," *Studies in Midwestern History* 2, no. 11 (October 2016), 139–49.
6. Margery Beck, "Historians Seek Revival of Studying the Midwest," Associated Press wire story, March 8, 2014; Donald Liebenson, "New Journal Focuses on Midwest History," *Chicago Tribune*, October 24, 2014; "Literary Journal 'Midwestern Gothic' Paints a Portrait of the Region," Michigan Public Radio, April 16, 2015.
7. Jon K. Lauck, *From Warm Center to Ragged Edge: The Erosion of Midwestern Literary and Historical Regionalism, 1920–1965* (Iowa City: University of Iowa Press, 2017) and Jon K. Lauck, ed., *The Midwestern Moment: The Forgotten World of Early Twentieth-Century Midwestern Regionalism, 1880–1940* (Hastings NE: Hastings College Press, 2017).
8. Bill Glauber, "A Bar Full of Academics, a Few Old-Fashioneds, and Donald Trump Spur Midwest History Resurgence," *Milwaukee Journal-Sentinel*, July 24 2017.

FINDING A NEW MIDWESTERN HISTORY

PART 1

The Midwest as a Region

1

The Birth of the Midwest and the Rise of Regional Theory

Michael C. Steiner

Some imaginative Easterners caught glimpses of it at the Exposition, where Eastern culture and accent was swallowed up and lost in the mighty flood of the middle West, unknown and inarticulate, but tremendous in its mass.—HAMLIN GARLAND, 1894

Although the Midwest seems a fixture in the constellation of American regions, it has had a surprisingly brief history and a nomadic existence. In the long view of history, what we now consider the Midwest is a recent invention. As recognized today, the region consists of twelve states: the five states of the Old Northwest (Ohio, Indiana, Illinois, Wisconsin, and Michigan) with Minnesota, Iowa, Missouri, and the eastern (tallgrass prairie) edges of the Dakotas, Nebraska, and Kansas thrown in for good measure.[1] It wasn't until the last years of the nineteenth century that this vast territory containing a fifth of the nation's area and a third of its population was referred to as the "Middle West" and its inhabitants began to think of themselves as "Middle Westerners." Until then, this great interior with many overlapping subsections had been inhabited and shaped by a complex sequence of long-standing Indigenous cultures and relatively recent waves of colonizing settlers.

Known by numerous Native names for thousands of years prior to European colonization—and variously called *Pays d'en Haut* by French voyagers, and the Ohio Valley, Mississippi Valley, the Northwest, the Old Northwest, the Great West, or the Middle Border by subsequent settlers—the area we now think of as the Midwest, lacked a distinct regional consciousness and commonly accepted name until the 1890s. To trace the "birth" of the Midwest as we know it and to explore its early role as a seedbed of regional theory and practice, it is import-

3

ant to place this recent slice of human history within a deeper, long-standing perspective.

The Indigenous Background

The land that would be widely considered the Middle West by 1900 has a deep human history and rich Indigenous past that has been minimized, silenced, and hidden from view. The present-day region is the latest configuration in a complex layering of cultures and names stretching back many thousands of years. As Doug Kiel argues, the region's most common historical narratives are driven by a "deep-seated notion that the Midwest and its history belong to Euro-Americans." Drawing attention to the shamefully neglected Indigenous Midwest—both as historical foundation and ongoing presence—Kiel emphasizes that the region suffers from a "cultural geography of colonial amnesia" largely obliterating the Native presence from public consciousness. Asserting that "today's Midwest is a product of the frontier having erased its own tracks," Kiel urges us to recall this repressed history and acknowledge its impact on the present.[2]

It is essential to appreciate the profound Native presence in the Midwest while also recognizing its regrettable absence in the minds of most of its non-Native inhabitants. In addition to uncovering this long-standing influence, we must also see the "Midwest" as a recently imposed construct, "a U.S. spatial category that is defined, in part, by the national project of replacing Indigenous societies."[3] Despite the myth of the region as a blank slate for intrepid pioneers, the land that we now consider the Midwest has a complex history of textured homelands stretching back at least eleven thousand years before the Euro-American frontier. Beginning with the retreat of the continental ice sheets of the Wisconsin Glaciation that had sculpted the landscape and carved the watercourses north of the Ohio and east of the Missouri River, a complex sequence of Native cultures inhabited and shaped much of this sprawling terrain of forests and prairies. Uncovering the number of pre-Columbian inhabitants of this expanse over time is notoriously difficult and subject to heated debate. But recent demographic scholarship indicates that prior to European contact at least two million Native Americans were living in North America east of the Mississippi, with roughly 125,000 inhabiting the Great Lakes region of that larger territory, creating a rich mosaic of agricultural and hunting-and-gathering-based societies.[4]

The Mississippian and Mound Building cultures that flourished in the Ohio and Mississippi River watersheds between AD 800 and 1400 reflect the density and sophistication of but one phase of the pre-Columbian Midwest. The city of Cahokia, built in the rich Mississippi bottomlands opposite present-day St. Louis during the thirteenth and fourteenth centuries, reached a peak population of twenty thousand by AD 1350, making it by far the largest city in North America until Philadelphia had that number of inhabitants in the 1770s. It wasn't until the 1770s that the combined Euro- and African American population of the North American colonies exceeded two million, equaling the number of Native Americans who had lived in the same territory before 1492 and prior to the massive population collapse brought by the frontier. These are a few examples of the deep human history of this vast interior before it became the Middle West in the minds of its more recent inhabitants.[5]

The territory lying between the Ohio River and the Great Lakes and stretching from the Allegheny Mountains to the Mississippi River is an immense middle ground that experienced many centuries of human history before it became the Middle West. From Cahokia in the fifteenth century to Chicago in the nineteenth century, from the interaction of French voyageurs and Native inhabitants in the 1660s and '70s to the migration of millions to the nation's new industrial heartland in the 1880s and '90s, the landscape that would be thought of as the Middle West experienced sweeping transformations. It is a long history, serving as a hidden foundation to the rise of regional consciousness and birth of the Midwest as we know it at the end of the nineteenth century. To fully portray this vast panorama or to completely depict a briefer regional era could take a lifetime. The more modest goal of this chapter is to trace the emergence of the Middle West as a place in the minds of Americans and its impact on regional thought in the late nineteenth and early twentieth centuries.

Finding a Name for a Place

A number of scholars have convincingly argued that the present-day notion of the "Middle West" entered the national consciousness in the thirty-year period between the 1880s and 1910s.[6] Among these scholars, James Shortridge has pushed the analysis deeper, uncovering the first use of the term Middle West in Timothy Flint's 1827 account of religious awakenings in what Flint described as "the middle western states: chiefly in Tennessee."[7] This initial north-south ordering of space, with Tennessee and Kentucky occupying a middle position between the Old Northwest and the Old Southwest, shifted westward by the eve of the Civil War in the 1850s, with Kansas and Nebraska emerging as the new Middle West situated between the new Northwest in the Dakotas and new Southwest in Texas and the Indian Territories. By the 1890s, the Middle West shifted once again, this time northeastward, to its present-day, twelve-state location stretching from Ohio to the prairie states.[8]

This may be a familiar story to specialists in midwestern history; what may be less familiar is the role that a generation of intellectuals, writers, and artists played at the creation of the Midwest, acting as midwives and architects to shape not only awareness of the region but also of regionalism and regional theory in general. Their first public use of the label "Middle West" can be seen as marking the birth of the region as we know it. To trace the use of words is much more than an etymological exercise. Words are artifacts, and the introduction of a new word or label offers deep historical insight, marking the "birth" of an idea and a place. "Language is not just a medium, like a water pipe," architectural historian Witold Rybczynski has argued, rather "it is a reflection of how we think . . . the introduction of words into language marks the simultaneous introduction of ideas into consciousness."[9]

The naming of things and regions are significant events, indicating that an inchoate thing or place has become a *self-conscious* concern, an object of deliberate thought and public attention. Underscoring the power of names on the land, Henry Nash Smith stressed the need for a series of "collective representations"—shared images of a Virgin Land, Garden of the World, Yeoman Republic, Plantation South, Wild West—to give meaning to settlers of the vast American interior. "History cannot happen," Smith argued, "without images which simultaneously express collective desires and impose coherence on the infinitely numerous . . . and varied data of experience." In equally compelling words, Keith Basso has asserted that "place-names are among the most highly charged and richly evocative of all linguistic symbols," and concludes, "We are, in a sense, the place-worlds we imagine."[10] Recognizing a name is a powerful precipitant, bringing an embryonic concept or a formless space into public consciousness, and this process took place in the territory that became the Middle West in the decades following the Civil War.

Beginning in the 1890s and peaking during World War I, a remarkably varied group of self-conscious midwesterners began using the term Middle West and fashioned distinctive images of their emerging region. Many also used their sense of this new region to develop prescient theories of regionalism, becoming among the first to do so in American intellectual history. There were many inklings of this turn-of-the-century birth of midwestern identity and regional thought. Elizabeth Raymond has traced the emergence of a widespread "prairie craze" to the 1820s and "a growing body of romantic prairie paeans" over the next several decades, usually penned by travelers and tourists, thrilled by the "oceanic openness" of the seemingly endless rippling grasslands.[11]

Although pervasive use of the term Middle West did not emerge until late in the nineteenth century, Martin Ridge has argued that even before the Civil War, the inhabitants of the Old Northwest "began to think of themselves as different. They were not part of the South, the East, or the Far West or the mountains and plains."[12] Other scholars, including Carl Sauer and Christopher Phillips, have traced the emergence of the label "Middle Border" to the Ohio and Mississippi Valleys during the decades leading to the Civil War and discussed how it gave way to the broader notion of the Middle West in the decades following the war.[13] This rising awareness found voice in several native sons who predicted the land's future significance and mapped its contours. In 1862, for example, Abraham Lincoln foresaw the "great interior region" that we now think of as the Midwest as "the great body of the republic"; and beginning in the late 1860s, fellow Illinoisan John Wesley Powell (1834–1902)

The Birth of the Midwest 7

was the first to systematically map the natural and cultural regions of North America, dividing the nascent Midwest into the "Lake-Plains" and the "Prairie-Plains."[14]

Lincoln and Powell's great interior region quickly captured the imaginations of two great American visionaries, Walt Whitman and Louis Sullivan. Following the common practice of ignoring Indigenous history, the great poet and fledging architect voiced early versions of midwestern manifest destiny, envisioning the great interior as an enormous blank slate and future global pivot point brimming with power and potential. Of his first ecstatic glimpse at the age of seventeen of the sprawling prairie, vast lake, and sweeping "dome of the sky" as his train approached Chicago, in November 1873, Sullivan recalled: "Here was power—power greater than the mountains. . . . Here in full view was the light of the world, companion of the earth, a power greater than the lake and the prairie below." Six years later, after an 1879 railroad journey through Indiana, Illinois, and Missouri, sixty-year-old Whitman exuberantly proclaimed the tallgrass prairies as "America's most characteristic landscape," "the theater of our great future," a beacon to the world, and the heart and soul of the nation.[15]

Such early prophecies and epiphanies laid the groundwork for a flowering of regional thought and practice beginning in the 1890s when a generation began to think of themselves as Middle Westerners. This identity emerged from both the country and the city. During the same moment in the late 1890s when, as Raymond argues, "the agricultural Prairie Midwest had become the normative American environmental symbol," Chicago rivaled and in many ways surpassed New York as the nation's urban ideal.[16] Beginning in the early 1890s and culminating by 1920, a number of intellectuals, artists, and public figures from both urban and rural places helped create midwestern identity and American regional theory. They were part of a climate of opinion and moment in history that encouraged people to reflect upon the land around them. In tracing this regional birth process we will see how, in less than a generation, a once vague and variously labeled landscape grew from an amorphous space, "unknown and inarticulate, but tremendous in its mass," into a distinct and powerful place seen as the dynamic center and "apotheosis of American civilization."[17]

Many of the first generation of self-conscious midwesterners came from the rural Upper Midwest, specifically from Wisconsin and Illinois and with a scattering from Iowa and Minnesota. This early group included a remarkable concentration in or near the small town of Portage, in the Wisconsin River valley, where the Wisconsin and Fox Rivers nearly meet, and marking the historic link between the Mississippi and St. Lawrence watersheds. Frederick Jackson Turner, John Muir, Robert M. LaFollette, Frank Lloyd Wright, Zona Gale, and Georgia O'Keefe were all born in the 1860s, '70s, or '80s and lived their formative years in or within a forty-mile radius of this town of roughly five thousand people.[18] Other significant Wisconsinites of this generation include Laura Ingalls Wilder, who spent a significant portion of her childhood in the coulee country near Pepin, and Norwegian-born cultural theorist Waldemar Ager, who lived most of his life in Eau Claire. Two powerful cultural critics who would move to the neighboring states of Minnesota and Iowa as small children were Norwegian-American Thorstein Veblen, born near Milwaukee in 1857, and Hamlin Garland, born in the coulee country near La Crosse in 1860. Norwegian immigrant novelist and cultural critic Ole Rølvaag, who lived most of his productive career in Northfield, Minnesota, contributed to this group of writers and regional theorists.[19]

The urban Midwest also played a central role in the birth of midwestern consciousness, and Chicago was the focal point. This broad-shouldered, bursting-at-the-seams metropolis, founded by black French Canadian trader Jean Baptiste Point du Sable in the 1780s, had become within a century a spectacle of feverish expansion and yawning inequalities. With its disturbing contrasts between palaces along Lake Shore Boulevard and hovels behind the Union stockyards, between skyscrapers and slaughterhouses, Chicago was, in William Cronon's words, a great vortex "both glorious and abhorrent at the same time."[20]

Beginning in the late 1880s and coming into focus during the decade following the 1893 World's Columbian Exposition, an extraordinary number of cultural movers and shakers came of age in Chicago. Progressive reformers Jane Addams and John Peter Altgeld; black civil rights activists Ida B. Wells and Reverdy Ransom; novelists Hamlin Garland, Sherwood Anderson, and Theodore Dreiser; poets Harriet Monroe, Vachel Lindsay, and Carl Sandburg; philosophers Veblen and John Dewey; architects Louis Sullivan and Frank Lloyd Wright—all helped shift the nation's cultural center westward and expressed critical affection for their turbulent city and emerging region. Skyscrapers and prairie homes, modern poetry and naturalistic novels, egalitarian hopes and rampant inequalities—all grew from the tumultuous multiethnic ferment of Chicago and its hinterlands.[21]

Three Architects of Midwestern Identity and Regional Theory

Three figures stand out as pioneering midwestern regionalists. Architect Frank Lloyd Wright (1867–1959), radical writer Hamlin Garland (1860–1940), and historian Frederick Jackson Turner (1861–1932) created influential images of their emerging region. They were among the first to label it the Middle West and were—along with their California contemporary Josiah Royce (1855–1916)—the first Americans to develop self-conscious regional theories and aesthetic expressions. All three were rural midwesterners with Wisconsin roots whose childhood memories shaped their thought. And each used Chicago as a precipitant and the Columbian Exposition as a platform for their regional expressions.

The 1893 exposition had a profoundly negative impact on Wright, spurring him to create what he saw as its antithesis: an organic architecture that seemed to grow from the prairies, woods, and rolling hills of his native region. As a fledgling architect from rural Wisconsin and newly arrived in Chicago, where he worked as Sullivan's draftsman from 1887 until 1893, Wright was appalled by the pompous architectural eclecticism and abject kowtowing to European styles displayed throughout Daniel Burnham's Great White City. Declaring that "all that was fraudulent and crapulent" in American culture had risen to a feverish pitch at the exposition, and that "the nature of man was there reduced to the level of a clever trained animal," Wright resolved to build an indigenous architecture that would proudly reflect the land itself.[22]

Over the next eight years Wright experimented with materials and technologies and drew upon memories of his "beloved ancestral Valley" in Spring Green, Wisconsin, to develop the first "prairie house" with the publication of a seminal article in 1901 and the completion of the Ward Willets House in Highland Park in 1902. Wright's prairie house, with its horizontal earth lines, wide eaves, nuclear fireplace, functional use of local materials, and sense of organic rootedness, was his homage to the emerging Midwest and the nation's first distinctive, nonderivative architecture.[23] This regionally rooted aesthetic trumpeted the fact that, in Wright's words, "the real American spirit, capable of judging an issue for itself upon its merits, lies in the West and Middle West, where breadth of view, independent thought and a tendency to take common sense into the realm of art, as in life, are more characteristic."[24]

Like many of his early midwestern contemporaries, Wright looked back upon a nomadic childhood and longed for a sense of stability and community. His father, William Carey Wright, was an itinerant preacher, musician, and composer who dragged his family from one disappointment to another. By the time Wright was twelve, he had lived in six towns and had been brought from his birthplace in rural Wisconsin to Massachusetts to Iowa. His mother, Anna Lloyd Jones, came from a family of prosperous Welsh farmers settled in the Wisconsin River valley, and she resented the rootlessness of her married life. The most satisfying periods of Wright's childhood were spent with his mother's relatives at Spring Green, forty miles downriver from Portage. The summers with the extended Lloyd Jones family, from 1879 until 1886, and their expansive Unitarian faith, helped shape Wright's strong sense of self-assurance, family intimacy, and attachment to place. "I loved the prairie by instinct as a great simplicity," he would recall, "the trees, the flowers, the sky itself, thrilling by contrast," and he drew upon these memories when he entered the swirl of Chicago in the late 1880s and created the prairie house.[25]

Wright was the most prominent of a community of architects inspired by the youthful Midwest. In his 1908 manifesto, "In the Cause of Architecture," Wright recalled leaving his apprenticeship with Sullivan in 1893 and devoting the next seven years to creating a domestic architecture to match the new region. Remembering "how the 'message' burned within me, how I longed for comradeship," Wright credited a spirited discussion group of young architects who referred to themselves as the "New School of the Middle West" for helping him find his way. Recalling lively gatherings with Robert Spencer, Myron Hunt, Dwight Perkins, Walter Burley Griffin, and others, between 1893 and 1900, as "inspiring days . . . for us all," Wright, in a rare moment of humility, acknowledged their common effort toward an organic regional style and fundamental belief that "we of the Middle West are living on the prairie. The prairie has a beauty of its own and we should accentuate this natural beauty, its quiet level."[26]

While chaotic Chicago challenged Wright to evoke the simplicity of his prairie past, the tumultuous city and its boisterous 1893 exposition had a more positive impact on Hamlin Garland. Like Wright, Garland regretted his unsettled early years largely caused by a fiddle-footed father. Born on a farm in Wisconsin's Mississippi River coulee country, in 1860, young Garland lived a forlorn, migratory childhood filled with tension between his restless, horizon-chasing father and his homesick, security-craving mother. At Dick Garland's bidding, his family was perpetually packing up and heading west from one failed enterprise to another until they had scattered and their father had become a defeated old man "snowbound on a tactless plain."[27] Garland lamented the deprivations of his rootless frontier childhood, and his early short story collection, the harshly realistic *Main-Travelled Roads* (1891), is filled with fierce indignation and deep yearning for a more settled and equitable collective life in the emerging Middle West.

Garland came of age as a writer and regionalist through a process of leaving and returning to his native ground. After becoming an established writer in Boston and New York in the late 1880s and early 1890s, he was drawn back to the ferment of the "Middle Border" by the Populist campaign of 1892 and by the Chicago World's Fair a year later. Unlike Wright, Garland was thrilled by the spectacle and assertive gusto of the fair, interpreting it as a symbol of his native ground gaining identity and dominance in the nation's cultural life. Using the fair as a platform to trumpet a newborn regional consciousness and pride, Garland gave a rousing talk on "Local Color in Fiction" there on July 14, 1893, two days after Turner had delivered his frontier essay from the same platform.

Garland's talk—expanded and published three months later as "The Literary Emancipation of the West" in a prominent literary journal *The*

Forum—was a brazen clarion call for the cultural independence and superiority of the rising Middle West. *The Forum* editor, Walter Hines Page, who two years later as editor of the *Atlantic Monthly* would solicit Turner's first essay on the Middle West, recalled "with glee" that Garland's 1893 polemic sparked a firestorm of "nearly a thousand editorial comments, commendatory and otherwise."[28] Like a midwestern Whitman sounding his barbaric yawp over the rooftops of the world, Garland announced the birth of a youthful all-embracing heartland culture free from the moribund elitism of the East. "Keep your past," the rising West tells the tradition-bound East, he declared. "Hug your tablets to your shirt-front; you are welcome to all that; we are concerned with the present, and the splendor of the future. . . . The youth of all nations are in the fight." Foreseeing Chicago as the flash point for this first truly American culture that "must be democratic and progressive . . . and stand for a mighty people who will not abide slavish genuflections before any idol," Garland boldly proclaimed: "There is coming in the land the mightiest assertion in art of the rights of man and the glory of the physical universe ever made in the world. . . . It will be born of the mingling seas of men in the vast interior of America. . . . Stand up, O young Men and women of the West! Stand erect! Face the future with a song on your lips and the light of the broader day in your eyes."[29]

The youthful bravado of a region coming of age reached full voice with the 1894 publication of *Crumbling Idols: Twelve Essays on Art and Literature*. A landmark in midwestern identity and regionalist theory, *Crumbling Idols* may have marked the first time the term Middle West appeared in print to designate this emerging region.[30] One of the nation's earliest regionalist manifestos, it also contained one of the first full-scale theories of cultural regionalism penned by an American.[31] Garland's fiery tract was pathbreaking not only for labeling the Middle West but also for advocating, presciently, a decentralized "provincialism" with "literary centers all over the nation" more than a decade before Josiah Royce argued for a "wise provincialism" as a key component of his hope for a "beloved community."[32]

Garland's allusion to the work of Frederic Mistral and the French decentralists, who had coined the term and concept of "regionalisme" in the 1850s, appeared more than a generation before Lewis Mumford would reintroduce this concept and the word "regionalism" to an American audience in 1917.[33] Garland's vision of an emerging region where "there is the mixture of races . . . a great heterogeneous, shifting, brave population, a land teeming with unrecorded and infinite drama" would be echoed by subsequent midwestern regionalists. His general faith that "it is the differences which interest us; the similarities do not please, do not forever stimulate and feed us as do the differences" would be amplified by a later generation of cultural pluralists.[34]

Frederick Jackson Turner was also an architect of midwestern identity and regional theory, and the Columbian Exposition also served as a platform for his sense of his native ground. On the hot summer evening of July 12, 1893, a few days before Garland's talk and a few hours after Buffalo Bill Cody's Wild West Show had dazzled crowds just outside the exposition grounds, the thirty-one-year-old from Portage delivered what would become the most influential essay written by an American historian, making him arguably the most celebrated and reviled historian since Karl Marx.[35] Painting a dramatic image of the centuries-long "colonization of the Great West," Turner asserted that the immigrants' rough-and-tumble contact with untrammeled nature obliterated old cultures and demanded a new one in its place. This revitalizing immersion at "the outer edge of the wave, the meeting point between savagery and civilization," he announced to an identity-hungry nation, had forged our national character and explained everything distinctive about American culture.[36]

Turner's sweeping vision of intrepid pioneers wrestling with wilderness and becoming a new more vital people in the process has captured the public imagination. What is forgotten in light of this appealing, action-filled creation story is that Turner's 1893 essay was in essence a deeply disturbing funeral sermon. "The frontier has gone," he told his sweltering audience at the very end of his talk, "and with its going has closed the first period of American history."[37] The second period, he came to believe, would involve settling the land, cultivating regional identities, and creating a healthier culture after so many generations of restless wandering.

Primarily known for his youthful frontier thesis, Turner devoted most of his life to foreseeing how stable societies would sprout from the ashes of the ever-retreating frontier and to developing a comprehensive theory of the transition from frontier to region, with the emerging Midwest as the keystone and bedrock for this larger theory and process.[38] "As the frontier advance drew to a close," he would argue by the 1920s, "as these provinces were no longer regions to be crossed or merely to be exploited, but home-sections of permanent settlers, the final stage was reached." Coming to grips with the death of the frontier, it was time to establish roots, to shape raw space into familiar place, and to create a mosaic of regional cultures whose variety and cooperation would invigorate the nation as a whole. In a profound statement of regionalist faith, Turner envisioned a vibrant nation in which "we shall find strength to build from our past a nobler structure, in which each section will find its place as a fit room in a worthy house."[39]

The Midwest became the central room in this worthy house and the model for Turner's larger frontier-regional theory. During the first thirty years of his life, however, the Midwest remained a room in flux, a half-built frontier annex. Growing up in this unfinished region as it took shape, Turner was a participant in the very process he later analyzed. Like Garland and Wright, his theories were shaped by his childhood landscapes. Memories of the rolling prairies interlaced with oak and pine forests of the upper Wisconsin River valley and of Portage—as it transitioned from a tumultuous frontier settlement to a more stable community during his early years in the 1860s and '70s—all left indelible impressions, molding Turner's sense of the frontier, region, and Midwest as he came of age in the 1880s and beyond. Reminiscing in greater detail than Garland or Wright, Turner remembered a mosaic of Winnebago, Norwegian, Welsh, Scottish, Irish, Swiss, and German communities in and around his hometown, and he drew upon these memories to see the region as a matrix of cultural diversity and bulwark against the leveling forces of mass culture.[40]

Late in life, he recalled that Portage "had all types from a negro family named Turner, to an Irish 'keener' who looked like a Druid." "It was a town," he continued, "with a real collection of types from all the world. . . .

They mixed too. And respected and fought each other. When I went to Europe, it was familiar. I had seen it in Portage."[41] Echoing Garland's praise of diversity within the Midwest and using imagery that would cheer his contemporary Jane Addams and a slightly younger group of cultural pluralists, including Ager, Rølvaag, Horace Kallen, and Randolph Bourne, Turner concluded in his last publication that the midwestern states "were not to be a melting pot, with a fusion of manifold ingredients, but rather a mixing bowl, with a process of adjustment, of giving-and-taking. . . . In this plastic society, all the various stocks intermingle, but they do not lose their separate individualities."[42] He also visualized the region or "section," to use his terminology, as a shield from surges of mass emotion. With Harvard colleague Royce in mind, Turner wisely asserted that "the world needs now more than ever the vigorous development of a highly organized provincial life to serve as a check upon mob psychology on a national scale, and to furnish that variety which is essential to vital growth and originality."[43]

In addition to developing prescient theories of regionalism and cultural pluralism rooted in the Midwest, Turner joined Garland in becoming among the first to publicly announce the birth of the region. The term Middle West, as we've seen, had been loosely used and variously located throughout much of the nineteenth century, and the label for the region as we know it today was first published by Garland in 1894. Turner closely followed Garland's lead. A series of letters and articles written between 1896 and 1901 reveals his evolving sense of the Middle West. On July 14, 1896, Walter Hines Page, who had solicited Garland's first regionalist essays three years earlier and was now editor of the *Atlantic Monthly*, invited Turner to contribute an essay on the historical-geographical background to the Populist insurgency.[44]

Turner responded enthusiastically, and his essay, "The Problem of the West," published two months later, brimmed with descriptions of a vital new region—still labeled the "Old Northwest"—that would mediate between the established East and the turbulent West and serve as the balance wheel of the nation. This nascent region, Turner argued, "holds the balance of power. . . . It has more in common with all the parts of the nation than has any other region. It understands the East, as the East does not understand the West." The splendor of the White City on the shores of Lake Michigan typifies the region's "growing culture as well as its capacity for great achievement" and demonstrates its future as the "Center of the Republic" and the "open-minded and safe arbiter of the American destiny."[45]

Buoyed by this article, Page wrote to Turner on August 22, 1896, proposing that he contribute a series of essays on "the characteristic parts of the country—the Middle West, the South, and New England, and perhaps we shall add the trans-Rocky-Mountain region as a fourth."[46] *Dumb* Page's invitation opened a floodgate of ideas, with Turner dashing off an exuberant letter on August 30, 1896, detailing his thoughts about regionalism in general and the Middle West in particular. This remarkable outpouring has been praised as "the high-water mark" of nineteenth-century American regional thought, and it expressed, among other things, Turner's belief "that the time is ripe for some such survey" because "we have reached a turning point in our national life—with the exhaustion of the supply of free lands." He also mused about the interplay between physiographic and cultural regions and the nation's emerging regional framework. Of particular interest are Turner's proposal to "divide the West into its proper regions and portray the spirit or personality of each" and his description of one of these new regions, the Middle West, as constituting the Old Northwest plus Minnesota and Iowa.[47]

Tuner never realized this ambitious project, but he did publish three essays over the next few years that established his vision of the Middle West and that would set a standard for how the region was perceived for several generations. In a paper delivered at the American Historical Association meeting in New York in December 1896, Turner emphasized that the West "requires analysis into the regions that compose it." Stressing that it is "especially important that the prairie portion of the middle West should no longer be ignored by historians," he concluded that "the Mississippi Basin, one vast area, covering a least half a dozen States, is almost virgin soil for the historian." In the last *Atlantic* article he would write for Page, published in April 1897, Turner declared, "The Old Northwest . . . is now the new Middle Region of the United States."

No long the western edge, this central region is now "the keystone of the American Commonwealth."[48]

Turner's fully conceived, panoramic vision of the region appeared four years later in the December 1901 issue of the *International Monthly*. Simply titled "The Middle West," this essay helped create the iconic image of the region as the nation's brawny, broad-shouldered industrial and agrarian heartland—a public perception and symbolic landscape that would last for generations. Turner's essay opened with the sweeping assertion that "the Middle West is the economic and political center of the Republic. At one edge is the Populism of the prairies; at the other the capitalism that is typified in Pittsburgh." Turner painted a vivid tableau of a mighty region emerging from humble beginnings. "The ideals of the Middle West began in the log huts set in the midst of the forest a century ago," he rhapsodized. "The pioneer dreamed of continental ambitions. The vastness of the wilderness kindled his imagination. He saw beyond the dank swamp at the edge of the great lake to the lofty buildings and the jostling multitudes of a mighty city." Pondering the future of this agricultural and industrial powerhouse, Turner stressed that "the task of the Middle West is that of adapting democracy to the vast economic organization of the present . . . to reconcile real greatness with bigness," and concluded, "If the ideals of the pioneers shall survive the inundation of material success, we may expect to see in the Middle West the rise of a highly intelligent society whose culture shall be reconciled with democracy in the large."[49]

Turner's vibrant portrait, along with Garland's fiery manifesto, Wright's firmly grounded prairie home, Sullivan's proud and soaring skyscraper, and many other turn-of-the-century heartland expressions gave birth to the Midwest and to American regional thought. These writers, artists, and intellectuals helped deliver the great interior region to public awareness, laying the foundations for future considerations and creations—for deeper, more complex, and constantly shifting visions of the Midwest and of American regionalism in general. How these pioneering midwestern regionalists paved the way for generations of regional thought constitute future chapters of an ongoing narrative. How subsequent groups of intellectuals and common folk, speaking from working-class, feminist, multiracial, and transnational perspectives, enriched our understanding of the Midwest and of American regionalism in general is a momentous story illuminating the rise and fall and possible rebirth of regionalism in our own times. In a larger sense, the Midwest's story of continual change and shape shifting is relevant to every cultural region of the nation and every human portion of the world.[50]

Notes

Among the many people who have helped shape this essay, I would especially like to thank David Good, Doug Kiel, Jon Lauck, Elizabeth Raymond, and Leila Zenderland for their invaluable advice and suggestions.

Epigraph: Hamlin Garland, "Literary Masters," in Garland, *Crumbling Idols: Twelve Essays on Art and Literature* (Chicago: Stone and Kimball, 1894), 177.

1. This twelve-state configuration, made up of East North Central and West North Central divisions, has been part of the United States Census since 1910. In 1984 the overarching regional label for the two divisions was changed from North Central to Midwest. See *History of the United States Census Bureau*, www.census.gov/history/www/programs/geography /regions_and_divisions.html.

2. Doug Kiel, "Untaming the Mild Frontier: In Search of New Midwestern Histories," *Middle West Review* 1 (Fall 2014): 10, 12, 14.

3. Doug Kiel and James F. Brooks, "Introduction: Reframing and Reclaiming the Indigenous Midwest," in "Indigenous Midwests," special issue, *Middle West Review* 3 (Spring 2016), vii.

4. On the deep Indigenous presence in what would become the Middle West and for specific demographics, see Daniel K. Richter, *Facing East from Indian Country: A Native History of Early America* (Cambridge: Harvard University Press, 2003), and Richter, *Before the Revolution: America's Ancient Pasts* (Cambridge: Harvard University Press, 2011). In *Facing West*, Richter lists peak pre-Columbian population totals eastward from the Mississippi on page 7 and in footnote 9, page 258. See Robert E. Ritzenthaler and Pat Ritzenthaler, *The Woodland Indians of the Western Great Lakes* (Prospect Heights IL: Waveland Press, 1991), 11–14, for estimates of the Indigenous population of the Great Lakes area before European contact. Accounts of Native American populations before and after European contact in the Great Lakes region include Richard White: *The Middle Ground: Indians, Empires, and Republics in the Great Lakes Region, 1650–1815* (New York: Cambridge University Press, 1991), and Russell Thornton, *American*

Indian Holocaust and Survival: A Population History Since 1492 (Norman: University of Oklahoma Press, 1987). I am indebted to Doug Kiel of Northwestern University, for his generous advice regarding pre-Columbian demographics.

5. For Mississippian and Cahokian demographics, I am indebted to David F. Good's comprehensive essay "American History through a Midwestern Lens," in *Wirtschaft and Gesellschaft* 38, no.2 (2012): 435–47, and to Timothy Pauketat's *Cahokia: Ancient America's Great City on the Mississippi* (New York: Viking-Penguin, 2009). For the number of North American colonists and slaves reaching two million by the 1770s, see Richter, *Facing East, 7.*

6. James R. Shortridge, *The Middle West: Its Meaning in American Culture* (Lawrence: University Press of Kansas, 1989); Jon Gjerde, *The Minds of the West: Ethnocultural Evolution in the Rural Middle West, 1830–1917* (Chapel Hill: University of North Carolina Press, 1997); Carl Ubbelohde, "History and the Midwest as a Region," *Wisconsin Magazine of History* 78 (Autumn 1994): 35–47; Andrew R. L. Cayton and Susan E. Gray, "The Story of the Midwest: An Introduction," in *The Identity of the American Midwest: Essays in Regional History*, ed. Cayton and Gray(Bloomington: Indiana University Press, 2001), 1–26; Wilbur Zelinsky, *Not Yet a Placeless Land: Tracking an Evolving American Geography* (Amherst: University of Massachusetts Press, 2011).

7. Shortridge, *Middle West,* 16.

8. James Shortridge, "The Origin and Expansion of the Regional Name," in his *Middle West*, 13–26 and throughout. John Fraser Hart's "The Middle West," in *Regions of the United States*, ed. Hart (New York: Harper and Row, 1972), 258–82, is a classic analysis of the emergence of the present-day Midwest.

9. Witold Rybczynski, *Home: A Short History of an Idea* (New York: Penguin Books, 1986), 20. In an early plea for a "linguistic turn" in history, Owen Barfield argued that "in our language alone the past of humanity is spread out in an imperishable map, just as the history of the mineral earth lies embedded in layers of its outer crust . . . language has preserved for us the inner, living history of man's soul." Barfield, *History in Words* (1953; repr., Grand Rapids MI: William B. Erdmans, 1967), 18.

10. Henry Nash Smith, Virgin Land: The American West as Symbol and Myth (Cambridge MA: Harvard University Press, 1950), xi and throughout. The longer quotation is from Smith's preface, ix. Keith H. Basso, *Wisdom Sits in Places: Landscape and Language Among the Western Apache* (Albuquerque: University of New Mexico Press, 1996), 76, 7.

11. C. Elizabeth Raymond, "Middle Ground: Evolving Regional Images in the American Midwest," in Johannes W. Bertens, Theo d.'Haen, and Ineke Bockting, eds., *Writing Nation and "Writing" Region in America*, vol. 33 of *European Contributions to American Studies* (Amsterdam: Vu University Press, 1996): 98 and throughout.

12. Martin Ridge, "How the Middle West Became America's Heartland," *Inland* 2 (1976): 13.

13. Carl O. Sauer, "Homestead and Community on the Middle Border," *Landscape: Magazine of Human Geography* 12 (1962): 3–7; Christopher Phillips, *The Rivers Ran Backwards: The Civil War and the Remaking of the American Middle Border* (New York: Oxford University Press, 2016).

14. See Kenneth Winkle, "'The Great Body of the Republic': Abraham Lincoln and the Idea of a Middle West," in *The Identity of the American Midwest*, ed. Andrew Cayton and Susan Gray, 111–22; John Wesley Powell, *The Arid Regions of the United States* (1879; repr., Harvard MA: Harvard Commons Press, 1983), and John Wesley Powell, *The Physiographic Regions of the United States* (1895; repr., Cambridge MA: Belknap Press of Harvard University Press, 1962).

15. Louis Sullivan, *The Autobiography of an Idea* (New York: Press of the American Institute of Architects, 1924), 196–97; Walt Whitman, "The Prairies" and "America's Characteristic Landscape," in *The Works of Walt Whitman: The Collected Prose*, ed. Malcolm Cowley (New York: Farrar, Straus and Giroux, 1969), 139–40, 149. For an insightful analysis, see Ed Folsom, "Walt Whitman's Prairie Paradise," in *Recovering the Prairie*, ed. Robert F. Sayre (Madison: University of Wisconsin Press, 1999), 47–60.

16. Raymond, "Middle Ground," 111.

17. Hamlin Garland, "Literary Masters," in Garland, *Crumbling Idols*, 177; Randolph Bourne, "A Mirror for the Middle West" (1918), reprinted in Bourne, *The History of a Literary Radical and Other Papers* (New York: S. A. Russell, 1956), 286.

18. For a brilliant analysis of Portage and its intellectuals—especially Tuner, Muir, and later Sigurd Olson and Aldo Leopold—see William Cronon's "Landscape and Home: Environmental Traditions in Wisconsin," *Wisconsin Magazine of History*, 74 (Winter 1990–91): 83–105. "Rarely," Cronon observes, "has so unlikely a landscape evoked such passionate responses from figures of such intellectual importance" (93).

19. For a thoughtful discussion of the Wisconsin-based environmental visions of Turner, Veblen, Muir, and Leopold, see Wilbur R. Jacobs, "The Great Despoliation: Environmental History," *Pacific Historical Review* 47 (Feb-

ruary 1978): 1–26. E. Bradford Burns's *Kinship with the Land: Regionalist Thought in Iowa, 1894–1942* (Iowa City: University of Iowa Press, 1996), includes an insightful discussion of an early generation of Iowa-based regionalists, beginning with Garland in the 1890s.

20. William Cronon, *Nature's Metropolis: Chicago and the Great West* (New York: W. W. Norton, 1991), 20.

21. Among the extensive literature on Chicago and the emerging Midwest in the 1890s, two classic books stand out: Ray Ginger's *Altgeld's America: The Lincoln Ideal and Changing Realities* (New York: Funk and Wagnalls, 1958) and William Cronon's *Nature's Metropolis*.

22. Frank Lloyd Wright, "Roots," in *Frank Lloyd Wright: Writings and Buildings*, selected by Edgar Kaufmann and Ben Raeburn (New York: New American Library, 1960), 33.

23. Frank Lloyd Wright, "A House in a Prairie Town," *Ladies Home Journal*, February 1901. See Robert C. Twombley, "Saving the Family: Middle Class Attraction to Wright's Prairie House, 1901–1909," *American Quarterly* 27 (March 1975): 57–72, for a thoughtful discussion of Wright's reaction to Chicago and the prairie house as a regional expression.

24. Frank Lloyd Wright, preface to *Studies and Executed Buildings* (Florence, Italy, 1910; repr., Palos Park IL: Prairie School Press, 1975), 4.

25. Wright, *An Autobiography* (1943; repr., Scottsdale AZ: Rizzoli, 1992, in *Frank Lloyd Wright: Collected Writings*), 2:198. Wright's maternal uncle, Jenkin Lloyd Jones (1843–1918), one of the most influential Unitarian theologians of the late nineteenth century, who lived and preached in Spring Green and Chicago, had a deep impact on his nephew's intellectual growth and aesthetics.

26. Frank Lloyd Wright, "In the Cause of Architecture" (1908), reprinted in *In the Cause of Architecture: Essays by Frank Lloyd Wright for Architectural Record, 1908–1952*, ed. Frederick Gutheim (New York: Architectural Record Books, 1975), 54, 55. See H. Brook Allan, *Frank Lloyd Wright and the Prairie School* (New York: George Braziller, 1984), for a detailed account of the creation of the "New School of the Middle West" between 1893 and 1900.

27. Hamlin Garland, *A Son of the Middle Border* (New York: Macmillan, 1917), 43–46 and throughout.

28. For Page's account of the controversy sparked by Garland's essay, see Keith Newlin, *Hamlin Garland: A Life* (Lincoln: University of Nebraska Press, 2008), 183.

29. Hamlin Garland, "Literary Emancipation of the West," *The Forum* (October 1893): 163–66.

30. See *Crumbling Idols*, 7, 13, and 177, for Garland's pioneering use of the label "middle West."

31. See Michael C. Steiner, "Region, Regionalism, and Place," in *Oxford Encyclopedia of American Cultural and Intellectual History*, ed. Joan Shelley Rubin and Scott Casper (New York: Oxford University Press, 2013), 2:275–88, for wider discussion of the history of American sectional and regional thought. For an earlier analysis, see Fulmer Mood, "The Origin, Evolution, and Application of the Sectional Concept, 1750–1900," in *Regionalism in America*, ed. Merrill Jensen (Madison: University of Wisconsin Press, 1951), 5–98.

32. Garland, *Crumbling Idols*, 153; Josiah Royce, *Race Questions, Provincialism, and Other American Problems* (1908; repr., Freeport NY: Books for Libraries Press, 1967). Echoing Garland, Ohio-born William Dean Howells also promoted a decentralized culture and praised the rising creativity of "the Great Middle West" in "American Literary Centers" (1897), published in Howells, *Literature and Life: Studies* (New York: Harper and Brothers, 1902).

33. Garland, *Crumbling Idols*, 6; Lewis Mumford describes his discovery of French regionalist thought and his introduction of the word and concept of regionalism to an American public in 1917 in his *Sketches from Life* (New York: Dial Press, 1982), 163–64, 214, 335.

34. Garland, *Crumbling Idols*, 15, 57. Garland emerges as a significant figure in two insightful studies of pluralism and regionalism in the late nineteenth and early twentieth centuries. See Carrie Tirado Bramen, *The Uses of Variety: Modern Americanism and the Quest for National Distinctiveness* (Cambridge: Harvard University Press, 2000); and Tom Lutz, *Cosmopolitan Vistas: American Regionalism and Literary Value* (Ithaca NY: Cornell University Press, 2004).

35. Assessing the enduring vitality of the frontier thesis, Martin Ridge asserted, "No historian since Karl Marx has received so much criticism of his work. Certainly, no American historian's works . . . have been subjected to such probing analysis and interpretation." Ridge, "Frederick Jackson Turner: His Broader Legacy," unpublished paper, presented at a conference on "Turner and His Frontiers: Legacies and Opportunities," Madison, Wisconsin, November 12, 1993.

36. Frederick Jackson Turner, "The Significance of the Frontier in American History" (1893), in Turner, *The Frontier in American History* (New York: Henry Holt, 1920), 1, 3.

37. Turner, "The Significance of the Frontier in American History," 38.

38. For detailed discussions of Turner's surprisingly neglected frontier-regional theory, see Michael C. Steiner, "The Significance of Turner's Sec-

tional Thesis," *Western Historical Quarterly* 10 (October 1979): 437–66; Steiner, "Frederick Jackson Tuner and Western Regionalism," in *Writing Western History: Essays on Major Western Historians*, ed. Richard Etulain (Albuquerque: University of New Mexico Press, 1991), 103–35; and Steiner, "From Frontier to Region: Frederick Jackson Turner and the New Western History," *Pacific Historical Review* 64 (November 1995): 479–501.

39. Turner, "Geographic Sectionalism in American History" (1926), in Turner, *The Significance of Sections in American History* (New York: Henry Holt, 1932), 197–98; Turner, "Sections and Nation" (1922), in Turner, *Significance of Sections in American History*, 339.

40. Turner to Constance L. Skinner, March 15, 1922, reprinted in Ray Allen Billington, *The Genesis of the Frontier Thesis: A Study in Historical Creativity* (San Marino CA: 1971), 215–16.

41. Turner to Carl Becker, December 16, 1925, reprinted in Billington, *Genesis of the Frontier Thesis*, 240.

42. Turner, *The United States, 1830–1850: The Nation and Its Sections* (New York: Henry Holt, 1935), 286.

43. Turner, "The Significance of the Section in American History" (1925), in Turner, *Significance of Sections in American History*, 45.

44. Walter Hines Page to Frederick Jackson Turner, July 14, 1896, cited in Merrill Jensen, ed., *Regionalism in America*, 91.

45. Turner, "The Problem of the West" (1896), in Turner, *Frontier in American History*, 221.

46. Walter Hines Page to Frederick Jackson Turner, August 22, 1896, reprinted in Merrill Jensen, ed., *Regionalism in America*, 91–92.

47. Frederick Jackson Tuner to Walter Hines Page, August 30, 1896, reprinted in Merrill Jensen, ed., *Regionalism in America*, 92–96. Fulmer Mood's praise of this as "the high-water mark" is on page 96.

48. Turner, "The West as a Field for Historical Study," *Annual Report of the American Historical Association* (Washington DC: American Historical Association, 1896), 283. Turner, "Dominant Forces in Western Life" (1897), in Turner, *Frontier in American History*, 222.

49. Turner, "The Middle West" (1901), in Turner, *Frontier in American History*, 127, 153, 155, 156.

50. For a vivid discussion of the Midwest's decline from broad-shouldered powerhouse in the 1920s to scorned flyover country by the 1960s, and how the region's future identity remains in flux, see Jon K. Lauck, *From Warm Center to Ragged Edge: The Erosion of Midwestern Literary and Historical Regionalism, 1920–1965* (Iowa City: University of Iowa Press, 2017).

2

How Nature and Culture Shaped Early Settlement in the Midwest

James E. Davis

The interplay of cultural factors and geographical factors in the settlement process is timeless. The discipline of geography studies features on or near the surface of the earth and relationships among those features. It includes anything that can be seen, heard, felt, smelled, tasted, or imagined. When humans locate houses, farms, towns, and other elements of the built environment, they take into account, on the one hand, their cultural desires and, on the other hand, geographical realities. Certain guiding principles shaped the interplay of cultural desires and geographical realities in influencing where settlers located houses, towns, and other elements of the built environment. Few midwestern settlers had much formal education, but they were intelligent, eager to learn, and able to take into account understandings of geography, cultural desires, and guiding principles in constructing their built environment.

This interplay of cultural desires and geographical realities affected settlement at three places: at falls or rapids on navigable rivers; on the inside and the outside of bends in rivers; and on farmsteads.[1] The dynamics of cascading water, water sweeping around river bends, and variations of winds, sunlight, and elevations heavily influenced the built environment. Distinct guiding principles influenced settlement at these three sites.

Cascading water in falls or rapids on navigable rivers produced head-of-navigation sites. A head-of-navigation site occurred where rough, rushing water prevented large vessels from continuing upstream and most smaller vessels from continuing downstream. Heads of navigation in the East occurred where rivers flowed from the erosion-resistant rocks in the Piedmont and rushed into the softer sandy Atlantic Coastal Plain. At the points where the rushing water hit the sand, the sand was swept away, creating falls or rapids at those places. Every navigable river flowing from the Appalachians to the Atlantic had a head-of-navigation site. Head-of-navigation sites in the Midwest include Keokuk and Sioux City in Iowa, and Portage in Wisconsin.

A line connecting those sites is known as the "fall line," which in the East runs from Milledgeville, Georgia, on the Oconee River to Lowell, Massachusetts, on the Merrimack River. A similar fall line connects head-of-navigation sites on the tributaries flowing into the Ohio River from Illinois, Indiana, and Ohio. Elsewhere in the Midwest, heads of navigation produce fall lines, albeit less well-defined than the fall line in the East.

The fall line is highly significant in that it spawned towns at or near the falls or rapids on these rivers and impacted overall settlement. Most of these towns became county seats, some became state capitals, and one became Washington DC. Cities on the fall line soon sported at least fourteen of the eighteen or so basic functions of cities. Because vessels could not navigate the falls or rapids, cargoes were offloaded, carried around the rough water, and then reloaded onto other vessels. This offloading and reloading required portage services to move the cargo. Portaging required oxen or mules, workers, the means to clear paths, and wagons, carts, and pallets.[2] This involved feeding and housing workers and animals and servicing and repairing equipment. Because vessels were sometimes unavailable for reloading for further shipment, cargo had to be stored, which necessitated warehouses. Warehouses and workers needed protection, which required coercive government and which motivated these places to obtain county seats, complete with courts, sheriffs, jails, a newspaper of record, surveyors, lawyers, abstract offices, and related activities. These, in turn, led to fine taverns, inns, liveries, and hotels. Such places attracted early telegraphs and then railroads. Livestock in each town's hinterland triggered stockyards, slaughtering, and meat-packing, as well as such allied industries as cooperage, tanning, harness, and soap industries. Threats produced small forts, usually perched on a resistant rock outcrop just upstream, and some forts became arsenals. Warehoused goods triggered wholesaling and retailing functions, accompanied by banking and insurance activities. Schools and churches sprang up, some communities becoming religious centers and college towns. Academies, lyceums, art galleries, museums, and opera houses soon adorned communities. Over time, these towns developed recreational and entertainment facilities. And some ultimately became part of the industrial-educational-defense complex.

Rushing water spawned manufacturing. Mills, usually overshot mills, popped up for sawing timber, grinding grain, spinning wool and cotton, and powering trip hammers.[3] Mill ponds and mill runs stored and channeled water for mills.[4] Trip hammers assisted metal-working and repair facilities, and rope works served vessels. Smithing served many needs. By 1860 coal-fired steam engines supplemented water power, and they allowed manufacturing where no rushing water was found. Often within a generation, costly canals and locks bypassed the falls, enabling vessels to avoid the cascading water.

Durable rocks just upstream from falls avoided erosion. Before long, these rocks supported the foundations of bridges that spanned the streams. These bridges linked road systems that connected cities on the fall line and other communities popping up on the line between the rivers. Ferry services just below the falls provided similar links. Where great distances separated the rivers, new counties were created, each with its county seat.

Cities on the fall line benefited from being "edge settlements." Being on the edges of two regions, they easily tapped both regions' resources and served both hinterlands' markets. Moreover, river navigation allowed them to tap distant regions. Edge settlements enjoyed protection from disasters that afflicted other communities. For example, if parasites devastated crops, animals, or timber downstream from the fall line, settlers could fall back on resources upstream.

The quality of rivers influenced whether or not head-of-navigation sites produced major cities. A democracy of rivers does not exist; some are better than others. For example, rivers with estuaries are more likely to produce significant head-of-navigation cities than rivers without estuaries. Similarly, rivers with many navigable tributaries are more likely to produce such cities than rivers with few navigable tributaries. Conversely, north-flowing rivers in the Northern Hemisphere generally flood twice yearly, in late spring and late summer, which severely inhibits settlement. In addition, rivers used as boundaries—especially international boundaries—are almost always underused rivers or misused rivers; inevitable political squabbles degrade and distort human activities on such rivers. In the Midwest, only the Red River flows north, and the St. Marys, St. Clair, and Detroit Rivers are the only significant rivers used as international boundaries. Generally amiable relations between the United States and Canada benefit both the Midwest and Canada.

Bends in navigable rivers produced the second category of sites. Towns built on the outside of bends had compelling advantages and some disadvantages, and towns built on the inside of bends had a few advantages and severe disadvantages.

Towns on the outside of river bends were perched relatively high on river bluffs, which protected them from floods. Their height, moreover, gave them cooling, drying, life-saving breezes, which suppressed flies and mosquitoes and fetid odors. Elevation provided aesthetically pleasing vistas, enhanced defense, and allowed merchants to spot approaching vessels and be the first to learn what was for sale on the spot. Water on the outside of river bends moves fast, preventing debris and sandbars from accumulating, providing deep-water docks, and powering saw mills, grist mills, and industrial trip hammers. These towns enjoyed huge hinterlands, allowing for large markets and diverse resources and room for expansion. In addition, portages, roads, canals, or railroads linked such towns to distant rivers, lakes, and railroads.

But towns on the outside of bends had some disadvantages. Fast currents eroded river banks, often severely. Townsfolk struggled to keep the banks—and the towns—from being eroded and swept away. Occasionally, currents swept entire towns downstream, sometimes virtually overnight. Swift currents, moreover, made docking tricky and dangerous, and they often slammed logs and other debris into docks and docked vessels. High river banks that provided flood protection, drying breezes, and nice vistas, were steep, making movement of goods and people up and down difficult, expensive, and sometimes dangerous. The construction of warehouses, stores, and dwellings at the foot of bluffs created "lower" towns and partially alleviated this problem, albeit at the risk of floods and erosion. Although the large hinterland encouraged expansion, soil on bluffs was often marginal and cut by gullies, and water supplies there were sometimes limited, unpredictable, or of poor quality. Furthermore, destructive winds and icy blasts pounded structures, livestock, and crops on bluffs. Finally, bluffs sometimes lacked sizable timber stands.

Towns located on the inside of river bends had some advantages. They had rich, alluvial soil, high in organic matter and near the water table. Fish, waterfowl, wood supplies, and other resources abounded. Currents were relatively slow, and sharp winds were rare. Fortifications across the meander neck thwarted attacks.

But such towns suffered severe disadvantages as well. Massive floods devastated them, marshes and decaying vegetation stifled them, and the high water table complicated the construction and maintenance of sizable buildings. Although vegetation was thick, timber quality was problematic, consisting of willows, cottonwoods, and other "trash" trees. Slow and inconsistent currents produced sediment buildup, inhibiting shipping and moving the inside river bank farther and farther from the town. Relatively calm water also attracted debris and sewage. Impure water, sultry air, and swarms of insects triggered lethal diseases. Warm months brought few drying, cooling breezes. Aesthetics were often gloomy. Shallow, sluggish water and debris severely curtailed water power and manufacturing. Enemy artillery on the opposite bank posed threats. Such towns suffered from constricted hinterlands, few land links to the outside world, and little room for expansion.

Another threat, sometimes catastrophic, loomed over towns on both sides of the river. Meandering rivers often burst through their meander necks, immediately carving new river channels, which are sometimes miles from their original channel. This process left once-prosperous towns sitting on stagnant sloughs miles from the newly created main channels. Nevertheless, the advantages enjoyed by towns located on outside bends outweighed disadvantages of such locations and were much greater than advantages enjoyed by towns located on inside bends. Consequently, settlers founded few towns on the inside of river bends.

Rivers and culture combined to produce other towns. Railroads crossing navigable rivers gave birth to towns, giving shippers and travelers the option of at least four routes. Moreover, trains needed water, and often where tracks crossed dependable creeks on the Great Plains, communities popped up to store water for locomotives. Moreover, towns sprang up at the head of railroad construction, where cargo had to be offloaded and put onto wagons or other means of transportation. Similarly, hamlets and villages grew where trains had scheduled stops.

Hoping to tap two or more regions via "edge settlement," town founders located settlements at or near the confluence of rivers. St. Louis benefited from being just downstream from the confluence of the Mississippi, the Missouri, and the Illinois Rivers. Early portaging between two navigable rivers produced one or more towns along the portage path, such as Fort Wayne and South Bend. Some cities flourished at the heads of bays, especially if the bays sported navigable rivers, which was true of Green Bay, Wisconsin, and Bay City, Michigan. Detroit and other cities thrived from choke-point locations, where lake navigation is funneled through constricted waters. Some towns were originally extractive, pulling from the earth or water fish, timber, rock, coal, or oil.

Some towns became county seats or territorial or state capitals, which gave them enormous and sustained advantages over rival towns, which triggered innumerable "court house" wars. They had governmental officials, lawyers, surveyors, realtors, newspapers of record, fine hotels and restaurants, and other advantages. Their influence often attracted railroads, businesses, and other activities. Farms and other properties near county seats were usually worth more than similar properties near other towns.[5]

Clearly, head-of-navigation sites, river bends, and other geographical factors heavily influenced settlement and urban growth, as did prevailing winds, sunlight, and variations of elevation. At the microlevel, prevailing winds, sunlight, and variations of elevation influenced the locations of farmsteads and their development as early farms had no air-conditioning, central heating, electricity, or life-saving wire-mesh window screens. Some principles that influenced decision-making at the farmstead level apparently operated at the town and city level as well.

Farmers located farmsteads on hills and ridges, hoping to gain several advantages: avoid floods; enjoy cooling and drying breezes, breezes that drove away lethal flies and mosquitoes and dried barnyards and areas near doors; enjoy aesthetically pleasing views; detect straying livestock, broken fences, approaching strangers, and other irregularities; secure tactically significant heights for defense; and avoid wasting relatively productive land. At the same time, however, settlers located farmsteads, especially their houses, below the crests of hills or ridges and on the lee sides of prevailing winds to escape violent winds and icy blasts and to reduce time and energy required for walking up steep slopes. However, such locations often increased erosion, the likelihood of debilitating falls of people and livestock, and the distance to public roads and dependable water supplies. They also crimped farmstead expansion.

Prevailing winds and variations in sunlight during the year influenced the locations of the built environment on farmsteads. Wind roses in the Midwest generally show that prevailing winds are from the west, warm southerly breezes and icy northern winds notwithstanding. The prevailing winds are westerlies.

Accordingly, wherever possible, farmers located farmsteads east and south of trees, the trees serving as windbreaks. To minimize odors, flies, jarring noises, and the threat of fire spreading from barns to houses, farmers located barns and barnyards downwind from houses, placing most of them somewhere along an arc from northwest of houses to southeast of houses. Similarly, to maximize the morning sun's drying powers, farmers located barnyards and hog lots east and south of barns. Wanting to dry barnyards quickly, they planted few trees east or south of barnyards, often removing existing trees. Depending upon soil conditions, barnyards sloped between three and seven degrees, usually to the east or south, some sloping in both directions and always away from houses, the doors of key structures, and oft-used lanes.

Farmers designed houses carefully. Wanting to enhance warmth and light in rooms used during the day in winter months, they maximized sunlight there, saving fuel and effort and reducing danger from fire. Whenever possible, living rooms or parlors and dining rooms were located toward the south and west. During winter some rooms were closed off, the kitchen becoming the focal point of household activities. Kitchens on the east side of houses caught warming sunlight during winter, but in the summer strategically planted deciduous trees east of the house shaded the kitchen and the ground near the kitchen.

Farmers planted deciduous trees south, southwest, and west of houses, as well, but far enough away to prevent summer storms from toppling them onto their houses. Such trees rarely shaded houses, but they shaded the ground south and west of houses, and westerly and southerly breezes swept over the cooled ground and cooled houses downwind. Moreover, to assist this cooling and reduce dust, the first true lawns on farmsteads were disproportionately south and west of houses.

Smokehouses were often northeast of houses, and between them and the kitchens were woodsheds. Smokehouses, woodsheds, and privies were usually within sixty feet of houses. Woodsheds stored wood for heating, cooking, and other uses. During the first cold spell, usually by mid-January, annual hog kills occurred, near the smokehouses and woodsheds for convenience. This reduced the time and effort required to stock smokehouses and keep fires going. Hog kills were often communal affairs, lasted for days, and involved sustained fires, belching clouds of eye-watering smoke, foul odors, and (significantly) copious fiery sparks from wood fires. Westerly and northerly winter winds prevented odors, smoke, and dangerous sparks from swirling around houses. These winds also drove away smoke from daily smokehouse operations.[6] Kitchen doors often faced east, and woodshed doors and smokehouse doors usually faced south, which facilitated drying.

Hen houses were typically elongated structures with east-west axes, which maximized southern sunlight. They were near farmhouses, reducing effort required to feed chickens and gather eggs. Sometimes, a deciduous tree or two shaded hen houses from afternoon sun. Most poultry yards were between the house and the hen house, allowing people to keep watch and to throw garbage with comparative ease into the yards. Despite noises and smells generated by poultry, farmers located hen houses upwind from farmhouses, putting up with odors in order to hear racket if predators attacked the chickens.

Farmers situated wells near houses, uphill and away from barnyards, poultry yards, and other sources of pollution. Often, a second well was sunk near the barn. Deciduous trees shaded the paths between houses and wells. Privies were usually sited discreetly behind houses, often blocked from view by vegetation.

Farmhands sometimes lived in the original cabin, or later in specially built houses often called cottages, or in neighboring cabins purchased for their use, but ofttimes they lived in additions with separate entrances. Despite usually being lower-class, nonfamily males, hands ate with the owner and his family, the few exceptions to the contrary occurring on farms operated by recent European immigrants, who soon learned to allow hands to eat with their families. This practice in the Midwest persisted well into the twentieth century.

Gardens were close to houses. To enhance the morning sun's drying powers and promote good drainage, gardens sloped three or four degrees eastward, southeastward, or southward. Women and children tended gardens, starting right after the morning sun burned off the dew, before predators arrived, and before it got hot. To keep dirt off plants, farmers located gardens upwind from dusty roads and lanes. Sometimes trees lined the north and northwest sides of gardens, but few appeared on the east or south sides.

Fencing was important. Fences performed two main functions: keeping animals confined and keeping predators out. Fences kept animals in fields, but they also channeled the movement of animals from one place to another. Post-and-board fencing north and west of farmsteads also served as snow breaks. As finances permitted, post-and-board fences appeared along the road, presenting to passersby evidence of neat, prosperous farms. Post-and-board fences lining driveways from roads to houses presented additional evidence of prosperity. By the late 1880s, after prices of metal plummeted, wrought iron fences enclosed some front yards.

Prevailing winds influenced where crops were grown. For months every year, farmers plowed and harrowed and then planted, cultivated, and harvested corn and other row crops. These activities generated billowing dust and swarms of insects. Consequently, farmers rarely planted row crops upwind from farmhouses. They also avoided moving herds of livestock upwind from houses, especially on windy days. Farmers usually reserved fields upwind from houses for wheat, barley, rye, oats, hay, clover, pastures, and timber lots. Some planted fragrant orchards upwind.

Farmsteads with similar functions located north, south, east, and west of roads suggest much. The emerging grid system of roads in the Midwest heavily influenced farmstead location and layout. Farmsteads north and east of roads often differed from those south and west of roads. To minimize dust, noise, mosquitoes and flies, and wind-driven smells from stagnant water in roadside ditches, settlers situated houses downwind from roads (north and east of roads) farther from roads than houses located upwind (south and west of roads).[7] Although people imperfectly understood causal relationships between stagnant water and disease, they knew to avoid stagnant water in ruts in roads and adjoining ditches and winds that blew over them.

Settlers tried to locate houses upwind from their loop driveways. Planted windbreaks bordered the farmsteads' northern and western edges, about a hundred feet to one hundred and fifty feet from the structures they protected. Windbreaks initially included existing trees and quickly planted, fast-growing trees. Soon, however, settlers planted a mix of fast-growing and slow-growing trees, harvesting the fast-growing trees as slow-growing trees matured. Some farmers mixed conifers with deciduous trees if the windbreaks served as snow breaks. Farmers oriented living rooms toward sunlight and turned houses south of roads forty-five degrees to maximize sunlight in the living room. Kitchens faced east or southeast to catch morning sun in winter and escape afternoon sun in summer. Deciduous trees to the east and southeast protected kitchens from morning summer sun but admitted winter sun. Woodsheds were near kitchens and smoke houses, often between them. Wells were close to kitchens and were sometimes incorporated in houses either by being moved or by being enclosed by additions to houses. Despite such arrangements, no arrangement was perfect. Some arrangements were better than others, but even the best had tradeoffs in convenience, safety, expense, and efficiency.

The guiding principles mentioned above shaped midwestern farmsteads, but what was true in Ohio was not necessarily true in Nebraska, and what was true in Cairo, Illinois, was not necessarily true in Grand Rapids. Unusual variations occurred. For example, settlers responded to obnoxious neighbors or unsightly scenes on neighboring farms by planting trees in unusual places or orienting houses differently, thereby distorting some guiding principles. Moreover, one settler in Illinois, originally from Maryland, successfully replicated the geography of his Maryland farm, though he knew he was creating certain inefficiencies. Ethnic considerations altered guiding principles among English settlers in Edwards County, Illinois, and among German settlers in Madison County, Illinois.[8] Sometimes ignorance of guiding principles produced variations. Also, farmers built new structures, moved or tore down others, or saw them destroyed by fire or storms. New livestock, new crops, new roads, and new technologies (such as barbed wire and windmills) eroded some guiding principles and created new ones.[9]

Some guiding principles may have applied to towns. It's possible, for example, that prevailing winds shaped midwestern towns. Very likely, wealthy people built their fine homes upwind from central business districts, factories, and railroads. They wanted to minimize wind-driven smells, smoke, and noise from railroads, mills, tanneries, breweries, meat-processing establishments, and smithing operations. And they wanted to avoid wind-driven dust and lethal sparks from such places. Today, all things being equal, many large, gracious homes built in the 1800s are west and south of downtowns, only rarely east and northeast. Horse and mule droppings imbued dust in the streets with memorable qualities. Townsfolk loathed this fine dust and its smell, especially after warm rains. Consequently, perhaps, houses on the north and east sides of streets were set back from streets farther than houses on the south and west sides. Similarly, wealthy townsfolk built fine homes on hills, ridges, and river bluffs to avoid floods and lethal dampness and to enjoy lovely views and cooling breezes, breezes that suppressed mosquitoes and flies and dissipated smell and smoke. Poor townsfolk, on the other hand, lived in low-lying parts of towns, which flooded, had stagnant water, smelled, and were sultry and muddy and full of mosquitoes and flies. Moreover, they lived usually downwind from smoky, smelly, noisy industries, industries that spewed particulate matter, including lethal sparks. In suggesting that some guiding principles pertained to towns, I hope further research will either corroborate or refute these findings.

Finally, the guiding principles mentioned above are only that: guiding principles. They are not immutable, eternal, deterministic laws. Local conditions, personal preferences, quirks, desires, ignorance, new technologies, and the passing of time distorted or weakened these principles. Even so, towns and farmsteads reflect the dynamic interplay of nature and culture as shaped by focused intelligence and serious decisions. Towns and farmsteads may appear haphazardly located and formed, but their varied locations and complex shapes are not products of random forces or mushy thinking. Towns and farmsteads continue to reflect the ongoing powerful interplay of culture, nature, guiding principles, and focused intelligence. They challenge us to pause, reflect, and see the familiar in new and exciting ways.

Notes

1. An understanding of agrarian location theory begins with Johann Heinrich von Thunen. A landowner in the early 1800s in northern Germany, he developed over decades insightful understandings of why certain crops and livestock were raised in specific places and not in other places. He assumed an environment with a featureless plain, only one market, no public subsidies such as roads, and highly informed and motivated farmers. Similarly, an understanding of urban location theory begins with Walter Christaller, whose trailblazing work in the 1930s laid foundations for subsequent urban studies. He, too, envisioned a featureless plain on which settlements of various sizes would develop according to Central Place Theory. Over time, he posited, the boundaries of the regions served by each urban place would assume hexagonal shapes, nature's most efficient "packing" shape.

   This chapter does not assume featureless plains. Rather, it assumes irregularities in the landscape and stresses how humans founded towns and established and operated farms according to irregularities in elevation, dynamics of stream flow, prevailing winds, and seasonal and diurnal sunlight. Numerous conversations I have had over decades with farmers and with people raised on farms throughout the Midwest greatly enhanced this chapter. These people provided fine insights concerning the creation of farmsteads, the production of crops, and the raising of livestock, the dynamics of farm activities, and the formation of towns in the nineteenth century.

2. For a succinct account of hardships associated with portaging and for the dangers involved with "shooting" the rapids to avoid portaging, see Ralph

H. Brown, *Historical Geography of the United States* (New York: Harcourt, Brace, 1948), 176 and 241. Basic functions of cities include government, defense, manufacturing, extraction, storage, wholesale, retail, finance, transportation, communication, education, culture, religion, health, recreation, entertainment, tourism, and retirement.

3. Water flowing under the wheels powered undershot mills. They were not as efficient as overshot mills, however, and few were built after 1800. In overshot mills, water fell onto the blades or buckets of the wheel, gravity providing the motive power. Most early mills were located on small streams. By the 1850s, metal gears and rods, leather belts, and improved mill ponds and improved mill runs made mills more powerful, larger, and more dependable. They had fewer breakdowns and less damage from logs and other objects racing down the mill runs. For more on mill developments, see George Rogers Taylor, *The Transportation Revolution, 1815–1860* (New York: Harper and Row, 1951), 222–24. For a sophisticated account of mill developments and their impact on societies, see James E. Vance Jr., *The Role and Structure of the City in the Geography of Western Civilization* (New York: Harper and Row, 1977), especially 322–38.

4. Steam-powered mills enabled mills to operate far from flowing water wherever timber for fuel could be had. By the Civil War, coal powered some engines, and water turbines began to replace waterwheels. Water-powered mills in western portions of the Midwest often suffered from insufficient water supplies especially in late summer and early fall, when demand surged. Water-powered mills in the Upper Midwest often suffered damage or reduced efficiency from the effects of ice.

5. For a good account of county-seat wars and what was at stake, see Daniel J. Boorstin, *The Americans: The National Experience* (New York: Random House, 1965), 165–67. For those that were waged in Illinois, see James E. Davis, *Frontier Illinois* (Bloomington: Indiana University Press, 1998), 320–28. For those county-seat wars that raged between just two settlements, see Patrick Allan Pospisek, "'The Rivalship of Insignificant Villages': Springfield, Illinois, and Town Development in the Old Northwest, 1817–1840," *Historical Geography* 38 (2010): 107–29. Settlements that lost often became ghost towns and utterly vanished. Despite the high stakes and ruined fortunes, lethal violence was virtually unknown. Farms far from county seats suffered disadvantages, many either failing as a result or not appreciating in value as rapidly as those better located.

6. Within a short time, many farms sported a grindstone, which was usually located near the woodshed and the smokehouse and which sharpened

axes, sickles, knives, and other implements. Not far from the kitchen and near the place of the hog kill was the ash bin. Ashes were used for a variety of purposes, including the making of soap and dyes.

7. Some evidence suggests that ethnicity influenced how far people located their houses from public roads. For example, Germans may have located their houses farther from public roads than others. If this is true, the reason for it is not readily apparent, but it may have had something to do with Germans' aversion to dust, dirt, and odors. In any case, many travelers in the nineteenth century claimed that German farmsteads were neat, trim, and clean.

8. An enduring classic study of farmsteads is Glenn T. Trewartha, "Some Regional Characteristics of American Farmsteads," *Annals of the Association of American Geographers* 38, no. 30 (September 1948). It deals with location, frequencies, shapes, and sizes of various farmstead structures, farmstead architecture, topography, and other facets of farmsteads in various regions of the United States. Significant regional differences are obvious. Methodology is also discussed. This work spawned many subsequent studies.

9. Daniel Halladay's patent in 1854 was for a self-governing windmill that could draw water from a hundred feet or more below ground. He was from Connecticut, but soon moved to Illinois, where he had access to a huge and growing market. Windmills provided water for humans, livestock, and crops, and for water tanks for locomotives, especially in places in the western portions of the Midwest, where streams were either absent or unreliable. Abundant, reliable water supplies attracted railroads, sharply increasing the value of farms near railroad stations and stops. Improvements in windmills in the nineteenth century included tails that directed them into the wind, steel blades after the Civil War, curved blades, self-lubricating windmills by the early 1900s, and governors that kept windmills from disintegrating during windstorms. Widespread electrification by the 1930s ended the need for most windmills.

3

First Cousins

THE CIVIL WAR'S IMPACT
ON MIDWESTERN IDENTITY

Nicole Etcheson

Among the successful authors who graced Indiana's golden age of literature was Meredith Nicholson who wrote an account of the Midwest, or West, as he called it in 1918. Upon being charged that his "West" much resembled Kentucky, he asserted that this "does not distress me a particle, for are not we of Ohio, Indiana, and Illinois first cousins of the people across the Ohio?"[1]

The association of the Lower Midwest with the South remains not only strong, but strongly negative. The *New York Times* titled an article discussing Indiana's conflicted reaction to the outbreak of the Civil War "Up South."[2] Several comments on the *Disunion* blog, where the article appeared, referenced the Ku Klux Klan, one of which noted that "Indiana had the strongest KKK, and essentially picked the Governor in 1924. The head of the KKK, D. C. stephenson [*sic*], who was from Indiana."[3] Two others expanded on the Klan theme, although one did acknowledge that the Klan of the 1920s was a different organization than the Southern Klan of Reconstruction. But all agreed on the Southern influence on the state. One commentator wrote, "As a Hoosier by birth, I used to comment that the Mason-Dixon line ran through Muncie IN."[4] And another pithily observed, "So THAT's what's wrong with Indiana. Thanks."[5]

There is both truth and misunderstanding in this continued association between the Midwest and South. The Lower Midwest states such as Indiana, Ohio, and Illinois were settled heavily by people of the Upland South. This resulted in a strong Southern influence on material culture, social values, and politics. The Civil War forced a rejection of the South, however, if not in sentiment then in policy. Midwesterners accepted that the South had to be subordinated and northeastern abolitionist values adopted for the good of the Union. After the Civil War, the Lower Midwest solidified its position as a place in the middle: despite a continued identification with the South, substantive differences in race relations nonetheless made the Midwest a distinctively non-Southern place.

Nineteenth-century Americans understood connections between regions as determined by two factors among many: the origins of the settlers and the culture established by those settlers. The work of Gregory Rose has demonstrated that the Lower Midwest was settled heavily by upland southerners. We know that migration routes led across or down the Ohio River from states such as North Carolina, Virginia, and Kentucky. The 1850 Census, the first to give us place of birth, tells us that roughly 10 to 20 percent of lower midwesterners were born in such Upper South states, and that another 50 to 60 percent were born in their respective midwestern state. As for Ohioans, Hoosiers, or Illinoisans who listed one of those states as their birthplaces in 1850, most likely had parents born in Kentucky or another Southern state.[6]

Culture is a little more amorphous. It can include foodways, log cabin construction, and values such as manliness and honor. Best known, however, as the blog posts indicate, is the convergence of attitudes on race. We know that racism was an American, not merely a Southern or midwestern, phenomenon. For example, Prudence Crandall, who was hounded into jail for admitting black students to her female seminary, lived in Connecticut.[7] Ellis Mitchell, a free black traveling with two whites, found that he was made to eat in the kitchen in both Ohio and Virginia. Despite his companions' pleas that Mitchell was not their servant, that he owned property, and was a "respectable gentleman," an Ohio tavern keeper declared, "He can't eat at my table with white folks."[8] Recent scholarship has made us aware that there were interstices in the system of white supremacy, which some Southern free blacks exploited. Eva Sheppard Wolf has chronicled the decades-long effort of Samuel Johnson, who petitioned the Virginia legislature to allow himself and his family to remain in the state even though Virginia law required free blacks to emigrate. Despite their indeterminate status, the Johnsons lived in the state as free blacks.[9]

Despite the many commonalities in population, culture, and racial attitudes that parts of the Midwest shared with the South, the Civil War opened a gap between the regions. The origins of disunion can be traced back to the founding of the republic, as Elizabeth R. Varon has done, but she does devote over a third of her book to the 1850s, reaffirming that decade's primacy as the pivotal era of sectional conflict. In discussing the Compromise of 1850, her concern is with the extremes of North and South: Daniel Webster's "apostasy" for accepting a fugitive slave law; William H. Seward's defense of a "higher law"; and the dying John C. Calhoun's defiance of threatened Northern "subjugation."[10] In Indiana, Governor Joseph A. Wright repudiated such sectionalism, declaring that "Indiana takes her stand in the ranks, not of Southern Destiny, nor yet of Northern destiny. She plants herself on the basis of the Constitution."[11] At the same time, however, some in the state were beginning to demand a Northern spirit. A Centerville, Indiana, meeting protested the 1850 Compromise, especially its fugitive slave bill, for "yielding of rights on the part of the North to the supercilious demands of Southern slaveholders."[12]

Years of turmoil over slavery in the territories produced increasing calls for the North to stand up for itself. The breakup of the Democratic Party occurred because Northern Democrats could not stomach measures that appealed to Southern Democrats, such as the Kansas-Nebraska Act and the effort to force the proslavery Lecompton Constitution on Kansas. Lecompton especially drove some midwestern politicians past their breaking point. Illinois senator Stephen A. Douglas, who had authored the pro-Southern Kansas-Nebraska Act, refused to support a proslavery constitution for a territory where free-state settlers were the majority. One of Douglas's supporters, John Givan Davis of Indiana, got into a shouting match in Congress with William Smith of Virginia over the Hoosier's refusal to support Lecompton. Since President James Buchanan had made Lecompton a test of party loyalty, Smith accused Davis of using the "language of rebellion," to which Davis replied, "It is the language of a freeman, and not the language of a slave."[13]

By the election of 1860, young politician John Hanna was promising voters in Indiana that, although the new Republican Party would respect the rights of the South, he wondered whether "the North had no rights which should be respected."[14] In his classic monograph *Free Soil, Free*

Labor, Free Men, Eric Foner has laid out the ideology of the Republican Party, a Northern party with no adherents in the Deep South. This Republican Party ideology combined "resentment of southern political power . . . [and] a commitment to the northern social order and its development and expansion." The social order could be ugly in its racism, but it opposed slavery at the very least for being if not an immoral social system then one inferior in its economic effects to the Northern free-labor system. While Republican presidential candidate Abraham Lincoln obtained none of the popular vote in nine Southern states, he received 55 percent of the midwestern popular vote, slightly lower than the 60 percent popular vote he got in the northeastern states.[15]

The occasional midwesterner with strong Southern ties might go south and fight for the Confederacy. Henry Lane Stone, whose family moved from Kentucky to Indiana when he was nine, left the state in 1862, crossed into Kentucky, and joined the Confederate cavalry under John Hunt Morgan. The next year, when Morgan raided Indiana and Ohio, Stone "engaged in a hostile invasion of my adopted State."[16] But it was much more common for midwesterners of Southern descent to fight on the Union side. Stone's own two brothers, much to his chagrin, were in the Union army. Fifty-seven percent of military-aged Hoosiers enlisted in the Union army, a number that could not have been achieved without men of Southern ancestry.[17]

Nonetheless, antiwar Democrats, known as Copperheads, after the midwestern snake, were a substantial minority in the region. It is difficult to know to what degree huzzahing for Jeff Davis, or violently resisting the draft, reflected actual support for the Confederacy or merely anger and disaffection with the Lincoln administration and its policies. These policies included the first conscription in United States history; other infringements of civil liberties, such as suspending the writ of habeas corpus and jailing Democratic newspaper editors; instituting the Whig party economic program; and emancipation.[18]

Copperheads had some sympathy with the South. Hoosier John Runyan said, "The Northern soldiers have gone South just to steal the Southern men's property, and he didn't blame the rebels to kill them, and he would kill them if he were in their places."[19] Runyan may have belonged to the Knights of the Golden Circle (KGC) or the Sons of Liberty, secret societies of armed men who organized to stop the draft. Spies infiltrated the Indiana KGC and Governor Oliver P. Morton had several of its leaders arrested in August 1864. Some of the KGC's leaders may have been in league with Confederate agents. At its most elaborate, the plan involved coordinated uprisings in Illinois and Indiana, the liberation of Confederate prisoners from camps in Chicago and Indianapolis, and perhaps even the creation of a Northwest Confederacy—a separate midwestern government that would ally with the South.[20] But even if the KGC leadership was involved in an active plot to aid the Confederacy, the adjutant general of Indiana, W. H. H. Terrell, concluded that many members "never knew the treasonable schemes into which they were intended to be driven."[21]

Among the complex motivations prompting pro-Southern midwesterners, race and the draft loomed large. Copperheads blamed the war on "antislavery fanatics" in the Republican Party. The Emancipation Proclamation merely proved that the Lincoln administration had instigated the war to end slavery.[22] In Putnam County, Indiana, Democrats resolved: "That we believe that our Fathers established this Government for the benefit of the white man alone; and in considering the terms of settlement of our national troubles we will look only to the welfare, peace and safety of the white race, without reference to the effect that settlement may have upon the condition of the African."

These Democrats feared that emancipation would allow the movement of "a worthless negro population," which would "settle in the free States, contrary to the will of the people." Whites and blacks living in the free states would lead to placing "the two races upon terms of perfect equality."[23] Accusations that emancipation would lead to social equality culminated during the 1864 election in an anti-Republican pamphlet that invented the word "miscegenation" for racial intermarriage. The pamphlet was the work of New York Democrats, but it was taken up by many Northern Copperheads, including Ohio congressman Samuel Cox, because it seemed self-evident that the Republican policy of "perfect social equality of black and white . . . can only end in this detestable doctrine of—miscegenation!"[24]

Midwesterners often accepted emancipation as a military necessity. Indiana soldier W. H. McIlvain explained, "*Slavery is the cause of this war*, which no one will deny. It is also the *life* and *sinew* in supporting and prolonging this war. . . . The Proclamation is simply a *military necessity*. It is bound to cripple the rebellion, for every healthy negro that we take from them, makes one soldier less in the ranks."[25] Aden Cavins had mixed feelings about the Proclamation: he admired the president's firmness is going through with it, but felt it would have little good effect on the slaves, whom he deemed too ignorant, lazy, and shiftless to put it to good use. But he believed "that we ought to strip the rebels of everything," including slaves, either to win the war or as punishment for rebellion.[26]

While her soldier husband was away in the Union army, Mary Vermilion stayed with his Copperhead relatives in Indiana. She agreed with their racism, telling a family member that she didn't like "niggers" either. But she sought to counter his apprehensions about what emancipation would mean. Mary forced him to confess that he had not "*seen* a negro since the Proclamation" or even heard of one in the neighborhood, countering white fears that Northern states would face an influx of former slaves once emancipation occurred.[27] Vermilion's outspokenness reveals that women engaged in political discussion as well as the volunteer activities, such as nursing and organizing for the United States Sanitary Commission, for which they were better known.[28]

Vermilion was able to persuade her relative that some of his fears were illusory. However, while large numbers of freed slaves did not materialize, the threat of conscription was a real one. Mary Vermilion linked Copperhead activity to determination "to resist the draft."[29] In the Indiana treason trials, Elliott Richardson testified that the Sons of Liberty intended to stop the draft and other violations of civil liberties.[30] In Sullivan County, Indiana, members of the Sons had resolved to "resist the draft, by force of arms, if necessary, because they were not willing to submit to the government. They decided that the conscript law was unconstitutional and they would not obey it."[31]

Throughout the North, men armed themselves to resist the draft. Congress passed the Enrollment Act in the spring of 1863. Draft officers began compiling the list of eligible young men. Resisters threatened and even

shot at enrollment officers. Women protecting their menfolk set dogs or
threw boiling water on them. According to historian Jennifer L. Weber,
the Provost Marshal General Bureau reported thirty-eight enrolling officers killed and sixty wounded throughout the country. In New York
City, for several days in early July 1863, mobs of working-class, mostly
Irish men and women prevented the holding of the draft lottery. Over
one hundred people were killed in what was, up to that date, the most
deadly riot in American history. Most of the dead were rioters, killed by
soldiers brought in to suppress the riot, but almost a dozen blacks were
killed by the mob, which sometimes mutilated their bodies. The New
York City draft riots became the best-known act of draft resistance and
showed how the rage unleashed by conscription intersected with that
unleashed by emancipation. But, as historian Joan E. Cashin has written,
"There was a great deal of small-scale violent resistance" to the draft.[32]

The Copperheads provoked enormous animosity from their fellow
midwesterners who saw them as being as much traitors as the Con-
federates. McIlvain vowed, "*Death! O! how I do like to administer this
medicine to traitors.* I want every man in the North who sympathizes
with rebellion drafted. If they wont [*sic*] fight in battle, they will make
breastworks for Union soldiers!"[33] Josiah Williams, also an Indiana soldier, was among troops sent to New York in August to prevent further
draft resistance. He relished the job, writing, "We are the boys to do it."[34]
Back in the Midwest, soldiers on furlough often got into fights with Copperheads. During an 1864 Democratic rally in Greencastle, Indiana, Lt.
John Cooper attacked a Copperhead who was hallooing for Jeff Davis
and beat him with a billiards cue. (The assembled Democrats, including
women, then turned on Cooper, who had to flee for his life.)[35]

Ultimately, the draft was intended to stimulate volunteering rather
than actually conscript large numbers. Many men failed to show up,
failed the medical exam, received family hardship exemptions, paid
commutation, or bought a substitute.[36] The draft was not the threat it
appeared to be and resistance subsided. And, of course, the end of the
war brought the end of the draft.

But the end of the war did not mean the end of the pro-black agenda,
far from it. The Civil War swept away midwestern black laws. African

Americans did take advantage of the war's disruption to make their way into neighboring states—black Missourians into Kansas and Iowa and black Kentuckians into Ohio and Indiana. Even upper midwestern states such as Wisconsin, Iowa, and Minnesota saw their small black populations quadruple in the years after the Civil War. In addition to the individual initiative shown by slaves who escaped into the North, Union troops or the government even organized efforts to send black refugees to Northern communities. Some midwesterners welcomed the new arrivals as workers able to stanch a labor shortage, while others feared competition for jobs. In the Midwest, however, recently eman-cipated slaves and free blacks still had to win the rights of citizenship and suffrage.[37]

Certainly midwestern African Americans believed that the war, and their participation in it, entitled them, if not to "perfect equality," then to citizenship and rights previously denied them. William Gibson, a veteran of the Twenty-Eighth United States Colored Troops, argued that black soldiers deserved "the rights and privileges due to other cit-izens."[38] Soldiers of the Sixtieth U.S. Colored Infantry, mustering out in Davenport, Iowa, resolved that, without the rights of citizenship, "our well-earned freedom is but a shadow." While black men pursued the vote, women were more likely to press for integrating schools and public transportation.[39]

The war's end is a particularly good moment for capturing the diver-gence in regional views about race relations. White Southerners had not yet assimilated the idea of emancipation. Freedmen's Bureau records indi-cate that whites continued to physically punish workers, often refused to pay them, and sometimes declared "that black people are not free."[40] Christopher G. Memminger suggested to President Andrew Johnson that freedom did not mean that blacks might not be kept as laborers. He suggested an apprenticeship system. Congress required the Southern states to ratify the Thirteenth Amendment, emancipating the slaves, and the Fourteenth Amendment, granting African American citizenship, as conditions of Reconstruction. Despite the requirements, some South-ern states refused to accept the amendments.[41] During Reconstruction, whites used violence and intimidation, in what Eric Foner has called a "wave of counterrevolutionary terror," to undo the political gains made by African Americans.[42] Starting with Mississippi's 1890 constitution, Deep South states began to disfranchise African Americans by means of literacy tests, understanding clauses, poll taxes, residency requirements, grandfather clauses, and other seemingly race-neutral legal and constitutional measures, all of which had a devastating impact on black voting (as well as that of poor whites).[43]

In the Midwest, there was considerable resistance to the advancement of black rights. From at least 1864 on, Indiana Republicans engaged in a rear-guard action, denying that the Emancipation Proclamation or the Thirteenth Amendment would lead to black citizenship and black voting. As late as 1868, after the Reconstruction Acts had given Southern freedmen the vote, Indiana Republicans declared that, in the North, voting qualifications would still be set by the states. By implication, if Indiana did not want to enfranchise blacks, it would not have to. After the Civil War, black suffrage measures were defeated in Minnesota, Kansas, and Ohio, although Wisconsin, Minnesota, and Iowa did enfranchise blacks before the Fifteenth Amendment made that national. Some midwestern states resisted black enfranchisement to the end. Indiana ratified the Fifteenth Amendment only after Democrats twice resigned from the state legislature in order to break the quorum and prevent ratification.[44] Nonetheless, Peter Kolchin argues that the war turned Northerners toward sympathy to "loyal southerners," namely blacks. The war also made Northerners determined to break the Slave Power and committed them to "an unusually far-reaching effort to transform the entire southern social order."[45]

Despite their ambivalence toward black rights, once established there was no going back in the Midwest. In their World War II–era study of blacks in Chicago, St. Clair Drake and Horace R. Cayton noted that migrants from the South found a "color line," but one "far less rigid than in the South." They could vote and many public spaces were not segregated.[46] The Midwest had segregated schools, as evidenced by the title of the famous school desegregation case: *Brown* v. *Topeka Board of Education*. But when the Supreme Court ordered desegregation, massive resistance was a Southern tactic. Instead, the North would have battles in cities such as Indianapolis and, even more bitterly, Boston, over busing children to achieve racial parity in the schools. But as Ronald P. Formisano has argued in the case of Boston, ethnicity and neighborhood loyalties have been as much a part of resistance to busing as race.[47] Nor did the Midwest attempt to disfranchise blacks as did the South. An African American student at Ball State University, in reminiscing about coming of voting age, recalled asking his father how it felt to cast that first ballot. Having turned twenty-one in Florida before the civil rights era, his father had not even attempted to register, knowing it would be futile, and did not vote until moving to Indiana in middle age.

Neither did the resurgence of the Ku Klux Klan in the 1920s indicate a convergence of the Midwest and the South. As James H. Madison has pointed out, the first Klan of Reconstruction and the segregationist third Klan both promoted white supremacy. The early twentieth-century second Klan, popular in Indiana and other parts of the North, was primarily anti-immigrant and anti-Catholic. This is not to say that white Southerners were open-minded about everyone except blacks. When Georgians lynched Leo Frank, a Jew, for raping and murdering thirteen-year-old Mary Phagan, they chose to believe the testimony of the black janitor, Jim Conley, who may have been the real murderer. Certainly, midwesterners had antiblack prejudices. As Madison has documented, the 1930 Marion, Indiana, lynching was racially motivated, but the Klan was "dead" in Indiana by the time a mob hanged Abe Smith and Tom Shipp. Lawrence Beitler's horrific photograph of the bodies has become the iconic lynching photograph, often misidentified as having occurred in the Deep South.[48] The second Klan arose for distinctively different reasons than the first and third Klans that were dominant in the South. Blog commentators are incorrect to conflate antiblack sentiment in Indiana with the second Klan.

Bound by historic ties of kinship and fellow feeling on issues such as race, the Midwest may be distinct, while not always differing completely, from the South. Opened in 1962, during the Civil War centennial and on the south side of town, Muncie, Indiana's new high school became the Rebels, complete with Confederate flag. A black alumnus prefers to remember the mascot as symbolizing rebellion against the town's other high school, Muncie Central. A school board member believed the flag had meaning to many Munsonians with family roots in Tennessee. Nonetheless, racial tensions led to the retirement of the flag and its replacement with a cannon as the mascot.[49] Ball State students, coming from other parts of Indiana, are generally surprised to find an Indiana school called the Rebels. Muncie Southside might be the exception that proves the rule: a small reminder of the Midwest's historic links to the South in a region where those ties have attenuated over time.

Notes

1. Meredith Nicholson, *The Valley of Democracy* (New York: Charles Scribner's Sons, 1918), 264.
2. Nicole Etcheson, "Up South," September 25, 2011, http://opinionator.blogs .nytimes.com/2011/09/25/up-south/#more-106165.
3. From macculloch, September 26, 2011, http://opinionator.blogs.nytimes .com/2011/09/25/up-south/#more-106165.
4. Todd Ianuzzi, September 26, 2011, http://opinionator.blogs.nytimes.com /2011/09/25/up-south/#more-106165; blasmaic, September 26, 2011, http:// opinionator.blogs.nytimes.com/2011/09/25/up-south/#more-106165.
5. Ty, September 26, 2011, http://opinionator.blogs.nytimes.com/2011/09/25 /up-south/#more-106165.
6. Gregory S. Rose, "Upland Southerners: The County Origins of Southern Migrants to Indiana by 1850," *Indiana Magazine of History* 82 (September 1986): 242–63; Nicole Etcheson, *The Emerging Midwest: Upland Southerners and the Political Culture of the Old Northwest, 1878–1861* (Bloomington: Indiana University Press, 1996), 2–3.
7. Etcheson, *Emerging Midwest*, 4; James Brewer Stewart, *Holy Warriors: The Abolitionists and American Slavery* (New York: Hill and Wang, 1997), 665.
8. Levi Coffin, *Reminiscences of Levi Coffin* (Cincinnati: Robert Clark, 1880), 120–25.
9. Eva Sheppard Wolf, *Almost Free: A Story about Family and Race in Antebellum Virginia* (Athens: University of Georgia Press, 2012).
10. Elizabeth R. Varon, *Disunion! The Coming of the American Civil War, 1789–1859* (Chapel Hill: University of North Carolina Press, 2008), 216–21.
11. Emma Lou Thornbrough, *Indiana in the Civil War Era, 1850–1880* (Indianapolis: Indiana Historical Society, 1995), 49.
12. Thornbrough, *Indiana in the Civil War Era*, 48.
13. Nicole Etcheson, *Bleeding Kansas: Contested Liberty in the Civil War Era* (Lawrence: University Press of Kansas, 2004), 175. The classic account of

the disintegration of the Northern Democrats is Roy F. Nichols, *The Disruption of American Democracy* (New York: Macmillan, 1948).

14. *Putnam Republican Banner*, January 25, 1860.

15. Eric Foner, *Free Soil, Free Labor, Free Men: The Ideology of the Republican Party before the Civil War* (New York: Oxford University Press, 1995), 310; "Election of 1860," *The American Presidency Project* (1999), http://www.presidency.ucsb.edu/showelection.php?year=1860.

16. Henry Lane Stone, *"Morgan's Men": A Narrative of Personal Experiences* (Louisville: Westerfield-Bonte, 1919), 12–13.

17. E. Polk Johnson, *A History of Kentucky and Kentuckians: The Leaders and Representative Men in Commerce, Industry and Modern Activities* (Chicago: Lewis, 1912), 647–49; Thornbrough, *Indiana in the Civil War Era*, 124.

18. Jennifer L. Weber, *Copperheads: The Rise and Fall of Lincoln's Opponents in the North* (New York: Oxford University Press, 2006); Stephen E. Towne, "Killing the Serpent Speedily: Governor Morton, General Hascall, and the Suppression of the Democratic Press in Indiana, 1863," *Civil War History* 52 (March 2006): 41–65.

19. Dollie to [William], April 16, 1863 in *Love amid the Turmoil: The Civil War Letters of William and Mary Vermilion*, ed. Donald C. Elder III (Iowa City: University of Iowa Press, 2003), 78.

20. Weber, *Copperheads*, 148–49. See Stephen E. Towne, *Surveillance and Spies in the Civil War: Exposing Confederate Conspiracies in America's Heartland* (Athens: Ohio University Press, 2015) for the most complete and convincing account of Copperhead subversive activities.

21. W. H. H. Terrell, *Indiana in the War of the Rebellion: Report of the Adjutant General*, 8 vols. (1869; repr., Indianapolis: Indiana Historical Society, 1960), 1:379–80.

22. "Public Meeting of the Union Men of Putnam County," *Indianapolis Daily State Sentinel*, April 15, 1861; Meeting of Putnam County Democrats, *Parke County Republican*, March 11, 1863.

23. Meeting of Putnam County Democrats, *Parke County Republican*, March 11, 1863.

24. Weber, *Copperheads*, 160–61.

25. *Putnam Republican Banner*, April 2, 1863.

26. *War Letters of Aden G. Cavins, Written to his Wife Matilda Livingston Cavins* (Evansville IN: Rosenthal-Kuebler, n.d.), 30–33, in Aden G. Cavins, Alumni Files, Archives and Special Collections, DePauw University, Greencastle.

27. Dollie to [William], March 11, 1863, in *Love amid the Turmoil*, ed. Donald C. Elder, 68–69.

28. See Jane E. Schultz, *Women at the Front: Hospital Workers in Civil War America* (Chapel Hill: University of North Carolina Press, 2004), and Judith Ann Giesberg, *Civil War Sisterhood: The U.S. Sanitary Commission and Women's Politics in Transition* (Boston: Northeastern University Press, 2000).

29. Dollie to [William], July 15, 1863, in *Love amid the Turmoil*, ed. Donald C. Elder, 166–67.

30. Samuel Klaus, ed., *The Milligan Case* (New York: Da Capo Press, 1970), 325–26. See also, Robert Churchill, "Liberty, Conscription, and a Party Divided: The Sons of Liberty Conspiracy, 1863–1864," *Prologue* 30 (Winter 1998): 295–303.

31. Weber, *Copperheads*, 128–29.

32. Eugene C. Murdock, *One Million Men: The Civil War Draft in the North* (Westport: Greenwood, 1971), 42–43; Weber, *Copperheads*, 105; Iver Bernstein, *The New York City Draft Riots: Their Significance for American Society and Politics in the Age of the Civil War* (New York: Oxford University Press, 1990); Joan E. Cashin, "Deserters, Civilians, and Draft Resistance in the North," in *The War Was You and Me: Civilians in the American Civil War*, ed. Joan E. Cashin (Princeton: Princeton University Press, 2002), 262–85, esp. 273.

33. *Putnam Republican Banner*, April 2, 1863.

34. J. C. Williams to Parents, August 20, 1863, Josiah C. Williams Letters, Manuscripts of the Indiana Division, Indiana State Library, Indianapolis.

35. Weber, *Copperheads*, 147; *Daily Wabash Express*, August 2, 1864.

36. J. Matthew Gallman, *The North Fights the Civil War: The Home Front* (Chicago: Ivan R. Dee, 1994), 68–70.

37. The black population of Kansas rose from less than 1 percent to almost 9 percent; the black population of Indiana doubled from 1860 to 1870. James R. Shortridge, *Peopling the Plains: Who Settled Where in Frontier Kansas* (Lawrence: University Press of Kansas, 1995), 29; Etcheson, *A Generation at War*, 167; Leslie A. Schwalm, *Emancipation's Diaspora: Race and Reconstruction in the Upper Midwest* (Chapel Hill: University of North Carolina Press, 2009), 2, 66, 81, 175.

38. Edwin S. Redkey, ed., *A Grand Army of Black Men: Letters from African-American Soldiers in the Union Army, 1861–1865* (Cambridge: Cambridge University Press, 1992), 223–25.

39. Schwalm, *Emancipation's Diaspora*, 180–206.

40. "Cases Adjudicated by the Freedmen's Bureau Superintendent at Gordonsville, Virginia," August 16–September 13, 1865, in *Freedom: A Documentary History of Emancipation, 1861–1867*, series 3, vol. 1, *Land and*

Labor, 1865, ed. Steven Hahn et al. (Chapel Hill: University of North Carolina Press, 2008), 523–27.

41. Christopher G. Memminger to Andrew Johnson, September 4, 1865, in *The Papers of Andrew Johnson,* vol. 9, *September 1865–January 1866,* ed. Paul H. Bergeron et al. (Knoxville: University of Tennessee Press, 1991), 22–26; Michael W. Fitzgerald, *Splendid Failure: Postwar Reconstruction in the American South* (Chicago: Ivan R. Dee, 2007), 29, 34, 45.

42. Eric Foner, *Reconstruction: America's Unfinished Revolution, 1836–1877* (New York: Harper and Row, 1988), 425.

43. Edward L. Ayers, *The Promise of the New South: Life after Reconstruction* (New York: Oxford University Press, 1992).

44. Thornbrough, *Indiana in the Civil War Era,* 240, 242–44; Foner, *Reconstruction,* 223.

45. Peter Kolchin, "Reexamining Southern Emancipation in Comparative Perspective," *Journal of Southern History* 81 (February 2015): 14–15.

46. St. Clair Drake and Horace R. Cayton, *Black Metropolis: A Study of Negro Life in a Northern City* (New York: Harcourt, Brace, 1845), 99–128, 276.

47. James T. Patterson, *Brown v. Board of Education: A Civil Rights Milestone and Its Troubled Legacy* (New York: Oxford University Press, 2001); James H. Madison, *Hoosiers: A New History of Indiana* (Bloomington: Indiana University Press, 2014), 314–15; Ronald P. Formisano, *Boston against Busing: Race, Class, and Ethnicity in the 1960s and 1970s* (Chapel Hill: University of North Carolina Press, 1991).

48. Madison, *Hoosiers,* 242–46; Leonard Dinnerstein, "Leo Frank Case," *New Georgia Encyclopedia* (2003), http://www.georgiaencyclopedia.org/articles/history-archaeology/leo-frank-case; James H. Madison, *A Lynching in the Heartland: Race and Memory in America* (New York: Palgrave, 2011), 4–41, 115–16.

49. John M. Coski, *The Confederate Battle Flag: America's Most Embattled Emblem* (Cambridge: Harvard University Press, 2005), 207; Thomas St. Myer, "Confederate Flag Is Part of the History at Southside," *Muncie Star Press,* June 8, 2014.

PART 2

The Midwest's People

4

Native Americans and Midwestern History

Susan E. Gray

How do we shoehorn Indigenous histories and traditional homelands—
which range over the center of the continent without particular regard
for either international or state and provincial boundaries—into the
twelve-state area today usually considered the Midwest? Viewed from
the vantage point of its history before the arrival of Europeans, the Indigenous "Midwest" presents a sprawling complexity rivaling that of the
American region. Far from static, this precontact history featured migration as revealed both in origin stories and archaeological evidence, such
as the westward movement of the ancestors of the Anishinaabeg, also
known as the Three Fires of the Ojibwe (Chippewa), Odawa (Ottawa),
and Boodewaadaamii (Potawatomi), up the Ottawa River and into the
area around northern Lake Huron by about AD 1000. From there they
spread out to occupy a homeland, Anishinaabewaki, that extended from
the eastern Great Lakes to the prairie West on both sides of what became
the international border between Canada and the United States.[1] To the
south of the Anishinaabeg lived other Algonquian-speaking peoples;
to the west, Siouan speakers, the other major language group of the
Indigenous Midwest. Three economic complexes characterized this vast
expanse, ranging from more sedentary economies based on agriculture
in the south to more migratory ways of life in the north that were largely
reliant on hunting and gathering. By about AD 1000 the northern climatic limits of corn growing (144 frost-free days) had been reached in
an economic transition zone between the northern and southern complexes, whose occupants combined the growing of corn, squash, and
beans with gathering, fishing, maple sugaring, and the hunt. In general,
the more sedentary and agricultural the economy, the more complicated
the social order, including political roles for women who controlled
agricultural production.[2]

This precontact Indigenous history of the Midwest is remote from the history of the American region; if mentioned at all in state histories, it appears only briefly onstage as a warm-up act before the curtain goes up. In histories of the American Midwest, the role of Indigenous peoples usually begins with contact with Europeans in the seventeenth century and ends with their loss of political autonomy with the conclusion of the War of 1812 and the solidification of American authority in the region. Midwestern histories have long treated Native Americans as irrelevant to the business of white settlement after 1815 and as having ceased to play a role in the development of the region by the Civil War, if not earlier. This discursive removal of Indigenous peoples from formal histories and popular writings alike ostensibly reflected their physical absence from the region as a result of the federal policy of removal inaugurated by the 1830 Indian Removal Act, a plan to relocate all Native Americans living east of the Mississippi to west of the river. But as Patrick Wolfe has forcefully pointed out, the "logic of elimination" has many practical applications.[3] In the Midwest, the discursive technique for disappearing Indigenous people proved as effective as forcible bodily removal, because it was applied to the entire region, including those areas where the federal policy failed or was never imposed, and took no account of Indigenous peoples who began to remove themselves west of the Mississippi in the face of encroaching white settlers as early as the 1790s.[4]

Why has the dominant narrative of midwestern history been predicated on the absence of people who have endured, in growing numbers, in the region to the present day? At the center of this conundrum lies the contrast between the stasis of the narrative—Indians gone, white settlement completed, region integrated into nation—and the mobility of Indigenous peoples and of the region itself. Peter Iverson has characterized Native American history as a "map in motion," and so, too, is the history of the Midwest as a region.[5] Exploring where and how these two maps overlap helps to resolve the puzzle posed by the midwestern narrative. This chapter thus has two objectives: to consider the ideological context of the removal of Indigenous peoples from midwestern history, and to examine the roles they actually played in the political and economic development of the region as colonial subjects, laborers under industrial capitalism, and sovereign nations. Instead of dwelling on the period before 1815, this chapter evokes a nineteenth- and twentieth-century story that is still with us today.

References to the Midwest as the twelve-state region composed of the five states of the Old Northwest (Ohio, Indiana, Illinois, Michigan, and Wisconsin) and seven other states lying, for the most part, west of the Mississippi River (Minnesota, Iowa, Nebraska, Kansas, Missouri, and North and South Dakota) are fairly recent, following the decision of the Federal Census Bureau to switch its designation of the area from North Central region to Midwest in 1984. This expansive definition of the Midwest makes the region's history part of both the trans-Appalachian West and the trans-Mississippi West, a fact also reflected in the history of the term "Midwest" itself. As James R. Shortridge has shown, the travel writer Timothy Flint coined the term in the early nineteenth century to refer to Kentucky and Tennessee, or the middle of the trans-Appalachian West, then drawing tens of thousands of emigrants from the Eastern Seaboard. By the 1880s, the Midwest had made its way to the high plains then being settled, where it again served as a simply geographical referent denoting the middle of the trans-Mississippi West. During the national depression of the 1890s, however, the Midwest acquired a new moral charge that associated it with youth, public virtue, and agrarianism in contrast to the corrupt, aged, industrial East. Endowed with such attributes, the Midwest returned east, where it became synonymous with the Old Northwest in the writings of Frederick Jackson Turner and others. This last migration was no quiet movement of a useful geographical referent, but a triumphal, ideological march; in its new home in the Old Northwest, the Midwest was celebrated as the most American of regions, its history epitomizing American nation-building. Alas, by the 1920s, epitome for many Americans turned to epithet, as the Midwest acquired a second set of more negative connotations without losing the first, more positive one: the most American of regions was now also a land of small towns, bourgeois conformity, and boredom. These two images have remained attached to the Midwest to the present day, and to the extent that the positive depiction has prevailed, it is because the

Midwest has fled the industrial and urban decay along the Great Lakes for its old, and far more rural, home west of the Mississippi.[6]

Histories of the Midwest as a region, as opposed to histories of states belonging to the region, first emerged in the late nineteenth and early twentieth centuries, precisely the period when the Midwest and the Old Northwest merged as geographical referents. These regional histories reflected the view of the first professionally trained historians, including Turner, that state boundaries were artificial units for analytical purposes, and that scholars should instead focus on regions defined by such natural features as rivers, lakes, and mountains.[7] Turner's own equation of the Midwest with the Old Northwest, for example, conformed to his bounding of the region by the Appalachian Mountains to the east, the Mississippi River valley to the west, the Ohio River valley to the south, and the Great Lakes to the north. Of these physical delineators, he was most interested in the great river valleys.[8]

Not coincidentally, the eastward migration of the Midwest and the shift from state to regional frameworks in historical writing occurred in tandem with a new period in relations between Indigenous peoples and Americans. In the last decades of the nineteenth century, the federal government completed its military conquest of Indigenous lands and peoples and embarked on a systematic campaign to reduce sovereign nations to colonial subjects through confinement on reservations, tutelage of Indigenous children in boarding schools, and allotment in severalty of tribal lands. The success of American settler society was now part of the national narrative, and since the Midwest was the regional metonym for the United States, national and regional stories with respect to Indigenous peoples merged. Turner was far from alone in making violent conquest of Indigenous lands and peoples the centerpiece of American nation-building. But the story that he and others, such as Theodore Roosevelt in *The Winning of the West*, told was neither new nor original.[9] The job of conquest was now finished, but it had long been underway.

By the late nineteenth century, the success of American settler society was already an old story in the Midwest and eastern United States. The midwestern version, as James Buss has shown, drew on older state histories and pioneer historical society writings to fashion a narrative of Indigenous conquest and physical removal from the region following the War of 1812.[10] This narrative begins with the fur trade and the clash of French and British imperial ambitions around the Great Lakes in the seventeenth and eighteen centuries. But it is most concerned with the period from the close of the American Revolution to 1815 and with the wresting of the states of Ohio, Indiana, and Illinois from wilderness occupied by savage beasts and savage men. By the end of the period, the Ohio River valley emerges as the apotheosis of an Indian-less landscape of white settlement. So powerful and long-lived has this story proved that R. David Edmunds opens his introduction to *Enduring Nations*, a pathbreaking 2008 collection of essays about Indigenous peoples in the Midwest, by taking direct aim at it: "Most residents of Ohio, Indiana, or Illinois are unaware of the Indian people living in their midst or that these people and their forebears played a major role in the history of the region and the American nation. Yet the demographics of the region refute these assumptions." According to the 2000 Census, "17.4 percent of all Native Americans in the United States currently live in the states of Minnesota, Wisconsin, Michigan, Ohio, Indiana, and Illinois."[11]

Two elements of Edmunds's indictment deserve particular attention: first, he singles out residents of the Lower Midwest (Ohio, Indiana, and Illinois) as singularly unaware of Indigenous people in the past or present; and second, he defines the Midwest as the Old Northwest plus Minnesota, a portion of which was included in the original federal designation of the territory. The geographical dimensions of Edmunds's argument thus mirror the old story of the Old Northwest as the Midwest. This alignment returns us to the conundrum of how to restore Indigenous people to midwestern history when both people and region remain in motion to this day. In the old narrative of the Midwest, the discursive disappearance of the Indigenous people was predicated on their physical departure from the region. Although not infrequently depicted as the melancholic drifting away of a dying race, removal was more practically a formal federal policy congressionally enacted in 1830.[12] On paper, the scope of the policy was breathtaking—nothing less than the ethnic cleansing of the eastern United States. In practice, however, the relocations, brutal as they could be, were complicated and incomplete. Nor were all removals involuntary ones at federal directive. Beginning in the 1790s, as Stephen Warren and John P. Bowes have shown, many Shawnees, Delawares, Wyandots, and Potawatomis in the Lower Midwest, sought sanctuary west of the Mississippi where, with the advance of white settlement across the river, they ultimately faced repeated relocations at the hands of the federal government—from Missouri, to Kansas, and finally to Indian Territory in the present-day state of Oklahoma.[13]

No fewer than four of the twelve essays in *Enduring Nations* treat Indigenous-white relations in the Lower Midwest between the War of 1812 and the implementation of the federal program of removal in the 1830s and 1840s, all of them emphasizing the attempts by Indigenous peoples to adjust to life in the midst of white settlement. Ginette Aley's analysis of the intersection of internal improvement schemes and federal Indian policy in early nineteenth-century Indiana, and James Buss's analysis of the efforts of Wyandot and Miami peoples in Ohio and Indiana to buy land as a way of evading removal, also help to disrupt the older narrative predicated on the inevitability of white settlement and its incompatibility with Indigenous ways.[14]

Despite this corrective, however, it must be admitted that the settlement narrative does describe, however imperfectly, a historical reality for the Lower Midwest. In contrast, the early histories of Michigan and Wisconsin, in which failure of removal is a signal episode, suggest a different story. The tale is economically told in three maps in the *Atlas of Great Lakes Indian History*, edited by Helen Tanner. The first shows the Indigenous subsistence patterns alluded to at the outset, in relation to the 144 frost-free days required for agriculture. Although not intended for this purpose, the map thus depicts the limits of grain-based, mixed agriculture as practiced by Euro-American and European settlers. In Michigan, the map traces a line from roughly the base of Saginaw Bay west to present-day Muskegon. West of Lake Michigan, the line loops south from Green Bay almost to the Wisconsin River and then moves north again along the Mississippi to the St. Croix River valley. The second map shows Indian reservations in the Great Lakes region between 1783 and 1889. In the Old Northwest—the five-state region encompassed by the three maps—the largest reservations are concentrated in northern Michigan and Wisconsin. Over time these were much diminished by federal allotment and private white rapacity that stripped them of their resources, such as timber. Nevertheless, in the nineteenth century, Indigenous peoples in the Upper Midwest retained enough access to land and resources to sustain the seasonal rounds that were the mainstay of their economies. The third map therefore shows many of their villages in 1870 scattered north of the 144 frost-free days' line in Michigan and Wisconsin. Only a few villages in Michigan appear on the map below the lines, and only one in Ohio, three in Indiana, and none in Illinois. Thus, the failure of removal in the Old Northwest was directly related to the failure of whites to impose in the north country the commercial agrarian landscape that they so successfully realized in the Ohio River valley.[15]

The maps also point to the story of the imposition of American power over Anishinaabewaki, a story that distinguishes the history of Indigenous-settler relations in the Upper Midwest from that of the Lower Midwest. Their contours follow closely the boundaries of three major treaties in which Anishinaabeg ceded millions of acres of their homeland in the United States to the federal government. In the 1836 Treaty of Washington, Odawas and Ojibwes yielded the western half of the Lower Peninsula north of the Grand River and the eastern half of the Upper Peninsula in exchange for temporary reservations, annuities for twenty years, and funding for schools, missions, and agricultural implements. It guaranteed the "usual privileges of occupancy" of the entire ceded area to the Anishinaabeg "until the land is required for settlement."[16] The following year, Ojibwes in northwestern Wisconsin and east central Minnesota ceded thirteen million acres to the federal government, also in exchange for twenty years of annuities and a guarantee of their use-rights to the cession. This guarantee differed from the one extended to the Michigan Anishinaabeg in that it was not predicated on the absence of white settlers, but spelled out the resources most valuable to the Ojibwes: "hunting, fishing, and gathering the wild rice."[17] Finally, in 1842, Ojibwes ceded an additional ten million acres— the western half of Michigan's Upper Peninsula and adjacent territory across the northern tier of Wisconsin. The treaty promised the Indians annuities for twenty-five years and confirmed "the right of hunting with the usual privileges of occupancy."[18]

Three features of these treaties stand out. The first is the Anishinaabeg's insistence on continued access to their resources throughout the ceded areas. The second is that none of these treaties was compacted under pressure from white settlers for Indigenous lands, hence the federal government's willingness to guarantee Anishinaabeg use-rights. Only in the Grand River valley at the southern end of the Lower Peninsula portion of the 1836 cession were settlers clamoring for the expulsion of Indigenous occupants. Henry Rowe Schoolcraft, the federal negotiator for the Treaty of Washington, could guarantee Anishinaabeg use-rights until the land was required for settlement precisely because he believed that it would not be required for the foreseeable future. The federal government's interest in the 1836, 1837, and 1842 treaties was not in promoting agricultural settlement, but in opening the north country to industrial development—the logging of vast stands of red and white pine and the extraction of iron and copper ore. Indeed, the 1837 treaty became popularly known as the Pine Tree Treaty, while the 1842 accord was expressly intended to secure "mineral lands."[19]

This privileging of the profits of extraction over farm-making and town platting, however, did not mean that federal and local officials did not reserve the right to relocate the Anishinaabeg at will. None of the treaties promised removal, but they all made clear that the Indians occupied the ceded areas at the pleasure of the president, and none offered permanent reservations. Moreover, the treaties did promote the arrival of whites in the region with ambitions for personal advancement and state-building. These circumstances culminated in a signal act of ethnic cleansing, one that has occupied a central place in Anishinaabeg historical memory and cultural consciousness to this day.

This grisly example of the intertwining of settler colonial desire and federal Indian policy took place in 1850 at Sandy Lake, located on the Mississippi River in central Minnesota. At issue was the removal of Ojibwes from the new state of Wisconsin and the relocation of the Indian agency on Madeline Island at the western end of Lake Superior to Sandy Lake. Alexander Ramsey, governor of the newly organized Minnesota Territory, in concert with other leading Minnesota politicians, was greatly interested in moving the Lake Superior Ojibwes to Sandy Lake as a way of tapping treaty annuity monies and generally reaping the financial benefits of government funding for the new agency to be established there. Ramsey and his cohorts secured federal approval of their plan by presenting evidence that the Lake Superior Ojibwes were harassing white settlers when the opposite was probably the case. Ramsey then arranged for the Ojibwes to travel very late in the fall to Sandy Lake to collect their annuities, the idea being to trap the Indians there over the winter when the waterways froze and they could not use their canoes to return home. Thousands of Ojibwes came on time for the payment from the Upper Peninsula and northern Wisconsin and Minnesota, only to find neither annuities nor promised provisions waiting for them. They starved for six weeks at Sandy Lake before payment and wholly inadequate provisions arrived; perhaps one-third of all adult Lake Superior Ojibwe men and women died at Sandy Lake or while they struggled on foot to return home. Four years later, in the second Treaty of La Pointe, after strenuous Anishinaabeg petitioning of the federal government, supported by white settlers in Wisconsin and Michigan, the Lake Superior Ojibwe received reservations in the homelands at L'Anse, Ontonagan, and Lac Vieux Desert in Michigan; La Pointe, Lac Courte Oreilles, and Lac du Flambeau in Wisconsin; and Grand Portage, Fond du Lac, and Bois Forte in Minnesota.[20]

The 1854 treaty reflected a shift in federal Indian policy away from removal and toward civilization as represented by Christian missionizing on the reservations and boarding school educations for young Anishinaabeg. The program of civilization also entailed the imposition of white notions of private property. The 1855 Treaty of Detroit finally put an end to the uncertainty that signatories of the 1836 Treaty of Washington had endured over whether they would be allowed to remain in Michigan, but at the price of allotments of land for Anishinaabeg heads of households in designated areas. The treaty foreshadowed the 1887 Dawes General Allotment Act forced on both the Lake Superior Ojibwe reservations and those subsequently established in Minnesota—Mille Lacs and Leech Lake, as well as White Earth, an only partially successful attempt to consolidate Ojibwes in the state in a single, large homeland.

Only Red Lake, also in Minnesota, escaped allotment, although it lost nearly three million acres of land.[21]

Allotment meant loss of resources, not only of land but also of access to game, fish, ricing lakes, and maple groves for sugaring. The seasonal round required movement around specific sites for specific purposes—the antithesis of settler life in places fixed by property ownership. Nevertheless, over the last decades of the nineteenth century and into the twentieth century, the Anishinaabeg persisted in their pursuit of traditional lifeways. Increasingly, however, they combined the seasonal round with wage labor in the extractive economy that took shape in northern Michigan, Wisconsin, and Minnesota based on lumbering, mining, and commercial fishing. Lumbering companies sought to hire skilled Anishinaabeg lumberjacks; Ojibwe men and women worked in the Lake Superior fisheries. Ojibwe women gathered and sold to white settlers the blueberries that flourished in the cutover. When the tourist industry emerged in the early twentieth century, Anishinaabe men found work as guides, while their wives and sisters sold Indigenous handicrafts and worked as maids in northern resorts. Prompted by state tourist boards, whites flocked to Indian pageants.[22]

The price of the extractive economy of the northern Great Lakes was environmental degradation, further impeding the Anishinaabe pursuit of the seasonal round. Commercial overfishing depleted stocks, turning abundance into scarcity. Clear-cut lumbering led to erosion and runoff that polluted waterways, not to mention outbreaks of massive fires in the slash. Damming projects altered water levels, destroying beds of wild rice that Anishinaabeg women had harvested for generations. By the late nineteenth century, the damage wrought by ruthless resource extraction was plain to Anishinaabeg and whites alike. But the response to it by state and federal authorities hardly took into consideration Anishinaabeg subsistence needs. Alongside state and federal reforestation efforts, newly established state conservation agencies imposed limits on hunting and fishing that made sense for white sportsmen, but none at all for Anishinaabeg who hunted and fished to live. Game wardens patrolled the woods, fining, jailing, and occasionally shooting Anishinaabeg, all the while denying their treaty use-rights.[23]

Conditions worsened for the Anishinaabeg during the Great Depression of the 1930s. At White Earth, for example, most residents found themselves dependent on poverty relief programs. Severe want forced many Anishinaabeg families to split up so that they could sustain themselves. Parents sent their children to boarding schools where they knew they would be clothed and fed. Many Anishinaabeg men and women found employment through the federal Works Progress Administration and the Civilian Conservation Corps–Indian Division. As Brenda Child has shown, one CCC-ID program in particular demonstrates the far-reaching effects of the Depression and the federal relief programs on Anishinaabeg lives. Wild rice management became a focus of state and federal relief programs. Without taking into consideration that the harvest was women's traditional work, the rice camps that the CCC-ID, Works Progress Administration, and the Minnesota State Forest Service established hired Ojibwe men, to such an extent that producing and harvesting wild rice had become a male gender role by the end of World War II, reconfiguring a fundamental element in the Anishinaabe seasonal round.[24]

During World War II, many Anishinaabeg, like other Indigenous people throughout the United States, left the grinding poverty of the reservation and sought to remake their lives in cities, where they found employment in defense and other war-related occupations. This movement to the cities has remained a fact of Indigenous life to the present day; in 2000, about four in five Indians were living off-reservation in urban areas. In the Upper Midwest, Chicago, Detroit, and especially Minneapolis rapidly acquired Indigenous populations. After the war, the rural-to-urban migration accelerated, thanks to new federal termination and relocation policies, both of which were intended to end federal responsibility for Indian tribes. One tribe chosen for early termination were the Menominees of Wisconsin, whose forest reservation was supposed to help them to succeed economically on their own. Instead, the tribe lost much of its land base and forest, gaining little in return. Designed to work in tandem with termination, relocation offered basic assistance to Indians seeking employment in approved relocation cities like Minneapolis, such as a bus or train ticket and a first month's rent.

By the time that termination ended in the early 1970s, Minneapolis had become home to the largest Indigenous population in the United States.[25]

Those who relocated to urban areas in the 1950s and 1960s did not lose their ties to their home reservations, but added to them new connections among urban dwellers, creating new networks linking tribes in both urban and rural areas. Out of these networks, and in response to termination, rose a new generation of activists. The American Indian Movement (AIM) was founded in 1968 in Minneapolis. The focus of this activism was self-determination, which meant in part forcing the federal government to live up to its treaty obligations. In 1964, the newly formed National Indian Youth Council (NIYC) targeted the failure of state and local officials in the Pacific Northwest to observe treaty rights for tribal fishing that had been reaffirmed by Congress in 1954. In response to the arrests of fishers for working out of season and without a license, the NIYC staged "fish-ins" over the next decade to assert tribal treaty rights. The protests culminated in the 1974 *Boldt* decision, which upheld the rights outlined in the 1854–55 treaties to award one-half of the catch to coastal tribes. When commercial and sport-fishing interests howled, Washington state officials dragged their feet in implementing the new regulations. A 1995 federal ruling extended the *Boldt* decision to include one-half of the shellfish in Puget Sound. When they tried to collect the shellfish, Squamish people found themselves under fire, the bullets flying over their heads.[26]

A parallel story unfolded in Anishinaabewaki. Beginning in the late 1970s, all three of the major cession treaties in Anishinaabewaki specifying use-rights—the treaties of 1836, 1837, and 1842—became flashpoints in white-Indian relations in the Upper Midwest and were litigated in federal court. In Michigan, the 1836 treaty became the subject of a series of decisions known as *U.S. v. Michigan et al.* In Wisconsin, Indigenous use-rights conferred in the 1837 and 1842 treaties were affirmed in *Lac Courte Oreilles Band v. State of Wisconsin (Voigt)*. The 1837 treaty was again the subject of litigation in Minnesota in *Mille Lacs Band et al. v. State of Minnesota* and *Fond du Lac Band et al. v. Carlson et al.* Ultimate affirmation of treaty rights came in a 1999 U.S. Supreme Court ruling.[27]

These cases did not happen in a vacuum, but were shaped by the determination of tribal members to take direct actions in support of their treaty rights, defying state fish and game regulations and rancorous, sometimes violent, public outcry over the notion of "special rights" for Indians. This was particularly the case in Wisconsin in the wake of the *Voigt* decision, when angry white citizens repeatedly harassed Lac du Flambeau spear fishers, shouting epithets and bearing signs reading "Save a Walleye—Spear an Indian." The demonstrations were only halted when Lac du Flambeau successfully sued the loudest of the organized protestors, Stop Treaty Abuse–Wisconsin, for racially motivated violations of their civil rights.[28]

There is no question that these cases have collectively spurred a period of political and cultural revitalization in Anishinaabewaki, helping to affirm heritage and to heal old wounds. *Minnesota v. Mille Lacs* was argued before the U.S. Supreme Court in December of 1998, nearly 150 years to the month after the disaster at Sandy Lake. To commemorate the joining of past and present, Anishinaabeg organized the Waabanong Run, a 1,000-mile relay from Lac du Flambeau Reservation to Washington DC, with the runners arriving in time to hear the case argued in court. After the decision in favor of the tribes was announced the following March, Anishinaabeg conducted healing ceremonies at Sandy Lake and arranged for the erection of a monument at the site.[29]

Finally, the revitalization of Anishinaabewaki has ushered in a new chapter in the history of Indian-white relations in the Upper Midwest. Put simply, where once Anishinaabeg were marginal to the point of invisibility for whites, they are now political actors to be reckoned with. Successful defense of their treaty rights has allowed the Anishinaabeg to pursue an active role as environmental stewards of Anishinaabewaki, thereby asserting their status as sovereign nations and devotion to cultural values predicated on the husbanding of natural resources. To this end, intertribal organizations engage with state and national authorities to oversee an array of environmental concerns, including fish and game populations, water levels and quality in the Great Lakes and inland waters, and climate change. In Michigan, for example, the Chippewa Ottawa Resource Authority (CORA) superintends the fishing rights of the five tribal signatories of the 1836 treaty.[30] Farther west, the Great Lakes Indian Fish and Wildlife Commission (GLIFWC) is an agency of eleven Michigan, Wisconsin, and Minnesota signatories of the 1836, 1837, 1842, and 1854 treaties "with services related to natural resource management and conservation; legal and policy analysis; public education; and intergovernmental relations."[31] Organizations like CORA and GLIFWC attest to the endurance and resurgence of Anishinaabewaki, an Indigenous homeland, despite the formidable challenges that settler society and state have posed to its integrity. Anishinaabewaki remains today a map in motion, whose history is also a vital part of the history of the Midwest.

Notes

1. The term "Anishinaabe" (plural Anishinaabeg) needs come clarification. It is most associated in the United States with the Ojibwe people of the western Great Lakes but, as the editors of *Centering Anishinaabeg Studies* explain, "it's a word that also exists as Aninawbe, Anishinape, Anicinape, Neshnawbé, Nishnaabe, Nishnawbe, Anishishinaube, and Nishinabe— just to name a few. Each lives in a locality, history, and context. . . . What brings these terms together . . . are the similarities, connections, and overwhelming number of ties that emerge when they are considered in relationship. Like strands and points of an interconnected web, these specific and shared names are what communities know now as Ojibwa, Ojibwe, Chippewa, Ojibway, Saulteaux, Mississauga, Nipissing, Potawatomi, and Odawa (and others) use to describe *themselves*." Jill Doerfler, Niigaanwewidam James Sinclair, and Heidi Kiiwetinepinesiik Stark, eds., *Centering Anishinaabeg Studies: Understanding the World through Stories* (East Lansing: Michigan State University Press, 2013), xvii. On the Anishinaabe origins story, see William W. Warren, *History of the Ojibwe People* (1885; repr., St. Paul: Minnesota Historical Society, 1984), 76–82.

2. Maps of precontact Indigenous economies may be found in Helen Hornbeck Tanner, ed. *Atlas of Great Lakes Indian History* (Norman: University of Oklahoma Press for the Newberry Library), 13–23.

3. Patrick Wolfe, "Against the Intentional Fallacy: Legocentricism and Continuity in the Rhetoric of Indian Dispossession," *American Indian Culture and Research Journal* 36, no. 1 (2012): 3–45.

4. On the "removed Indians" of the lower Midwest, see John P. Bowes, *Exiles and Pioneers: Eastern Indians in the Trans-Mississippi West* (New York: Cambridge University Press, 2007) on the experience of Shawnee, Dela-

ware, Wyandot, and Potawatomi peoples west of the Mississippi. See also Stephen Warren, *The Shawnees and Their Neighbors, 1795–1870* (Urbana: University of Illinois Press, 2009).

5. Peter Iverson quoted in Bowes, *Exiles and Pioneers*, 6.

6. James R. Shortridge, *The Middle West: Its Meaning in American Culture* (Lawrence: University of Kansas Press, 1980). See also Andrew R. L. Cayton and Susan E. Gray, "The Story of the Midwest: An Introduction," in Cayton and Gray, eds., *The American Midwest: Essays in Regional History* (Indianapolis: Indiana University Press, 2001), 1–26.

7. Derek K. Everett, *Creating the American West: Boundaries and Borderlands* (Norman: University of Oklahoma Press, 2014), 4–5.

8. See, for example, Frederick Jackson Turner, "The Middle West," "The Ohio Valley in American History," and "The Significance of the Mississippi in American History," in *The Frontier in American History* (1920; repr., Tucson: University of Arizona Press, 1986), 126–204.

9. Despite his earlier adventures in the Dakota Badlands, Roosevelt focused, like his contemporary Turner, on the history on the trans-Appalachian West. *The Winning of the West*, 4 vols. (1894; repr., Lincoln: University of Nebraska Press, 1995).

10. James J. Buss, *Winning the West with Words: Language and Conquest in the Lower Great Lakes* (Norman: University of Oklahoma Press, 2011), especially 165–211. A comparable account for the eastern United States is Jean M. O'Brien, *Firsting and Lasting: Writing Indians Out of Existence in New England* (Minneapolis: University of Minnesota Press, 2010).

11. R. David Edmunds, "Introduction: A People of Persistence," in *Enduring Nations: Native Americans in the Midwest*, ed. R. David Edmunds (Urbana: University of Illinois Press, 2008), 1–2.

12. On the trope of the "dying race," see Philip J. Deloria, *Playing Indian* (New Haven: Yale University Press, 1998), 62–70. On the federal policy of removal, see Francis Paul Prucha, *The Great Father: The United States Government and the American Indians* (Lincoln: University of Nebraska Press, 1986), 64–107; Ronald N. Satz, *American Indian Policy in the Jacksonian Era* (Lincoln: University of Nebraska Press, 1975), and "Indian Policy in the Jackson Era: The Old Northwest as a Test Case," *Michigan History* 60, no. 1 (Spring 1976): 71–93.

13. Warren, *The Shawnees and Their Neighbors, 1795–1870*; Bowes, *Exiles and Pioneers*. See also Bowes's discussion of the complexity of removal as a process in John P. Bowes, *Land Too Good for Indians: Northern Indian Removal* (Norman: University of Oklahoma Press, 2016).

14. Essays on the removal era in the Lower Midwest in Edmunds, ed., *Enduring Nations* include Thomas Burnell Colbert, "'The Hinge on Which All Affairs of the Sauk and Fox Indians Turn': Keokuk and the United States Government," 54–71; Stephen Warren, "The Ohio Shawnees' Struggle against Removal, 1814–30," 72–93; Bradley J. Birzer, "Jean Baptiste Richardville: Miami Métis," 94–108; and Susan Sleeper Smith, "Resistance to Removal: The 'White Indian,' Frances Slocum," 109–23. Ginette Aley, "Bringing about the Dawn: Agriculture, Internal Improvements, Indian Policy, and Euro-American Hegemony in the Old Northwest, 1800–1846," in *The Boundaries between Us: Natives and Newcomers along the Frontiers of the Old Northwest Territory, 1750–1850*, ed. Daniel P. Barr (Kent OH: Kent State University Press, 2006), 196–218. See also the essays in the same volume by Donald H. Gaff, "Three Men from Three Rivers: Navigating between Native and American Identity in the Old Northwest Territory," 143–60; Bruce P. Smith, "Negotiating Law on the Frontier: Responses to Cross-Cultural Homicide in Illinois, 1810–1825," 161–77; Phyllis Gernhardt, "'Justice and Public Policy': Indian Trade, Treaties, and Removal from Northern Indiana, 1826–1846," 178–95; and Thomas J. Lappas, "'A Perfect Apollo': Keokuk and Sac Leadership during the Removal Era," 219–35. James J. Buss, *Winning the West with Words*, 73–96; and "Imagined Worlds and Archival Realities: The Patchwork World of Early Nineteenth-Century Indiana," in *Beyond Two Worlds: Critical Conversations on Language and Power in Native North America*, ed. James Buss and C. Joseph Genetin-Pilawa (Albany: State University of New York Press, 2014), 97–116.

15. Tanner, ed., *Atlas of Great Lakes Indian History*, Map 4—Subsistence Patterns, 20–21; Map 31—Reservations, 1783–1889, 164–65; Map 33—Indian Villages, ca. 1870, 176–77.

16. Treaty with the Ottawa, etc., dc.library.okstate.edu/digital/collection/kapplers/id26292.

17. Treaty with the Chippewa, 1837, dc.library.okstate.edu/digital/collection/kapplers/id26332.

18. Treaty with the Chippewa, 1842, dc.library.okstate.edu/digital/collection/kapplers/id26383.

19. Charlie Otto Rasmussen, *Ojibwe Journeys: Treaties, Sandy Lake and the Waabanong Run* (Odanah: Great Lakes Indian Fish and Wildlife Commission Press, 2003), 16.

20. This account of the Sandy Lake tragedy follows Brenda J. Child, *Holding Our World Together: Ojibwe Women and the Survival of Community* (New York: Penguin, 2012), 65–81. See also Rasmussen, *Ojibwe Journeys*, 16–21.

21. Child, *Holding Our World Together*, 78–82.

22. Brenda J. Child, *My Grandfather's Knocking Sticks: Ojibwe Family Life and Labor on the Reservation* (Minneapolis: Minnesota Historical Society Press, 2014), 85–124; Bradley J. Gills, "The Anishinabeg and the Landscape of Assimilation in Michigan, 1854–1934" (PhD diss., Arizona State University, 2008); Chantal Norrgard, *Seasons of Change: Labor, Treaty Rights, and Ojibwe Nationhood* (Chapel Hill: University of North Carolina Press, 2014), 20–42, 63–127; Aaron Shapiro, *The Lure of the North Woods: Cultivating Tourism in the Upper Midwest*, 2013), 97–103.

23. Norrgard, *Seasons of Change*, 43–52; Rasmussen, *Ojibwe Journeys*, 22–24.

24. Child, *Holding Our World Together*, 98–120; Child, *My Grandfather's Knocking Sticks*, 161–92.

25. Child, *Holding Our World Together*, 139–59. On the early history of Menominee lumbering, see Brian C. Hosmer, *American Indians in the Marketplace: Persistence and Innovation among the Menominees and Metlakatlans, 1870–1920* (Lawrence: University of Kansas Press, 1999).

26. Roger L. Nichols, *Indians in the United States and Canada: A Comparative History* (Lincoln: University of Nebraska Press, 1998), 300, 317.

27. Ann McCommon-Soltis and Kekek Jason Stark, "Fulfilling Ojibwe Treaty Promises: An Overview and Compendium of Relevant Cases, Statues, and Agreements," in *Minwanjimo: Telling a Good Story*, ed. LaTisha A. McRoy and Howard J. Bichler (Odanah WI: Great Lakes Indian Fish and Wildlife Commission, 2011), 48–63. On the cases, see Susan E. Gray, "Indigenous Space and the Landscape of Settlement: A Historian as Expert Witness," in "The Historian as Expert Witness," special issue, *Public Historian* 37, no. 1 (February 2015): 54–67; Charles E. Cleland, *Faith in Paper: The Ethnohistory and Litigation of Upper Great Lakes Indian Treaties* (Ann Arbor: University of Michigan Press, 2011); and James M. McClurken et al., *Fish in the Lakes, Wild Rice, and Game in Abundance: Testimony on Behalf of Mille Lacs Ojibwe Hunting and Fishing Rights* (East Lansing: Michigan State University Press, 2000).

28. Larry Nesper, *The Walleye War: The Struggle for Ojibwe Spearfishing and Treaty Rights* (Lincoln: University of Nebraska Press, 2002); Patricia Loew and James Thannum, "After the Storm: Ojibwe Treaty Rights Twenty-Five Years after the *Voigt* Decision," *American Indian Quarterly* 35, no. 2 (Spring 2011): 161–91.

29. Rasmussen, *Ojibwe Journeys*, 43–66.

30. Chippewa Ottawa Resource Authority, http://www.1836cora.org. Members include the Bay Mills Indian Community, Grand Traverse Band of Ottawa

and Chippewa Indians, Little Traverse Bay Bands of Ottawa Indians, Little River Band of Ottawa Indians, Little Traverse Bay Bands of Odawa Indians, and Sault Ste. Marie Tribe of Chippewa.

31. Allison M. Dussias, "At the Margins: Border Tribes' Struggles to Protect Reservation Lands, Waters, and Communities," in Tribes, Land, and the Environment, ed. Sarah Krakoff and Ezra Rosser (Burlington VT: Ashgate, 2012): 126; http://www.glifwc.org. See also Larry Nesper, "Twenty-Five Years of Treaty Rights and the Tribal Communities," in Minwaajimo, ed. McRoy and Bichler, 288–326. Members of the GLIFWC include the Bay Mills Indian Community, Keweenaw Bay Indian Community, Lac Vieux Desert Band (Michigan); Bad River, Lac Courte Oreilles, Lac du Flambeau, Red Cliff, St. Croix Bands, and Sokagon Chippewa Community (Wisconsin); Fond du Lac and Mille Lacs Bands (Minnesota).

5

American and European Immigrant Groups in the Midwest by the Mid-Nineteenth Century

Gregory S. Rose

By 1850 the Old Northwest was a region of significant contrasts and one clearly undergoing transformation. Some contrasts were environmental. The climate differed notably from south to north and east to west in strength of the seasons, intensity of winter and summer temperatures, and amount of precipitation and snowfall. The region's natural vegetation varied accordingly, with coniferous forests on the north, hardwoods to the east and south, and prairie grasslands to the west. Topography could be hilly or flat, and soil quality and drainage ranged from quickly drying sandy soils to clayey soils holding moisture in low spots. These environmental conditions impacted settlement, the extent and prosperity of farming, the agricultural economy, and the resources to be exploited.

Some of the region's contrasts were linked to varying levels of economic development. The five Old Northwest states contained 4.5 million people, almost 20 percent of the United States total, but individual state populations differed widely, from 1.98 million in Ohio (including 115,000 in Cincinnati, the sixth largest city in the United States) to just over 300,000 in Wisconsin.[1] Different stages of development appeared among and within the states: frontier subsistence settlement; sustainable, self-sufficient farming; agriculture increasingly reliant on external markets; urbanization and incipient industrialization. Population density can gauge these contrasts. According to the 1880 Census, eighteen persons per square mile represented the minimum population density necessary for the establishment of successful agricultural settlement. By this measure, successful agricultural settlement advanced decade by decade from the east and southeast to the west but by 1850 not much farther north than the middle of Michigan's Lower Peninsula or halfway to Lake Superior in Wisconsin.[2] Harsher environmental conditions in the north limited white settlement to locations often associated with colonial-era fur trading posts, portage spots, and military forts. Also within and among states, notable contrasts appeared by 1850 in levels of commercialization, urbanization, and industrialization.

Another set of contrasts was demographic and geographic. The non-Native American population invading the region in increasing numbers following the Revolutionary War—immigrants born within the United States or coming from foreign nations—arrayed themselves in rather distinctive patterns across the Old Northwest, reflecting many factors such as geographic and transportation accessibility, timing of migration, and availability of attractive and affordable land.[3] The region's African American population, distinctive but numerically small in 1850, was distributed in patterns reflecting economic opportunity and additional factors such as assistance, social acceptance, and safety.

This chapter examines the origins of the Old Northwest's mid-nineteenth-century population primarily through birthplace data from the 1850 Census.[4] Given population size and development levels in some states, 1850 may seem late for exploring the pioneer era. However, that census is considered our first modern enumeration due to its comprehensiveness and the advanced procedures employed to complete the constitutionally mandated task of enumeration. And of greatest importance for this discussion, for the first time the census recorded the demographic and social characteristics of all family members, not just heads of households, including each inhabitant's state or country of birth.[5] Local assistant marshals (or enumerators or canvassers), hired to collect the data door to door and guided by detailed instructions, asked the required questions of every person at every residence and recorded their responses.[6]

While the census act required that respondents provide accurate information to the enumerator or face a fine or misdemeanor charge, no proof was required.[7] Despite good intentions, not every inhabitant was included. Native Americans, locally significant especially in the northern Old Northwest, were excluded from the census if they were "Indians not taxed" living on sovereign reservations.[8] Accuracy of data depended on the knowledge and intention of the person providing information and the carefulness of the person recording it. Some inhabitants did not know their birthplace; others did but obfuscated for a variety of reasons—fleeing legal difficulties or debts or family or slavery. Canvassers faced language barriers or resistance or absence, and some cut corners by not returning to count missed individuals or by avoiding remote locations or dangerous neighborhoods.[9]

An initial distinction can be made between the portion of the population born in each state, such as Illinois natives residing in Illinois, and the portion born elsewhere, such as Pennsylvania natives living in Ohio. By removing those born in their state of residence from the nativity calculations for Illinois, for example, the remainder represents immigrants from other parts of the United States and abroad. As thus defined, the immigrant population for Illinois included settlers born in other Old Northwest states, such as Ohio or Indiana. These states could be major sources of population, but that was not always the case. In Indiana, for example, 27.3 percent of all immigrants came from Ohio, making them by far the state's largest single source. Yet in Wisconsin, the four other Old Northwest states together accounted for just 9.1 percent of immigrants.

Across the Old Northwest, the division between the proportion of the total population born in each state and those born elsewhere was almost exactly fifty-fifty (see the table in this chapter). But considerable state-to-state variation existed in this split, reflecting each state's age and development. In longer-settled and older states, greater percentages of inhabitants were born in state, while immigrant proportions were higher in the newer recently settled states. In Ohio (1803 statehood), settlers born in state comprised 61.1 percent of the population while 38.9 percent were immigrants. For Indiana (1816) the proportions were 52.7 percent and 47.3 percent; in Illinois (1818) they were 39 percent and 61 percent. In Michigan (1837), 34.3 percent of settlers were in-state natives and 65.7 percent immigrant; for Wisconsin (1848) the values were 17.9 percent and 82.1 percent, respectively. Immigrant parents of inhabitants born in the state significantly influenced their children's cultural or ethnic identity, perhaps more deeply than percentages might suggest. The degree to which a Hoosier born of parents from North Carolina carried her family's cultural identity may be hard to ascertain but it was present and likely different or less pronounced than the ethnic identity maintained by the Wisconsin-born son of Bavarian immigrants speaking German at home, in church, and in the community.

Mapping the distribution of the immigrant population reveals how settlers sorted themselves out in the Old Northwest. But because the Old Northwest's population in 1850 was unevenly distributed, maps comparing groups on the basis of the population percentage represented by particular immigrants must be approached with some caution. Hamilton County, in the southwest corner of Ohio and encompassing Cincinnati, was home to 156,844 people in 1850 and was the most densely populated county in the Old Northwest, with 380 persons per square mile. At the other extreme, large swaths of northern Michigan and Wisconsin were sparsely inhabited and divided into hugely sized counties. Just sixteen non-Indian inhabitants lived in Schoolcraft County in Michigan's Upper Peninsula at a population density of 0.002 persons per square mile. Combining large territorial extent, low population, and just a handful of immigrants from a particular state or country could push that group's percentage of the population above the Old Northwest's regional average, making their significance appear, cartographically at least, greater than it was numerically.

Nineteenth-century migrants chose settlement locations using a number of decision factors, particularly in an era when most movers engaged in agriculture and when the yeoman farm—carved from the forest or prairie, developed and worked by the family, and the basis of the family's prosperity and inheritance—formed the conceptual ideal.[10] What was the agricultural potential of their new home? Could familiar crops and animals thrive in the new destination? Were family or friends already there or interested in migrating to form a cluster and support group in the howling wilderness? Where was land cheaply available for those with limited means? Migrants to the Old Northwest states did not go blindly into the backcountry. They perused emigrants' guides, gazetteers, pamphlets, newspaper articles, and personal and published letters.[11] Some documents recommended and others discouraged settlement in certain states or regions, and some states actively recruited domestic and overseas immigrants.

The birthplaces of immigrants to and within the Old Northwest can be separated into three basic regional groupings: the North, including all states north of the Mason-Dixon Line and the Ohio River as well as states of origin within the Old Northwest other than the state being examined (that is, Illinois residents with Illinois birthplaces were not immigrants but Indiana natives living in Illinois were); the South, including all states south of the Mason-Dixon Line and the Ohio River; and foreign, including all non-U.S. sources even within the Americas, such as Canada or Mexico. Across the Old Northwest in 1850, 53.1 percent of immigrants were northern natives, 21.7 percent reported birthplaces in the South, and 24.6 percent came from foreign lands (as the table shows). Considerable variation existed from state to state within the Old Northwest. In Michigan, 76.8 percent of immigrants were northern natives, 1.3 percent originated in the South, and 21.3 percent were foreign born, while immediately to the south in Indiana, the proportions were 48.5 percent, 38.6 percent, and 12.2 percent, respectively. Wisconsin had a different mix: 53.1 percent of arrivals hailed from the North, 2.3 percent had been born in the South, and 43.9 percent were foreigners.

Sources of inhabitants by 1850 (in percentages)

	Total population		Immigrant population birthplaces				
	Born in state	Immigrants	New England/ New York	Pennsylvania/ New Jersey	North*	South	Foreign
Illinois	39.0	61.0	20.2	8.8	48.8	28.8	21.4
Indiana	52.7	47.3	7.9	11.8	48.5	38.6	12.2
Michigan	34.3	65.7	64.0	5.9	76.8	1.3	21.3
Ohio	61.1	38.9	20.0	29.0	50.5	19.8	29.1
Wisconsin	17.9	82.1	39.5	4.6	53.3	2.3	43.9
Old Northwest	50.2	49.1	25.4	15.5	53.1	21.7	24.6

*North includes Old Northwest States other than the one listed.

Source: Table created by author using data collected by author from microfilms of the 1850 manuscript censes (Records of the Bureau of the Census, RG 29, M432).

United States Natives

Figure 1 displays the leading regions within the United States—North, Midland, and South—providing all immigrants to each Old Northwest county. The Midland typically combines with the northern region, because Pennsylvania and New Jersey are north of the Mason-Dixon Line, to permit a basic North/South differentiation. However, the Midland was identified separately here to highlight the impact of Pennsylvania natives among immigrants to Ohio and, less so, northern Indiana, compared to the impact of New Yorkers and New Englanders on Michigan, Wisconsin, and northern Illinois.[12] Yankees from New England and New York also were the leading population groups in a scattering of counties across northern Ohio (especially in the Western Reserve area of the northeast) and extreme northern Indiana. Southerners concentrated in the southern two-thirds of Indiana and Illinois.[13]

Counties having New Englanders above the Old Northwest average of 7.7 percent of immigrants were distributed similarly to northerners with two additions: an area of central Ohio including Franklin County and surrounding it on the east, north, and west, and another group of counties in southeastern Ohio outward from Marietta, the "capital" of the territory purchased by the Boston-based Ohio Company of Associates.[14] New Englanders comprised especially significant portions of the immigrant population in Michigan (12.1 percent) and Wisconsin (11.2 percent).[15] Within the Yankee region, counties with above-average percentages of Vermont natives (2.3 percent of Old Northwest immigrants) were arrayed almost identically to northerners. Unusual concentrations of settlers native to Vermont and Massachusetts (2.1 percent of immigrants) also appeared in central and southeastern Ohio counties, but the Massachusetts born tended not to congregate as far north in Michigan or as far west in Wisconsin as northerners. Inhabitants born in Connecticut (1.9 percent of immigrants) largely mirrored the distribution of New Englanders in central and southeastern Ohio, but were especially prevalent in northeastern Ohio, where the Connecticut Western Reserve—lands granted to families who lost property during the Revolutionary War—was located.[16] In some counties there, 15 to 20

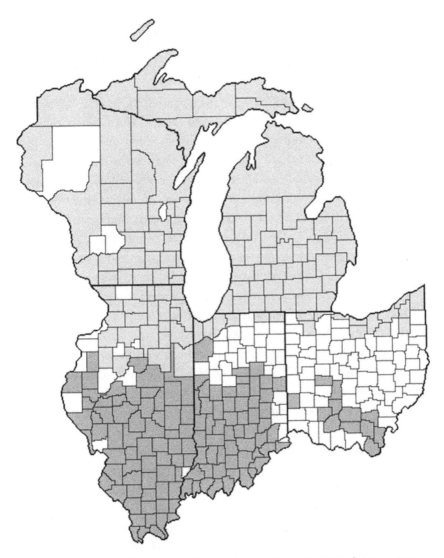

Fig. 1. Leading birthplace region for immigrants from the United States, 1850. Light gray denotes counties where northerners (New England and New York) exceeded 25.4 percent of the immigrant population; white denotes counties where midlanders (Pennsylvania and New Jersey) exceeded 15.5 percent of the immigrant population; dark gray denotes counties where southerners exceeded 21.7 percent of the immigrant population. Figure created by author using data collected by author from microfilms of the 1850 manuscript censes (Records of the Bureau of the Census, RG 29, M432).

percent of immigrants had Connecticut birthplaces. These natives also were found in Michigan's southern Lower Peninsula but away from the lakeshores, almost exclusively in extreme southeastern Wisconsin, and in northern Illinois.

Settlers with New York birthplaces comprised the largest single state element, at 17 percent, of immigrants to the Old Northwest. Counties with New Yorkers above the region's average were nearly identical to those with northern natives. That Michigan was described as "New York's Daughter State" is confirmed by the fact that every county in the Lower Peninsula had above-average concentrations of immigrants from the Empire State.[17] Indeed, 51.9 percent of Michigan's immigrant population had been born in New York, and in four counties—Calhoun, Shiawassee, Genesee, Midland—over two-thirds of immigrants were New Yorkers. Most of the eastern two-thirds of Wisconsin was heavily settled by New York natives who reached over 40 percent of immigrants in five counties. Not every Upper Peninsula county contained above-average percentages of New Yorkers, nor did most of western Wisconsin. The few New York–influenced counties in Indiana were in the north as were the greater number in Illinois, while New Yorkers extended about one range of counties farther south from the Lake Erie shore in Ohio than did the northern-dominated counties.

Pennsylvanians were by far the largest component of the Midland population group, accounting for 13.4 percent of immigrants to the Old Northwest. Pennsylvanians in Ohio (25.9 percent of immigrants) were so influential that their concentration exceeded the Old Northwest average in nearly every county except three in the extreme south (including Hamilton County/Cincinnati) and a line along Lake Erie where New Englanders and New Yorkers were strongest. Many Ohio counties had large proportions of Pennsylvanians, including Wayne with 65.2 percent. Midland and Pennsylvanian patterns were nearly the same in Indiana, but in northwestern Illinois more counties had Pennsylvania than Midland natives above average. Only two Wisconsin counties exceeded the norm for Pennsylvanians. Everywhere except Ohio, immigrants from New Jersey (2.1 percent of the total) generally concentrated in different locations than Pennsylvanians. The majority of Ohio counties held

New Jersey natives in higher-than-average concentrations, especially in the Symmes Purchase area of southwestern and west central Ohio between the Little and Great Miami rivers.[18] There, New Jersey natives accounted for 20.8 percent of Warren County's immigrants. Immediately west, many New Jersey natives lived in counties along the southeastern border of Indiana and scattered in northeast and north central parts of the state. Two groups of counties in the southeastern Lower Peninsula of Michigan had many New Jersey natives, and they were comparatively common in west central Illinois.

Migrants from the South, who comprised 21.7 percent of the total immigrant population, were highly concentrated in the southern two-thirds of Indiana and Illinois plus a line of counties extending toward west central Ohio from its southernmost point on the Ohio River. No Michigan or Wisconsin county was inhabited by southerners to a level greater than the Old Northwest average. By accounting for 7 percent of the birthplaces, Virginia supplied the largest southern immigrant population to the Old Northwest. While the patterns of southern and Virginian concentration counties were very much the same in Indiana, except for the southwestern-most counties where Virginia natives were fewer, in Ohio and Illinois noticeable differences in their distributions appeared. In Ohio, which had just a few southern-dominated counties, 11.3 percent of immigrants had birthplaces in Virginia and nearly every county in the southern two-thirds of the state housed Virginia natives in excess of the Old Northwest average, including five counties where Virginians comprised over 40 percent of immigrants, four of which were within the Virginia Military District.[19] A checkerboard of Illinois counties with percentages of Virginia immigrants above the average appeared within the southern immigrant region. No county in Wisconsin or Michigan housed Virginian natives in concentrations greater than the Old Northwest average, but one Indiana county, along the southwestern Michigan border, did. Natives of Maryland, accounting for 2.5 percent of Old Northwest immigrants, were found in greater-than-average concentrations in nearly every Ohio county. They also appeared in a line of counties along Indiana's eastern border and halfway down the Ohio River. Elsewhere in Indiana and Illinois, only scattered counties contained numerous Marylanders.

Inhabitants with Kentucky birthplaces formed 6 percent of the Old Northwest's immigrants. A line of Ohio counties along the Ohio River, running westward from the state's southern tip and directly across the river from Kentucky, contained Bluegrass natives in excess of the region's average, but nowhere else in the state did Kentuckians concentrate. Indiana and Illinois counties with Kentucky natives residing in greater than Old Northwest average percentages were distributed in a pattern similar to that of all southerners. Settlers born in Kentucky were especially prevalent in the southwestern two-thirds of Indiana. They formed the state's largest immigrant group, accounting for 15.1 percent of settlers not born in Indiana and just under 45 percent of that population in five counties. Whereas in Illinois the distribution of Virginia-influenced counties was patchy, counties dominated by Kentuckians formed a nearly solid block in the southern two-thirds of the state. This aligned with the proportions of Illinois immigrants from Kentucky, 9.8 percent, compared to the 4.9 percent from Virginia. In about ten Illinois counties, Kentucky natives formed over 25 percent of the immigrants. No counties in the northeastern third of Indiana, northern Illinois, Michigan, or Wisconsin were inhabited by Kentuckians in proportions exceeding the Old Northwest average.

North Carolina natives, who accounted for 2.3 percent of Old Northwest immigrants, were distributed in generally the same pattern as southerners in Ohio and especially in Indiana, where North Carolina natives and Quaker religious adherents were closely associated.[20] North Carolinians comprised 7 percent of Indiana's immigrants, reaching 18.1 percent of immigrants in Wayne County (including Richmond) and a maximum of 31.4 percent in Orange County. In Illinois, the distribution of southerners and North Carolinians was roughly the same, although counties with North Carolina–born settlers were typically found farther south. One county in Michigan—Cass—also contained North Carolinians above the Old Northwest average, the only one in that state or Wisconsin that did. Cass County had a distinctive history as a location settled by Quakers and large numbers of free blacks.[21] Immigrants born in Tennessee lived in concentrations greater than the Old Northwest's average in most counties that held southern natives in higher percentages, although the Tennessee-influenced counties shifted farther west in Indiana and were not as continuous. In Illinois, nearly every county in the southern two-thirds of the state was inhabited by Tennessee natives in above-average proportions. A couple of counties across from St. Louis that did not contain Kentucky-born immigrants in high percentages did hold concentrations of Tennessee natives.

The African American population of the Old Northwest was comparatively small in 1850, totaling 45,195, or 1 percent of all inhabitants. Even more than for the general population, the number and birthplace locations for African Americans in the 1850 Census may be inaccurate.[22] Additional factors beyond those causing others to avoid census enumerators affected this population. Many whites thought African Americans should be excluded from the Old Northwest. They experienced official discrimination due to "black laws" and their safety was endangered by escaped slave catchers.[23] They lived in urban centers (at a higher percentage than the general population) and in rural environments, often in remote settings on marginal lands.[24] Ohio housed over half of the Old Northwest's African Americans, who formed 1.3 percent of its total population. The second largest number lived in Indiana, accounting for 1.2 percent of inhabitants. Most African Americans resided in southwestern Ohio and southeastern Indiana counties and cities, including Columbus, Cincinnati, Richmond, and New Albany. Other smaller population centers included Detroit, Indianapolis, and Chicago as well as rural areas of southwestern Ohio, southeastern Indiana, and southwestern Michigan.

Just over 46 percent of African Americans had Old Northwest birthplaces, slightly less than for the general population. Of those born elsewhere, the vast majority (almost 99 percent) were United States natives. They had distinctively southern origins: 83.6 percent of the immigrants (compared to 21.7 percent for the total population) were born in the South while just 14.3 percent came from the North. Even in Michigan, where northerners dominated among the general population, more African American immigrants were southerners than northerners. Leading birthplaces for African Americans were Virginia (39.6 percent of the total), North Carolina (16.7 percent), and

Kentucky (10.7 percent). Counties with the largest group of African Americans coming from Virginia concentrated in the same areas of the southern Old Northwest as all Virginia immigrants, especially in Ohio, where Virginia was the largest source in nearly every rural and urban county except for a cluster in the northwest. Virginian blacks populated counties encompassing Detroit and Chicago, across from St. Louis, occasional counties scattered across Indiana and Illinois, and a few in Wisconsin and Michigan. Southwestern Michigan, centered on Cass County, received many manumitted slaves and free African Americans from Virginia and North Carolina, and Quakers.[25] Counties with North Carolina–born African blacks as the largest group heavily concentrated in east central and central Indiana, also an area of major Quaker population.[26] African American natives from Kentucky were the largest group in most counties strongly settled by all Kentucky natives, including a number in Indiana and a few in Ohio along the Ohio River, but primarily in Illinois. New York natives, only 2.5 percent of African American immigrants, were very strongly concentrated in the northern Old Northwest.

Foreign Natives

Across the Old Northwest, 24.6 percent of the immigrant population was foreign born, and three of the states had similar percentages. Ohio, with the largest total population in the Old Northwest, had the largest number of international immigrants, 220,940, and a slightly above-average percentage of 29.1. Michigan housed the fewest, 55,643, accounting for 21.3 percent; Illinois had almost the same proportion, 21.4 percent, but a larger number, 111,131. Indiana and Wisconsin were outliers. In Indiana, only 12.2 percent of immigrants were foreign natives and its number, 56,846, was the second smallest. Apparently the state was not especially attractive to foreign immigrants, confirming Governor Joseph Wright's contemporary statement that "there is less known abroad, this day, of Indiana . . . than any other State of the Union of her age and position."[27] Comparatively new Wisconsin, achieving statehood just in time for a major influx of German and Irish immigrants fleeing economic and political hardships at home, was much more attractive. It held the largest proportion of foreign born within the immigrant population (43.9 percent) and in number almost as many as Illinois.

Urban and rural counties inhabited by foreign-born immigrants greater than the Old Northwest's average appeared throughout the region while showing clear concentrations (figure 2). Nearly every Wisconsin county displayed an above average percentage—close to half state's immigrants were foreign natives—as did most counties in the Upper and northern Lower Peninsulas of Michigan. The Chicago region of northeastern Illinois and the southwest across from St. Louis contained many foreign natives. Indiana counties with concentrations of foreign-born settlers were found in the southwest, encompassing areas around Evansville, Vincennes, and Terre Haute, along the Ohio River, including New Albany, and in the northeast around Fort Wayne. In southeastern Michigan, counties enclosing Detroit and Monroe held foreign percentages above the Old Northwest average, but Yankee farmers dominated the south central peninsula. High proportions of foreign natives appeared in Ohio's rural counties and in counties containing Cincinnati, Columbus, Cleveland, and Toledo.

Germany, then consisting of numerous principalities and states but typically treated in the census as a single entity, was the leading foreign source of settlers in the Old Northwest, accounting for 10.3 percent of all immigrants.[28] As was the case for all foreigners, German immigrants in above-average concentrations appeared in counties surrounding the urban centers of Chicago, Cincinnati, Columbus, and Detroit; southwestern Illinois counties across from St. Louis; and Indiana counties along the Ohio River. Areas of largely rural settlements throughout the Old Northwest also were deeply influenced by Germans. In Wisconsin, 15.6 percent of the immigrant population was German, and they formed dominant percentages in the eastern counties of Washington (57.8 percent), Manitowoc (42.3 percent) and Milwaukee (38.6 percent). Another well-known area of German population appeared in the center of Michigan's Lower Peninsula, including settlements of and around Frankenmuth, where they formed 31 percent of immigrants in Saginaw County. A number of northwestern Ohio counties contained major percentages of German natives, such as Auglaize (56.4 percent),

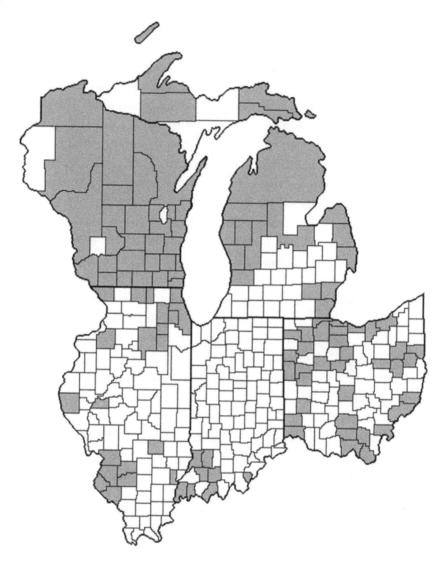

Fig. 2. Foreign birthplaces above the Old Northwest average. Dark gray denotes counties where foreign-born settlers exceeded 24.6 percent of the immigrant population. Figure created by author using data collected by author from microfilms of the 1850 manuscript censes (Records of the Bureau of the Census, RG 29, M432).

Mercer (38.7 percent), and Putnam (34.3 percent). Germans in Illinois concentrated in a line of counties along the Illinois River and the Ohio River in southern Indiana but were few in most of Indiana, eastern Illinois, and Michigan's southwestern Lower Peninsula.

Natives of "Ireland" were identified as such in the 1850 Census. Whether they were Protestants from Northern Ireland who had migrated there during the previous century, largely from Scotland, or Roman Catholics from there or other parts of Ireland, cannot be distinguished.[29] According to this inclusive category in the census, 5.7 percent of the Old Northwest's immigrants originated in Ireland. Many arrived with few resources and found employment as laborers in cities, on docks, on canals or railroads, and in mines and forests; others became farm laborers or farmers. Irish natives in above-average percentages were conspicuously absent from most of Indiana and east central and southeastern Illinois. They were more common in northeastern Illinois around Chicago and in southwestern Illinois across from St. Louis, in southwestern and eastern Ohio, and around the shoreline areas of Michigan's Lower Peninsula, including Detroit. Nearly every Wisconsin county housed concentrations of Irish-born immigrants.

Settlers born in England accounted for 3.6 percent of immigrants to the Old Northwest. Natives of Scotland (0.8 percent of the total) and Wales (0.5 percent) were separately identified in the census, but if collected with the English as natives from Great Britain they represented 4.9 percent of all immigrants.[30] Few Indiana counties housed concentrations of English immigrants, and the same held true for most adjacent parts of Ohio and Illinois. A group of above-average counties in extreme southwestern Indiana and southeastern Illinois contained places established by natives of England, including the English Settlement in Illinois, led by Morris Birkbeck and George Flowers, and Robert Owen's New Harmony, Indiana.[31] Two other areas of Illinois contained natives of England in high proportions: the northeast around Chicago and across from and north of St. Louis in the southwest. English-influenced counties appeared in eastern and northeastern Ohio, the southeastern Lower Peninsula of Michigan, and most of the eastern two-thirds of Wisconsin. Another distinctive English population consisted of Cornish miners working copper and iron reserves in Michigan's Upper Peninsula and lead ores in southwestern Wisconsin and northwestern Illinois.[32]

While Canadian-born immigrants were not the next largest international group in the Old Northwest—they accounted for only 1.9 percent of foreign settlers—their distribution was distinctive. Nearly every county in Wisconsin and Michigan (where they constituted 5.4 percent of immigrants) housed natives of Canada in above-average percentages: 1,953 Canadians formed 52.2 percent of immigrants in Michigan's Sanilac County.[33] But only a few far northern counties in Ohio, Indiana, and Illinois (except for Calhoun County in the west) held above-average percentages of immigrants from Canada.

Changes by 1860

By 1860 some substantial changes in immigration sources had occurred, especially for the foreign born. A major increase in immigration to the United States and the Old Northwest occurred during the 1850s, especially from Ireland and Germany. New arrivals numbered 2.6 million in the 1850s, compared to 1.7 million in the 1840s. And changes across the decade occurred within the Old Northwest states. The original immigrants were passing away or migrating elsewhere while the number and proportion of their children born in state grew. Reflecting the fecundity of settlers, the numbers native to each Old Northwest state grew and their proportion of the population expanded by 2 to 4 percent except in the newest—Wisconsin—where it grew by 14 percent. As the number of immigrants to each state continued to increase, their relative proportions changed because the foreign arrivals outpaced those native to the United States: foreign-born immigrant proportions typically increased by about 10 percent as the United States–born proportions of immigrants decreased. Although the United States–born immigrant proportion declined in Wisconsin, Michigan, and northern Illinois, where settlement was more recent, their actual number continued to enlarge between 1850 and 1860. The number of New Yorkers in Wisconsin increased from 70,810 to 120,637; in Michigan they grew from 135,533 to 191,128; in Illinois their number enlarged from 67,740 to 121,508. But in the older states of Ohio and Indiana, the number of settlers native to some domestic immigrant sources decreased during the decade. Kentuckians in Indiana fell from 70,554 to 68,588. Ohio was the home of fewer Virginians in 1860 than in 1850 (75,874 compared to 85,718) and fewer Pennsylvanians (174,764 compared to 196,889).

Because of their numeric and proportional growth, foreign-born settlers had a greater impact on the Old Northwest in 1860 than in 1850. Immigrants from the various German states formed the largest component of the foreign-born population in 1850 and in 1860, with the social, political, and economic turmoil associated with the Revolution of 1848 encouraging even greater numbers to join their compatriots already living in the region, especially in Wisconsin.[34] German natives in the Old Northwest region increased from 231,979 in 1850 (10.3 percent of immigrants) to 528,394 (15.7 percent) in 1860. Wisconsin witnessed a major influx, from 39,159 Germans (15.6 percent of immigrants) to 123,879 (23.4 percent); Ohio also saw a notable enlargement, from 14.9 percent to 20.8 percent. Many Irish had arrived before the worst of the potato famine years in the mid and late 1840s, resulting in an already considerable number of settlers native to Ireland by 1850: 127,924 or 5.7 percent of the region's immigrants. But their impact intensified during the next decade to number 268,904 or 7.8 percent of immigrants in 1860. Irish natives in Illinois and Ohio expanded most significantly, perhaps due to increasing urbanization. In Ohio, the Irish immigrant proportion grew from 6.7 percent in 1850 to 9.5 percent in 1860; in Illinois, the increase was from 5.4 percent to 8.7 percent. England, the third-largest source of foreign immigrants to the Old Northwest in both census years, increased its numbers but its percentage grew less compared to other foreign sources, rising from 3.6 percent in 1850 to 4.2 percent in 1860. In every state, England accounted for moderately more immigrants, although in Wisconsin their numbers increased but their percentage among birthplaces fell, from 7.8 percent in 1850 to 5.8 percent in 1860.

In most cases, immigrants made conscious choices about where to settle in the Old Northwest. The timing of the urge to move and the availability of new land in the region, particularly of government acreage recently opened for sale, impacted the migrants' decisions. Ohio was the "first west," followed by Indiana, Illinois, Michigan, and Wisconsin, but some lands proved more attractive than others and areas did not open in strict chronological order. Nearness of the new destination and access routes were important factors channeling migration. Before the Erie Canal opened and without regularly passable roads crossing northwestern Ohio's Black Swamp, "plenty of good land was still available in Ohio, Indiana, and Illinois, [so] there was little incentive for the pioneer to brave the hazards involved in getting to Michigan."[35] Virginians and Pennsylvanians came into Ohio via the Ohio River or various land routes. Southern Indiana and Illinois were connected to Kentucky and Tennessee via the Ohio or Mississippi Rivers. Numerous Upstate New Yorkers reached Michigan via the Erie Canal and the Great Lakes, and those water routes linked the immigrant port of New York City to Wisconsin. Paths within the states—rivers, roads, canals, incipient railroads—brought access to formerly inaccessible lands or carried migrants across recent frontiers to the newest and most attractive edges of settlement. Many migrants chose environmentally similar areas featuring familiar climates, vegetation, and topography, such as Kentucky and southern Indiana and southern Illinois or Upstate New York and Michigan's southern Lower Peninsula. While the countryside today may not directly tell us that nineteenth-century immigrants John Smith came from England or New York and Johanna Schmidt came from Pennsylvania or Germany, their ethnic impact on the cultural landscape remains in the names they gave new towns and counties, the styles used to build homes and farms, and the decisions employed in arranging the environment.[36] And the birthplaces of immigrants collected in the 1850 Census confirm what is still evident in the cultural landscape they created.

Notes

1. J. D. B. DeBow, *The Seventh Census of the United States: 1850* (Washington DC: Robert Armstrong, Public Printer, 1853), 818, 30, 917.
2. John Fraser Hart, "The Middle West," in *Regions of the United States*, ed. John Fraser Hart (New York: Harper and Row, 1972), 260n5; John Fraser Hart, "The Spread of the Frontier and the Growth of Population," in *Man*

and Cultural Heritage: Papers in Honor of Fred B. Kniffen, ed. H. J. Walker and W. G. Haag (Baton Rouge: Louisiana State University Press, 1974), 73–81; Charles O. Paullin, *Atlas of the Historical Geography of the United States* (Washington DC: Carnegie Institution of Washington and American Geographical Society of New York, 1932), plate 77.

3. Malcolm J. Rohrbough, *The Land Office Business: The Settlement and Administration of American Public Lands, 1789–1837* (New York: Oxford University Press, 1968).

4. This author collected a full set of birthplace data for Michigan and Wisconsin from microfilms of the manuscript census schedules for 1850: F. G. Bohme, *Twenty Censuses: Population and Housing Questions, 1790–1980* (Washington DC: General Printing Office, 1979); Bureau of the Census, "National Archives Microfilm Publication M432," in Record Group 29 (Washington DC: National Archives). Data for Ohio, originally collected by H. G. H. Wilhelm, were supplemented with information collected by this author from an additional review of the microfilmed census schedules: Hubert H. G. Wilhelm, *The Origin and Distribution of Settlement Groups: Ohio, 1850* (Athens OH: printed by the author, 1982). Data for twenty-one (now twenty-two) counties in northern Indiana, originally collected by Elfrieda Lang, were supplemented with information collected by this author from an additional review of the microfilmed census schedules for those counties and this author collected a full data set for the remaining seventy counties: Elfrieda Lang, "An Analysis of Northern Indiana's Population in 1850," *Indiana Magazine of History* 49, no. 1 (1953): 17–60. Partial data for Illinois, limited to United States–born adult males over the age of twenty, was collected by Douglas K. Meyer and expanded through information collected by this author to cover the balance of the Illinois population: Douglas K. Meyer, "Native-Born Immigrant Clusters on the Illinois Frontier," *Proceedings of the Association of American Geographers* 8 (1976): 41–44.

5. Robert G. Barrows, "The Manuscript Federal Census: Source for a 'New' Local History," *Indiana Magazine of History* 69, no. 3 (1973): 184; Gregory S. Rose, "Information Sources for Nineteenth-Century Midwestern Migration," *Professional Geographer* 37, no. 1 (1985): 66–72.

6. Hyman Alterman, *Counting People: The Census in History* (New York: Harcourt, Brace, and World, 1969), 195; Margo J. Anderson, *The American Census: A Social History* (New Haven CT: Yale University Press, 1988), 34–38, 42–43; Margo Anderson, "The U.S. Bureau of the Census in the Nineteenth Century," *Social History of Medicine* 4, no. 3 (1991): 505–6; DeBow,

The Seventh Census of the United States: 1850, xxi–xxvi; Statistical View of the United States: Being a Compendium of the Seventh Census (Washington: A. O. P. Nicholson, 1854), 17; Loretto Dennis Szucs and Matthew Wright, "Census Records," in The Source: A Guidebook to American Genealogy, ed. Loretto Dennis Szucs and Sandra Hargreaves Luebking (Provo UT: Ancestry, 2006), 157; Carroll D. Wright and William C. Hunt, History and Growth of the United States Census (Washington DC: Government Printing Office, 1900), 41–43, 45.

7. Szucs and Wright, "Census Records," 161; Wright and Hunt, History and Growth of the United States Census, 44.

8. Alterman, Counting People, 66.

9. Alterman, Counting People, 70–72; Barrows, "The Manuscript Federal Census," 189–91; Barnes F. Lathrop, "History from the Census Returns," Southwestern Historical Quarterly 51, no. 4 (1948): 304–5; J. B. Sharpless and R. M. Shortridge, "Biased Underenumeration in Census Manuscripts: Methodological Implications," Journal of Urban History 1, no. 4 (1975): 412–15, 20; Szucs and Wright, "Census Records," 160–61; Wright and Hunt, History and Growth of the United States Census, 43–44.

10. Gregory Rose, "Yeoman Farmer," in The American Midwest: An Interpretive Encyclopedia, ed. Richard Sisson, Christian Zacher, and Andrew Cayton (Bloomington: Indiana University Press, 2007), 85–88.

11. Morris Birkbeck, Notes on a Journey in America from the Coast of Virginia to the Territory of Illinois, to Which Is Added Letters from Illinois, 1818 (New York: Augustus M. Kelley, 1971); William Darby, A Tour from the City of New York, to Detroit in the Michigan Territory, Made between the 2d of May and the 22d of September, 1818 (New York: Kirk and Mercein, 1819); Timothy Flint, A Condensed Geography and History of the Western States, or the Mississippi Valley, 2 vols. (Cincinnati: E. H. Flint, 1828); Charles Fenno Hoffman, A Winter in the West. By a New-Yorker, vol. 1 (New York: Harper and Brothers, 1835); J. M. Peck, A New Guide for Emigrants to the West, Containing Sketches of Ohio, Indiana, Illinois, Missouri, Michigan, with the Territories of Wisconsin and Arkansas, and the Adjacent Parts (Boston: Gould and Lincoln, 1836).

12. Gregory S. Rose, "The Southern Midwest as 'Pennsylvania Extended,'" East Lakes Geographer 23 (1988): 53–70.

13. John C. Hudson, "North American Origins of Middlewestern Frontier Populations," Annals of the Association of American Geographers 78, no. 3 (1988): 395–413; Richard Lyle Power, Planting Corn Belt Culture: The Impress of the Upland Southerner and Yankee in the Old Northwest (Indianapolis: Indiana Historical Society, 1953); Gregory S. Rose, "The National

Road Border between the North and the South in the Midwest by 1870," *Geoscience and Man* 25 (1988): 159–67.

14. Ray Allen Billington, *Westward Expansion: A History of the American Frontier*, 4th ed. (New York: Macmillan, 1974), 208–15; Barrows, "The Manuscript Federal Census," 215–18; Malcolm J. Rohrbough, *The Trans-Appalachian Frontier: People, Societies, and Institutions 1775–1850* (New York: Oxford University Press, 1978), 66–67; Gregory Rose, "Yankees/Yorkers," in *The American Midwest: An Interpretive Encyclopedia*, ed. Richard Sisson, Christian Zacher, and Andrew Cayton (Bloomington: Indiana University Press, 2007) 193–95.

15. Stewart H. Holbrook, *The Yankee Exodus: An Account of Migration from New England* (Seattle: University of Washington Press, 1950).

16. Gregory Rose, "Western Reserve," in *The American Midwest: An Interpretive Encyclopedia*, ed. Richard Sisson, Christian Zacher, and Andrew Cayton (Bloomington: Indiana University Press, 2007).

17. Arthur Pound, "Michigan, New York's Daughter State," *New York History* 23, no. 3 (1942): 283–97.

18. Billington, *Westward Expansion*, 231–32.

19. Gregory Rose, "Virginia Military District," in *The American Midwest: An Interpretive Encyclopedia*, ed. Richard Sisson, Christian Zacher, and Andrew Cayton (Bloomington: Indiana University Press, 2007), 174–75.

20. Gregory S. Rose, "Quakers, North Carolinians and Blacks in Indiana's Settlement Pattern," *Journal of Cultural Geography* 7, no. 1 (1986): 35–48.

21. John Cox Jr., "The Quakers in Michigan," *Michigan History* 29, no. 4 (1945): 512–21; Harold B. Fields, "Free Negroes in Cass County before the Civil War," *Michigan History Magazine* 44, no. 4 (1960): 375–83; George K. Hesslink, *Black Neighbors: Negroes in a Northern Rural Community* (Indianapolis: Bobbs-Merrill, 1968); Roma Jones Stewart, "The Migration of a Free People: Cass County's Black Settlers from North Carolina," *Michigan History* 71, no. 1 (1987): 34–38; James O. Wheeler and Stanley D. Brunn, "An Agricultural Ghetto: Negroes in Cass County, Michigan, 1845–1968," *Geographical Review* 59, no. 3 (1969): 317–29.

22. David T. Thackery, "African Americans in the Federal Census," in *The Source: A Guidebook to American Genealogy*, ed. Loretto Szucs and Sandra Hargreaves (Provo UT: Ancestry, 2006), 211.

23. Paul Finkelman, "Slavery and the Northwest Ordinance: A Study in Ambiguity," *Journal of the Early Republic* 6, no. 4 (1986): 343–70; Stephen Middleton, *The Black Laws in the Old Northwest: A Documentary History* (Westport CT: Greenwood Press, 1993).

24. Cheryl Jennifer LaRoche, *Free Black Communities and the Underground Railroad: The Geography of Resistance* (Urbana: University of Illinois Press, 2014).

25. Fields, "Free Negroes in Cass County before the Civil War"; Hesslink, *Black Neighbors*; Stewart, "Migration of a Free People."

26. Rose, "Quakers, North Carolinians and Blacks in Indiana's Settlement Pattern."

27. Richard Lyle Power, "Wet Lands and the Hoosier Stereotype," *Mississippi Valley Historical Review* 22, no. 1 (1935): 34.

28. Wolfgang Kollmann and Peter Marschalck, "German Emigrants to the United States," in *Dislocation and Emigration: The Social Background of American Immigration*, ed. Donald Fleming and Bernard Bailyn, Perspectives in American History (Cambridge: Harvard University Press, 1973) 499–544.

29. David Noel Doyle, "The Irish in North America, 1776–1845," in *Making the Irish American: History and Heritage of the Irish in the United States*, ed. J. J. Lee and Marion R. Casey (New York: New York University Press, 2006) 213–52; David Noel Doyle, "Scots Irish or Scotch-Irish," in *Making the Irish American*, ed. Lee and Casey, 151–70.

30. Charlotte Erickson, "British Immigrants in the Old Northwest, 1815–1860," in *The Frontier in American Development: Essays in Honor of Paul Wallace Gates*, ed. David M. Ellis (Ithaca: Cornell University Press, 1969) 323–56; Maldwyn A. Jones, "The Background to Emigration from Great Britain in the Nineteenth Century," in *Dislocation and Emigration: The Social Background of American Immigration*, ed. Donald Fleming and Bernard Bailyn, Perspectives in American History (Cambridge: Harvard University Press, 1973) 3–92.

31. Billington, *Westward Expansion*, 284–85; Birkbeck, *Notes on a Journey in America from the Coast of Virginia to the Territory of Illinois*; Ralph H. Brown, *Historical Geography of the United States* (New York: Harcourt, Brace and World, 1948), 245, 48–52; Rohrbough, *Trans-Appalachian Frontier*, 163, 65.

32. Brown, *Historical Geography of the United States*, 304–5, 12–15; Russell M. Magnaghi, *Cornish in Michigan* (East Lansing: Michigan State University Press, 2007), 5–15; William E. Van Vugt, *Britain to America: Mid-Nineteenth Century Immigrants to the United States* (Urbana: University of Illinois Press, 1999), 79–93.

33. Gregory S. Rose, "The Origins of Canadian Settlers in Southern Michigan, 1820–1850," *Ontario History* 79, no. 1 (1987): 31–52; R. K. Vedder and L. E. Gallaway, "Settlement Patterns of Canadian Emigrants to the United States, 1850–1960," *Canadian Journal of Economics* 3, no. 3 (1970): 476–86.

34. Carl Wittke, *Refugees of Revolution: The German Forty-Eighters in America* (Philadelphia: University of Pennsylvania Press, 1952).

35. Willis F. Dunbar and George S. May, *Michigan: A History of the Wolverine State*, 3rd ed. (Grand Rapids MI: Wm. B. Eerdmans, 1995), 159.

36. Henry Glassie, *Pattern in the Material Folk Culture of the Eastern United States* (Philadelphia: University of Pennsylvania Press, 1968); John A. Jakle, Robert W. Bastian, and Douglas K. Meyer, *Common Houses in America's Small Towns: The Atlantic Seaboard to the Mississippi Valley* (Athens: University of Georgia Press, 1989); Fred Kniffen, "Folk Housing: Key to Diffusion," *Annals of the Association of American Geographers* 55, no. 4 (1965): 114–23; John Leighly, "Town Names of Colonial New England in the West," *Annals of the Association of American Geographers* 68, no. 2 (1978): 233–48; Wilbur Zelinsky, "Classical Town Names in the United States: The Historical Geography of an American Idea," *Geographical Review* 57, no. 4 (1967): 463–95; *The Cultural Geography of the United States* (Englewood Cliffs NJ: Prentice-Hall, 1973).

6

Civic Life in a Midwestern Community

Paula M. Nelson

On the afternoon of June 4, 1888, Oliver Russell of Canton, Dakota Territory, lawyer, president of Dakota Savings and Loan, manager of the Dakota National Guard's Second Regimental Band, and Civil War veteran, suffered a brief chest pain while visiting with a probate judge. The pain faded and Russell went home in apparent good health. He went to bed as usual, but his gasping for breath woke his wife at 5:00 a.m. the next morning. She sent for the doctor, but there was nothing he could do. Oliver Russell, pillar of the community, died at 5:15 a.m., June 5, age forty-six.

Russell's funeral was held in his home. His lodge, the Knights Templar of Sioux Falls, an affiliate of the Masons, led the procession of Canton Masons, the Grand Army of the Republic post, Company B of the National Guard, the regimental band, and mourners, past the band shell and concert/theater hall, now draped in black crepe, en route to the cemetery. The band played a dirge as "sixty carriages" and "an immense number of foot passengers" trekked behind the organized groups. At the grave, the Knights Templar performed their final rituals, while the Masons and Civil War veterans cast flowers and evergreens down to the casket. Company B fired a three-volley salute. Then "the company quietly slipped away, leaving only the dead in possession of their great campground."[1]

The story of Oliver Russell's death and funeral provides insights into civic life in the Midwest of the late nineteenth century. In 1831–32 Alexis de Tocqueville, the observant French aristocrat, studied American culture on a grand tour of North America. He accorded great significance to the meteoric rise in the number and scope of voluntary associations in America, operating outside of government control or compulsion, which had no analog in Europe:

Americans of all ages, all conditions, all minds constantly unite. Not only do they have commercial and industrial associations in which all take part, but they also have a thousand other kinds: religious, moral, grave, futile, very general and very particular, immense and very small. . . .

As soon as several of the inhabitants of the United States have conceived a sentiment or an idea that they want to produce in the world, they seek each other out; and when they have found each other, they unite. From then on, they are no longer isolated men, but a power one sees from afar, whose actions serve as an example; a power that speaks, and to which one listens. . . . In order that men remain civilized or become so, the art of associating must be developed and perfected among them in the same ratio as equality of conditions increases.[2]

Voluntary associations and institutions, including the family, the church, ladies' aids, charity groups, lodges, and neighborly helpfulness, were at the core of midwestern towns in the nineteenth century and the first half of the twentieth. Such groups helped society function and reinforced the moral values and direction of the community. Civic society includes organizations promoting the welfare of their communities.[3] Those who worked to provide public buildings or to attract railroads are in this category. In the twentieth century, Kiwanis, Lions, Rotary, or commercial clubs, would also belong. Jonah Goldberg, a contemporary political writer, describes the concept thus: "Civil society is where life happens."[4] Although economic change and population decline have undermined the viability of small towns and rural areas in the Midwest, and diminished membership in organized institutions in some places, the sense of community and helpfulness remains.

This chapter will examine voluntary associations and civic organizations in South Dakota, primarily in the community of Canton and its surrounding area. Settlers began to arrive in the territory in 1861, but the largest influx, the Great Dakota Boom, did not begin until 1879 and ended within a decade. A second settler boom began after 1900 in the western part of the state and ended by 1911. A much smaller rush brought potential farmers into the western counties in the late 1920s. All stages of these settlement movements were comprised mostly of people from the older Midwest, who brought voluntary associations of many kinds with them. European immigrants migrated as well, with their own traditions and cultures.[5]

Civic society in South Dakota was shaped by the later time period of its settlement. Don Harrison Doyle explains in *The Social Order of a Frontier Community: Jacksonville, Illinois, 1825–70* that the Second Great Awakening, and the rise of reform movements it prompted during the early nineteenth century, sent New England missionaries to places like Illinois, "the West" of that era. They hoped to fight the social disorder that they perceived as dangerous to western communities. Their plan: to inspire locals to build stronger families, churches, schools and other institutions like those in New England. They brought a moral urgency to the construction of schools for the young and academies for advanced education. Their belief that intemperance was the source of many evils helped prompt political solutions to the alcohol problem. Local governments then created laws to control alcohol. Social and governmental coercion also drove some private voluntary associations toward temperance and prohibition.[6] By the time settlers from the eastern Midwest reached Dakota Territory, the religiosity and world view of New Englanders in Illinois and elsewhere had imprinted itself on the middle-class social order.

Canton, Dakota Territory, was first established in 1867, with the two railroads arriving in 1879. The town grew steadily after that. In 1880, 635 people resided in the town; in 1900 the population had tripled to 1,943. Canton was built on the banks of the Big Sioux River, the border between Iowa and Dakota Territory. Town residents were generally midwesterners, with earlier family origins in New England, Pennsylvania, and New York, or they were Norwegians, either immigrants or first-generation Americans moving from Wisconsin, Iowa, or Minnesota.[7] The blend of cultures shaped Canton life. American merchants hired Norwegian-speaking clerks to attract Norwegian customers. The three-member county board always had one Norwegian, and the county officers always included a Norwegian Register of Deeds. The Congregationalists built the first church with Presbyterians, Methodists, Episcopalians, and an independent church following. Before they could afford church buildings, the various denominations met in the courthouse. The Norwegians initially had two churches, both Lutheran, which represented the division between the Norwegian Synod, a reflection of Norway's state Lutheranism, and a pietistic Haugean offshoot. The two churches combined in 1902.[8]

Canton, like other towns and rural neighborhoods, had an informal social world based on custom, tradition, and need, and a formal social order arranged around organized groups and institutions. Both helped sustain cultural values. The informal social world existed, in part, because people lived in close contact with others. Manners and proper behavior helped keep the peace. This was a world of observation. Residents of the town walked to their destinations. They saw neighbors and strangers passing by their homes or met them on the streets of the business district. Windows and doors stood open in the summer. Voices carried. People had to haul or pump water, which brought them outside. Householders chopped wood for the cookstove in the yard or near the back door. Women did the laundry or churned on the back porch in milder weather. Children played in yards or in the dirt side streets, where grass often grew. Many people boarded in hotels or in the homes of others. Employees sometimes lived with their employers. The families of merchants might live above or behind their stores, and unmarried male clerks sometimes slept in the shops where they worked and ate at hotels or restaurants.[9]

Daily life was quite public. Close proximity could bring trouble, especially when livestock and chickens invaded neighbors' gardens. The local excursion boat captain punched a neighbor when they argued over a pig pen. The poor captain lived between the two families in town who still kept pigs. Summer's hot, humid weather made the stench unbearable and frustration led to fisticuffs. The neighbor pressed charges.[10]

Close proximity also led to heroism. The requirements of neighborliness prompted action in times of crisis or peril. Jake Williams was out getting wood one day when his house caught fire. Inside, his wife was completely bedridden. The Golden brothers, on their way home, saw the smoke, called for help, then ran into the house. They carried Mrs. Williams out of the house, bed and all, and brought them both to a neighbor's. Other neighbors came running, took the children to safety and hauled out any household goods that they could reach. The Williams family was left with a bed, a stove, and not much else, but no lives were lost. The community then raised money to help them rebuild.[11]

Close proximity also meant that unusual noise attracted attention. A man who attacked his wife in their Beloit, Iowa, home, brought the neighbors running. They pulled the wife to safety and pummeled the abusive husband. On other occasions men abusing their animals brought neighbors over to stop the violence.[12]

Much of what we know about Canton comes from its newspaper columns. One of the town's papers, the *Sioux Valley News*, had a single editor for twenty-eight years. The paper began publication in 1872; in January of 1877, Newman C. Nash purchased the operation and remained at the helm until his death in February 1905. N. C. Nash was born in Upstate New York. The family moved to Rock County, Wisconsin, to farm when N. C. Nash was seven. Nash was a Civil War veteran, a temperance man, and Congregationalist. He was a keen observer of his community and fearless in his commentaries on child behavior, drunken rowdies, cruelty to animals, wife beating, marital or social scandals, neighborhood discord, officials who did not do their jobs, and any other social or cultural issue that he saw or that readers brought to his attention. Nash's office was busy with printing work, in spite of occasional boycotts from those stung by his remarks, and with visitors, male, female, young, and old, who enjoyed quick chats.[13]

One of Nash's interests throughout his career was maintaining a reasonable order in the town. Although the maintenance of law and order is generally considered a government function, in the absence of police departments or sheriffs' offices, residents stepped in to protect the peace. In the earliest years, the Lincoln County sheriffs lived in Canton, so "the law" was usually available. In 1876, however, county voters elected Albert Dixon, who lived on his farm some distance from town. He appointed deputies, but none were from Canton. One of the deputies, a Norwegian farmer, drank heavily and caused considerable disorder in the town. Alcohol fueled many of the troubles in Canton. Editor Nash, in the summer of 1879, complained that "drunks paraded the streets" and interrupted religious meetings going on in the city. "What is the use of a sheriff if he lives so far in the country as to be beyond reach to quell disturbances that occur after nightfall?" Nash complained. When a minister held tent meetings downtown, drunken "rowdies" threw stones at the tent and disrupted the services. Nash wrote that "several citizens went out and tried to identify the boys. Three were spotted." Nash knew that publicity and identification of culprits helped end disorder. In this case, men who did not want to attend the tent meetings volunteered to do "picket duty" to keep rowdies away.[14]

On another occasion, Nash wrote of "another whiskey row, of which there have been so many." Austin Olson drank all day, becoming loud and profane. In the absence of the sheriff, town "boys" decided to drive Olson and his drinking neighbors out. They loaded the men into their wagons and pointed them toward home. The drinking farmers came right back. Then "someone hit one town man with a bottle. Olson pulled a knife." Cooler heads prevailed and the miscreants left for home. Nash called for the election of a different sheriff and the appointment of deputies who did not drink. "Olson is a terror to his neighborhood and a frequent problem in town," Nash concluded.[15]

Even after Canton incorporated in 1881 and had city councilmen to appoint marshals, local citizens had to assist him to subdue the disorderly or chase burglars. Nash praised those who helped the lone marshal and condemned those who stood by when their help was needed. Canton's location on the Big Sioux River, directly across from Beloit, Iowa, provided criminals an easy escape from local authorities.[16]

There were many organized voluntary groups in South Dakota committed to serving individuals or the community; churches were the most obvious and best known. Women's groups, such as ladies' aids or mission societies, especially flourished. Lodges, however, also engendered strong attachments among their members, and their emphasis on moral teachings and upstanding behavior helped sustain a culture of character. Lodges were omnipresent in towns of the late nineteenth and early twentieth centuries, but the specific purposes they filled are not well understood today.

Don Harrison Doyle argues that churches and political parties "institutionalized *divisions* of faith and ideology within the community."[17] Lodges, on the other hand, along with other voluntary associations, "integrated" men of varying ethnicities, classes, and religious and political beliefs. Lodges, while emphasizing the spiritual in a broad sense, forbade discussions of politics or religion. Lodges also provided their members with some security in a mobile nation, where people moved to new places with no family ties or support. In times of illness or other crises, lodge members relied on other lodge members, perhaps total strangers, to aid them.[18]

The Masons represented the oldest and most complex of these organizations, offering three basic degrees and several other options for "master" masons to advance through the work. Because many American Founders were Masons, the lodge held considerable prestige.[19] The International Order of Odd Fellows was a younger institution with just three steps or degrees. In general it was less mysterious and more welcoming. These two fraternal organizations were the first in Canton.[20]

The Masons comprised several divisions, including the Scottish Rite and York Rite lodges, but all welcomed Masons from other branches. All Masons shared a common moral code and character. The three core Masonic principles were Brotherly Love, Relief (or Charity), and Truth. The four cardinal virtues of the organization were Fortitude, Prudence, Temperance, and Justice. Masons expressed core principles through symbols that originated with stone cutters of long ago, whose guilds provided the model for Masonic lodges. Masons wore jewelry embellished with the square, compass, level, gauge, and trowel, each of which expressed a key value. The square, for example, indicated "square actions through the 'square of virtue.'" The compass, which created lines and boundaries, reflected self-control and restraint.[21]

What role did Masonry play in civic life? Masons promoted unity, a sense of the sacred, a commitment to brotherhood and fellowship based on equality, as well as individual character development. The requirement of secrecy in rituals, signs, and words helped build trustworthiness and dependability. Members who could not keep lodge secrets were not honest or reliable, important values in a brotherhood. Masons suspended or expelled members who violated the moral code of the chapter. Those who followed the moral code of the lodge developed self-discipline, enhanced reputations, built stronger families and improved opportunities for upward mobility.[22] Lodge membership also provided a "temperate and purified" place for men to socialize away from the demands of family.[23]

The Order of the Eastern Star was founded in 1850, creating a place for women among the Masons. The order had both male and female members. The lodge offered degrees based on the stories of biblical women and by 1876 had developed a complex system of officers and rules. Men in the lodge had to be Master Masons, the women had to be related to a Master Mason, although relationships could include stepmothers or children, nieces and others outside nuclear family ties. On occasion the Masons and the Order of the Eastern Star met together for social events.[24]

The Independent Order of Odd Fellows, or IOOF, the second lodge founded in Canton, began in eighteenth-century England as a group that provided charity for others without claiming recognition for themselves. Some labeled them "Odd Fellows" as a result, and the name stuck. By 1819 the IOOF also had lodges in North America. Their precepts were simple but profound. Members must follow a Supreme Being, as master of the universe. The group's motto provided their philosophy: one must pursue "Friendship, Love and Truth." Members committed themselves to "improve and elevate the character of humanity through service and example." The Odd Fellows philosophy reflected the truth of human nature. Members contemplated difficult questions: "How am I going to spend my life?" they asked, in light of "the frailty and inevitable decay of human life and the fact that wealth has no power to stop the sureness of eventual death." The lodge emphasized the brotherhood and sisterhood of all, temperance and chastity in thought and deed, respect for oneself and others, generosity, and mental clarity. The Rebekahs were the associated women's lodge. The name came from Rebekah, who in the book of Genesis, offered water to a stranger and to his camels. The Odd Fellows and Rebekahs often socialized together.[25]

Masons who settled in the Canton area organized the Silver Star chapter of the Ancient Free and Accepted Masons in 1874, when the town had few residents and no railroad. Canton men organized the Centennial Chapter of the Independent Order of Odd Fellows in 1876, also before the full flowering of the town. In 1883, another branch of the Masons organized the Siroc Chapter.[26] Oliver Russell, whose lodge brothers marched with his body to the grave, belonged to a branch of the Masons in Sioux Falls, the Knights Templar, among whose missions was the defense of Christianity. Russell caught the train to Sioux Falls, twenty-two miles away, to enjoy the rituals and brotherhood of the Knights. He also belonged to the Canton lodges.[27] The Canton Masons organized the Order of the Eastern Star in the 1890s.[28] Local lodges all belonged to the Grand Lodges of their particular orders. Representatives from Canton traveled to Yankton, Sioux Falls, or Rapid City to meet with Masons from other towns, creating a network of relationships across the state. The Odd Fellows used a similar Grand Lodge structure. Many men in the Canton area belonged to more than one well-established lodge as well as newer lodges or those devoted primarily to insurance, as they developed in the later nineteenth century. Several Canton men held elective office in the various Grand Lodges of the state, as well. N.C. Nash led the state Grand Lodge of Odd Fellows in the mid-1890s, for example.[29]

Other Canton lodges included the Good Templars, organized as Rescue Lodge number two in 1876, a temperance lodge that enrolled both men and women, and the Ancient Order of United Workmen, organized in 1880. This was the first of the fraternal benefits organizations, where the primary goal was member insurance for illness, or for death benefits. Over time the AOUW nationally evolved into the Pioneer Mutual Insurance Company. By the 1890s Canton had a Modern Woodmen lodge, Knights of Pythias organization, and an Ancient Order of the Pyramid lodge.[30]

Lodges were sometimes controversial. Secret rituals and elaborate officer titles, such as "Worshipful Master," added an element of mysticism that some believed threatened Christianity or the social and political order.[31] In Canton in the 1890s, the Lutheran minister sermonized against lodges over a period of many months. N.C. Nash, loyal member of the Masons, Woodmen, and Odd Fellows, defended lodges in his newspaper. Nash argued that lodges supported the practice of religion and helped sustain its members and the communities of which they were a part. Nash, himself, was a deeply religious Congregationalist, who loved to hear the Gospel taught and attended tent meetings and church services for a variety of denominations, including the Salvation Army, Seventh Day Adventists, and Catholics. He appreciated the brotherhood his lodges encouraged, the sociability they fostered, and the charity they offered for others. As editor he had the opportunity to encourage charitable actions and to report on them.[32] In one dramatic case, a young mother died when the stairs in the family's rented home crumbled as she came down, throwing her to the ground and killing her. The family was new in town but the husband was an Odd Fellow. Lodge members came at once to help the man who was crushed by his wife's death and unable to function. They cared for the small children, assisted with funeral arrangements, and helped him take the train with his children to his parents' home. When members faced hard times or crisis, members of many kinds of lodges filled a vital role.[33]

Although lodges continued to play a role in the social world of midwestern life well into the twentieth century, changing economic and cultural circumstances reduced their influence on the civic community. Author Stanley Coben, critical of the "Victorian cult of character," made a long list of Victorian cultural characteristics that nineteenth-century lodges and other groups would have heartily endorsed: "dependably self-controlled, punctual, orderly, hardworking, conscientious, sober, respectful of other Victorians' property rights, ready to postpone immediate gratification for long-term goals, pious toward a usually friendly God, a believer in the truth of the Bible, oriented strongly toward home and family, honorable in relations with other Victorians, anxious for self-improvement in a fashion which might appear compulsive to modern observers and patriotic."

This culture was gradually transformed into a more materialistic consumer culture by the potent conformist pressures of big business, advertising, and the values and interests of urban cultural elites. Independent businessmen and small-town merchants no longer had the social or economic authority they enjoyed in the nineteenth century. One result was a new kind of civic group, the service club. The largest and most successful were the Rotary Club, the Lions Club, and Kiwanis, all headquartered in Illinois, until Kiwanis moved to Indianapolis in 1982. Rotary was the first to organize when a young lawyer, Paul Harris, found himself in Chicago, trying to build a practice and make connections. He came from a small town and found the city difficult to navigate. He built his club for individual merchants, small businessmen, and professionals, with sociability and shared business and trade as goals. The Rotary, founded in 1905, was the result. The members, male only, met once a week for lunch, rotating from office to office. Harris readily shared his idea, which caught on quickly. More Rotary Clubs appeared in larger midwestern cities and then spread to smaller cities. In 1911 Rotary dropped the business-exchange program after critics complained about restrictions on trade. Clubs began to emphasize community service as members expressed interest in doing good works.[34]

Imitators sprang up. The Kiwanis Clubs, also male only, began in Detroit in 1914. Built at first on an exchange of business plan, the organization shifted its focus to community service. The Kiwanis made Chicago its headquarters and began to develop clubs in smaller cities in Illinois and elsewhere. The Lions Club organization, like the others male only, began in Chicago in 1917, a service club from the beginning. The Lions organized clubs in smaller towns, with under five thousand residents. Many organizers of the Rotary and Kiwanis Clubs were traveling salesmen who represented wholesalers based in large cities. They traveled to medium-sized cities and small towns, selling merchandise to merchants. Satisfied members of Rotary or Kiwanis themselves, they advertised the possibilities found in the organizations. The Lions Club home office hired organizers to visit smaller towns and won memberships there.[35]

Why were business/service clubs so successful in the post–1910 era? The new order of corporate consolidation and bureaucratic organization, along with Progressive reformers' efforts to manage change and reform society, prompted this new kind of civic engagement. Dramatic civic projects, such as bringing a railroad to town, or building a courthouse and giving it to the county, as Canton men had done in the 1870s, was no longer possible.[36] Lodges, focused on the fraternal and local, no longer had the same appeal in a rapidly changing, urbanizing world, where social problems appeared to exist everywhere. Small-town businessmen worried that their authority and influence had disappeared. They hoped to build their communities and their bottom lines through service clubs better suited to the times. Through the Rotary, Kiwanis, or Lions Clubs they cooperated with one another, learned new ideas, and served their communities. For most, the important focus was local; service clubs provided opportunities to boost the hometown. The informality of club social life certainly had an appeal as well. As Jeffrey A. Charles writes, however, joining one of the three major service clubs was in essence joining a national organization, whose priorities would shape all the small places businessmen hoped to protect. "Ironically . . . their attempt to preserve local identity may have aided the standardization of community life. . . . Thus every town had its Lions pancake breakfast, its Kiwanis ballfield, its Rotary park."[37]

The centralizing forces of the American economy and growing mass culture continued to reshape midwestern life and create a new order, one that N. C. Nash and the founders of Canton would not recognize. Civic life and lived experience provide useful tools for examining all levels of social interaction and organization in midwestern communities and the social changes that have continued to redefine the levels and types of individual and local group participation. Male-only service clubs, for example, began to admit women in 1987, when the Supreme Court ruled that private clubs whose members made business contacts at meetings could no longer exclude women.[38] The rise of electronic media, radio, movies, and television provided new entertainment choices that reduced participation in voluntary associations, and with television, kept people at home far more than before. The rise of high school sports in the 1920s provided entertainment, but also opportunities for voluntarism and community commitment. Today in the Midwest, parental commitment to their children's sports, along with the rise of two-income families, has reduced their participation in church and community groups. Those organizations struggle to find active members. Lower birth rates and small-town population decline means that a Lutheran church in

Gaylord, Minnesota, who for years had Easter breakfasts served by the youth group Luther League, no longer has enough youth to continue the tradition. Detailed study of civic life and voluntary associations, then and now, highlights change in the lived experience of individuals and communities, its causes and repercussions. The Midwest provides rich ground for such study.

Notes

1. *Sioux Valley News* (Canton, South Dakota), June 8, 1888.
2. *Democracy in America*, by Alexis de Tocqueville; translated, edited, and with an introduction by Harvey C. Mansfield and Delba Winthrop (Chicago: University of Chicago Press, 2002 paperback ed.): 489, 492.
3. "Civic Society," accessed April 20, 2015, https://www.collinsdictionary.com /dictionary/english/civic-society; "The difference between civil and civic," January 30, 2018, https://senscot.net/the-difference-between-civil-and-civic/.
4. Jonah, Goldberg, "Moral Heroism without Morality," accessed January 30, 2018, http://www.nationalreview.com/g-file/416443/moral-heroism -without-morality-jonah-goldberg.
5. Herbert S. Schell, *History of South Dakota*, 3rd ed. (Lincoln: University of Nebraska Press, 1975), 158–74; Paula M. Nelson, *After the West Was Won: Homesteaders and Town-Builders in Western South Dakota, 1900–1917* (Iowa City: University of Iowa Press, 1986); Paula M. Nelson, *The Prairie Winnows Out Its Own: The West River Country of South Dakota in the Years of Depression and Dust* (Iowa City: University of Iowa Press, 1996).
6. Don Harrison Doyle, *The Social Order of a Frontier Community: Jacksonville, Illinois, 1825–70* (Urbana: University of Illinois Press), 23–38, 156–93.
7. *The History of Lincoln County South Dakota* (Freeman SD: Lincoln County History Committee, 1985), 1–15, 17–26. Census data from U.S. Bureau of the Census, *Tenth Census of the United States*, 1880; *Twelfth Census of the United States*, 1900.
8. *Sioux Valley News*, September 2, 1876; *History of Lincoln County*, 160–62.
9. *Sioux Valley News*, February 22, 1879; April 23, 1880; *Tenth Census*, 1880; *Twelfth Census*, 1900.
10. *Sioux Valley News*, September, 8, 1899.
11. *Sioux Valley News*, December 9, 1876.
12. *Sioux Valley News*, August 18, 1877; November 24, 1877.
13. *Memorial and Biographical Record of Turner, Lincoln, Union, and Clay Counties South Dakota* (Chicago: George A. Ogle, 1897), 66–68; *Sioux Val-*

ley News, every issue has one or more of the elements listed in this paragraph. The paper of February 24, 1877 lists all of his visitors from the start of his editorship in one paragraph.

14. *Sioux Valley News*, July 12, 1879; August 30, 1879; April 30, 1880; May 21, 1880; July 22, 1881.

15. *Sioux Valley News*, September 24, 1880; February 24, 1899.

16. *Sioux Valley News*, July 19, 1889.

17. Doyle, *Social Order of a Frontier Community*, 178.

18. Doyle, *Social Order of a Frontier Community*, 178–83.

19. Teresa Lynn, *Little Lodges on the Prairie: Freemasonry and Laura Ingalls Wilder* (Austin TX: Tranquility Press, 2014), 17–37.

20. "About Us," accessed April 24, 2015, http://www.ioof.org/about_us/What's _a_Odd_Fellow?

21. "Difficult Questions about Masonry," accessed April 24, 2015, http://web .mit.edu/dryfoo/Masons/Questions/difficult.html. Also http://www.mit .edu/dryfoo/masonry. See also http:// www.dummies.com/how-to/content /figuring-out-what-freemasons-believe-in and http://www.masonicinfo.com.

22. Lynn, *Little Lodges on the Prairie*, 46–49.

23. Doyle, *Social Order of a Frontier Community*, 178.

24. Lynn, *Little Lodges on the Prairie*, 73–84.

25. Odd Fellows informational website, accessed April 24, 2015, http://www .ioof.org.

26. *History of Lincoln County*, 202; *Sioux Valley News*, July 20, 1876; August 15, 1883.

27. "Knights Templar," accessed April 27, 2015, http://www.masonicinfo.com /templars.htm.

28. *Sioux Valley News*, first mention of the Order of the Eastern Star, February 18, 1895.

29. *Sioux Valley News*, May 18, 1894, Nash elected head of IOOF Grand Lodge.

30. *Sioux Valley News*, August 25, 1876; AOUW information comes from a retrospective report in the *Sioux Valley News*, July 19, 1881.

31. Lynn, *Little Lodges on the Prairie*, 41–48.

32. *Sioux Valley News*, August 20, 1879; August 12, 1892; October 25, 1901; February 1, 1879.

33. *Sioux Valley News*, August 17, 1883.

34. Stanley Coben, *Rebellion Against Victorianism: The Impetus for Cultural Change in 1920s America* (New York: Oxford University Press, 1991), 4; see also Jeffrey A. Charles, *Service Clubs in America: Rotary, Kiwanis, and Lions* (Urbana: University of Illinois Press, 1993), 2–4.

35. Charles, *Service Clubs*, 9–85.

36. *Sioux Valley News*, May 4, 1876; May 25, 1876, for courthouse building; February 5, 1878, for railroad organization.

37. Charles, *Service Clubs*, 6; 1–85 and throughout.

38. "High Court Rules That Rotary Clubs Must Admit Women," by Stuart Taylor Jr., *New York Times*, May 5, 1987, http://www.nytimes.com/1987/05/05/us/high-court-rules-that-rotary-clubs-must-admit-women.html, accessed January 23, 2018; "Kiwanis Becomes a Co-ed Organization," https://kiwanis.org/about/history/kiwanis-becomes-a-coed-organization, accessed January 23, 2018; Nelson, *Prairie Winnows Out Its Own*, 89, 110–14 for radio, 86–87 for school sports and activities; for "lived experience" concerning local sports and Luther League, my champion volunteer mother, Marie Main, of Gaylord, Minnesota.

7

Politics in the Promised Land

HOW THE GREAT MIGRATION SHAPED
THE AMERICAN MIDWEST

Jeffrey Helgeson

Between about 1910 and the mid-1970s, millions of black southerners migrated to the Midwest, seeking the promise of jobs and freedom in the North, as well as refuge from the violence and lack of opportunity in the Jim Crow South. In 1910, 89 percent of the nation's black residents resided in the South. But by midcentury, one-third of black Americans lived in the North, and by the end of the migration, in the early 1970s, the number of African Americans in the North was nearly equal to the number in the South—10,216,000 versus 10,673,000.[1] Roughly half of the black southern migrants headed for the Midwest, most of them going to the region's large cities. The largest single interstate migration after World War II was from Mississippi to Illinois, with Chicago becoming host to a black metropolis of over 1.1 million African Americans by 1970. Over time, increasing numbers of migrants settled in the smaller towns of the region, but this was a migration defined by the search for a promised land in the industrial, urban Midwest. The migration to the Midwest was part of a much larger movement from the South to the North and West, and from the country to the city. Black Americans had been among the most rural of American people, but by 1970, only 18 percent of black Americans lived in the rural South.[2] In this process, migrants transformed everything from American religion and popular culture to the hierarchies that defined life in urban neighborhoods, at work, and in politics. As African Americans became the nation's most urban citizens, nothing was left untouched.

Regions are to some extent political projects, and the Great Black Migration had a polarizing influence on the making of the Midwest. This is, after all, a region rooted in European-American settlers' nineteenth-century displacement of Native Americans and their plans for an intentionally white republic free of the evils of slavery and racial tensions. In the twentieth century, the mass migration of black southerners to the region came to be understood by social scientists and policymakers, as well as in popular opinion, as a problem to be diagnosed and treated. The persistence and pervasiveness of racial inequality and segregation were just too apparent to ignore. And for many, the migrants themselves were the problem; they seemed to bring a "backward" rural culture unprepared for complex urban life. Cultural and behavioral explanations of the problems in American cities, however, proved to be misleading and demonstrably false, or at least grossly insufficient. And so an extensive literature on the racism of American life has described the individual and structural forces that have created and constantly re-created what some have called "American Apartheid."[3]

Undeniably, the Great Black Migration has polarized politics in the Midwest. The dominant responses to the migration empowered the forces of white working- and middle-class politics that reenergized and reshaped twentieth-century American conservatism. Yet the migrants also energized the social protest that made the modern civil rights movement possible. The Great Migration thus facilitated white Americans' movement to the suburbs and the reconstruction of the South during and after the 1960s. As a result, much of the urban Midwest—the major destinations of the migration—has become deindustrialized, deunionized, and increasingly isolating and antagonistic to working-class black residents. Descendants of the twentieth-century migrants, therefore, are now moving again. This time they are going to the suburbs and smaller towns of the Midwest, as well as to the economic and political powerhouses of postindustrial America now concentrated in cities in the South and Southwest.[4] The Great Migration, therefore, did not initiate racial tensions in the Midwest, but the migrants brought to the surface the aspects of the region that made it both a land of hope and a place of profound disappointment in black Americans' diasporic movement in search of freedom and opportunity.

In part to compensate for the focus on the migration as a source of social "problems," some observers have set out to document the migrants' achievements, and there is much to celebrate in this history. Many of the individuals, both well-known and obscure, who made the southern diaspora what it was, did their work in the Midwest. Who can imagine an American culture without the music that found a popular audience by being recorded and broadcast in Kansas City, St. Louis, Chicago, and Detroit? How different would the history of American media be without outlets ranging from the *Chicago Defender* and *Jet* and *Ebony* magazines to the scores of regional and local black newspapers and radio stations that both spoke to a black public and brought black voices to the American public more broadly? How much narrower would American political discourse have been without the radical press that black writers helped sustain?[5] And how could one miss the influences of black politics on the Midwest? Black politics has defined midwestern politics from Ida B. Wells's crusades against lynching (which she based in Chicago after being run out of Memphis) to the rise of Michelle and Barack Obama from Chicago to the White House.[6] The post-Emancipation generation engaged in critical civil rights struggles and constructed the first black political machines. Black voters and politicians were crucial to the New Deal coalition at the local and national levels. Influential activists based in the Midwest, many of whom are still not well-known, were also at the heart of the labor and civil rights movements between the 1930s and the 1960s, as well as the Black Power struggles of the 1960s and 1970s and the electoral organizing to increase black political representation from the late 1960s to the present.[7] The pantheon of black midwesterners who profoundly shaped American culture, politics, and social life is much too long to list here.

It is important to recognize those who overcame exclusion to transform modern American life, but merely celebrating their individual accomplishments does not get to the heart of the migration's influences on the Midwest. To stop there would be to risk seeing the outstanding individuals as exceptions to the rule that the migrants and migration were ostensibly "the problem." The real problem, however, was that black southerners—self-selected for their ambition and grit—flocked to the Midwest in search of a "promised land," only to find a region defined in large part by structural and individual racism. It is in the tensions between freedom and oppression, opportunity and subordination, movement and segregation, resistance and accommodation that black migrants and their descendants constructed their cultural, political, and social force. Properly understood, the migration must be seen as a project of both individual and group liberation. To move was to make a deliberate decision—based on personal circumstances as much as historical contexts—to take a chance on networks with friends and relatives, to leave behind the Jim Crow South for the unknown of the North, to risk that one's dreams in the promised land would be for naught. For all too many, the move brought a realization that the Midwest was, in the words of one woman who moved to Cincinnati after World War II, "no promised land" at all.[8]

Richard Wright, perhaps the most famous literary migrant to the Midwest, captured the migrants' characteristic ambivalence about their new homes. "On the plantations," Wright mused in 1941, "our songs carried a strain of other-worldly yearning which people called 'spiritual'; but now our blues, jazz, swing, and boogie-woogie are our 'spirituals' of the city pavements, our longing for freedom and opportunity, an expression of our bewilderment and despair in a world whose meaning eludes us."[9] The meanings of life in the Midwest eluded them for the same reasons they elude us: because the complexity of the region defies simple definitions. For black southerners arriving in Detroit's "Paradise Valley," Chicago's South or West Side Black Metropolis, Cleveland's Flats, Minneapolis's Phillips neighborhood—or in Gary, Indianapolis, Springfield, Muncie, Omaha, or Grand Rapids—for them the Midwest was both more open and more closed than the Jim Crow South had been. And so every aspect of the migration's influences on the Midwest must be seen with an eye to the tensions between "the longing for freedom and opportunity" and the profound limits on that freedom and opportunity that always threatened to engender "bewilderment and despair."

Such tensions are ongoing. Just before Christmas 2014, the *Fond du Lac Reporter* published a story on the racism that African Americans face in the Wisconsin city every day. "While Fond du Lac may not be Ferguson, Missouri," the infamous site of clashes between protestors and police that autumn in the midwestern suburb, "racism is showing up in subtle, and sometimes not-so-subtle forms."[10] This conclusion about the racism in the Midwest, and the haunting reference to corroborating events in Ferguson, came from Christopher Cross, an African American nurse who moved to the town after discharging from the navy. Cross revolted in disgust at the racist lawn figurines in his neighbors' yards, and he had to paint over the stenciled "rows of watermelon slices and pickaninnies" previous owners left on the kitchen walls in his new home. Just as concerning, he noted that there were no black business owners listed in the town's 2010 census. And, as in Wisconsin and the Midwest as a whole, racial disparities abound in the housing, the labor market, and the education and criminal justice systems. Cross had not given up on his dreams of a more open community in this city of 100,000 people on the southern shore of Lake Winnebago. But his neighbors and city officials worried that things were going to get worse before they got better. Tensions were growing as locals worried about the arrival of new black residents from cities like Milwaukee and Chicago. A new migration, from cities to suburbs and small towns across the Midwest has been creating new tensions.[11]

Stories like Cross's can be found throughout what was once the nearly all-white hinterland of midwestern cities, as the destinations of the twentieth-century Great Migration become places to flee in an ongoing search for a better life. This new movement of black midwesterners provides a new imperative to study the dynamics of the previous century's migration. To understand the migration's influence on the Midwest requires more than just celebrating the past. Studying the history of the Midwest is necessarily a political project. Incorporating a black history perspective may help this historical project become, in the words of the late Manning Marable, "a critical force for change" that may, to quote Pero Dagbovie, "help improve, reform, democratize, and enrich American culture and society."[12]

Lessons from the Past

Before the Great Black Migration, many white settlers had envisioned what we now think of as the Midwest as the great hope for a republic of white independent producers. In order to protect this land of "free soil" and "free labor," the states in the region passed antebellum "black laws" with special taxes and other restrictions on black newcomers; three states—Indiana, Illinois, and Iowa—even prohibited black migration into their territories.[13] "Racial prejudice," noted Alexis de Tocqueville, "appears to me stronger in the states that have abolished slavery than in those where slavery still exists, and nowhere is it shown to be as intolerant as in states where slavery has always been unknown."[14] Fear of emancipation resounded through antebellum white America. Tocqueville thought the North would be insulated from the potential racial conflicts after emancipation. "In the North," he wrote, "when whites fear being intermingled with blacks, they are scared of an imaginary danger."[15] He was wrong about that, but he was right when he declared, "The more the whites of the United States are free, the more they will seek to isolate themselves."[16] Black residents of the Midwest in the nineteenth century became the foil against which white working-class men and women, especially the more recent immigrants, defined their "white" racial identities. Black midwesterners thus became victims of racial discrimination in the economy and politics, as well as the targets of a racist popular culture, the most popular form of which featured white actors in blackface denigrating black men and women in minstrel shows.[17] From the outset, the Midwest has been a place of constant racial tension punctuated by bouts of racial violence that change in their specifics but have never quite gone away. The eventual mass migration of black southerners to the Midwest would only intensify whites' general impulse to racial separation.

The Midwest, then, began as a region defined largely by resistance and antagonism to black newcomers. But that was not the whole story. Black runaways made it to what they saw as a land of freedom north of the Ohio River, aided by allies on the Underground Railroad.[18] Many continued on into Michigan and then Canada. But the region's growing towns were heterogeneous enough to provide pockets of safety, tolerance, and even abolitionist advocacy. The Midwest has manifested a kind of begrudging openness to black migrants, as refugees from slavery and Jim Crow, and as workers in industrial boomtowns. It is important to recognize how newcomers to the Midwest saw the region as a place of real possibility.

It is also essential to keep in mind that the migration was not propelled by social and economic forces alone. The migrants were present at the making of the migration. Black leaders in the Midwest and in the South helped frame the desire for the migration. In some few cases, local community leaders in the South organized entire towns to move north together. And the *Chicago Defender*, distributed by black Pullman Porters throughout the South, sang the praises of the migration as a step toward the liberation of the race. Moreover, individual migrants helped build the momentum, becoming important links in a "chain migration," either persuading relatives, friends, and acquaintances to move to the North or facilitating their counterparts' self-driven flight from the South.[19] Consequently, over the course of the migration era, migrants became increasingly likely to move from the Deep South and to make the transition in one move, rather than in steps, as previous migrants had done.[20]

The migrants were agents of their own history, but they encountered powerful forces of segregation, subordination, and exclusion. The scale of the migration, alone, made social conflicts inevitable. The Great Black Migration was far from the largest migration in the United States of the twentieth century, but it was the most visible. In fact, more white southerners moved to the North between the 1910s and the 1970s, and the general drift of the American population from the East to the West dwarfed both northward migrations. Nonetheless, the Great Black Migration stood out for a number of reasons. First, unlike their Euro-American counterparts, black migrants to the Midwest settled in densely populated and segregated urban neighborhoods concentrated in a few large cities.[21] And in those cities, black migrants moved into segregated communities that became only increasingly isolated from white, Latino, and Asian residents. Consequently, the Great Black Migration remained more conspicuous than other movements that were larger in sheer numbers. Black migrants were more visible, and black urban communities took on an explanatory importance as observers sought to understand the fate of American cities as they rose and fell.

The history of the black migration to the Midwest, then, teaches us that public responses to such visible migrations must seek to counter invidious comparisons. The middle decades of the twentieth century marked the peak of sociological thought and urban planning that defined the migrants as "problems" requiring "adjustment" to the city. The adjustment paradigm fostered individualistic responses to societal dilemmas and created a rationale for urban planning as an exercise in cordoning off the problem while investing resources elsewhere. Yet the migrants actually defied the assumptions about them as "backward" and "maladjusted" to urban life. Despite the stereotypes of black migrants, extensive and repeated studies have shown that postwar migrants were actually better educated than their northern-born counterparts, and that they fared better in terms of their individual and family well-being. To the extent that migrants struggled, on the whole they struggled after prolonged exposure to the segregation, discrimination, and exploitation in their new northern home cities.[22]

The persistence of segregation and inequality in the Midwest has been the result of choices individuals and institutions have made. As people continued to arrive in big cities, tensions rose. After World War II, many historians have argued, policymakers chose to reinforce the color line, constructing what Arnold Hirsch called the "second ghetto" in Chicago and other midwestern cities. Postwar segregation and the rise of the urban crisis by the late 1960s and 1970s were not inevitable, natural phenomena. Individuals and institutions sustained segregation, discrimination, and exclusion from opportunity. They moved jobs and other investment away from central cities, while white middle- and working-class families moved to booming metropolitan areas where black Americans were unwelcome. This is not just a story about what black migrants and their descendants lacked. It is also a story about the ways that segregation made black families vulnerable to those who would extract capital from black communities through predatory housing speculation and the manipulation of slum clearance and urban renewal in the decades after World War II.[23]

The black Midwest has always been more complex than it has been presumed to be. The migrations to cities like the Chicago-Gary metropolitan region, Detroit, St. Louis and East St. Louis, Cleveland, Columbus, Kansas City, and Milwaukee were the most conspicuous. But there were significant migrations to Grand Rapids, Indianapolis, Bloomington-Normal, Peoria, and the Quad Cities. Even smaller cities and towns, such as Muncie, Indiana; Harvey, Illinois; and River Rouge, Michigan, received a fair share of migrants.[24] One historian has estimated that approximately 15 percent of black migrants moved to suburbs of major northern cities between 1915 and 1940.[25] Endless variations on migrants' experiences took place in the black Midwest.[26]

Any historian of the Midwest would be skeptical of the notion that smaller communities were in any way "simpler." Such relatively small but complex black towns included Richard Pryor's Peoria, Illinois, which remained the subject of his comedic genius throughout his legendary and culturally radical career. It was in Des Moines, Iowa; Driscoll, North Dakota; and the University of North Dakota that Era Bell Thompson found the drive to make it in the world of journalism in Chicago and to become *Jet* and *Ebony* magazines' African correspondent during the era of decolonization.[27] And it was in Lorain, Ohio, that the Nobel Prize–winning novelist Toni Morrison found inspiration for her first, profoundly influential novel, *The Bluest Eye*. And Morrison credits her childhood in that small midwestern town, where her family lived among the diverse European immigrant communities of the 1930s and 1940s, for her particular views on race and the politics of art. Her childhood in that town meant that when she went off to Howard University and then the publishing industry in New York, she was wary of the politics of black nationalism, and she did not see the need to make her work overtly political. Her youth in Lorain inspired in her instead a desire to write novels that would convey the traditions and narratives of black life, embracing the complexity and heroic character of everyday black life, without offering easy refuge in the sensational or in proposed sociological solutions to the problems of racism. Her midwestern background, then, contributed to what one critic recently called Morrison's radical literary mission:

> Here, blackness isn't a commodity; it isn't inherently political; it is the race of a people who are varied and complicated. . . . It is a project . . . [that] has allowed Morrison to play with language, to take chances with how stories unravel and to consistently resist the demand to cre-

ate an empirical understanding of black life in America. Instead, she makes black life—regular, quotidian black life, the kind that doesn't sell out concert halls or sports stadiums—complex, fantastic and heroic, despite its devaluation. It is both aphorism and beyond aphorism, and a result has been pure possibility.[28]

The presence of a radical midwestern vision of pure possibility and creativity like the one Toni Morrison has forged must be weighed against the persistence of racial inequity, exclusion, and exploitation today.

Incorporation into existing political and economic institutions, moreover, did not necessarily bring real power or progress. The migration facilitated black class formation and the concomitant political, economic, and cultural differentiation within sprawling black communities. The idea that class conditioned black migration and urbanization and, therefore, the evolution of the Midwest, prevents any vision of the region framed in terms of a unitary black "community." An understanding of intraracial class differentiation helps explain everything from day-to-day tensions in black neighborhoods to the particular political culture black residents created in midwestern cities.

The development of class differences between black residents of the Midwest must be seen in light of the deindustrialization of the region, which began with the slow movement of jobs and industry to the suburbs as early as the 1920s and accelerated with the rapid decline of American urban manufacturing during and after the 1970s. Just as black workers won access to good, blue-collar jobs in factories and on the railroads in the Midwest, those jobs disappeared. And with the loss of those good jobs, in a context where suburban zoning laws and selective gentrification of urban neighborhoods have continued to preserve residential segregation, high concentrations of black poverty have become increasingly isolated. As sociologist Robert Sampson has argued recently, in contrast to postmodern arguments about the "placelessness" of contemporary life, neighborhoods that had once been the midwestern destinations of the Great Black Migration represent the enduring significance of local conditions, and perceptions of local conditions, in shaping the quality of life of urban residents.[29]

The tragic dimensions of the migration are clear. In many ways, the migration was a disappointment for both individual and collective aspirations for racial progress. The consequences have been devastating, as black urban neighborhoods—no matter how hard they have fought for their quality of life and for political power—have not had access to an authority capable of radically redistributing opportunity. From the perspective of black metropolitan communities, state power all too often has been a tool for an outsider to sustain exclusion from opportunity. For instance, as celebrated legal scholar William J. Stuntz has explained, largely white suburban voters have imposed a discriminatory and excessively punitive criminal justice system upon central city black communities, with devastating consequences.[30] Local democracy and local capitalism have too infrequently helped residents of central cities, even as local control provided means for suburbanites to protect their perceived economic and cultural interests.

Rather than coinciding with the creation of a more open, more liberal city, the Great Migration was part of a dual migration of black Americans from the South to northern cities and of white urbanites, and employers, from the cities to the suburbs. Responses to the Great Migration, argues Jon Teaford, thus helped fragment the American metropolis. The push for reform in American metropolitan areas has "repeatedly collided with the implacable realities of social and ethnic separation: most Americans desired not a unified metropolis, but a fragmented one, where like-minded people lived together untroubled by those of different opinions, races, or lifestyles. . . . Thus, Americans opted for the dissolution of the city and with the aid of the automobile, created the dispersed and fragmented metropolitan world of the late twentieth century."[31]

Making matters worse, most of the cities in the Midwest to which black southerners moved were "inelastic," meaning that they could not easily expand through annexation or other means. "An inelastic area has a central city frozen within its city limits and surrounded by growing suburbs. It may have a strong downtown . . . but its city neighborhoods are increasingly catch basins for poor Blacks and Hispanics."[32] Or, as geographer D. W. Meinig has put it, "There was a strong territorial dimension to all these levels of assumed or ascribed identities. . . . Amid the intensive complexities of modern metropolitan life, Americans seek to conduct their more personal social life" in homogenous spaces.[33]

Consequently, and despite all attempts to foster good will or democratic urban planning, the dominant responses to black migration have meant that the politics of midwestern metropolitan regions have been defined in large part by turf battles. Implicit assumptions about the migration, and explicitly racist responses to the migrants, together created a poison pill that destroyed the hopes for a desegregated city, even in the midst of the postwar era's massive economic growth, but especially when deindustrialization, public disinvestment in cities, the nation's discriminatory drug war, and the housing crisis imposed by predatory lending stripped resources from many black neighborhoods in the decades after the migration reversed course out of midwestern cities.

Toward a More Open Midwest

The cumulative effects of the migration and the responses to it created new discourses of race, class, gender, and space that have fundamentally shaped the course of American history. The migrants made for convenient scapegoats for both well-meaning reformers and less sympathetic observers seeking to use the tensions over the migration and black poverty to their advantage. The migration energized arguments about black "social disorganization" and the "culture of pathology" among the "underclass." The migration thus played into the hands of those who attributed urban problems to the ostensible deviousness of the black "scab" worker or "the welfare queen," or who chalked up the presence of multigenerational poverty to the "maladjusted" rural migrant lost in the concrete jungle, inevitably becoming the "thug" or "gangster" and threatening all good citizens both on the streets and in their lamentable "rap culture."[34] At the same time, the migration must also be seen as energizing the democratic, anti-racist, egalitarian strains of American popular discourse. The migration also gave rise to a rich political vocabulary that connected racial inequality in American cities to class and gender inequities and to global dynamics of racial imperialism. For those who could see through explanations of inequality and segregation in the city that blamed the victims, the migration has been a seed ground for oppositional worldviews founded upon finding common ground in a shared awareness of structural inequality and upon pride in the achievements of the excluded and exploited.

The tensions between these evolving discourses have been pervasive. When critical voices argued that external forces created and sustained segregation and discriminatory, exploitative systems of labor, housing, education, and criminal justice, the critics were targeted as outsiders. As Richard Wright put it, "they assail us as 'trouble-makers' . . . say we speak treasonably . . . solemnly assert that we seek to overthrow the government . . . [and] brand us as revolutionaries when we say that we are not allowed to react to life with an honest and frontal vision."[35] Yet the critics of American inequality themselves have often claimed the mantle of true Americanism. The great Chicago writer Saul Bellow remembered that Ralph Ellison reflected on the reciprocal relationship between black and white society: "I tell white kids that instead of talking about black men in a white world or black men in a white society, they should ask themselves how black *they* are, because black men have been influencing the values of the society and the art forms of the society."[36] Or, as black Chicago poet Margaret Walker put it, "Who are you, America, but me?"[37]

The main lesson of the black Midwest is that this is a region with a history and present deeply divided by the fact that some people's opportunity has depended upon others' exclusion. "It is the centrality of the Afro-American experience that makes its past so significant," Benjamin Quarles has argued. And as is the case for black history as a whole, the history of the Great Black Migration is "a past that has a sobering but redemptive quality for our nation, not as an escapist journey to some gossamer glory of bygone days, but possibly as a vehicle for present enlightenment, guidance, and enrichment."[38] With this view in mind, we must interrogate the past, not merely celebrate it, in order to foster the possibility of openness as a bulwark against the impulse to protect the certainties of racial isolation and inequality.

Notes

1. D. W. Meinig, *Global America, 1915–2000*, vol. 4 of *The Shaping of America: A Geographical Perspective on 500 Years of History* (New Haven: Yale University Press, 2004), 180 and 225.

2. Meinig, *Global America*, 4:226.

3. Douglas S. Massey and Nancy A. Denton, *American Apartheid: Segregation and the Making of the Underclass* (Cambridge: Harvard University Press, 1993).

4. James N. Gregory, *The Southern Diaspora: How the Great Migrations of Black and White Southerners Transformed America* (Chapel Hill: University of North Carolina Press, 2005), xii.

5. Isabel Wilkerson, *The Warmth of Other Suns: The Epic Story of America's Great Migration* (New York: Vintage, 2011), 531.

6. Nell Irvin Painter, foreword to *The Great Migration in Historical Perspective: New Dimensions of Race, Class, and Gender*, ed. Joe William Trotter (Bloomington: Indiana University Press, 1991), x.

7. For a good introduction to an extensive literature, see Thomas J. Sugrue, *Sweet Land of Liberty: The Forgotten Struggle for Civil Rights in the North* (New York: Random House, 2009).

8. Beverly A. Bunch-Lyons, "'No Promised Land': Oral Histories of African-American Women in Cincinnati, Ohio," Oral History, special issue, *OAH Magazine of History* 11, no. 3 (Spring 1997): 9–14.

9. Richard Wright and Edwin Rosskam, *12 Million Black Voices* (1941; repr., New York: Basic Books, 2002), 128.

10. Sharon Roznik, "Racism in Fond du Lac: Man's Small-Town Ideal Shattered," *Fond du Lac Reporter*, December 18, 2014, http://www.fdlreporter.com/story/news/local/2014/12/13/racism-fond-du-lac-mans-small-town-ideal-shattered/20352847/.

11. John Sullivan, "Black America Is Moving South—and to the 'Burbs: What's It Mean?" *Colorlines*, October 10, 2011, http://www.colorlines.com/articles/black-america-moving-south-and-burbs-whats-it-mean; and Robert Gutsche Jr., "The Black Pleasantville Migration Myth: Moving from a City Isn't Pleasant," *Guardian*, March 28, 2014, http://www.theguardian.com/commentisfree/2014/mar/28/black-migration-from-city-inequality.

12. Pero Gaglo Dagbovie, *African American History Reconsidered* (Urbana: University of Illinois Press, 2010), 47.

13. Eric Foner, *Free Labor, Free Soil, Free Men: The Ideology of the Republican Party before the Civil War* (New York: Oxford University Press, 1995), 261; and Iowa Pathways, "African Americans in Iowa, 1838–2005," http://www.iptv.org/iowapathways/mypath.cfm?ounid=ob_000238, accessed May 18, 2015.

14. Alexis de Tocqueville, *Democracy in America*, trans. and ed. Harvey C. Mansfield and Delba Winthrop (Chicago: University of Chicago Press, 2000), 329.

15. De Tocquville, *Democracy in America*, 343.

16. De Tocqueville, *Democracy in America*, 342.

17. David Roediger, *The Wages of Whiteness: Race and the Making of the American Working Class*, new ed. (New York: Verso, 2007); and Eric Lott, *Love and Theft: Blackface Minstrelsy and the American Working Class*, 20th ed. (New York: Oxford University Press, 2013).

18. Eric Foner, *Gateway to Freedom: The Hidden History of the Underground Railroad* (New York: W. W. Norton, 2015).

19. James R. Grossman, *Land of Hope: Black Southerners and the Great Migration* (Chicago: University of Chicago Press, 1991).

20. Darlene Clark Hine, *Hine Sight: Black Women and the Re-Construction of American History* (Bloomington: Indiana University Press, 1994), 94. See also Ira Berlin, *The Making of African America: The Four Great Migrations* (New York: Penguin, 2010), 170; and Steven A. Reich, *Encyclopedia of the Great Black Migration* (Westport CT: Greenwood Publishing, 2006), 531.

21. Meinig, *Global America*, 4:182 and 4:227.

22. Wilkerson, *Warmth of Other Suns*, 529–30; and Gregory, *Southern Diaspora*, 106.

23. Arnold R. Hirsch, *Making the Second Ghetto: Race and Housing in Chicago, 1940–1960* (New York: Cambridge University Press, 1983); Thomas. J. Sugrue, *The Origins of the Urban Crisis: Race and Inequality in Postwar Detroit* (Princeton: Princeton University Press, 1996); and Beryl Satter, *Family Properties: How the Struggle Over Race and Real Estate Transformed Chicago and Urban America* (New York: Picador, 2010).

24. Mark Wyman, "Origins of the Bloomington-Normal Black History Project," McLean County Museum of History, accessed May 12, 2015, http:// mchistory.org/research/resources/blackhistory/origins.php.

25. Andrew Wiese, "The Other Suburbanites: African American Suburbanization in the North before 1950," *Journal of American History* 85, no. 4 (March 1999): 1495–1524.

26. Dorothy Schwieder, Joseph Hraba, and Elmer Schwieder, *Buxton: A Black Utopia in the Heartland* (Iowa City: University of Iowa Press, 2003), 210.

27. Jeffrey Helgeson, *Crucibles of Black Empowerment: Chicago's Neighborhood Politics from the New Deal to Harold Washington* (Chicago: University of Chicago Press, 2014), 91.

28. Rachel Kaadzi Ghansah, "The Radical Vision of Toni Morrison," *New York Times Magazine*, April 8, 2015, http://www.nytimes.com/2015/04/12/magazine/the-radical-vision-of-toni-morrison.html?_r=0.

29. Robert J. Sampson, *Great American City: Chicago and the Enduring Neighborhood Effect* (Chicago: University of Chicago Press, 2013).

30. William J. Stuntz, *The Collapse of American Criminal Justice* (New York: Belknap Press, 2013).

31. Jon C. Teaford, *Twentieth-Century American City* (Baltimore: Johns Hopkins University Press, 1993), 169, quoted in Meinig, *Global America*, 4:254.

32. David Rusk, *Cities without Suburbs*, 2nd ed. (Washington DC: Woodrow Wilson Center Press, 1995), 47, quoted in Meinig, *Global America*, 4:253.

33. Meinig, *Global America*, 4:152–53.

34. Elijah Anderson, "The White Space," *Sociology of Race and Ethnicity* 1, no. 1 (2015): 10–21.

35. Wright and Rosskam, *12 Million Black Voices*, 130.

36. Saul Bellow, preface to John F. Callahan, ed., *The Collected Essays of Ralph Ellison* (New York: Modern Library, 2003), xi.

37. Jeffrey Helgeson, "Who Are You, America, But Me?" in *The Black Chicago Renaissance*, ed. Darlene Clark Hine and John McCluskey Jr. (Urbana: University of Illinois Press, 2012).

38. Benjamin Quarles, *The Negro in the Making of America*, quoted in Dagbovie, *African American History Reconsidered*, 71.

PART 3

The Iconic Midwest

8

Midwestern Small Towns

John E. Miller

Writing in 1923, Minnesota-born Thorstein Veblen famously characterized the country town as being "one of the great American institutions;
perhaps the greatest, in the sense that it has had and continues to have
a greater part than any other in shaping public sentiment and giving
character to American culture."[1] For the first three centuries or so of
American history, for the vast majority of the population, small towns
had been the centers of economic activity, the pillars of society, and the
heartbeat of culture. What was true for the country as a whole seemed
doubly true of the Midwest, the region of the country that more than
any other was associated with and defined by life in its small towns.

Iconic status became attached to Mark Twain's Hannibal, Willa Cather's
Red Cloud, James Whitcomb Riley's Greenfield, Thomas Hart Benton's
Neosho, Sinclair Lewis's "Main Street," Sherwood Anderson's "Winesburg, Ohio," Garrison's Keillor's "Lake Wobegon," Laura Ingalls Wilder's "Little Town on the Prairie," and John Cougar Mellencamp's "Small
Town." These kinds of places are deeply embedded in American thought,
memory, and folklore, inspiring songs, poems, literature, and art. And
there's the rub. Any objective consideration of midwestern small towns
must distinguish between the image they present, on the one hand, and
the reality of things, on the other—between people's memories, construc-
tions, likes and dislikes, on the one hand, over against the realities of
small-town history and development as best as can be described and analyzed to the degree any observer can be objective about it, on the other.

So let us stipulate at the outset, along with the cultural critic Max
Lerner, the almost universal ambivalence with which both small-town
insiders and outside observers have regarded these small towns. "The
phrase 'small town,'" Lerner wrote, "has come itself to carry a double
layer of meaning, at once sentimental and condescending. There is still

a belief that democracy is more idyllic at the 'grass roots,' that the business spirit is purer, that the middle class is more intensely middling. There is also a feeling that by the fact of being small the small town somehow escapes the corruptions of life in the city and the dominant contagions that infest the more glittering places."[2] Nostalgia—and its opposite, knee-jerk criticism—are always tempting lures. But we should remain on guard to try to avoid both as best we can.

It may seem counterintuitive to begin by talking about the images we hold in our heads about small towns rather than about the actual places that inspire that imagery. To a large degree, however, the symbols and myths that attach to small towns are the primary basis for people's understandings of the phenomenon, especially since, in twenty-first century America, more than 80 percent of all Americans live in metropolitan areas. Back in horse-and-buggy days, and even when train travel and automobile navigation of "blue highways" provided at least quick glimpses of small towns to travelers passing through them, people could pick up a sense of what such towns were like. Now, when travelers rumble past at seventy or eighty miles an hour on the interstate, pausing at quick stops for gas and burgers, or fly over at thirty-five thousand feet, they have little or no chance to formulate much of an impression of these places. Novelist Diane Johnson's recent book, *Flyover Country*, underscores the point.

The myth of small-town goodness, neighborliness, mutuality, and goodwill was a direct descendant of Thomas Jefferson's agrarian myth of rural virtue and superiority.[3] William Jennings Bryan, a son of Salem, Illinois, restated the notion memorably at the historic 1896 Democratic national convention that nominated him for the presidency of the United States. Defending the small-town/rural order against the encroaching tentacles of urban America, he implored, "Burn down your cities and leave our farms, and your cities will spring up again as if by magic; but destroy our farms, and the grass will grow in the streets of every city in the country."[4] The single most influential purveyor of the small-town myth may well have been the beloved Indiana poet James Whitcomb Riley, who apotheosized small towns and rural life in sentimental poems such as "Home-Folks," "When the Frost Is on the Punkin," "The Old

Swimmin'-Hole," and "The Little Town o'Tailholt." His popularity and stature attained such great proportions that at his death, in 1916, the whole country paused to honor his memory. Nostalgia for the small-town way of life remained strong enough in 1938 to spur enthusiastic popular response to Thornton Wilder's appreciative tribute to it in his play *Our Town*. But the mid to late 1910s, referred to by the historian Henry F. May as "the end of American innocence," probably mark, if such a period can be pinpointed, the height of the small town's appeal and the beginning of the myth's demise.[5]

Images of the small town that embedded themselves in the nation's collective consciousness could be found in poems like Riley's, as well as in songs, magazine articles, short stories and novels, paintings, photographs, sermons, political speeches, and the like. Local newspaper photos of baseball teams, Fourth of July parades, prize pigs and pies at county fairs, high school graduations, and scenes of troops heading off to war at the local railroad depot were reproduced later in county history books, television documentaries, and volumes of photographs, ranging from historian Michael Lesy's dark *Wisconsin Death Trip* to writer Sherwood Anderson's sunnier *Home Town*.[6] As time went by, more Americans probably acquired their ideas about small-town life from movies like *State Fair* and *The Music Man* than they did from personal experience.

If a single representative image of midwestern small towns had to be chosen, it might well be a long shot taken down Main Street from the railroad depot, showing a block or two (or more) of stores forming walls on either side and converging at some vanishing point in the distance. Warm memories of Marceline, Missouri, Walt Disney's hometown between ages four and nine, prompted him to install Main Street as the entry point to both Disneyland in 1955 and Walt Disney World in 1971. Meredith Willson's memories of parades on Main Street and of all the important gathering spots in Mason City, Iowa, inspired him to write a musical play about his hometown—a bouquet to small towns everywhere. When people approached towns from a distance in horse and buggy or in a car or on a train, they were usually presented with a horizontal image—wider for larger towns, narrower for smaller ones—which served to reinforce the standard egalitarian image of life in small towns. With regard to the vertical dimension, the tallest structures on the horizon were usually church spires, representing the religiosity of communities; grain elevators, reflecting their commercial nature; and water towers, indicators of the collective spirit of populaces that provide necessary services for themselves through democratic political processes. A hotel or some other structure of four stories or more would be a sign of a community or of individuals within it of some wealth or pretension.

The visual images people retain of small towns and the mental images they store in their minds are always more or less accurate, more or less fantastic. Interpretations of the small-town way of life range from Meredith Nicholson's *The Valley of Democracy* (1918), with its generally positive vision of friendly, hardworking, virtuous, and democratic small-town dwellers in Indiana, to Sinclair Lewis's 1920 bombshell of a book, *Main Street*, based on mordant memories of growing up in Sauk Centre, Minnesota. In his particular case, time healed many wounds, and by 1931 he could write for his old high school yearbook that in spite of all the criticisms he had directed at small-town life, based on memories of his school days there, it had been "a good time, a good place, and a good preparation for life."[7] For him as for many others, when it came to small towns, ambivalence ruled.

In shifting our attention from image, myth, and symbol to the realities of small-town life, the actual places in which midwesterners grew to maturity were, in the first instance, just that—*places*. For all the variation that the Middle West's several thousand small towns presented to the world, from Ohio in the east to Kansas, Nebraska, and the Dakotas in the west, they presented a general similarity of appearance to the world, something that has often been commented upon. In keeping with their predominantly commercial origins, aesthetics were not usually a high priority. "Business districts made little pretense to beauty," Lewis Atherton piquantly observed.[8] Rather, efficiency and practicality mattered most. Towns were functional, and the stores on Main Street performed a variety of practical functions; thus, the familiarity and redundancy of so many descriptions offered up in newspaper stories, fictional accounts, local history books, and scholarly tomes on the look of small towns. Sinclair Lewis's description of *Main Street* protagonist Carol Kennecott's thirty-two-minute initial walk up and down the main business street in the imaginary town of Gopher Prairie, Minnesota, provides a classic example of this phenomenon. Calling Gopher Prairie's central business street "the continuation of Main Streets everywhere," Lewis went on to catalog the Minniemashie House hotel, a "tall lean shabby structure" catering to traders and traveling salesmen; Dyer's Drug Store, with its "greasy marble soda-fountain"; the Rosebud Movie Palace, showing a film called *Fatty in Love*; Howland and Gould's Grocery, with Knights of Pythias, Maccabees, Woodmen, and Masonic lodges located in rooms above on the second floor; Dahl and Oleson's Meat Market; a jewelry shop with "tinny looking" wrist watches; several saloons; a tobacco shop; a clothing store, its dummies like "corpses with painted cheeks"; The Bon Ton Store; Axel Egge's General Store; Sam Clark's Hardware Store; Chester Dashaway's House Furnishing Emporium; Billy's Lunch; a dairy; a produce warehouse; Ford and Buick garages; an agricultural implement dealer; a feed store; Ye Art Shoppe; a barber shop and pool room; Nat Hicks's Tailor Shop, on a side street off Main Street; the post office; the State Bank; the Farmers' National Bank; and a score of similar stores and businesses.[9] With some variation in particular kinds of businesses and considerable differences based on the sizes of the towns being considered, this could have been a description of almost any midwestern small-town business district that catered primarily to farmers during the last several decades of the nineteenth century and the first several of the twentieth.

Towns like the fictional Gopher Prairie or its real life inspiration, Sauk Centre, certainly could vary in their appearance, modernity, efficiency, and sociability, but what mattered more in the opinions that people harbored of them were the attitudes and predilections that they brought with them. Whereas Carol Kennicott was inclined to employ words like "drab," "forbidding," "muddy," "dismal," "rickety," "greasy," "sleazy," "broken," and "curdled" in describing what she encountered, Bea Sorenson, a young woman straight off the farm, after viewing the same sights, used words like "swell," "fine," "lovely," "big," "high," "dandy," and "elegant." Carol herself was conflicted from the very beginning, allowing that many of the things that she observed were indeed "pleasant," "new," "neat," "clean," "shiny," "pure," and even "exquisite."

The most notable design aspect of small towns was the grid layout to which most of them adhered. The earliest towns established north of the Ohio River during the late 1700s and early 1800s may have developed in unplanned fashion at the outset, and topographical peculiarities, such as rivers, lakes, valleys, and hills may have boxed some of them in on one or more sides. For the most part, however, the grid was easily expandable, as new additions were tacked on to original plats in serial fashion. In practice, this brought about a paradoxical situation: standardized plats dictated uniform widths of lots, streets, and alleys, resulting in what many perceived to be highly boring vistas. Within those parameters, however, the marketplace allowed owners of land and buildings to do pretty much what they pleased with their properties, subject to certain zoning restrictions and regulations adopted over time. The cookie-cutter appearance of many town plats, especially in the western parts of the region in places established after 1880, was usually the result of railroad companies imitating the work of the Illinois Central Railroad during the 1850s, when its subsidiary land company laid out main streets parallel to the tracks and assigned identical street names in town after town. The Chicago and Northwestern Railroad's Western Town Lot Company worked in similar fashion during the 1880s in South Dakota, but in this case almost all of the Main Streets were drawn perpendicular to the railroad, making them "T-towns." Geographer John C. Hudson goes a step further in classifying railroad towns in north-central North Dakota into three categories: symmetric, orthogonal, and T-towns.[10]

Grand urban designs with large streets, elaborate fountains and structures, and impressive buildings, such as those contained in Daniel Burnham's extensive 1910 Chicago Plan, were almost entirely absent in small towns. But even as individual entrepreneurs made their decisions, things got sorted out in predictable ways. For example, livery stables, lumber yards, coal lots, and many of the hotels in small towns tended to congregate near the railroad tracks. Banks often bought up higher-priced corner lots. Desirable locations on Main Street frequently went to general stores, drug stores, hardware stores, and newspaper offices. In most cases, doctors', dentists', and lawyers' offices, along with other business offices and apartments, went into second-floor spaces above the various stores. Churches, lodge halls, post offices, city halls, libraries, and other public buildings tended to be located at the edge of or near the downtown business district. The more elegant homes often congregated on a tree-lined street or on a hill. In general, however, there was much less class-based residential segregation in small towns than there was in large towns and cities, where class divisions were more prominent.

Courthouse squares, surrounded on all four sides by business blocks, were more common in the southern Midwest than in the northern part of the region. Courthouses, grade schools, high schools, and colleges tended to be located off to the side of downtown or in a prominent location like a park, grove of trees, or on a hill. Baseball diamonds, skating rinks, county fairgrounds, high school basketball courts, and other places of amusement were often built on the edge of the residential section at the time. Lower forms of entertainment, such as pool halls, saloons, and brothels, tended to be set apart informally from the more respectable parts of town, but there were always exceptions to every rule.

The arrival and maturation of the automobile did some major reconfiguring of townscapes. Hitching posts disappeared from downtown streets, city councils were pressed to gravel or hard-surface the main business streets and some of the side streets, many stores went out of business over time as town residents often opted to shop in towns farther down the road that had more variety and better deals, and everything tended to spread out more, reducing the gravitational pull of the town center. With more highway traffic, downtown hotels gave way to tourist camps and motels on the edge of town, and cafés and restaurants made room for franchised fast-food operations. Automobile and farm equipment dealers, bowling alleys, gas stations, and other businesses catering to car traffic formed commercial "strips" that tended to take on the same look, making it difficult to tell one town from one another, although town boosters continued to plant welcome signs out at the edge ("Welcome to Lake Preston: The Town Designed with You in Mind"), and, almost inevitably, a wall bearing the logos of churches and/or civic groups, such as Rotary, Kiwanis, Lions, Altrusa, 4-H, and Girl Scouts announced to travelers that this was a progressive, go-getting community.

As these observations suggest, no discussion of small towns can proceed very far without noting the importance of history, or time. While it may have seemed to many that small towns never changed, in fact they all were dynamic change agents in many respects; the only questions were whether those changes would be faster or slower and whether they would be for the better or for the worse. When considering local history, it is always tempting to focus primary attention on how towns were founded and on the early years of development, being sure to mention the first examples of everything but often not bothering to consider very much how things were constantly changing, decade by decade. But for small towns, as for everywhere else, history—like place—matters.

This is not the place to attempt to give any kind of definitive survey of change over time, but a few observations are in order. Towns were founded for many reasons, but for the vast majority of the several thousand small towns in the Middle West, serving agriculture as a middleman for shipping out livestock and crops as well as for importing every sort of farm implement and input as well as consumer items for the home was the central function they performed and the primary reason for the various businesses that sprang up like weeds in spring. Of course, beyond serving as agricultural service centers, there were many other functions that small towns performed. Early on, they were often located along Indian trails or near Indian encampments or government forts. Location along transportation routes—roads, road interchanges, rivers, other navigable streams, and lakes—often explained why towns were where they were. When canals and railroads came along, there were huge incentives for towns to be built along them. In addition to business and commerce, town founders were also motivated by their desire to acquire a county seat, or even state capital designation, and the Midwest was especially well-known for its many county-seat "fights." As a rule, county-seat towns prospered more and grew larger than their competitors. Government facilities and activities of many types put money into residents' hands over time: post offices, K–12 schools, colleges and universities, prisons, mental health operations, hospitals, soil conservation offices, crop subsidies, the dispensing of Social Security and Medicare checks, and so forth. Oberlin College in Oberlin, Ohio; St. Olaf College in Northfield, Minnesota; and Knox College in Galesburg, Illinois, all benefited and helped establish the identities of the small towns that hosted them. Lumber mills, flour mills, meatpacking sites, and other food-processing facilities were all important. Tourism, hunting and fishing, casinos, sports facilities, and other kinds of recreational attractions all became more important functions of small towns after World War II.

The stories that towns told about themselves tended to resemble each other in myriad ways. There was a narrative arc to which many of them adhered: high hopes and aspirations in the beginning; a period of early growth and maturation, figuring out what the town could do best and sorting out the various individuals and groups in a hierarchical fashion; a series of challenges—economic, social, cultural—that townspeople either successfully or unsuccessfully negotiated; a gradual accommodation to reality—for most acceptance that they would never grow spectacularly, for others an ability to keep moving up or hold steady, and for many the growing realization that they were trapped in a continuing downward spiral. In some cases, some new product, factory, transportation development, or institution made for a major shift in direction.

Several broad but tentative generalizations can be proffered. In general, the larger towns have done substantially better than the smaller ones in thriving economically and holding onto or even increasing their populations. Towns below a thousand or five hundred in population are almost destined to decline and maybe even to cease to exist. One of the most prominent new functions of small towns is to provide living places for retirees and especially, if they have a hospital or nursing home and assisted living facilities, to provide health and assistance to the elderly sick. Beyond that, small towns within thirty (or even fifty) miles of large towns or cities often emerge as bedroom communities for the larger place. Cheap housing and being "a good place to raise children" continue to be two of the major attractions of towns on the urban fringe and the major reason why many of them are so relatively vibrant.

A second broad generalization is that towns located along major highways, and especially along interstates, have at least the potential for thriving and growth. This rule applies especially well to the state I live in, South Dakota, where the major areas of population growth and economic development are along the I-29 and I-90 corridors in the south-eastern sector of the state, with some additional vitality being shown along I-90 where it skirts the Black Hills in the western part of the state. One has to be careful, however, in this regard, for many, if not most, of the towns along interstates enjoy only modest advantage from gasoline and tourism sales to people traveling along the highway.

Beyond the themes of image, place, time (or history), and function, one can also examine how various kinds of structures affect small towns, having already talked a bit about physical structure, as embodied in place. Social structure, or class, is a perennial subject of interest for people living in small towns, as well as elsewhere. Americans have always been reluctant to admit the relevance of class distinctions or even to talk about them, and I would say this is doubly true of midwesterners. Residents of the region are, in fact, very much beholden to the notion of middle-class, bourgeois values, behaviors, and reputations.[11] With that said, most observers and analysts over time have detected the presence of class divisions and distinctions, maybe not as great as in the South, where the split between white slaveholders and black slaves, as well as non-slaveholding whites, was much more visible and real, or, for that matter, in New England and the Northeast, where much larger accumulations of wealth likewise made for a more visible aristocracy of wealth and position.

If small towns have always displayed class differences, it is also true that, in most circumstances, those differences have been less extreme than in more urbanized places. One or a few very rich families in a small town—say in a "company town" or in a place with a single large factory—can make for highly unequal distributions of wealth and income, but the very reality of small size generally places limits on the range of extremes that are likely or possible. Moreover, the very wealthy are less likely to be satisfied to live in small places containing fewer luxuries, less culture, and few people like themselves. What happened in most places was that, early on, an inner circle of families informally developed, joined by income, wealth, family position, prestige, and political power and influence. Not surprisingly, they tended to be WASPs (white, Anglo-Saxon, and Protestant) or of northern or western European descent (as opposed to deriving from southern and eastern Europe). If Protestant, they could most often be found in the pews of Episcopal, Methodist, Presbyterian, and Congregational churches. Usually drawn from the professions (lawyers, doctors, and perhaps college presidents), the banking community, and the more prosperous businesses, they often gravitated to leadership positions in local churches, government institutions, and voluntary organizations. Over the years, many people observed that an 80/20 rule operated when it came to voluntary organizational work, that is, 80 percent of the work got done by 20 percent of the people. It was from among those men and women in the 20 percent—generally leaders and "movers and shakers" who achieved high regard and respect in the community, which is as or more important than absolute income and wealth—that the social elite were drawn. In their studies during the 1920s and 1930s of "Middletown" (Muncie, Indiana), Robert and Helen Lynd reported the presence of a discernable "power elite" that in many ways "presided" over the community.[12]

Whereas economic distinctions and social structures were sometimes fuzzy and blurred, difficult to ascertain and hard to grapple with, gender divisions remained distinct and determinative far into the twentieth century, beginning to shift significantly only after World War II. This is not to say that women were not generally honored and respected, but it is to indicate that women's roles were clearly demarcated in many areas of life, and attempting to modify them or to end gender discrimination was extremely difficult. Again, it is important to note that women worked as hard as men, but usually at home, raising children, taking care of the household, maintaining gardens, participating in church societies and civic organizations, and usually for no pay. Some women worked with their husbands or took over family businesses after the husband died, a few owned business of their own (especially haberdasheries and beauty shops), and many served as waitresses, cooks, clerks in stores, and so forth. Black women generally worked as maids, and young immigrant women often worked as domestic help in middle- and upper-middle-class households. But outside of the home, the two occupations women were generally funneled into were school teaching and nursing. That changed after World War II, as increasing numbers of women moved directly into all areas of the economy. Just as in urban households, women broke down barriers that had existed for centuries and millennia, and life literally was transformed for half of the population (and for the other half, too, for that matter).

Social structures and barriers of all kinds came tumbling down during the 1960s and later, and small-town residents joined their more urbanized counterparts in bringing about one revolution after another. Once, men had gathered in veterans and fraternal organizations, baseball teams, hook-and-ladder squads, livery stables, pool halls, saloons, and other male preserves. Women, for their part, had mingled in church ladies' aids, women's book clubs and study groups, the WCTU (Women's Christian Temperance Union) and other reform-minded organizations, the women's suffrage movement, and in ladies' clothing shops. As the twentieth century wore on, some vestiges of gender segregation remained, but men and women now often joined together in church couples' clubs, Kiwanis, Lions, and Rotary Clubs, political organizations, charity drives, recreational activities, and the like.

All of these last-mentioned organizations and groups contributed to another major element of small-town life—a strong sense of community. Of course, not every small town was community-oriented or particularly outgoing, generous, and sociable. But one of the elemental realities of small-town life—then and now—was and is that it is lived on a human scale, where there is much more face-to-face interaction, a greater sense of reciprocity and responsibility for one's fellow human beings, and a greater likelihood of bonding with people one casually runs into rather than with people one chooses to associate with. Community is another word for neighborhood, another name for the kind of social relationships that require commitment, caring, and, yes, love. It is the kind of thing that drives some participants like the young Sinclair Lewis to despair regarding the nosiness, narrow-mindedness, provincialism, and conformity-producing interference that he wrote about in *Main Street*. Certainly, there are tradeoffs in any honest consideration of what small-town life means. But social observers from Ferdinand Tönnies (whose distinction between gemeinschaft—the more intimate, private, face-to-face relationships that constitute "community"—and gesellschaft—the looser, more public, aggregations that make up "society"—during the 1890s set the tone for all later discussions of community) to Thomas Bender (who reminds us that notwithstanding the corrosive effects of industrialization and urbanization on modern life, a sense of community has remained vibrant in recent years) have wisely concluded that community is one of the precious elements of small-town life and one of those that make it most attractive and desirable to residents.[13]

Having used most of the space available here without even mentioning other central constituents of society—church, school, and home—and all of the other institutions and practices that go into it, I will have to be satisfied merely to mention the kinds of other considerations that midwestern small-town life suggests. Hardly anything or little has been said here about race and ethnicity, about all of the voluntary organizations that make up a good part of small-town life, about recreation and leisure-time activities, and about politics and social control.

This has been one of those discussions that has remained largely at an abstract level with very few references to any real people, but, of course, history is made up of real people, and small towns are nothing if they are not collections of real people. History is often about leaders, people of influence and power, stories of success, and recognition of achievement. Most people, small-town dwellers or not, do not fit any of those categories. We want to know about town founders, people who make and shape towns, people who make a difference. But we also want to know about the people who are followers, the ones who "go along with the flow," the ones who make their lives and make a living. We want to hear their stories, too. We want to know where power lies and how it works. We know that much of life is about choice, and one of the major choices facing young people in small towns for many decades has been whether to stay or leave. That, in fact, may be the defining question of small towns and their futures, along with, "What can be done to give young people a choice of whether to leave or stay?"

Finally, for those who do stay or who choose to move down the road to another small town, we want to continue to ask, "Why?" What is it about small-town living that is so attractive to you that you have not joined the majority exodus out of town to join your metropolitan colleagues, who obviously rule the roost just now? The future of small towns is not set in stone. Reconstructing their past is something that we as historians are beginning to do better. We hope to become even better in the future.

Notes

1. Thorstein Veblen, "The Country Town," originally published in 1923 in *The Portable Veblen*, ed. Max Lerner (New York: Penguin Books 1976), 407.

2. Max Lerner, *America as a Civilization*, 2 vols. (New York: Simon and Schuster, 1957), 1:151.

3. Henry Nash Smith, *Virgin Land: The American West as Symbol and Myth* (Cambridge: Harvard University Press, 1950).

4. Bryan quoted in Richard Hofstadter, *The Age of Reform: From Bryan to F.D.R.* (New York: Knopf, 1955), 35.

5. Henry F. May, *The End of American Innocence: A Study of the First Years of Our Own Time, 1912–1917* (New York: Knopf, 1959).

6. Michael Lesy, *Wisconsin Death Trip* (New York: Pantheon, 1973); Sherwood Anderson, *Home Town* (New York: Alliance Book Corporation, 1940).

7. Lewis quoted in *The Man from Main Street: Selected Essays and Other Writings, 1904–1950*, ed. Harry E. Maule and Melville H. Cane (New York: Random House, 1953), 54.

8. Lewis Atherton, *Main Street on the Middle Border* (Bloomington: Indiana University Press, 1954), 49.

9. Sinclair Lewis, *Main Street* (New York: Signet-New American Library, 1920, 1961), 36–41.

10. John Hudson, *Plains Country Towns* (Minneapolis: University of Minnesota Press, 1985), 87–90.

11. Timothy R. Mahoney, *Provincial Lives: Middle-Class Experience in the Antebellum Middle West* (New York: Cambridge University Press, 1999).

12. Robert S. Lynd and Helen Merrell Lynd, *Middletown: A Study in Contemporary American Culture* (New York: Harcourt, Brace, 1929).

13. Ferdinand Tönnies, *Community and Society*, trans. Charles P. Loomis (New York: Harper, 1963); Thomas Bender, *Community and Social Change in America* (Baltimore: Johns Hopkins University Press, 1978), 4–12, 42–43.

9

The Agrarian Midwest

A GEOGRAPHIC ANALYSIS

Christopher R. Laingen

The Midwest is the agricultural powerhouse of the United States. In 2012 the twelve states that comprise the Midwest accounted for 40 percent of all U.S. farms, 37 percent of our country's farmland, 57 percent of its total cropland, and 46 percent of the market value of all agricultural products sold in the United States (51 percent of the market value of crops sold and 41 percent of the market value of livestock sold).[1] Corn and soybean acres in the Midwest account for 87 percent and 84 percent, respectively, of the nation's total, and 78 percent of the country's hogs. Less impressive, yet still peripherally important, are data that show that 42 percent of the country's wheat acreage, 42 percent of its cattle, and 35 percent of its milk cows originate here as well. While these percentages have undoubtedly changed since this region's landscape was first converted to agricultural uses, it is clear from all accounts that the Midwest is most strongly rooted in its Corn Belt tradition—a region within a region, if you will—that in and of itself has changed quite dramatically from the time when Corn Belt farming first leapt over the Appalachian Mountains and took hold in south central Ohio.

A discussion of agriculture, regions, and regional identity is well suited for geographic analysis. "Agriculture may well be the most comprehensive of geographic topics. It involves modification of both the biological (plants) and physical (soils, landforms) components of the environment, and it incorporates social and economic components with distinctive spatial manifestations. It is also dynamic, playing a major role in recent human history."[2] Geographers have relied upon regions to help them describe Earth and its various physical and human features for nearly as long as the discipline has existed.[3] Regions help to simplify the complex world in which we live. Further, regional boundaries and definitions are also, by their nature, fuzzy, complex, and dynamic.[4] Lines are put on maps to help us understand where one region ends and another begins. Regions are, however, quite complex, and are normally comprised of two parts: cores and peripheries. The core of a region contains the vast majority—and in a more densely packed manner—of the "thing(s)" that make the region what it is, whether those are physically (landforms, vegetation, and so on) or figuratively (cultural attitudes, identities, people-centric processes) present. Those patterns fade near a region's periphery and may disappear altogether before one enters the next region. The basic makeup of the geographic core of the Corn Belt has remained nearly intact since the turn of the twentieth century.

Two transformations have been occurring almost simultaneously within the Corn Belt's core, and more recently around its periphery. Internally, this transformation began slowly around World War I. Cash-grain farming originated on the Grand Prairie of Illinois and western Indiana, on the Des Moines Lobe of southern Minnesota and northern Iowa, and on the Maumee Plain of northwestern Ohio and northeastern Indiana, displacing the feed grains and livestock Corn Belt farming system. This internal evolution continued ever so slowly from World War I into the late 1970s and early 1980s. Small fenced fields got larger and fences were removed. Traditional farmers had a hard time making the transformation, and so did their children once they took over, having grown up knowing only one way of farming. But soon, they had no choice but to adapt to a new way of doing things—one that relied heavily upon artificial inputs, larger and more complex machinery, and which eventually led to today's computerized, globally focused, duoculture agricultural production system.[5]

Changes along the region's periphery have occurred more recently. Here, an expansion of the region, where land once thought to be too marginal because of mostly environmental limitations related to soil fertility and/or climatic barriers of temperature and precipitation, has transformed other types of cropping systems to one that is increasingly focused on corn and soybean production. Conversely, the region has contracted in other peripheral areas, where mostly topographical barriers preclude the use of large-scale, modern machinery and land use practices.

Corn Belt Geography

The geographic bounds of the Corn Belt, however they have been defined over nearly the past century, have changed very little (figure 3). The vernacular region we call the Corn Belt has been in existence since the late 1800s and, as will be discussed later, could be as easily referred to today as the Corn-Soybean Belt.[6] In 1892 *The Nation* first printed the term "Corn Belt," and in 1903 Harvard University economist T. N. Carver wrote of "a tolerably compact strip where corn is the principle crop, and which may properly be called the corn belt."[7] Later that year Carver again referred to the region as "the most considerable area in the world where agriculture is uniformly prosperous."[8] These early references probably refer to areas of western Ohio and central Indiana, where the first hints of what would become the contemporary Corn Belt were found.[9]

Two areas of prime agricultural land west of the Appalachians that settlers encountered in their westward journey were the Miami and Scioto River valleys of southern and southwestern Ohio.[10] Seeds of European grains and pasture grasses were brought there, as were livestock breeds—crosses made by breeding indigenous animals with those imported from Europe. Large corn crops found in these early centers of the feed grain–livestock farming system stimulated interest in breeding animals that could consume more corn during a time when demand for beef, pork, and lard was growing. This first Corn Belt farming system was essentially the practice of fattening beef cattle and hogs on corn.

Though the Scioto and Miami valleys are, to this day, still heavily entrenched in Corn Belt agriculture, the eastern margins of the Corn Belt have ebbed back from the hills of western Appalachia and the northern Ozarks, whose steep slopes a century ago could be farmed with horse-drawn equipment, but are too treacherous and cumbersome for large-scale, modern machinery.[11] Many of these acres have been converted back to non-cropland uses such as pastureland, while many thousands of acres, especially in regions such as northern Missouri and even southern Iowa, have been enrolled in government-supported conservation programs, returning lands once cropped back to presettlement vegetation.[12]

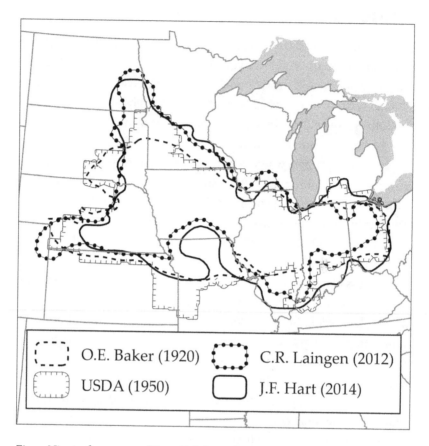

⌐ ‥ ¬ O.E. Baker (1920)	C.R. Laingen (2012)
⌐ ‥ ¬ USDA (1950)	J.F. Hart (2014)

Fig. 3. Ninety-four years of Corn Belt boundaries. Map produced by the author using data from the U.S. Census of Agriculture, various years.

Fast forward nearly three decades to the late 1920s, and the majority of the present-day Corn Belt had been settled and its prairies broken. In 1927 geographer and agricultural economist O. E. Baker, in a series of papers published in *Economic Geography*, was the first to draw and spatially define the region that he referred to as the Corn Belt.[13] Bounded on the north and east by the hay and dairying region, to the south and southwest by the hard winter wheat and corn and winter wheat regions, and to the west and northwest by the spring wheat region, the Corn Belt's boundaries were largely derived from climatological and topographical barriers: average summer temperature of sixty-six degrees (north), summer rainfall totals of over eight inches (west), and soil and topographic limitations already discussed (east, south).

To the north, both the land surface and the climate were constraints to anyone contemplating most agricultural endeavors. Youthful glacial topography prohibited the use of large machinery, especially in more recent decades, and the shortness of the growing season limited the profitability of crop production to the point where most farmers were not willing to risk losing their entire crop. If any agriculture did exist in the prairie-forest ecotone of the Upper Midwest, or even in the dense northern woods of Minnesota, Wisconsin, and Michigan, it was not Corn Belt agriculture. Such transition zones were where corn, soybean, and hog farms were replaced by dairy farms surrounded by small fields on hillsides, many growing any number of types of crops that supported the rest of the farm's more important activities such as dairying, selling "specialty crops" in local markets or along the roadside, or where non-farm farms existed on small tracts of land.[14] Here, hobby or weekend farmers would tend to a few dozen cattle or small fields after their week of work in town was done.

In 1950, using O. E. Baker's earlier work as a template, the U.S. Department of Agriculture drafted a map of the country that placed each county into one of nine farming regions, based primarily on the county's most common agricultural practice.[15] The Corn Belt, "Region V: Feed Grains and Livestock," was spatially similar to Baker's 1920s region, with new areas extending northward into Minnesota and South Dakota's spring wheat region, into Kansas's and Missouri's corn and winter wheat region, and a peninsula of newly included counties on either side of the Wabash River valley in both Illinois and Indiana.

On the western fringe of the region was another untapped frontier marked by an important barrier to corn and soybean farming: rainfall. Plains scholars have often defined the eastern margin of the Great Plains as the 98th meridian, and less frequently the 100th meridian— the boundary marking where fewer than twenty inches of precipitation fell, and where irrigation was necessary to grow row crops such as corn and soybeans (unless dryland corn was being grown for silage, to be cut while still green and fed to cattle in feedlots).[16] From 1950 to 2009, the U.S. Department of Agriculture reported that Kansas corn production increased from 85 million bushels to 561 million bushels. This increase was attributed to the expansion of both ditch/gravity and center-pivot irrigation. Ditch irrigation began in Kansas as early as 1881 near Garden City.[17] From 1959 to 1987, western Kansas's consumption of Ogallala– High Plains Aquifer water increased from 5.4 percent to 15.5 percent. Irrigated acres nearly quadrupled from 1959 to 1978, then decreased slightly in 1987 because of lower crop prices, higher energy costs, less water availability, and farm programs, such as the Conservation Reserve Program, that encouraged irrigators to set aside highly erodible land.[18]

While farmers have breached this western rainfall barrier effectively by using supplemental irrigation, irrigation of corn is a mostly recent endeavor that was unheard of in the traditional Corn Belt farming system, and for the most part is still exceptional. In 1950 there were 48,000 acres of irrigated corn that produced just over 17 million bushels in Corn Belt counties west of the 100th meridian. By 2007, within those same counties, there were just less than 2.6 million acres of irrigated corn that produced 596 million bushels.

On the Colorado piedmont and the South Platte River valley north of Denver, Earl C. Brookover (from Garden City, Kansas) was the businessman who initiated the shift of cattle feeding in the Corn Belt to the southern high plains.[19] Brookover realized the benefits of using irrigated crops to fatten cattle. After World War II, boxed beef production was slowly replacing small-town, small-scale packing plants and butcher shops that once provided meat to most Americans who did not live on a farm and so could not butcher their own. In 1951 Brookover constructed the first commercial feedlot on the north side of Garden City. Within ten years, its capacity grew to forty thousand head of cattle.

Early pioneers in high plains irrigation dammed up and diverted streams to provide water for flood irrigation. This meant that most irrigated lands were destined to be found in low-lying bottomlands. Technological developments after World War II allowed farmers to now pump water up from underground, specifically from the Ogallala–High Plains Aquifer that underlies much of western Kansas, Nebraska, Oklahoma, Texas, and eastern Colorado. Center-pivot irrigation meant that uplands, once impossible to irrigate using gravity-fed methods, could now be cropped. The convergence of center-pivot technology, an ever-growing density of larger and larger feedlots, the construction of meat processing facilities, and an ever-increasing demand from Americans for cheap beef quickly transformed the southern plains from a much-maligned agricultural region into a modern-day beef producing oasis. Beef cattle, once a staple on nearly every Corn Belt farm prior to World War II (in 1925 the average farm in the Midwest had sixteen head of cattle), have all but vanished from farms in the core of the modern Corn Belt, save for parts of western Iowa and Nebraska where medium-sized feedlots still operate. By 2012 beef cattle, especially those that were custom-finished and fattened on corn grown courtesy of the Ogallala–High Plains Aquifer, were relegated to a handful of counties on the western and southern Great Plains, leaving the average number of cattle per farm at numbers less than five, with most true corn and soybean farms having entirely liquidated their herds many decades ago. Cattle consume precious amounts of land that could otherwise be cropped, precious bushels of corn that could be sold, and precious hours of time. As most livestock farmers well know, there are no such things as vacations.

Hog farming is still a central part of Corn Belt agriculture, but production is markedly different from the early days of the feed grains and livestock Corn Belt. Hog farming in this region has its roots in the Miami (Ohio) River valley, where the settlement of thousands of farmers familiar with this practice (from Pennsylvania, New Jersey, Virginia, and Maryland) had occurred in the late 1700s and early 1800s. Pasture and farm-raised hogs (eventually an animal of both European and East

Indian ancestry) were walked to Cincinnati, in many instances for more than one hundred miles, to other farmers nearer to Cincinnati who specialized in fattening them on corn prior to slaughter, which mimicked cattle production in the Scioto Valley of southern Ohio. Packinghouses were established in Cincinnati in 1818, and by midcentury, hogs from Indiana and Kentucky added to the half a million hogs reported by meatpacking plants in both Cincinnati ("Porkopolis") and Covington, Kentucky, towns that soon became ground zero for the production of not only meat products derived from hogs, but also fuel-lard, candles, soaps, cosmetics, and lubricants.

Hog processing diffused throughout the region as Corn Belt agriculture moved west, encouraged in large part by the Homestead Act of 1862. Before long, cities such as Chicago (the "Hog Butcher of the World" from the 1860s to mid-1900s), St. Louis, Kansas City, Omaha, and Sioux City, Iowa, boasted both hog and cattle processing facilities. Moving processed beef and pork by barge was overtaken by rail in the middle and late 1800s, and stockyards, like South Chicago's along the Lake Michigan lakeshore. By 1864 there were a half-dozen in the city, which either sold the livestock to meatpackers in the city, or facilitated their shipment to markets farther east. By the 1880s, eight million head of livestock were being shipped annually to Chicago, and by 1890s that total exceeded thirteen million.[20] This trend began the creation of a select group of companies that would continue to transform the Corn Belt's livestock processing industry during the next century—companies such as Hammond, Morris, Armour, and Swift: "Big-city union stockyards were only an intermediate step in the evolution of meat packing's geography, because the packer's best interest focused on obtaining animals that were as recently removed from the range or feedlot as possible. What permitted Chicago's rise as a packing center was thus exactly the same as permitted Omaha's or Sioux City's. And as the Corn Belt moved west, so did the packing industry."[21]

What Has Changed?

The modern Corn Belt, especially its core, has been slowly transformed from 1950 to 1982.[22] Many factors influenced this transformation, including the hybridization of seed and use of fertilizers, pesticides, herbicides, and fungicides, loss of farms and the increasing size of farms, agricultural specialization (mono- and duoculture farming practices), and international and domestic agronomics.[23] Meanwhile, the region was steadily shifting from a mixed-crop-and-livestock farming system to one that is highly specialized and focused on cash-grain farming.[24] These trends continue today, along with new innovations and socioeconomic driving forces that continue to impact this region's agricultural footprint.

Without question, the most impressive and important change on the agricultural landscape of the Corn Belt has been the gradual adoption of a corn and soybean (cash-grain) farming system as opposed to the earlier feed grains and livestock system (figure 4). During the eighteenth century, German farmers brought to this country a corn and hog farming system that was transplanted many times over—first to Pennsylvania and then farther west to Ohio. From there, it diffused across much of the present-day Corn Belt. Corn and hog farmers grew crops in a standard three-year rotation: corn (a feed grain) in the first year; oats or wheat (a food grain) in the second year; and alfalfa or clover (soil-building legumes that they cut for hay) in the third year.

Farmers used their corn to fatten cattle and hogs, their principal source of income, sold some of their wheat for cash, but fed their oat and hay crops to horses, which were their principal workstock. Horses and oats, an animal and a crop that have essentially disappeared from the agricultural landscape of the Corn Belt, go hand in hand. A one-thousand-pound working horse required ten pounds of oats per day. There are thirty-two pounds of oats in a bushel, which means that one bushel of oats would last three days. In a year, then, a horse would consume 121 bushels. In the 1920s, the average per-acre yield for oats was twenty bushels, so each horse would require about six acres of oats to sustain their feed base for the year. On average, most farms would have kept four horses for draft work. All told, six acres of oats per horse multiplied by four horses equals twenty-four acres of cropland annually devoted to oats, or about 15 percent of a farmer's cropland. This "back of the napkin" math is right on. In 1925, midwestern farms averaged 3.95 horses per farm (there were 9.6 million total horses), and of

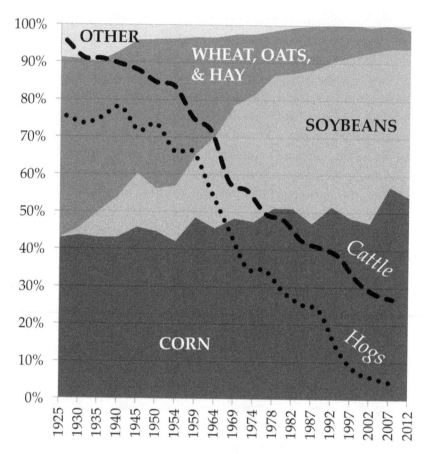

Fig. 4. Crop types as a percentage of harvested cropland area and the percentage of farms that raised hogs (dotted line) and cattle (dashed line) in Iowa, Illinois, and Indiana, 1925 to 2012. Graph created by author using data from the U.S. Census of Agriculture, various years.

the region's harvested cropland, 16 percent of it (31.4 million acres) was devoted to growing oats. Eighty-seven years later in 2012, there were 1.1 million horses and only 651,410 acres of oats, an 89 percent and 98 percent reduction, respectively, largely because of the advent of tractors.

With respect to crop types that have been grown in the Corn Belt over the past century, corn acreage has increased only slightly, from comprising just over 40 percent of the region's harvested cropland, to just over 50 percent. Rotational crops such as wheat, oats, and hay, once found on over 40 percent of the region's farmable landscape, have been decimated, falling to less than 10 percent, and having been steadily replaced by soybeans. Corn and soybean farmers also gradually chipped away at not only the amount of cropland they planted to oats and other hay crops used to feed their livestock, they also began to transform noncrop farmland (e.g., pastureland) reserved for their livestock, so as to further increase their base acreage of tillable cropland.

Livestock production during this period could be described as imploding, on one hand, while on the other hand as exploding.[25] In 1925 cattle and hogs were found on 96 and 76 percent of all Iowa, Illinois, and Indiana farms respectively. But by 2012 cattle were found on only 27 percent of those three states' farms, and hogs on a miniscule 5 percent of all farms. However, the number of cattle and hogs both grew during this period, with hogs increasing from thirty-seven million to forty-five million and cattle from twenty-nine million to thirty-eight million. As such, from 1950 to 2012, with farmers in the Corn Belt, in general, selling off their livestock herds, farms that once only received 20 to 45 percent of their annual farm's income from the sale of crops were, in 2012, relying upon the sale of crops for 60 to 80 percent of their annual income.

Scholars who have focused on short-term intercensal changes have struggled to comprehend the region's long-term trends that capture with more clarity the essence of this region.[26] Within the core states of the region—Iowa, Illinois, and Indiana—corn has always played an important role and has been a dominant crop on the landscape, comprising 40 to 60 percent of all cropland harvested. In the early part of the twentieth century, the crops that farmers grew and the land uses they practiced were all geared toward the raising of livestock. The shift away from feed grain–livestock farming began in the 1920s with the introduction of soybeans as a cash crop.[27] The first area to embrace soybeans was the Grand Prairie region of east central Illinois, followed by other glacially flattened areas such as the Des Moines Lobe in north central Iowa and the Maumee Plain of northwestern Ohio and northeastern Indiana, where, by the 1960s, soybeans comprised no less than one-third of all harvested cropland; in subsequent decades soybeans became ubiquitous across the Corn Belt. Quietly, over many decades, soybean production increased to the point where it has achieved nearly equal status with corn—and in some states, such as Ohio, soybeans have outpaced corn (with respect to acres harvested) in seven of the last nine agricultural censuses.

The Changing Fringe

Much of the recent change in the Corn Belt's geography has been on the region's western and northwestern fringes. Since 1950, the center of gravity of corn acres harvested has moved first north and then west, with an even more recent trend to the northwest (figure 5 inset map). The northerly push from 1950 to the late 1970s was caused by corn farmers in the South abandoning their farming efforts because of inhospitable agricultural conditions for growing row crops (infertile soils, undulating topography, and land better suited for pasture or other nonagricultural uses) coupled with ever-increasing yields farther north in better-suited soil and climate conditions.[28] In the late 1970s irrigation on a large scale drew ever-increasing acres of corn farther and farther west, especially in states such as Nebraska and Kansas, and stretching even farther west into eastern Colorado where the Ogallala–High Plains Aquifer had first been tapped a few decades prior.

More recently, from 1997 to 2012, the region has been pulled in a northwesterly direction because of changes in cropping practices in the eastern Dakotas. In and around the James River valley (shaded in gray in figure 5), local, regional, and global-scale driving forces have been changing the appearance of the contemporary agricultural landscape. As the world's appetite for corn and soybeans continues to increase, the Dakotas' agricultural landscape has been quietly transformed. One driver, the 1996

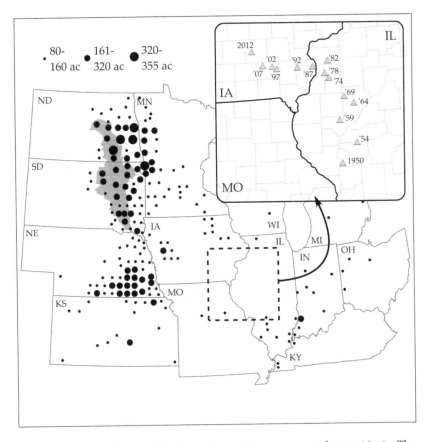

Fig. 5. New acres of corn and soybeans in 2007/2012 compared to 1978/1982. The James River watershed is shown in gray. Inset map shows the spatial trend of the mean center of gravity of harvested corn acres from 1950 to 2012, similar to what the U.S. Census Bureau releases every ten years with the Census of Population results. Map and analysis by author using data from the U.S. Census of Agriculture, various years.

FAIR Act (the Farm Bill), decoupled a significant portion of farm program payments from production decisions. What this meant was that farmers no longer had to plant certain crops to be eligible to receive government payments and/or crop insurance. They were now free to plant the crops that would yield them the highest returns.[29] Modern crop genetics had also created varieties of both corn and soybeans that would mature during the north country's short growing season, though not as high yielding as in the more southerly core of the Corn Belt.[30]

The southern portion of the James River valley has long been entrenched in Corn Belt agriculture. For decades, counties from Sanborn County, South Dakota, south to the Missouri River have planted nearly 30 percent of their cropland to corn. Evidence of this early Corn Belt status can be seen in Mitchell, South Dakota—home to the Corn Palace and the Mitchell (high school) Kernels.

But just to the north, some major changes are occurring. From LaMoure County, North Dakota, south to Spink County, South Dakota, these counties have, over the past five decades, seen marked increases in the amount of cropland devoted to growing corn—in some cases, nearing the 20 percent change mark.[31] This area's agricultural landscape has not changed much in terms of use. In 1954, 80 percent of the land was cropland and the remaining 20 percent was pastureland. In 2012, that proportion was more or less unchanged; but the proportion of corn and soy to other grains has changed dramatically. Too flat to drain, yet too poor to crop, much of the pastureland has remained pastureland. The remaining 80 percent that was used in the 1950s for growing wheat, oats, barley, flax, rye, and only meager acreages of corn grows an ever-increasing volume of corn and soybeans (in some cases over 75 percent of the cropland), with oats, barley, flax, and rye having been essentially erased from existence, again, thanks in large part to the 1996 (Freedom to) Farm Bill.

To handle this ever-growing demand for corn- and soy-based products, new, state-of-the-art infrastructure in this region has recently been built to help facilitate the storage, processing, and movement of massive amounts of grain—mostly corn and soy—to destinations as far away as Asia, opening up new and expanding global and domestic agricultural markets to the farmers of this region. One such facility, located just east of Andover, South Dakota—capable of storing three million bushels of corn, soy, and wheat—is part of the James River valley's new agricultural landscape, and brought to fruition through an investment initiative driven by the South Dakota Wheat Growers cooperative called "Connecting to Tomorrow." These shuttle loader terminals can load 110-car-unit trains bound for Pacific Northwest ports in less than eight hours. They also serve other distant domestic agricultural rail markets such as ethanol facilities in Illinois, Nebraska, and Missouri, and livestock producers in Missouri, Texas, and Arkansas.[32]

Farther south, in southeastern Nebraska, sixteen counties grew 160 to 320 more acres of corn and soybeans per square mile of cropland in 2007 and 2012 than they did in 1978 and 1982. Here, the loss of small grains such as oats, barley, flax, and rye was not the culprit, but rather the loss of sorghum (and to a lesser extent wheat). Sorghum is a crop that is well suited for southeastern Nebraska's arid conditions and undulating topography, where to grow corn or soybeans would necessitate the installation of irrigation technology. However, with the rise of the importance of corn-fed livestock in this part of the state, and more recently, in the 1990s and 2000s, a growing demand for corn-based ethanol, demand for the more energy-dense, corn-based feed has outpaced the demand for sorghum-based feed among producers of both cattle and hogs.

Indeed, the agricultural landscape of the Corn Belt's western fringe is changing, albeit slowly. Today's landscape is a mosaic of the old—the barbed-wire fence, grazing cattle, bales of hay, pastureland, and fields of wheat—alongside the new—the towering grain elevator and the ever-increasing presence of corn and soybeans. To the casual passerby these changes appear benign. However, such changes signal to those studying the rural landscape that global forces are no longer foreign to even the most secluded agricultural regions of our country.

Many drivers of change have transformed agriculture in the Midwest over the past two centuries. For over one hundred years traditional Corn Belt farmers specialized in growing crops used to fatten both hogs and cattle for sale on the market, which in turn sustained other aspects of their working farm. As the region spread northwestward from Ohio and Indiana, pockets of cash-grain agricultural production, focusing first on corn and then on corn and soybeans, diffused from their centers on the flat, fertile soils of the Grand Prairie, the Maumee Plain, and Des Moines Lobe, and eventually throughout the rest of the region. Livestock production, once dependent upon proximity to early processing centers in the eastern part of the region, has transitioned farther west as technological innovations such as rail transportation and refrigeration changed the locational importance of later centers of production such as Chicago, St. Louis, and Kansas City.

In the early 1900s, the introduction of soybeans and soybean-based products slowly transformed the region throughout the twentieth century at the great expense of small grains, pastureland, and small farms clinging to outmoded, small-scale systems of production. Today's modern midwestern farmers are cosmopolitan compared to their ancestors. Farmers are now part of a global agricultural system. Modern farmers are keenly aware of farm reports from countries like Brazil and Argentina who are competitors in growing the crops that are found ubiquitously across the Midwest. Very few are concerned with raising livestock, but those who are mass-produce them. Government policy and innovations in irrigation, drainage, crop genetics, fertilizer and chemical applications, global-positioning systems, and farm implements have further helped to create a landscape that, to the causal passerby, may not appear dramatically altered from the landscape of their grandfather or great-grandfather, but is one that has undergone an almost complete transformation in how and where the agricultural products the world now depends on are produced.

Notes

1. "Census of Agriculture," last accessed March 3, 2015, http://www.agcensus .usda.gov. All text, map, tabular, and graphical references to Census of Agriculture data found in this chapter were obtained here. From this URL, users may navigate to data from past censuses as far back as 1840 to as recent as 2012. The twelve states used in this chapter's agricultural analysis of the Midwest include Illinois, Iowa, Indiana, Kansas, Michigan, Minnesota, Missouri, Nebraska, North Dakota, Ohio, South Dakota, and Wisconsin.

2. W. E. Doolittle, "Agriculture in North America on the Eve of Contact: A Reassessment," *Annals of the Association of American Geographers* 82, no. 3 (1992): 386–401.

3. James R. Shortridge, *The Middle West: Its Meaning in American Culture* (Lawrence: University Press of Kansas, 1989).

4. Tyra A. Olstad, "Understanding the Science and Art of Ecoregionalization," *Professional Geographer* 64, no. 2 (2012): 303–8.

5. Philip M. Raup, "Reinterpreting Structural Change in U.S. Agriculture," in *Economic Studies on Food, Agriculture, and the Environment*, ed. Canavari et al. (Dordrecht, the Netherlands: Kluwer Academic/Plenum, 2002).

6. D. E. Napton, "Agriculture," in *The American Midwest: An Interpretive Encyclopedia*, ed. R. Sisson, C. Zacher, and A. Cayton (Bloomington: Indiana University Press, 2007).

7. T. N. Carver, "The Corn Growers," *The World's Work*, vol. 7 (n.p., 1903), 7:4127–37.

8. T. N. Carver, "Life in the Corn Belt," *The World's Work*, vol. 7 (n.p., 1903), 7:4232–39.

9. Roger F. Auch, Chris Laingen, Mark A. Drummond, Kristi L. Sayler, Ryan R. Reker, Michelle A. Bouchard, and Jeffery J. Danielson, "Land-Use and Land-Cover Change in Three Corn Belt Ecoregions: Similarities and Differences," *FOCUS on Geography* 56, no. 4 (2013): 135–43.

10. John C. Hudson, *Making the Corn Belt: A Geographical History of Middle-Western Agriculture* (Bloomington: Indiana University Press, 1994), chapter 1.

11. John Fraser Hart, *The Land That Feeds Us* (New York: W. W. Norton, 1991).

12. Data on changes in acres in the Conservation Reserve Program from 1986 to 2014 can be found here: http://www.fsa.usda.gov/programs-and-services /conservation-programs/reports-and-statistics/index.

13. O. E. Baker, "Agricultural Regions of North America: Part IV—The Corn Belt," *Economic Geography* 3, no. 4 (1927): 447–65.

14. John Fraser Hart, "Nonfarm Farms," *Geographical Review* 82, no. 2 (1992): 166–79.

15. U.S. Department of Agriculture, "Generalized Types of Farming in the United States," *Agricultural Information Bulletin No. 3* (Washington DC: U.S. Government Printing Office, 1950).

16. David J. Wishart, *The Last Days of the Rainbelt* (Lincoln: University of Nebraska Press, 2013).

17. S. E. White, "Ogallala Oases: Water Use, Population Redistribution, and Policy Implications in the High Plains of Western Kansas, 1980–1990," *Annals of the Association of American Geographers* 84, no. 1 (1994): 29–45.

18. D. E. Kromm and S. E. White, "Irrigation in the High Plains of Western Kansas," *Proceedings IRDC-90*, compilers James Byrne and Catherine Fleming (University of Lethbridge Water Resources Institute, 1991), 61–72.

19. J. F. Hart, *The Changing Scale of American Agriculture* (Charlottesville: University of Virginia Press, 2003), chapter 3, "Beef."

20. J. C. Hudson and C. R. Laingen, *American Farms, American Food: A Geography of Agriculture and Food Production in the United States* (Lanham MD: Lexington Books, 2016), 71.

21. Hudson, *Making the Corn Belt*, 134.

22. J. F. Hart, "Change in the Corn Belt," *Geographical Review* 76, no. 1 (1986): 51–72.

23. According to the 2007 Census of Agriculture, over 65 percent (265 million acres) of all U.S. cropland was treated with some type of commercial fertilizer, lime, or soil conditioner. In the Corn Belt region, over 72 percent (115 million acres) of all cropland was treated in 2007.

24. J. L. Anderson, *Industrializing the Corn Belt: Agriculture, Technology, and Environment, 1945–1972* (DeKalb: Northern Illinois University Press, 2009).

25. Owen J. Furuseth, "Hog Farming in Eastern North Carolina," *Southeastern Geographer* 41, no. 1 (2001): 53–64, and "Restructuring of Hog Farming in North Carolina: Explosion and Implosion," *Professional Geographer* 49, no. 4 (1997): 391–403.

26. J. F. Hart, "Change in the Corn Belt," *Geographical Review* 76, no. 1 (1986): 51–72.

27. K. Smith Howard, "The Midwestern Farm Landscape Since 1945," in *The Rural Midwest Since World War II*, ed. J. L. Anderson (Dekalb: Northern Illinois University Press, 2014).

28. John Fraser Hart, "Bovotopia," *Geographical Review* 97, no. 4 (2007): 542–49.

29. Bruce Babcock and Miguel Carriquiry, "Acreage Shifts Under Freedom to Farm," *Iowa Ag Review* 7, no. 1 (2001): 4–5.

30. Corn in east central North Dakota must mature in eighty to ninety days, while corn grown in central Illinois has over 120 days in which to mature. In 2014, Barnes County, North Dakota's average corn yield was 129 bushels per acre, compared with McLean County, Illinois, at 218 bushels per acre.

31. C. R. Laingen, "A Picture Is Worth 898 Words: Changing Agricultural Landscapes of the Dakotas," *focus on Geography* 57, no. 1 (2014.): 41–42.

32. Unit trains were first introduced by a joint venture between the Illinois Central Railroad and Cargill in 1966. The first train left Gibson City, Illinois, in the winter of 1967 bound for Cargill's export terminal in Baton Rouge, Louisiana. Though the train partially derailed while crossing a bridge, the trip was termed a success, and soon after two additional transport terminals were opened in Tuscola, Illinois, and Linden, Indiana. More information can found at http://minnesota.cbslocal.com/2015/04/09/cargills-great-unit-train-innovation/, last accessed on April 14, 2015.

10

The Role of Sports in the Midwest

David R. McMahon

> I thank God I was warring on the gridirons of the Midwest and not on
> the battlefields of Europe. I can speak confidently and positively that the
> players of this country would much more, much rather, struggle and fight
> to win the Heisman Award than the Croix de Guerre.—NILE KINNICK's
> 1939 Heisman Award speech.

If the study of the Midwest is to be revived, sports history must play an
important role in its revival. Sport has an unrivaled capacity to signify
and create regional identity even in our increasingly commercialized
and globalized age. At a time when the history of the Midwest is under-
appreciated, too little known and celebrated, and rarely found in school
curriculums, the sporting heritage of the Midwest is one of the region's
most significant and recognizable cultural resources.

There is no need to wait for the full maturation of a New Midwest History before spreading the word; as educators, we can promote the study
of the Midwest by teaching the history of sports in our classrooms. In
"Why Sports History Is American History," Mark Naison reasons: "In
the classroom, examples from sports can explain key events in American
history and help explore how people in American society have grappled
with racial, ethnic, and regional differences in our very diverse nation."
Naison rightly concludes that "sports history is a tremendously valuable
tool for bringing American history to life."[1]

For example, in my U.S. History Survey course, students learn that
before Ronald Reagan became president, he was a radio broadcaster for
WHO in Des Moines in the 1930s. As a sports broadcaster, he covered the
Iowa Hawkeyes in football and the Chicago Cubs in baseball (re-creating
Cubs games from the telegraph). He witnessed the abuse suffered by Ozzie
Simmons, the Iowa standout and one of the few black players in college

football at the time. Years later, Reagan recalled a game Simmons played against Illinois. After several late hits, his Iowa teammates threatened: "Do that to him once more, and we're gonna run you right out of the end of your stadium." Minnesota's rough treatment of Simmons in 1934 led to Floyd of Rosedale—one of the great rivalry trophies in college football. As Iowa prepared for the 1935 game, the Minnesota team was threatened with violence by Iowa fans and the governor. Tensions were eased only after the governors of both states agreed to bet a prize pig on the outcome. Each year a bronze pig is given annually to the winner of the Iowa-Minnesota game.[2]

The color line marred sports for much of the twentieth century. The drubbing of Drake's Johnny Bright in 1951 led to rule changes in college football and to greater awareness of discrimination in sports. Iowans like Bob Feller and J. L. Wilkerson played important roles in the integration of Major League Baseball. I share these episodes and others with college students, stories derived in part from my own research on blacks and sports in Iowa. Class time is also spent on the issue of gender equity. Students learn about the unintended consequences of reform by looking at how Iowa high school girls' basketball transitioned from six-on-six to the five-player game.[3]

But for students in Iowa City, the story of Nile Kinnick excites the most interest. An outstanding student-athlete at the University of Iowa, Kinnick won the 1939 Heisman Trophy; his acceptance speech elevated his standing as an exemplary son of the Midwest. His speech tells us a lot about the region on the eve of World War II. Personifying the transition from isolation to intervention as war clouds gathered, Kinnick later died in a flight-training accident during the war. An excerpt from the speech is played before every home football game in the stadium named in his honor: "I thank God I was warring on the gridirons of the Midwest and not on the battlefields of Europe. I can speak confidently and positively that the players of this country would much more, much rather, struggle and fight to win the Heisman Award than the Croix de Guerre."[4]

Toward a Sports History of the Midwest

In *The American Midwest: An Interpretive Encyclopedia*, Robert F. Bachin explains the role of sports in the Midwest: "Sports have always played an important part in structuring social relations. From the games of Native Americans to the outdoor winter sports of Scandinavian immigrants, the Midwest took on distinctive patterns of leisure and recreation." Bachin makes clear that "unlike the South," "where gambling and blood sports helped to define the rigid racial and social structure of slave culture, sports and recreation in the Midwest often extended opportunities for preserving cultural traditions and for penetrating ethnic and racial boundaries. Attitudes toward sport in the Midwest also differed from those in New England, where sports were frowned upon or avoided as mere idleness."[5]

While no comprehensive study of sports in the Midwest exists, essays in *The American Midwest* prove there is an identifiable history of sports in the Midwest. Native American and immigrant influences—especially Scandinavian, German, and Czech—and the advent of competitive games to hone skills needed for survival, combined with the land itself to create a distinctive sports culture. Midwesterners were leaders in conservation, intercollegiate athletics, coeducation and athletic opportunities for women, the development of the sporting goods industry, the development of professional baseball and football, the creation of urban playgrounds for kids, professional baseball for blacks, professional baseball for women; and midwestern colleges like the University of Iowa led the integration of collegiate sports, among other achievements.[6]

A key part of midwestern sports culture is intercollegiate athletics. The Big Ten is the oldest Division I athletic conference in the nation, and arguably the premier academic association. Huge and historic stadiums dot the landscape—the University of Michigan, Ohio State, and Penn State are among the largest in college football—and the Big Ten is the leading conference for college basketball games in terms of attendance. In televised sports, the launch of the Big Ten Network is considered one of the most successful in cable history; the network serves as a model for other conferences and teams seeking to enhance their media profile.[7]

Sports historian Daniel Nathan sums it up in his entry on intercollegiate athletics in *The American Midwest*: "Intercollegiate athletics has long been a prominent feature of Midwestern life, an activity universities and colleges use to promote themselves and foster community by giving people a reason to gather and cheer." The popularity of college football, basketball, wrestling, and ice hockey in Minnesota is obvious. "But intercollegiate athletics is not only about school and community spirit and vicarious glory, it is a multimillion-dollar-a-year industry frequently beset by corruption and hypocrisy." While there are many levels of intercollegiate competition, the Big Ten "is the most prestigious, influential, and publicized." "Indeed, for many people Big Ten football (and to a lesser extent men's basketball) defines midwestern intercollegiate athletics, though the conference also sponsors championships in twenty-four other sports, thirteen of them for women."[8]

In *Rooting for the Home Team: Sport Community and Identity*, an exemplary work that provides models for pursuing the sports history of the Midwest, Nathan describes what University of Iowa coaches and teams meant to Iowans, recalling his graduate student days at the university:

When I lived in Iowa, Dan Gable, Hayden Fry, C. Vivian Stringer, and Tom Davis were the most successful and prominent coaches at the university and probably in the state. They were all icons—well, maybe not Dr. Tom, whom I always liked, despite the incessant passing around the perimeter. These coaches were iconic for many reasons. It was not just that their teams won, especially Gable's, whose record over his twenty-one years as wrestling coach is unprecedented in any sport. With Gable at the helm, the Iowa wrestling team won 15 national titles (nine of them consecutively) and twenty-one straight Big Ten conference championships. Fry, Stringer, and Davis experienced success, too. But beyond the wins, which created opportunities to bask in reflected glory, many Iowa fans connected with, liked, and even admired these people because they personified things we valued—hard work, preparation, intensity, determination, perseverance, integrity, charm, and humility, at least in public, most of the time.... In the process, they helped us differentiate ourselves from others: from, say, Cyclones and Cornhuskers, Badgers and Buckeyes.[9]

Rooting for the Home Team is not primarily a book about the Midwest, but it provides examples of how sports create and maintain collective identity in the region. Academics interested in reviving midwestern studies should consult this book and the work of other scholars affiliated with the North American Society for Sports History (NASSH), the major professional organization for sports scholars.[10] Without serious attention to sports, the revival of Midwest history would be incomplete.

Critical Nostalgia and Sports

I think of myself as an accidental sports historian. I stumbled onto the field of sports history because I took on a research project that involved sports, not because I was directed to it by one of my mentors in graduate school. In fact, my mentors had taught me little about the history of sports. As important to me as the scholarship of sports history, is the fact that I grew up in the Midwest in the first place. Growing up in a small town in Iowa taught me the importance of sports and the role it plays in the formation of community identity. The focus of much of my research and teaching has been the interplay of sports, place, and memory.[11]

Scholars who spoke at the "Finding the Lost Region" conference echoed a point I had long believed. Nostalgia can actually be the starting point of critical analysis. For far too long, historians viewed nostalgia simplistically—and negatively, as the antithesis of historical thinking—using their influence to block or malign local history and the study of regions. In 1998 Jackson Lears wrote a powerful defense of nostalgia: "Renewed respect for nostalgia could provide a powerful antidote to linear notions of progress—by underwriting the conviction that once, at least, in some ways, life was more humane and satisfying than it is today."[12]

Begging the pardon of the reader, I would like to illustrate the point by discussing the history of sports in the small town where I grew up in the 1970s and 1980s, in particular as it pertains to the role of females in athletics, an important part of the Midwest culture. My nostalgia for Manilla, Iowa, has led me to consider critically the staggering changes that have occurred since the 1980s. In the 1970s and 1980s, Manilla had a population of about a thousand people. The high school was small, but it had a mighty tradition in athletics, particularly girls' sports. In recent years the town has suffered economic and population decline, and the school building I attended is now closed, threatening the town's very existence.[13] This is a familiar story in western Iowa and other rural parts of the state.

The highpoint in my town's history was winning the Iowa high school girls' basketball championship in 1974. I remember my older sister appearing in the state championship game on television. As she entered the contest late in the game, to the delight of the sell-out crowd at Veterans Auditorium in Des Moines, Frosty Mitchell, one of the tournament's broadcasters, said she was sixteen inches shorter than the tallest girl in the tournament: "a leprechaun in time for St. Patrick's Day."[14]

Despite playing only a minor role in the tournament, my sister Mickey was a minicelebrity by the time she came home from Des Moines. Fans wrote her letters and photographers took her picture, seeing in those pigtails the epitome of the Iowa girls' game. Other Manilla girls, like sophomore forward Jean Rostermundt, gained statewide recognition on the all-state team. Rostermundt was the tournament's leading scorer and won the free-throw shooting contest that year. In time, she became a pioneering college athlete at the University of New Mexico. The Lobos' first female athlete to be awarded a full athletic scholarship for four years, she was a four-time most valuable player in basketball while also excelling in track and field and cross country. She later played professional basketball and coached basketball and soccer to children while teaching health classes.[15]

That 1974 game rivals anything portrayed in *Hoosiers*, the classic Hollywood film about Indiana boys' high school basketball. Manilla's victory was one of the biggest upsets in tournament history. By the end of the game, the smallest school in the "Sweet Sixteen" had triumphed over Adel, the top-ranked team in the state and the previous year's runner-up. Near the end of the game, the broadcasters opined that Manilla's victory was forged during the cross country and track seasons the previous year.[16]

Manilla had been to the finals before, and would be there again—in 1976, and multiple times as part of consolidated school districts (Irwin-Kirkman-Manilla and IKM-Manning). But the announcers had been right when they connected Manilla's basketball title in 1974 to cross country and track and field. Tiny Manilla had won the state cross-country title in 1970, 1972, and 1973, and it accumulated six state outdoor track titles from 1967 to 1978, the period directly before and after the passage of Title IX, the pathbreaking legislation that mandated equal opportunities for girls in sports. The first all-state track championship for high school girls in Iowa was held in 1962: Manilla was runner-up in 1964; champions in 1967; runner-up in 1968; champions in 1969 and co-champions in 1970; champions in 1971; and champions in class 1A in 1977 and 1978, when a class system was instituted for high school girls' sports.[17]

Nostalgia for the community I grew up in is more than a sentimental longing for a former place and time—it is a historically informed sense of local community and shared identity. The female high school athlete was honored in the culture I grew up in. They were seen not so much as the equals of boys, but often our betters. My biggest local athletic heroes back then were young women, including my sisters, other relatives, neighbors, and friends. The rise to prominence of the female athlete has been a long time in coming, and not without hardship and struggle. Forty years after the passage of Title IX, a more progressive sports culture in the United States has resulted in the image of the dominating U.S. female athlete—as was proved at the Olympics in Rio.[18]

A local athlete worth noting is Robin Evans, who moved to Manilla to take advantage of the school's athletic programs in the 1970s. Transferring from nearby Carroll Community Schools, she excelled in basketball and running. Evans was instrumental in expanding athletic opportunity for girls in Iowa, especially in track and field. Known primarily as a distance runner, she was twice a state cross-country champion. In track, she was a champion as well and personally advocated for the mile run at a time when girls were limited to running the 880 event. One of the first high school girls to break the five-minute mile, she held numerous records at the time of her death in 2006. According to her obituary, Evans was rated in the top ten for women milers for three years, 1970–72, and was inducted into the Iowa Girls' High School Track Hall of Fame and the Iowa Association of Track Coaches Hall of Fame.[19]

The athletic career of Robin Evans teaches us that little communities like Manilla were often ahead of their urban counterparts when it came to opportunity for girls. In the early 1970s, a girls' weight-lifting team from Manilla demonstrated to other girls at the Iowa Girls Basketball Academy in Ida Gove the latest advanced techniques in sports training. Girls from each of the sixteen tournament districts in Iowa were chosen to attend the academy by the Iowa Girls High School Athletic Union. The brainchild of boat manufacturer Byron Godbersen, the academy featured speakers such as astronaut James Lovell and former Boston Celtic Bill Russell. The academy also offered athletic scholarships for girls.[20]

In retrospect, a solid foundation had been set for Manilla to win the 1974 state championship. The school's victory coincided with the zenith of what Max McElwain called "the most successful athletic activity for high school females in American history." Small, rural communities had adopted the six-on-six high school girls' basketball game as the premier community event at a time when progressive reformers had argued against interscholastic sports for young women. The game, ironically watched over mostly by men, such as E. Wayne Cooley, the head of the influential Iowa Girls High School Athletic Union, led to unprecedented levels of participation by female athletes by the early 1970s. According to McElwain, "Understanding Iowa six-player girls' basketball entails acknowledging its contradictions. It was an activity that was simultaneously conservative and progressive, and its extraordinary appeal and survival occurred precisely *because* [author's emphasis] of these contradictions. The contradictions that marked girls' basketball similarly characterized the larger Iowa culture."[21]

But the spectacle so long in development ended quickly. By the 1980s, the game that had done so much for Iowa girls was targeted for extinction by a new generation of reformers (and naysayers like *Des Moines Register* columnist Donald Kaul). With the demise of six-player girls' basketball, the luster of the annual state tournament was lost—and it hasn't recovered since. The end of six-on-six basketball in Iowa resulted in a strange kind of gender equity: "In 1993, more than twenty years after the passage of Title IX, 42 percent of participants of Iowa high school sports were female—the same percentage of women who compete nationally in college athletics today. But only a few decades earlier, 70 percent of Iowa girls had played one sport alone: basketball. Statistically speaking, Iowa and the rest of the country were finally equal."[22]

All-American Sports Writing in the Midwest

Nostalgia has also led me to consider a neglected topic of research: sports writing in the Midwest. Modern sports journalism has deep roots in the Midwest. Keith Cannon writes, "Sports journalists in the Midwest contributed significantly to the development of modern trends in sports reporting, including the use of investigative techniques and the role of sports media as promoters and sponsors of athletic events."[23] To my mind, sports writing has yet to receive its due.

My hometown can also lay claim to one of the best sports writers in the Midwest: Maury White, a sports writer and columnist for the *Des Moines Register* during its heyday. White personified the Midwest—in his work ethic, sports writing, and as a member of the so-called greatest generation. A proud descendant of Irish immigrants who made newspapering the family business, White took over as editor of the *Manilla Times* in high school when his father died unexpectedly during the Great Depression. While this delayed his entry into college for a time, he eventually enrolled at Drake University, where he played various sports, including football. In one notable contest he scored two touchdowns to defeat Iowa State.[24]

After graduating from Drake, White enlisted in the navy during World War II. When his service was over he began his career in journalism. He became master of the "Iowa angle," finding links to Iowa and Iowans in the great sport stories of the day. He was named sportswriter of the year in 1971, cementing his reputation as one of the finest sports writers in the country. From Super Bowls to Rose Bowls and the Olympics, including the 1972 Munich games, White covered the greatest sporting events in the world. At the time, the *Register* billed itself as Iowa's hometown newspaper, but it was also one of the country's best. Loyal readers tore through the "Big Peach" sports section and were treated to outstanding writing from a stable of scribes that included the father of bestselling travel writer Bill Bryson.[25]

White defended the status of the *Register* and his own place among sports writers in a letter he wrote in 1974: "Folks in the local Baseball Writers chapters simply don't have the foggiest idea of what are large and small papers, which actually cover sports and which are merely trying to get somebody a seat at the game." Arguing for a better seat in the press box for his paper, he noted that "the attached sheet of circulation figures are a pretty good clue that the *Des Moines Register* is worth having to come cover your event, and if you care to check it is frequently included in the lists of 'best' papers in the nation. I just ran down the list and there are only 16 cities in the nation who have larger Sunday papers." Another letter suggests problems with the Heisman Trophy ballots among midwestern voters, something that would cause a stir among partisan fans today.[26]

In another letter, a man from Birmingham, Alabama, wrote the *Register* to complement White on his even-handed and insightful coverage of the Sugar Bowl game between Notre Dame and Alabama. The man found the article in a discarded newspaper that was used to package some merchandise he bought from an Iowa firm. "Perhaps Mr. White's geographical detachment made it easier for him to write what I thought was a very balanced view, but I think he probably carries that attitude to all his writing, geographical distance to the contrary notwithstanding." Even to this accidental reader, White's journalistic talent was obvious.[27]

I met Maury for the first time in 1996 following a lecture he gave at the University of Iowa during a symposium on sports. He was joined at the podium by his colleague Tom Witosky, an investigative reporter who gained fame covering the Norby Walters sports agent scandal in the 1980s, involving Iowa running back Ronnie Harmon.[28] After his speech, I asked if I could interview him to learn more. During several visits to his home in Des Moines, Maury greatly expanded my knowledge of sports in the Midwest—usually over cups of coffee and glasses of Scotch. My interviews with him, and the personal correspondence and papers I obtained after his death in 1999, convinced me sports writers like him have yet to receive their due. The careers of sports writers and broadcasters from White's era provide a unique lens into midwestern life. More should be written about them.

Jim Leach, a thirty-year congressman from Iowa and former high school state wrestling champion, was a guest at a dinner party I attended recently. Inevitably, our conversation turned to sports. After sharing a few stories he asked me to name the battery of a certain Adel American Legion baseball team in the 1930s. Leach, the former chair of the National Endowment for the Humanities, smiled broadly when I gave him the correct response: the pitcher was Bob Feller and the catcher was Nile Kinnick.

As I explained to Congressman Leach, I could guess the answer because my mother had grown up in Van Meter, Iowa, the boyhood home of Bob Feller. On many occasions, the Hall of Fame pitcher had visited my grandfather—his greatest fan—when he returned to his hometown. Years later, I interviewed Feller about the history of black baseball in Iowa and the role he played integrating the game by organizing contests between white and black baseball players after World War II (stories I heard first from my grandfather). My nostalgia had led me to critically examine Iowa sports history. In the process, I gained a new appreciation for how Iowans, black and white, worked together to break down the color barrier in sports. The resulting essay was a modest contribution to the field of sports history.[29]

History, of course, is more than sentimental memories of the past. But nostalgia for the past can lead us to real insights and new understandings. The "Finding the Lost Region" conference proved the value of Midwest history. Some scholars might remain skeptical of our efforts, but this should not deter us. As scholars, we owe the best possible explanation of why the Midwest matters to the widest possible audience; as teachers, we owe our students the opportunity to know their history.

In particular, students should know the role sports played in creating a distinctive Midwest culture. They should know that the playing fields of the Midwest were important battlegrounds in the struggle for civil rights and gender equity. More research is needed on the history of the Midwest, including the sports history of the Midwest. But it is clear we have reached the end of the beginning of a national conversation about giving the Midwest its due. May the conversation begun in Grand Rapids be long lasting and of consequence.

Notes

1. Mark Naison, "Why Sports History Is American History," http://
gilderlehrman.org.history-by-era/reform-movements/essays/why-sports
-history-american-history. See also Robert F. Wheeler, "Teaching Sport as
History, History Through Sport," *History Teacher* 11, no. 3 (May 1978): 311–22.

2. See Ronald Reagan audio file, "Welcome to the Gridiron: 100+ Years of
Iowa Football," http://magazine.foriowa.org/gridironglory/index.cfm,
accessed February 4, 2018; Pat Borzi, "Trophy Tells a Tale of Rivalry and
Race, *New York Times*, November 25, 2010; and Mark Steil, "The Origin of
Floyd of Rosedale," Minnesota Public Radio, November 17, 2005.

3. The scholarly research on Iowa sports history is rich. See David R. McMahon,
"Pride to All: African-Americans and Sports in Iowa," in *Outside In: African-
American History in Iowa, 1838–2000*, ed. Bill Silag, Susan Koch-Bridgford,
and Hal Chase (Des Moines: State Historical Society of Iowa, 2001), 464–95;
Jaime Schultz, *Moments of Impact: Injury, Racialized Memory, and Reconcilia-
tion in College Football* (Lincoln: University of Nebraska Press, 2016); Zebulon
Baker, "'This affair is about something bigger than John Bright'": Iowans Con-
front the Jim Crow South, 1946–1951," *Annals of Iowa* 72, no. 2 (Spring 2013):
122–60; Max McElwain, *The Only Dance in Iowa: A History of Six-Player Girls'
Basketball* (Lincoln: University of Nebraska Press, 2004); and Shelley Lucas,
"Cornography: Selling Women's Professional Basketball in a Girls Basketball
State, *Annals of Iowa* 64, no. 2 (Fall 2005): 340–72.

4. Paul Baender, ed., *A Hero Perished: The Diary and Selected Letters of Nile
Kinnick* (Iowa City: University of Iowa Press, 1991), 33–37.

5. Robert F. Bachin, "Overview," in *The American Midwest: An Interpretive
Encyclopedia*, ed. Andrew R. L. Cayton, Richard Sisson, and Chris Zacher
(Bloomington: Indiana University Press, 2007), 869.

6. Bachin, "Overview," 869–72.

7. For more on the Big Ten Network, see http://www.btn.com. A disconcert-
ing note was sounded in Marc Tracy's, "As Big Ten Declines, Homegrown
Talent Flees," *New York Times*, October 3, 2014.

8. Daniel A. Nathan, "Intercollegiate Athletics," in *The American Midwest: An
Interpretive Encyclopedia*, ed. Andrew R. L. Cayton, Richard Sisson, and
Chris Zacher (Bloomington: Indiana University Press, 2007), 892–93.

9. Daniel Nathan, ed., *Rooting for the Home Team: Sport, Community, and
Identity* (Urbana: University of Illinois Press, 2013), 1–2.

10. Daniel Nathan is past president of the North American Society for Sport
History (NASSH), the organization that publishes *Journal of Sports History*,

and a prominent member of the Sports Studies Caucus at the annual meeting of the American Studies Association.

11. For example, see McMahon, "Remembering the Black and Gold: African Americans, Sport Memory, and the University of Iowa," *Sport in Society* 4, no. 2 (Summer 2001): 63–98.

12. McMahon, "Nostalgia," in *Encyclopedia of Local History*, ed. Carol Kammen and Norma Prendergast (Walnut Creek: AltaMira Press, 2000): 348–50; and Ray Cashman, "Critical Nostalgia and Material Culture in Northern Ireland," *Journal of American Folklore* 119, no. 472 (Spring 2006): 137–60. Perhaps this is why Jon Lauck discovered the field of midwestern studies in such "a sorry state" before he organized the Midwest History Association. See Jeff Charis-Carlson, "Is the Midwest Less Important Than Other Regions?" *Iowa City Press Citizen*, March 25, 2015.

13. Jeff Morrison, "Time Runs Out on Manilla School," *Des Moines Register*, June 20, 2014.

14. See YouTube for Iowa Public Television broadcasts of the state championship games uploaded by the Iowa Girls' High School Athletic Union, including the 1974 championship game between Adel and Manilla.

15. See "Jean Rostermundt Gurule," New Mexico Official Athletic Site, released August 18, 2011. See also the commemorative booklet "1974 State Champs: Manilla Hawkettes," published by *The Denison Bulletin* (in the author's possession).

16. See note 14 for television broadcast information.

17. See "State Track & Field Meet champions," at http://www.data .desmoinesregister.com, accessed February 4, 2018. Two signs outside of the town of Manilla list state championships in football, basketball, cross country, and indoor and outdoor track.

18. My sister Theresa (Mickey) was a member of the cross-country championship team of 1973; my sister Debra was a member of the 1978 state track and field champions; their aunt, Madonna (McMahon) Schwieso, was Manilla's first all-state girls' basketball player in the 1930s. For more on the Olympics in Rio, see Christine Brennan, "U.S. Women Are 'Killing It' at These Olympics," *USA Today*, August 2, 2016.

19. See Robin Evans's obituary in the *Nevada Journal*, April 6, 2006. She participated in basketball and track and field at Iowa State University before transferring to the University of Iowa.

20. McElwain, *Only Dance in Iowa*, 81–82.

21. McElwain, *Only Dance in Iowa*, 193, 187.

22. McElwain, *Only Dance in Iowa*, 186–87. The high school wrestling tournament is now the biggest draw in Iowa. See Mike Kilen, "Iowa Poll: Wrestling Reigns as King of Iowa Tourneys," *Des Moines Register*, February 20, 2015.

23. Keith R. Cannon, "Sports Writing," in *The American Midwest*: An Interpretive Encyclopedia, ed. Andrew R. L. Cayton, Richard Sisson, and Chris Zacher (Bloomington: Indiana University Press, 2007), 918–19.

24. See my paper, "The Newspaperman and the Historian: Maury White and the Making of Iowa Sports History," Northern Great Plains History Conference, St. Cloud MN, October 1999, and Maury White papers (both in author's possession).

25. See the article on Maury White's induction in the *Des Moines Register* Iowa Sports Hall of Fame: http://www.data.desmoinesregister.com. Today, the Maury White award is given to the most outstanding performer at the men's collegiate/invitational level at the Drake Relays in Des Moines. For a nostalgic tale about growing up in Des Moines, see Bill Bryson, *The Life and Times of the Thunderbolt Kid: A Memoir* (New York: Random House, 2006).

26. Maury White to Bob Wirz, December 13, 1974; Austin F. Melvin to Maury White, November 8, 1967, letters in possession of the author.

27. Edward W. Mullins to editor and publisher of the *Des Moines Register*, January 25, 1974.

28. Maury White and Tom Witosky lecture, "From Stone Age to Stonewalling: Half a Century of Sports Journalism," Iowa City, June 17, 1996. Witosky collaborated with Marc Hansen, another veteran *Register* sports writer, to chronicle the same-sex marriage decision in Iowa that was a landmark in the struggle for marriage equality. See *Equality Before the Law: How Iowa Led Americans to Marriage Equality* (Iowa City: University of Iowa Press, 2015).

29. McMahon, "Pride to All," 464–95.

PART 4

Midwestern Landscapes

11

The View from the River

ANOTHER PERSPECTIVE ON
MIDWESTERN HISTORY

Michael Allen

"Stand at the Cumberland Gap and watch the procession of civilization, marching single file—the buffalo following the trail to the salt springs, the Indian, the fur-trader and hunter, cattle-raiser, the pioneer farmer— and the frontier has passed by."[1] When Frederick Jackson Turner wrote these words in 1893, he was certainly correct in saying the mountain passes and early American trails were a course for civilization onto the trans-Appalachian frontier. Yet the midwestern river systems were also a course for that civilization and remain so today.

Indeed, one could take the above quote and substitute, "Stand where the Allegheny and Monongahela form the Ohio"; "Stand where the Ohio River joins the Mississippi"; "Stand beneath St. Anthony's Falls on Minnesota's upper Mississippi"; "Stand where the Missouri River is joined by the Kansas River"; or, "Stand near the juncture of the Missouri, Illinois, and Mississippi rivers." Moreover, one could supplement Turner's reference to the "fur-trader and hunter, cattle-raiser, the pioneer farmer" by adding mound builders, explorers, town builders, rivermen, soldiers, folk heroes, freedom fighters, governmental leaders, writers, artists, moviemakers, and musicians.

Midwestern Rivers and Urban Geography

In this chapter, readers will view the American Midwest through the lens of its rivers. Here I define the term "Midwest" in simple form. The Midwest is that region of the United States west of the Appalachians, south of the forty-ninth parallel and the Great Lakes, east of the ninety-eighth line of longitude, and north of both the Ohio River and the thirty-sixth line of latitude. HA!

Around 12,000 BC, the Great Ice Age came to an end in North America and as the huge glaciers slowly melted, the Midwest's myriad rivers slowly formed. To be sure, many midwestern northerly rivers drain Hudson's Bay, the Great Lakes, and the St. Lawrence flowing to the Atlantic. And the great Red River flows northward to Lake Winnipeg in Canada. Yet the Midwest core is defined by the Ohio, upper Mississippi, and lower Missouri River trunk lines and their numerous tributaries. These southwardly flowing rivers form the upper Mississippi valley—the historic and cultural midwestern heartland.

A quick look at a map of the modern Midwest reflects the importance of rivers in determining the urban landscape. Because rivers were essential for travel and trade, the Midwest's major towns arose along their banks until the invention of the railroad and internal combustion engine. As suggested above, Pittsburgh sits at the juncture where the Allegheny and Monongahela form the Ohio; Marietta, the first American settlement in the Old Northwest, was founded where the Muskingum joins the Ohio; and Cincinnati arose where the Miami River enters the Ohio. Were it not for a vast and inhospitable floodplain, Cairo, Illinois, at the juncture of the Ohio and Mississippi, might have become the great city that those who named it envisioned. On the upper Mississippi, the Twin Cities of Minneapolis and St. Paul sit where St. Anthony's Falls effectively end upstream navigation on the Father of Waters. St. Louis was founded just south of the points where both the Missouri and Illinois Rivers join the Mississippi; the Illinois River is itself formed near the suburbs of Chicago. And up the Missouri, Independence and Kansas City lie where the Kansas River makes its entry. A little farther upstream St. Joseph—"St. Joe"—sits astride the Missouri in that part of America where the Midwest slowly becomes the West.[2]

Mound Builders

Long before the arrival of European Americans, Indigenous Americans founded their own river towns. Commonly known as "Mound Builders," Hopewellian and Mississippian people inhabited what we call the Midwest for approximately two thousand years, from 400 BC to AD 1400.[3] First were the Hopewell Indians, who dwelt in today's Ohio, Wisconsin, Indiana, Illinois, western Pennsylvania, and New York, where they farmed maize ("Indian corn"), gathered nuts and berries, hunted deer, bear, and small game, and fished. Hopewell workers built large earthen mounds (roughly comparable to Egyptian, Aztecan, and Mayan pyramids) by hauling dirt in baskets strapped to their backs. The mounds served for defense, religious and burial rituals, and more.[4]

Much later, and in river valleys and river towns farther south, the Hopewell were supplanted by the Mississippians. They flourished from approximately AD 800 until the eve of European contact in the lower Mississippi Valley, including large portions of today's western Illinois and eastern Missouri. Mississippians also made their living hunting, fishing, and farming maize, beans, squash, gourds, and tobacco in the rich midwestern soil of the Mississippi River bottomlands. Mississippian men and women worshipped corn and the sunshine that made it grow in varied religious rituals and dances.[5]

The great Mississippian city was Cahokia, whose center lay on the east bank of the Mississippi River, a few miles from modern St. Louis. From approximately AD 700 to 1400, Cahokia arose and fell. At its peak, the city boasted some 120 mounds and ten thousand to fifteen thousand men and women. At the city's center stood Monk's Mound (a name that comes from later Europeans who named it after Catholic missionaries from the 1700s), which was 100 feet high with a 955-foot-by-775-foot base, equal to some of the Egyptian and Mesoamerican pyramids. Chiefs, the hereditary rulers, lived atop Monk's Mound, which hosted religious ceremonies, burials grounds, and human sacrificial rituals. Beneath was Cahokia's forty-acre "Grand Plaza," the community's social and market center.[6]

Mississippian decline began before European arrival, and by 1400 the Cahokia site was abandoned. Crop blight appears to be a major cause of decline, and there were droughts resulting in famine. Disease may have been a factor. All this combined with fierce warfare between chiefdoms. However, the Midwest fostered new groups of Indigenous human occupants. Archeologists and anthropologists debate the extent to which modern Woodland Indians are direct descendants of Hopewellian and Mississippian people.[7] Shawnee, Cherokee, Miami, Fox, Sauk, Peoria,

Wabash, Piankashaw, and Kickapoo arose in the Midwest and carried on through the early modern era before the Indian Removal Act of 1830.

Where's Hennepin?

Explorers and Soldiers

The major French explorers of the Mississippi Valley—Marquette, Jolliet, and LaSalle—all traversed the great rivers of the American Midwest. In 1673, more than a century after Spain's Hernando de Soto crossed the Mississippi in the Old Southwest, Father Jacques Marquette and Louis Jolliet set out to find a direct trade route to Asia. Marquette and Jolliet, a Catholic priest and a cartographer/hydrographer turned frontier fur trader, mirror France's religious, scientific, and economic motivations for exploration. The two sailed a small party down the Wisconsin River to the Mississippi where, according to the nineteenth-century historian Francis Parkman, they met Indian people and saw "buffalo . . . grazing in herds on the great prairies which then bordered the river." They continued south to the mouth of the Arkansas River. At last accepting the fact that the Gulf of Mexico, not the Pacific Ocean, lay at the Mississippi's mouth, Marquette and Jolliet slowly worked their way upstream, this time ascending the Illinois River to Lake Michigan, ending a 2,500-mile adventure near modern-day Chicago.[8] A few years later, New France's government sent the savvy Indian trader René-Robert Cavelier, the Sieur de La Salle, to descend the Illinois River and the entire length of the lower Mississippi, which he claimed for Louis XIV in 1682.[9]

England followed, battling the French and their Indian allies in a series of "colonial wars," where the upper Ohio River, near Fort Pitt (Pittsburgh), was a site of much bloodshed. These wars began in the early 1700s and ended with British victory in 1763, a year that ushered in the early trans-Appalachian expeditions of Daniel Boone and East Coast conflicts leading directly to the American Revolutionary War. While Boone fought the British and their Shawnee allies south of the Ohio, Virginia militiaman George Rogers Clark attacked on the Wabash River and the Illinois side of the Mississippi. Clark won the battles of Kaskaskia and Vincennes, and the new United States of America took possession of the trans-Appalachian West east of the Mississippi and north of Spanish Natchez by virtue of the Treaty of Paris of 1783.[10]

American independence served to increase, not diminish, the military role of midwestern rivers. In 1803 U.S. Army captains Meriwether Lewis and William Clark (George Rogers Clark's younger brother) sailed down the Ohio and up the Mississippi to Wood River, Illinois, where they wintered on the American side of the Mississippi while the U.S. Senate finalized President Jefferson's Louisiana Purchase. In 1804 the Lewis and Clark Expedition ascended the Missouri River, exploring former Spanish and French territory and crossing the Rockies to the Columbia River and the Pacific Ocean. Meanwhile, Colonel Aaron Burr descended the Ohio River in 1805, stopping at Harman Blennerhassett's island residence for a cash infusion before sailing southward and hanging a sharp left at Cairo. Of course, the former vice president's military commission had been retired during the American Revolution, and he most certainly lacked President Jefferson's blessing on his expedition. Burr commanded about sixty men on a flotilla of gunboats (constructed at Andrew Jackson's Cumberland River boatyard) when he was arrested by federal marshals in Natchez, Mississippi, in 1807. No one is quite sure what Burr aimed to accomplish, though it probably entailed a scheme to take Texas from Spain. Charged with treason, Burr was acquitted; he lived three more decades, long enough to hear the news in 1836 that Sam Houston had carried out much of his dream.[11]

Meanwhile, midwestern rivers provided the stage for the final defeat and removal of Ohio Valley Indians. At the juncture of the Tippecanoe and Wabash Rivers in 1811, warrior followers of Tecumseh and his brother Tenskwatawa, the Shawnee Prophet, fell to the forces of William Henry Harrison.[12] Twenty years later, Chief Black Hawk's War was fought on the Upper Mississippi, along and around the shores of modern-day Illinois, Minnesota, Iowa, and Illinois.[13] The final military role for midwestern rivers began in the early phases of the U.S. Civil War. General Ulysses S. Grant (a native of the Ohio River town of Point Pleasant) left his Mississippi River home in Galena, Illinois, in 1861 to lead Union troops on a campaign to cut the Confederacy in two by way of the Mississippi River and its tributaries. Grant began in Cairo, Illinois, and eastern Missouri. Crossing the Ohio in 1862, he captured rebel forts near the mouths of the Tennessee and Cumberland Rivers and began his long, hard journey to Shiloh, Vicksburg, and Chattanooga on the lower Mississippi and Tennessee Rivers.[14]

Riverboating

The first midwestern boatmen were the Hopewellians, Mississippians, and their Woodland Indian successors, sailing canoes and mud-and-stick "bullboats" along midwestern rivers to trade, make war, and connect with neighboring bands. After the American Revolution, a host of rivermen from the new U.S. republic appeared on the scene as part of an emergent export economy and "Great Migration" into the trans-Appalachian West. For eighty years, midwestern riverboating evolved and progressed on the Ohio, upper Mississippi, and Missouri Rivers and their tributaries, from nonmotorized craft—keels, flats, and rafts—to steamboats.[15] Much later, twentieth-century river improvements and locks and dams fostered important diesel-powered towboat commerce on midwestern rivers.

Keelboats—"keels"—most closely resembled what modern Americans would call a large sailboat or very small schooner. Keels were sleek, prowed (not flat-bottomed) boats, averaging sixty feet in length and eight feet in width. Because they drew only one to two feet of water, loaded keels could run the Ohio, Upper Mississippi, and Missouri Rivers' most shallow ("shoal") currents. Unlike raftsmen and flatboatmen, keelboatmen possessed the equipment and skills to move their crafts upstream as well as down. Through skill and muscle, they somehow sailed, rowed, pulled, and poled their boats against strong currents before the invention of steamboats.[16]

The ubiquitous flatboats—"flats"—made up 90 percent of the antebellum midwestern riverboat fleet. Their low cost and relative ease of construction meant an amateur boat builder could, for about fifty dollars, fashion a flatboat out of timber he felled himself in the surrounding forest. Flatboats were boxlike craft averaging fifty feet in length and twelve feet in width. Unlike the sleek keels, flatboats were extremely difficult to navigate; boatmen steered with a long stern oar (a "sweep") and smaller oars on the port, starboard, and bow. Flatboats ran in high water (early spring and late fall) to avoid running aground. Like keelboatmen, flatboatmen faced bad weather, fog, shoals, boulders, and floating debris, especially uprooted trees. Because flatboats had no keel and could only float downstream, at journey's end they were broken up and sold for scrap lumber.[17]

Flatboat cargoes varied and included corn (loaded as meal or, more often, distilled liquor), hearty fruits and vegetables (apples, potatoes, onions, etc.), salted pork, animal skins and dried venison. Tar, turpentine, saltpeter, tallow, beeswax, and hemp all floated downstream. Sometimes livestock was loaded and shipped on the hoof, and chickens sailed in crates. Although human chattel sailed as slave cargo on the lower Mississippi, there was little such trade on midwestern rivers above their confluence with the Ohio or, with the exception of Missouri, the Upper Mississippi. Interestingly, flatboats endured decades after the 1811 introduction of the steamboat to western rivers. Why? The steamboat offered flatboatmen a cheap ride home! Because of steamers, flatboatmen became commuters, keeping the cost-effective flatboat trade alive and well until railroads superseded all river craft. In the late nineteenth century, flatboats became the prototypes of modern steel river barges.[18]

Log and lumber rafts made up the third group of nonmotorized, midwestern river craft. Throughout the upper Ohio and upper Mississippi valleys, raftsmen moved newly cut timber to downstream sawmills; after the logs were milled, they often rafted the finished lumber to downstream markets. Raftsmen flourished in locales ranging from western Pennsylvania's Appalachians to Wisconsin's north woods. Rafts were large rectangular affairs, often three hundred feet long and composed of as many as two thousand logs. Raftsmen built their rafts—sometimes called "drifts"—in a manner similar to a modern barge tow. They first constructed a number of small rafts—"stringers," or "blocks"—and then pieced them together into the large navigable unit. To secure the logs, they strapped and pegged them together with hickory or other deciduous saplings and strips ("whaling"); some hardwoods required metal "chain dogs" instead of wooden pegs. Raftsmen formed the blocks into the larger raft using the same techniques. Although there was sometimes "smooth sailing" in high water, hazards and dangers always lay in wait. Raftsmen faced freezing rain, sleet and snow, fog, submerged sandbars, or shoals, boulders, and floating debris.[19]

Upper Mississippi and Wisconsin River rafting flourished during the rise of Nauvoo, the Mormon river city in western Illinois. In 1841–42, a company of Latter Day Saints logged and milled timber at a "pinery" on Winnebago Indian land abutting Wisconsin's Black River. On October 13, 1842, the Mormon prophet Joseph Smith Jr. wrote, "The brethren arrived from Wisconsin with a raft of about 90,000 feet of boards and 24,000 cubic feet of timber for the Temple and Nauvoo House." Soon a new logging crew departed to harvest, mill, and plane an 1843 crop.[20]

The average midwestern boatman or raftsman (nonsteam) was a white male of Anglo or Celtic ancestry, averaging twenty-eight years of age. While Indian, black, German, and French rivermen sailed the Mississippi on nonsteam craft, they were exceptions that proved the above rule. Women sailed and worked in significant numbers aboard family emigrant flatboats, not commercial craft. One can further divide the demographic group into four major professional categories—merchant navigators, professional boatmen, farmer flatboatmen, and common hands.[21] The most famous midwestern flatboatman was young Abraham Lincoln. Lincoln worked as an Ohio River ferryman and woodboatman, and in 1828 and 1831 he made flatboat trips to New Orleans, "getting the timber out of the trees and building a boat at Old Sangamon town the Sangamon River."[22]

Most nineteenth-century midwestern steamboats were workboats that did not sport the ornamental decorations, ballrooms, state rooms, and other luxurious amenities sometimes associated with the golden age of steam. Steamboats were mostly small (three hundred tons) sternwheelers, with shallow (two to three feet) drafts suitable for navigating low water depths. Powerful boilers made these sleek craft fast, dexterous, and dangerous. A steamer's average lifespan was five years. Unlike nonsteam craft, steamboats employed black freedmen. Boats carried ten-to-twelve-man crews, including a captain, pilot, engineer, mate, and deckhands. Women first entered the boating profession as cooks and maids aboard larger steamers. Upper Mississippi, Ohio, and Missouri steamboats ran whenever they could, but peak shipping was the same as for flats, keels, and rafts—the high water of late fall and early spring. Steamboatmen also faced dangers from fog and freezing temperatures, and from floating and sunken logs, cave-in banks, and shoals. During the antebellum years, an annual average of 365 steamboats worked the upper Mississippi River and its tributaries.[23]

By the mid-1820s, nationalists in the emergent Whig Party were advocating federal subsidies to make the western rivers more easily navigable. Congress created the "Army Engineers" (today's Army Corps of Engineers) to alleviate some of the worst river hazards through federally subsidized "internal improvements." For example, a young army lieutenant named Robert E. Lee blasted and drilled upper Mississippi rock beds to improve passage for steamboats near Keokuk, Iowa. But Lee's work was cut short, and one local complained in 1845 that it was "impossible to pass the [lower] rapids so long as the surface was ruffled by the wind, interfering with the Pilot's ability to watch for snags and rocks." True progress would come only in the postbellum period when the Corps blasted, dredged, and built enough wing dams to tame the infamous "Rock Island" and Keokuk stretches of the upper Mississippi.[24] Thus the stage was set for twentieth-century innovations and improvements such as locks and dams as midwestern steamboats gave way to modern diesel towboat commerce.

As the railroads slowly drew commerce away from the river towns, nostalgia set in, and rivermen rose to mythic proportions in the midwestern imagination. Stories of the historic Pittsburgh keelboatman Mike Fink, "King of the River," circulated in the popular press and almanacs. The public loved to read about Mike's adventures plying the Ohio and mighty Mississippi, fighting Indians, playing tricks on landsmen, and sharpshooting whisky cups off his fellow boatmens' heads! There was a dark side to Mike Fink's stories, which mirrors the violent and intolerant society that worshipped him, Davy Crockett, and other "half horse, half alligator" frontier folk heroes. Mike loved a good fight, always prefaced by a speech in which he announced his prowess: "I'm a land-screamer— I'm a water dog—I'm a snapping tur[t]le—I can lick five times my own weight in wild-cats." Later, Missourian Mark Twain lionized the Mississippi steamboatmen in *Life on the Mississippi* and wrote about the

"majestic, magnificent Mississippi" and memories of the daily com-
motion, the cry "S-t-e-a-m-boat a-comin'!" in his hometown of Hannibal, Missouri.[25]

Race, Politics, and the Environment

The Ohio, upper Mississippi, and Missouri Rivers and their tributaries played a major role in antebellum debates over slavery. In 1787 the
Confederation Congress designated the Ohio River as the dividing line
between the free territory of the Old Northwest and the Old Southwest,
outlawing slavery above the Ohio. After the Missouri Compromise, the
Mississippi River divided free Illinois from slaveholding Missouri, and
Missouri's northwestern Missouri River border did the same with Kansas
and Nebraska until 1854. While slaves were sold south in boats traversing
the Ohio and Mississippi Rivers bordering Kentucky and eastern Missouri, the famed Underground Railroad for escaping slaves pivoted on
passage north across the Ohio River. Indeed, two of the most memorable scenes in American literature are the slave woman Eliza's escape to
freedom via the frozen Ohio River in *Uncle Tom's Cabin*, and Huck and
Jim's raft journey to Cairo in *The Adventures of Huckleberry Finn*. An even
more gripping event actually happened in the Mississippi River town of
Alton, Illinois, where in 1837 an angry proslavery mob murdered abolitionist Elijah P. Lovejoy. Scottish immigrant Frances ("Fanny") Wright
expressed her radical antislavery and feminist beliefs in newspapers and
magazines she published astride the Wabash River in New Harmony,
Indiana, and along the Ohio River in Cincinnati, Ohio.[26]

From the 1820s to the modern day, politicians have identified with
midwestern rivers in their campaign autobiographies and platforms.
While Democrats boasted Nashville keelboat entrepreneur President
Andrew Jackson, Whigs countered with Henry Clay ("Harry of the
West"), who first migrated to Kentucky on an Ohio River flatboat. Clay
was joined by Davy Crockett, William Henry Harrison, the hero of
Tippecanoe, and, of course, Abraham Lincoln. It is interesting to note
that at least a dozen delegates to the 1850–51 Indiana Constitutional
Convention were former flatboatmen, and Whigs strongly advocated
Clay's "American System" and federally subsidized river improvements.

After the Whigs were replaced by the modern-day Republican Party, in 1854, Abraham Lincoln continued to call for internal improvements, including a transcontinental railroad. As the Republicans' 1860 Republican presidential candidate, Lincoln referred to his pioneer riverboating credentials, declaring, "I am not ashamed to confess that twenty-five years ago I was a hired laborer, mauling rails, at work on a flatboat—just what might happen to any poor man's son." Eight years later, Ulysses S. Grant received news of his election to the presidency at his Galena Upper Mississippi home.[27]

In 1884, eight years after Grant left the White House, Harry S. Truman was born near Independence, Missouri. Truman stands alongside Ronald Reagan, two twentieth-century U.S. presidents most influenced by midwestern rivers. Before he entered politics, Truman spent eleven years working his family's farm near Grandview, Missouri, growing corn, wheat, hay, oats, clover hay and horses, cattle, and hogs in the rich bottomland of the lower Missouri River valley. He later remembered their Grandview farm was the "finest land you'd ever find anywhere . . . I was very much interested in the creation of things that come from the ground." At work in the natural world, "farmers really all have time to think," Truman recalled, noting it was farmers who "have made it possible for us to have free government. That's what Jefferson was writing about."[28]

Ronald Reagan's midwestern roots and influences far outweighed those of his later Hollywood years and California lifestyle.[29] Born in 1911 in the pork and corn country of northern Illinois, Reagan spent six summers of his teenage and young adult life as a lifeguard on Illinois's Rock River, which flowed past his hometown of Dixon. "We just all remember him as Lifeguard," a Dixon woman recalled sixty years later. There is a striking photograph of Ronald Reagan in his lifeguard swimsuit, and there are many tales about the number of lives he saved from the swift Rock River current. Reagan supposedly cut notches in a beach log every time he rescued someone, and there were reportedly seventy-seven notches. This story (which is reminiscent of folktales about Daniel Boone carving his name on a tree at sites where he killed black bears), adds to Reagan's mystique as a true son of the American

Midwest. "I think the Rock River was the central symbol of his youth," states Ronald Reagan biographer Edmund Morris.[30]

Ironically, Henry Clay's American System and the Army Corps of Engineers ultimately fueled as many debates in the twentieth and twenty-first centuries as in the nineteenth. This began with the great flood of 1927, which led to Franklin D. Roosevelt's New Deal programs (most importantly the Tennessee Valley Authority) to control flooding while simultaneously generating electricity, fostering industrial development, and providing recreational opportunities in new lakes behind dammed rivers.[31] In less than forty years, however, a reaction set in from environmentalists expressing concern for midwestern river ecosystems. The Ohio, Upper Mississippi, Missouri, and their tributaries all fueled controversy as politicians debated the harm to plants and fish and humans of internal improvements. Environmentalists sharply criticized industrial pollution, flood control, locks and dams, and the environmental consequences of infrastructure, manufacturing, and transportation along the Ohio, Upper Mississippi, and Missouri Rivers and their tributaries.[32]

Arts, Movies, and Music

Finally, midwestern rivers have strongly influenced art and popular culture in works of literature, painting, movies, and music. While we rightly single out Mark Twain as the greatest Mississippi River author, in fact he learned his art from the antebellum newspaper and almanac authors of stories about Big Mike Fink and other alligator-horse folk heroes. In late nineteenth-century St. Louis, John Henton Carter became a popular Mississippi Valley newspaperman and novelist who adopted the pseudonym "Commodore Rollingpin," based on his experiences as a steamboat cook and steward. Carter published nine volumes of prose and poetry and hundreds of newspaper and magazine articles, including *Thomas Rutherton*, a novel about a young boy's first flatboat trip down the Ohio and Mississippi to New Orleans. Carter was writing at the same time as the "rural realist" writers emerged throughout the Midwest. Although the rural realists often painted a dark picture of the difficulties of farm and small-town living, their books also showed a love of the natural world and folk culture of the midwestern heartland. Rivers and river valley life were an essential component of rural realist portrayals, exemplified in the short stories of Hamlin Garland's *Main-Traveled Roads: Stories of the Mississippi Valley* (1891), Willa Cather's novels *O Pioneers!* (1913) and *My Ántonia* (1917), and the poems of Edgar Lee Masters's evocative *Spoon River Anthology* (1915).[33]

The midwestern rivers also adorned important American painting subgenres. Nineteenth-century landscape painters, including Hudson River School artists, turned their eyes westward to the upper Mississippi Valley and a new "local color" genre arose, depicting common midwestern folk in natural settings. From 1845 to 1855, George Caleb Bingham created his beloved river series, including *Western Boatmen Ashore* (1838), *Boatmen on the Missouri* (1846), *The Jolly Flatboatmen* (1846, 1848, 1857, 1878), *Raftsmen Playing Cards* (1847), *The Wood Boat* (1850), and *Mississippi Boatman* (1850), all featuring direct or reflected light ("luminism") on water, sky, and human characters.[34]

In the early twentieth century, Bingham was succeeded by Neosho, Missouri, painter Thomas Hart Benton (a great-nephew of the famed Jacksonian Senator), who painted large storytelling murals that combined elements of high and folk art to an end soon dubbed "regionalism." Benton's most stunning murals are *America Today* (1931), *The Arts of Life in America* (1932), *A Social History of Indiana* (1933), *A Social History of the State of Missouri* (1936), *Independence and the Opening of the West* (1962), and *The Sources of Country Music* (1975). Mural viewers are bathed in Benton's colorful images of steamboatmen, fiddlers, gospel musicians and female jazz singers, Huck Finn and Jim, Jesse James, midwestern farmers, and river-town folk. Then, too, there are depictions of slavery, lynching, Depression-era poverty, labor strife, the Ku Klux Klan, and the tragic black lovers Frankie and Johnny. Benton was joined, and influenced by, fellow midwestern painters Grant Wood (Iowa) and John Steuart Curry (Kansas), co-founders of the Prairie School of American regionalist art.[35]

Musical moviemakers painted a more idealized picture of the Midwest and its river towns in the classics *Meet Me in St. Louis* (1944), *State Fair* (1945), *The Pajama Game* (1957), and *The Music Man* (1962). Set on the eve of the 1904 St. Louis World's Fair, *Meet Me in St. Louis* stars Judy Garland and her castmates literally singing the praises of their midwestern river town (in comparison to New York City). *State Fair*, the first of three movies that might be called the "Iowa Musicals," portrays the annual Iowa State Fair as a spectacle as grand as that in St. Louis. Here, the Frake family follows the Des Moines River valley road through Ottumwa, Oskaloosa, and Pella, bound to enter their prize pig Blue Boy (and Ma's mincemeat) at the Iowa State Fair. *State Fair* celebrates American heartland values in the song "All I Owe Ioway." As one Iowan sings that he is planning to move to California, the chorus responds, "What a shame! . . . When you leave your native state / you'll be feeling far from great! / You'll be good and gosh-darn sorry when you go!"[36]

Dubuque, Iowa, on the upper Mississippi, is the setting for the movie musical *The Pajama Game*, based on *7½ Cents*, Richard Bissell's humorous 1953 novel about a labor dispute. A Dubuque native, Bissell worked in his father's clothing factory (which made pajamas) before shipping as a 1940s towboat pilot on the upper Mississippi, Ohio, and Illinois Rivers (Bissell also authored two towboat novels and an excellent 1973 river autobiography, *My Life on the Mississippi, or Why I Am Not Mark Twain*). The most famous of Iowa musicals, however, is *The Music Man*, a Broadway hit, with songs by Iowan Meredith Willson, made into a Hollywood movie five years after *The Pajama Game*. In this movie, a spellbinding con man named Professor Harold Hill (played by Robert Preston) arrives in the fictitious town of River City, Iowa, to start the "River City Boys Band." In the end, he is saved by love (Shirley Jones) and midwestern values, and comes to believe in his own dreams. The movie's finale is a marching band parading down River City's Main Street playing "Seventy-Six Trombones."[37]

Traditional New Orleans Jazz—"Dixieland Jazz"—came up the Mississippi to the Midwest via steamboat and especially the work of trumpeter Louis Armstrong, who was employed by St. Louis's famed Streckfus Steamboat Lines. Armstrong played Davenport, Iowa (where aspiring trumpeter Bix Beiderbecke listened in awe), and soon left the river to play in Chicago jazz clubs. Meanwhile, the Delta Blues migrated north by way of the Mississippi River, Illinois Central Railroad, and Highway

61, the "Great River Road" paralleling the Mississippi from New Orleans to the Twin Cities. All this music ascended the Missouri, and 1920s and '30s Kansas City witnessed the rise of a blues-driven subgenre—"Kansas City Jazz"—that took form in the work of Count Basie's big band and many other musicians. When, in the early 1950s, rock-and-roll music arose in the Mississippi Valley, St. Louis played an important supporting role by way of a young guitarist, singer, and composer named Chuck Berry. Berry fashioned rock-and-roll riffs and songs from a St. Louis musical childhood that he recalled was replete with blues, big band jazz, hillbilly music, and "pure harmonies of the Baptist hymns . . . blending with the stirring rhythms of true Baptist soul . . . Hallelujah!"[38]

Midwesterners also loved country music, and tens of thousands weekly tuned in to the Grand Ole Opry via the far-reaching radio waves of station WSM in Nashville. Young Garrison Keillor, born in 1942 in the upper Mississippi River town of Anoka, Minnesota, loved the Opry so much that he eventually created his own successful weekly musical radio show, *A Prairie Home Companion*. In St. Louis, John Hartford worked as a deckhand and pilot on Ohio and Illinois River towboats at the same time he was recording songs about diesel towboatmen, playing the bluegrass banjo, and helping to fashion a country music subgenre called "newgrass." On his Grammy-winning album *Mark Twang*, John Hartford invoked images of Illinois River towboatmen "makin' up barges, on a long hot summer's day."[39]

Another midwesterner, Bobby Zimmerman, listened to the Opry, blues, jazz, gospel, and rock and roll on his radio and phonograph in his Hibbing, Minnesota, home and dreamed of traveling down the Great River Road, Highway 61. As a young man, he left Minnesota, changed his name to Bob Dylan, and recorded folk music and an album entitled *Highway 61 Revisited* (1965). "Highway 61, the main thoroughfare of the country blues, begins about where I came from," Dylan later wrote, adding, "The Mississippi River, the bloodstream of the blues, also starts from up in my neck of the woods." Bob Dylan's reflections on the Mississippi River might be applied to many midwesterners and their rivers: "I was never too far away from any of it. It was my place in the universe, always felt it was in my blood."[40]

Notes

1. Frederick Jackson Turner, "The Significance of the Frontier in American History," in *Frontiers of Western History: The Origins, Evolution, and Future of the Study of Western History*, 2nd rev. ed., ed. Michael Allen and Mary L. Hanneman (Boston: Simon and Schuster, 2007), 42.

2. The major works are Richard C. Wade, *The Urban Frontier: Pioneer Life in Early Pittsburgh, Cincinnati, Lexington, Louisville, and St. Louis* (1959; repr., Chicago: University of Chicago Press, 1964); Timothy R. Mahoney, *River Towns in the Great West: The Structure of Provincial Urbanization in the American Midwest, 1820–1870* (Cambridge UK: Cambridge University Press, 1990); William Cronon, *Nature's Metropolis: Chicago and the Great West* (New York: W. W. Norton, 1991).

3. Brian M. Fagan, *The Great Journey: The Peopling of Ancient America* (London: Thames and Hudson, 1987), 242–48.

4. Fagan, *Great Journey*, 243; Jeffrey J. Jordan, "Aboriginal Cultures and Landscapes," in *A Geography of Ohio*, ed. Leonard Peacefull (Kent OH: Kent State University Press, 1996), 71.

5. Brian Fagan, *Ancient North America: The Archeology of a Continent* (1991; rev. ed., London: Thames and Hudson, 1995), 427–37; Fagan, *Great Journey*, 195–96, 241–42.

6. Timothy R. Pauketat, *Ancient Cahokia and the Mississippians* (Cambridge: Cambridge University Press, 2004) 67–95; "Cahokian Mounds" (October 2010), booklet, Cahokia Mounds State Historic Site, Collinsville IL, 6, 9, 13, 16–19; George R. Milner, *The Moundbuilders: Ancient Peoples of Eastern North America* (London: Thames and Hudson, 2004), 124–25, 132–36.

7. Fagan, *Ancient North America*, 450–52, 482–84; Pauketat, *Ancient Cahokia and the Mississippians*, 144, 157–59.

8. Francis Parkman, *The Discovery of the Great West: La Salle*, ed. William R. Taylor (1869; repr., New York: Little, Brown, 1956), 45–46, 50, 51–60; W. J. Eccles, *The Canadian Frontier, 1534–1760* (1969; rev. ed., Albuquerque: University of New Mexico Press, 1983), 103–7.

9. Eccles, *Canadian Frontier*, 105–7; Robert V. Hine and John Mack Faragher, *The American West: A New Interpretive History* (New Haven CT: Yale University Press, 2000), 47–48.

10. Hine and Faragher, *American West*, 80–87; John Mack Faragher, *Daniel Boone: The Life and Legend of an American Pioneer* (New York: Henry Holt, 1992), 35–37.

11. Marshall Smelser, *The Democratic Republic, 1801–1815* (New York: Waveland Press, 1968), 112–17 is an excellent overview.

12. R. David Edmunds, *The Shawnee Prophet* (Lincoln: University of Nebraska Press, 1983), 48–49, 72; Francis Paul Prucha, *The Great White Father: The United States Government and the American Indians* (Lincoln: University of Nebraska Press, 1984), 76–78.

13. Prucha, *Great White Father*, 253–58.

14. Ulysses S. Grant, *Personal Memoirs of U. S. Grant*, 2 vols. (1885–86; repr., New York: Tab Books, 1990), 1:174–88.

15. Michael Allen, *Western Rivermen, 1763–1861: Ohio and Mississippi Boatmen and the Myth of the Alligator Horse* (Baton Rouge: Louisiana State University Press, 1990), 58–63, 144–45.

16. Leland D. Baldwin, *The Keelboat Age on Western Waters* (Pittsburgh: University of Pittsburgh Press, 1941); Allen, *Western Rivermen*, 69–72.

17. Allen, *Western Rivermen*, 67–69.

18. Allen, *Western Rivermen*, 63–64, 145.

19. Gustave Giese, "The Rafting and Running of Lumber Down the Wisconsin and Mississippi Rivers to Southern Lumber Markets in Bygone Days" (typescript in the State Historical Society of Madison WI); George B. Engberg, "Who Were the Lumberjacks?" in *The Old Northwest: Studies in Regional History, 1787–1910*, ed. Harry N. Scheiber (Lincoln: University of Nebraska Press, 1969), 270–79; Allen, *Western Rivermen*, 155–56.

20. Joseph Smith, *History of the Church*, vol. 4 (Salt Lake City: University of Utah Press, 1956), 608–9; Smith, *History of the Church*, vol. 5, 169–70; Dennis Rowley, "The Mormon Experience in the Wisconsin Pineries, 1841–45," *BYU Studies* 32, no. 1 (1991): 1–25.

21. Michael Allen, "The Riverman as Jacksonian Man," *Western Historical Quarterly* 21 (August 1990): 305–20; Harry N. Scheiber, "The Ohio-Mississippi Flatboat Trade: Some Reconsiderations," in *The Frontier in American Development: Essays in Honor of Paul Wallace Gates*, ed. David M. Ellis (Ithaca NY: Cornell University Press, 1970), 277–98.

22. Abraham Lincoln, "New Haven Speech (1860)," in *Complete Works of Abraham Lincoln*, 12 vols., ed. John G. Nicolay and John Hay (New York, 1905), 5:361; Benjamin P. Thomas, *Abraham Lincoln: A Biography* (New York: Knopf, 1967), 16–18, 23–24.

23. Louis C. Hunter, *Steamboats on Western Rivers: An Economic and Technological History* (Cambridge MA: Harvard University Press, 1949) and Eric F. Haites, James Make, and Gary M. Walton, *Western River Transportation* (Baltimore MD: Johns Hopkins University Press, 1975), passim.

24. Haites, Make, and Walton, *Western River Transportation*; Isaac Lippincott, "A History of River Improvement," *Journal of Political Economy* 22 (July 1914): 640.

25. Allen, *Western Rivermen*, 12. Quotes from Emerson Bennett, *Mike Fink: Legend of the Ohio* (1852; repr., Upper Saddle River NJ: Prentice Hall, 1970), 28, and Mark Twain, *Life on the Mississippi*, Justin Kaplan, ed. (1883; repr., New York: Signet, 2001), 26.

26. James M. McPherson, *Ordeal by Fire: The Civil War and Reconstruction* (New York: Knopf, 1982), 2, 52, 58, 106; James Brewer Stewart, *Holy Warriors: The Abolitionists and American Slavery* (New York: Farrar Straus and Giroux, 1976), 75–77, 160–62.

27. Allen, *Western Rivermen*, 171; Lincoln, "New Haven Speech (1860)," *Complete Works*, 5:361; Thomas, *Abraham Lincoln*, 16–18, 23–24.

28. Alonzo L. Hamby, *Man of the People: A Life of Harry S. Truman* (New York: Oxford University Press, 1995), 3–24; Harry S. Truman and Merle Miller, *Plain Speaking: An Oral Biography of Harry S. Truman* (New York: Berkeley Publishing, 1973), 89–90.

29. "Author Peter Hannaford Reflects on Reagan's Early Years," *Libertas* 33 (Summer 2012): 5. See also Peter Hannaford, *Reagan's Roots: The Peoples and Places That Shaped His Character* (Bennington VT: Images from the Past, 2011).

30. Paul Kengor, "A River and a Church: The Making of a Leader," *Libertas* 32 (Spring 2011): 16–23; Lou Cannon, *President Reagan: The Role of a Lifetime* (New York: PublicAffairs, 1991), 180–82. Morris quote from Adriana Bosch, *Reagan*, 2 vols. (Boston, 1998), DVD, vol. 1.

31. Army Corps of Engineers, *History of Navigation in the Ohio River Basin* (Washington DC, 1983), 35–44.

32. Christopher Morris, *The Big Muddy: An Environmental History of the Mississippi and its Peoples from de Soto to Katrina* (New York: Oxford University Press, 2012).

33. Ruth Ferris, "John Henton Carter," unpublished essay, Ruth Ferris Collection, St. Louis Mercantile Library, box 19; John T. Flanagan, "John Henton Carter, alias Commodore Rollingpin," *Missouri Historical Review* 63, no. 1 (1968): 38–54; Hamlin Garland, *Main Traveled Roads: Stories of the Mississippi Valley* (1891; repr., New York: Kessinger, 1962); Edgar Lee Masters, *Spoon River Anthology* (1962; repr., New York: Collier Macmillan, 1962).

34. "The American Cousin," in Joshua C. Taylor, *America as Art* (Washington DC: National Collection of Fine Arts/Smithsonian Institution Press, 1976), 37–95; John Francis McDermott, "Jolly Flatboatmen: Bingham and his Imitators," *Antiques* 73, no. 3 (March, 1958): 267–69; E. Maurice Bloch, *George Caleb Bingham: The Evolution of an Artist* (Berkeley: University of California Press, 1967), 5–7. Some of the best reproductions of Bingham's

river series appear in Albert Christ-Janier, *George Caleb Bingham: Frontier Painter of Missouri* (New York: Harry N. Abrams, 1975).

35. Henry Adams, *Thomas Hart Benton: An American Original* (New York: Knopf, 1989) is the best overview. There are good reproductions of the mural sections in Adams and Matthew Baigell, *Thomas Hart Benton* (New York: Harry N. Abrams 1973), 111–35. See James M. Dennis, *Renegade Regionalists: The Modern Independence of Grant Wood, Thomas Hart Benton, and John Steuart Curry* (Madison: University of Wisconsin Press, 1998).

36. Phil Stong, *State Fair* (1932; repr., New York: Literary Guild/Century, 1950); *State Fair* (1945; repr., 2006), DVD, no. TCFHE, liner notes, and special features.

37. Richard Bissell, *7½ Cents* (Boston: Little, Brown, 1953); *The Pajama Game* (1957; repr., 2005), DVD, 70599; Richard Bissell, *My Life on the Mississippi, or Why I Am Not Mark Twain* (Boston: Little, Brown, 1973); Richard Bissell Induction File, National Rivers Hall of Fame, Dubuque IA; *The Music Man* (1962), DVD.

38. Joseph Streckfus Memoir, Streckfus Collection, Herman T. Pott Library and St. Louis Mercantile Library, University of Missouri, St. Louis, February 18, 1958, February 20, 1958; Chuck Berry, *Chuck Berry: The Autobiography* (New York: Harmony Books, 1987), 2. See Ross Russell, *Jazz Style in Kansas City and the Southwest* (Berkeley CA: University of California Press, 1971) and Nathan W. Pearson Jr., *Goin' to Kansas City* (Urbana: University of Illinois Press, 1987).

39. Garrison Keillor, "Onward and Upward with the Arts: At the Opry," *New Yorker*, May 6, 1974, 64; "20 Questions with Garrison Keillor," Country Music Television News, accessed May 17, 2015, http://www.cmt.com/news/1535357/20-questions-with-garrison-keillor/; John Hartford Induction File, National Rivers Hall of Fame, National Rivers Museum, Dubuque IA; John Hartford, *Mark Twang*, Flying Fish Record No.020, (Chicago, 1976), LP record.

40. Bob Dylan, *Chronicles: Volume One* (New York: Simon and Schuster, 2004), 240–41. See David Pichaske, *Song of the North Country: A Midwest Framework to the Songs of Bob Dylan* (New York: Bloomsbury Academic, 2010).

12

The Midwest's Spiritual Landscapes

Jon Butler

Lake Wobegon, Pastor Ingqvist, Our Lady of Perpetual Responsibility? Garrison Keillor has so successfully established Lake Wobegon as the epitome of midwestern religion and culture that it seems only academic to suggest that, maybe, there's more to the story. As Keillor's Catholics and Protestants head for church suppers and lime Jell-O salad, what does their religion really tell us?

Fiction establishes all but indelible cultural images. Nathaniel Hawthorne's *The Scarlet Letter*, Flannery O'Connor's *The Violent Bear It Away*, and Larry McMurtry's *Lonesome Dove* long have shaped the way we think about colonial New England, the modern South, and the late nineteenth-century West. But their models are far from simple, and Keillor has hinted at uneasy complexities in Lake Wobegon. He does not think that he said very much good about Pastor Ingqvist, has called Father Emil and Father Wilmer "stuffed shirts," and suggests amiable yet persistent Protestant-Catholic tensions in Lake Wobegon.[1]

If Lake Wobegon's winsome charm introduces readers to small-town midwestern religion, bumps and all, it probably obscures another fact: the Midwest was and still may be America's most religiously complex region. The argument admittedly is impossible to quantify. Still, from the time of the mysterious Cahokia settlement, past the nineteenth century, and up to the twenty-first, the numbers and varieties of religious expression and practice between Ohio and Nebraska and the Canadian border and Oklahoma defy the popular image of the Midwest as a pleasant Protestant blob with some Catholics and Jews thrown into the mix.

The real Midwest may not have been the Tower of Babel, but it comes close, with exuberant complications and bitter tensions. Even scratching out a few produces a very long sentence: multiple and not always compatible American Indian religious practices prior to European conquest; religious struggles between Indians and Christian missionaries after Europeans arrived; ethnically distinct Catholic worship; urban and small-town Jewish communities; anti-Catholicism and antisemitism; African Americans in multiple denominations and storefront churches; Christian-fueled racism; Adventists; the Church of God of Anderson, Indiana; the Westboro Baptist Church; Greek, Russian, and, recently, Eritrean Orthodox Christianies; Amish; Mennonites; the Nation of Islam; Bahá'í; spiritualists; Sunni and Shia Muslims; Sikhs (who attract little attention except from a murdering Wisconsin gunman intent on his own "racial holy war"); the quasi-communitarian settlement of Zion, Illinois, led by Scottish evangelical faith healer John Alexander Dowie; Chicago's Guy Ballard and his "I AM" movement, whose Saint Germaine Foundation is now headquartered in Schaumburg, Illinois; and the large Vietnamese, Hmong, and Somali communities that have transformed the urban Midwest culturally, visually, and religiously, much as Europeans did in the eighteenth and nineteenth century.[2]

Whither Lake Wobegon?

Linda Clemmons's lovely 2014 book, *Conflicted Mission: Faith, Disputes, and Deception on the Dakota Frontier*, approaches questions about religion and religions in exceptionally useful ways. A study of missionaries sponsored by the American Board of Commissioners for Foreign Missions between the 1830s and the 1862 Dakota War, *Conflicted Mission* reminds us of the radical transformations Europeans and Americans brought to the Midwest, the conflicts and the resolutions raised by those transformations, the importance of understanding individual motivations in all believers, the complicated importance of institutions, and government's role in shaping religion beyond the First Amendment's simple demands: "Congress shall make no law respecting an establishment of religion, or prohibiting the free exercise thereof."[3]

Conflicted Mission cannot comprehend all the Midwest's spiritual landscapes, and its focus on Indian missions may lead some historians to see it as narrowly tied to a history swamped by a rising agricultural and urban Midwest. But it may be a better guide than traditional linear approaches to religion in a vigorously heterogeneous region far from the powerful if conflicting images cast by Sinclair Lewis or Garrison Keillor.

Most importantly, *Conflicted Mission* describes a half-century of mixed motivations and complex behaviors everywhere easily seen in the violent 1862 Dakota War, with its several thousand American, European, and Indian casualties, the imprisonment of the surrendered Dakotas, the hanging of thirty-eight Indians for treason in Mankato, Minnesota, in 1862—the largest mass execution in American history—and the Dakotas' removal from Minnesota to what would become South Dakota and Nebraska. The missionaries eagerly told sponsors how the captured Dakotas sang Christian hymns as they left Fort Snelling a year later. But Clemmons explains that the singing was as much coerced as spontaneous and was "neither the unambiguously glorious future that the missionaries had envisioned when they first arrived in Minnesota in 1835, nor the image of hope and salvation that they promoted to the evangelical public in 1863."[4]

If exceptional religious diversity disfigured and enlivened the Midwest, this could occur because religion was and remained important. The Midwest took no back seat to New England, the South, and the West for spiritually stiff-necked demands. The 1862 Dakota War, for example, emerged from Indian resentment against conquest and missionaries and European and American convictions that pagan Indians deserved no "civilized" privileges. Seven years later President Ulysses S. Grant's euphemistically named 1869 "Peace Plan" assigned Indian reservations exclusively to Protestant and Catholic missionaries and banned traditional Indian religious practice, a ban in place until 1934. Reservations in Michigan, Wisconsin, Minnesota, Iowa, the Dakota territories, Nebraska, and Kansas, were assigned to Catholic, Congregational, Episcopal, and Hicksite and Orthodox Quaker missionaries, with one, in Iowa, assigned to Lutherans. The reservation system was not innocuous, and it created decades-long tensions between traditional Indian religious practices and the missionaries' Christianities. Hymn singing became a subtle yet persistent battleground for Ojibwe "religious sovereignty," for example—a small representation of the tensions between Christianity and traditional Ojibwe practice that underlie contemporary Midwestern Indian life and form central dilemmas in much contemporary Indian writing, such as Louise Erdrich's 1984 novel *Love Medicine*.[5]

Anti-Catholicism may first have been expressed along the Eastern Seaboard, but midwestern Protestants ran with it in the 1880s. The nativist American Protective Association emerged from a meeting in Clinton, Iowa, in 1887, and by the early 1890s shaped elections through supporters who disparaged the pope and Catholic Civil War veterans accused of desertion. In the 1920s a revived Ku Klux Klan attacked Catholics and Catholic institutions, including schools, supported a flagging Prohibition, and promoted winning Protestants for Indiana secretary of state, governor, U.S. Senate, and many members of the Indiana legislature, its demise stemming more obviously from its Grand Dragon's rape and murder convictions than a decline in anti-Catholic sentiment. In the same decades novelist Ole Rølvaag treated Catholic-Protestant tensions as progressively central to his powerful trilogy depicting the Norwegian immigrant experience, beginning with distrust between Norwegian and Irish settlers in *Giants in the Earth* and ending with the bitter collapse of Peder Holm's and Susie Doheny's mixed marriage in Rølvaag's third and final volume, *Their Father's God*.[6]

Journalist Carey McWilliams may have exaggerated when he tagged Minneapolis in 1946 as the "capital of anti-Semitism in the United States," but the Scandinavian city was antisemitic enough. Rev. William Bell Riley raged from the pulpit of Minneapolis's First Baptist Church against communists, booze, Catholics, and Darwin, but especially against Jews, stressing "the Jews' present position as rejectors of Christ and the eventual tools of the anti-Christ." Rev. George Mecklenburg of Minneapolis's Wesley Methodist Church criticized Jews and Jewish lobbyists in a radio talk on "Who Runs Minneapolis," Rev. Luke Rader regularly denounced Jews at Minneapolis's River Lake Gospel Tabernacle, and a 1938 political cartoon, "The Three Jehu Drivers," lampooned Farmer-Labor governor Elmer Benson as the dupe of prominent Minnesota Jews and graphically conveyed the antisemitism that stimulated widespread religious, employment, housing, and social discrimination against Jews in Minneapolis.[7]

THE "THREE JEHU DRIVERS"

Prepared and issued by R. J. Lloyd, 2728 Emerson Ave. So., Minneapolis, Minn., in behalf of better government.

Fig. 6. Cartoon "Three Jehu Drivers," 1938, Box 41, Jewish Community Relations Council of Minnesota Papers, Minnesota Historical Society. Courtesy of Minnesota Historical Society.

The prejudices lingered. Anti-Catholic sentiment filled a hand-typed letter sent to a rural Minnesota Democrat a week before the November 8, 1960, presidential election, warning that a victory for the Catholic John F. Kennedy would be "a defeat worse than that of open warfare" and enclosing anti-Catholic pamphlets from Minneapolis's Osterhuis Publishing Company (one thousand for $1.50), and Chicago's Good News Publishers (more expensive, five hundred for $5.50). Louis Malle's frequently touching 1985 PBS documentary, *God's Country*, focusing on Glencoe, Minnesota, demonstrated antisemitic embeddedness when a McCloud County, Minnesota, farmer suddenly looped into a dialogue about the international Jewish banking conspiracy to explain the Carter-era farm crisis. Religion stood on both sides of the 2012 effort to amend the Minnesota constitution to ban gay marriage, with support coming prominently from Catholic archbishop John Nienstedt and conservative evangelical Protestants, and opposition from a wide coalition of Protestant and Jewish clergy; voters rejected the amendment, 51 to 47 percent. Two years later, similar religious forces clashed in Indiana when a "Religious Freedom Restoration Act" allowed businesses to refuse gay customers, an act reversed following protests by Indianapolis businesses and many middle-road and liberal religious groups.[8]

Why antisemitism and anti-Catholicism generally declined after 1950 is an elusive question as much in the Midwest as elsewhere. Perhaps, like the rising acceptance of gays, lesbians, and gay marriage in the early twenty-first century, it came from knowing Jews and Catholics as individuals, at least in small and medium-sized midwestern towns if not in the Midwest's cities. Jews, mostly German and often merchants, first settled in small towns and cities from Ohio and Indiana into all the midwestern states, even homesteading in the Dakotas. They established synagogues in all the Midwest's big cities, from Cincinnati to Minot, but also in hundreds of small towns, such as the Minnesota Iron Range communities of Virginia, Chisholm, and Eveleth, including Hibbing, where Bob Dylan celebrated his bar mitzvah at Agudath Achim Synagogue in the 1950s, the building repurposed from a former Swedish Lutheran church.[9]

Catholics preceded Protestants as the Midwest's first Christians, migrating from Canada into Michigan and Wisconsin and Louisiana to Missouri, Iowa, and Wisconsin. But it was the massive numbers of German Catholics settling across the rural nineteenth-century Midwest—then Irish, German, Italian, and Polish Catholics settling in cities like Cincinnati, Chicago, Milwaukee, St. Louis, and St. Paul—that stamped the Midwest with its strongest Catholic identity. Rural Catholic communities ubiquitously evidenced what historian Kathleen Neils Conzen describes as "the trinity of farm, family, and church." In the cities, the Catholic parish system, with its large church and an attached Catholic school staffed by nuns, strengthened immigrant attachment to the church among first-and second-generation Irish, German, Italian, and Polish immigrants.[10]

East Coast Protestants flooded the Midwest beginning in the 1810s and continuing into the 1880s. Congregationalists, Methodists, Baptists, Presbyterians, and Episcopalians moved to and through Ohio, then fanned out across all the midwestern states in enormous numbers. They typically constituted the political and civic leadership of most midwestern states, cities, and rural counties well into the twentieth century. Their white-frame "country churches," many still standing, became ubiquitous features of the midwestern rural countryside, suggesting that they shared the Catholic "trinity of farm, family, and church," although they might hate to admit it. Midwestern small-town clusters of Protestant churches typically dominated town life, sharing it with the public school and staring suspiciously at a local Catholic church, when there was one, well into the 1960s.[11]

English, Welsh, Scottish, Danish, Norwegian, Swedish, and Finnish immigrants added massively to the Midwest's European Protestant ethos that began with early nineteenth-century German Lutheran and Reformed settlement. If they took second place in state politics to eastern Protestant migrants and their descendants, the European immigrants also clustered together in congregations throughout the Midwest, their congregations' religious and social needs in a region as unfamiliar to them as to all other European immigrants and American regional transplants. Their efforts sometimes succeeded and sometimes did not. Beret Holm exemplified the struggle, questioning journey and faith together in Rølvaag's *Giants in the Earth*, her religion both a salve and a thorn.[12]

Religion also produced conflict, not only external but internal as well. Scandinavian Lutherans found themselves disputing angrily over evangelical theology and the powers of laity, clergy, and denominations. By the 1890s first- and second-generation Lutherans had divided, almost accordionlike, into more than fifteen competing denominational bodies divided by theology, language, and ethnic consciousness. But after 1900, Lutheran bodies began to merge. Language and ethnic consciousness faded among second- and third-generation German, Finnish, Norwegian, Swedish, and Danish Lutherans, and denominational mergers increasingly fell along conservative and more liberal theological lines, conservatives aligning with the Missouri and Wisconsin Lutheran Synods, more liberal Lutherans ultimately coalescing in the Evangelical Lutheran Church of America.[13]

For a half century, between the 1880s and the 1930s, African American migration from the rural South to midwestern cities such as Cincinnati, Cleveland, Chicago, St. Louis, Milwaukee, and St. Paul transformed urban churches and migrants alike. Chicago's mainstream Baptist and African Methodist Episcopal churches swelled as the southern migration advanced. Olivet Baptist Church grew from six hundred members in the 1890s to over ten thousand by 1920, in part because the congregation recruited migrants and in part because the migrants responded to the power of institutions and a charismatic clergy in this new urban setting. As these congregations grew, hundreds of small storefront congregations with small followings, from ten to one hundred listeners, emerged throughout Chicago's South Side ghetto by the 1920s, their rented quarters reflecting the city's fluid real estate market. Their clergy and worshippers were poorer and far more modestly educated than those in the mainline churches; and women, such as Elder Lucy Smith of All Nations Pentecostal Church, led some of the storefront churches decades before they could be ordained in America's major African American and white denominations.[14]

Post-1980 migration transformed the Midwest's religious profile yet again, much of it stemming from nontraditional sources. The arrival of Soviet Jews; Mexican, Puerto Rican, and Central American Catholics and Pentecostals; Sikhs and Hindus from India; Catholic and traditionally Buddhist Vietnamese refugees; Hmong immigrants; and East African Muslims from Somalia and Orthodox Christians from Eritrea changed the Midwest's cities again, as well as its suburbs and smaller towns. Reaction to the immigrants and their religions varied. Hispanic and Somali immigrants met more resistance because they were poor as well as Catholic and Muslim. Hindus and Sikhs fared better because many were university educated and wealthier. Regrettably, how they all adapted traditional religious ways to varied American circumstances remains only skimpily studied.[15]

The Midwest's laidback, folksy image scarcely precluded exercising denominational leadership and authority. Congregationalist, Unitarian, and Jewish denominational bodies continued to place substantial authority in the hands of local congregations, and their statewide and regional bodies typically advised rather than dominated congregations, even when the advice could be sharp. Others replanted and expanded their authoritative group and denominational bodies, sometimes powerfully so. Methodists and Episcopalians replicated traditional hierarchical structure headed by bishops as thoroughly in the Midwest as elsewhere. Catholicism, famous within and without for its commanding hierarchical system, expanded it powerfully to the Midwest, most famously, or infamously, through articulate and charismatic figures such as Archbishop John Ireland of St. Paul, who served from 1888 to 1918, and Cardinal George Mundelein, who served in Chicago from 1915 to 1939. Asian religious and immigrant groups—Hindus, Sikhs, Vietnamese Buddhists, and Hmong—have formed community associations that support traditional religious practices, ceremonies, and rituals, emphasizing their preservation in family life.[16]

The Midwest has also housed national headquarters for American religious groups from the mid-nineteenth century forward. These include not just the three major Lutheran groups—the Evangelical Lutheran Church of America (Chicago), the Lutheran Church Missouri Synod (St. Louis), and the Wisconsin Evangelical Lutheran Synod (Milwaukee)—but the Christian Reformed Church (Grand Rapids); the Disciplines of Christ (Indianapolis); the United Church of Christ (Cleveland); the Church of the Brethren (Elgin, Illinois); the Church of God (Anderson, Indiana); the Nation of Islam (Chicago); the Community of Christ, renamed in 2001 from the Reorganized Church of Jesus Christ of Latter Day Saints (Independence, Missouri); the Church of the Nazarene (Lenexa, Kansas, a suburb of Kansas City); and the Bahá'í (Wilmette, Illinois), among others.[17]

Religious colleges, universities, and bible schools flourished in the Midwest. Isaac Mayer Wise established the nation's first seminary to train rabbis in Cincinnati in 1875, Hebrew Union College, which became and remains the most prominent Reform Jewish seminary in the nation. The nation's two most prominent Catholic and Protestant evangelical colleges—Notre Dame University and Wheaton College—were established in South Bend, Indiana, and Wheaton, Illinois, respectively. So many Catholic and Protestant colleges were strewn across the midwestern landscape that even when the weakest succumbed to the brutalities of college economics throughout the twentieth century, hundreds more remained. Bible schools also found the Midwest hospitable. Chicago's Moody Bible Institute, founded in 1887, was among the earliest; and if some transformed themselves into accredited colleges, many others still offer Bible-centered study to thousands of midwestern students.[18]

Not least, the Midwest has proven to be as religiously creative as any American region, perhaps more so, despite its reputation for boredom. For Indians, the sacred character of many midwestern locations has never receded, even if sustaining those beliefs has encountered a century and more of incursions and innumerable disputes with federal and state authorities and local property owners. Although Joseph Smith published the *Book of Mormon* in upstate New York in 1830, central events in Mormon history occurred in the Midwest, including the construction of the first two Mormon temples in Kirtland, Ohio, in 1836, and Nauvoo, Illinois, begun in 1841, and, most disastrously, Smith's assassination in Carthage, Illinois, in 1844. Charles Parham's ministries in Kansas led to healing and speaking in tongues that ultimately led to the creation of a Pentecostal movement whose followers worldwide now number in the millions. Detroit gave birth to the Nation of Islam in the 1930s. Chicago's Thomas A. Dorsey, a former nightclub pianist, is widely and rightly credited as the "father of the black gospel movement" that transformed

African American church music and popular music in the United States after 1930. More than a hundred formal Catholic shrines can be found across the Midwest; and in Necedah, Wisconsin, a Catholic convert, Mary Ann Van Hoof, drew one hundred thousand worshipers in 1949 and 1950 claiming to see the Virgin Mary at a site she and her followers turned into a shrine. The bishop of Lacrosse disavowed Van Hoof and the shrine in the 1950s, but both are honored today by the dissident Old Catholic Church, and the shrine still draws worshipers.[19]

And whither Lake Wobegon? If many midwesterners wittingly and unwittingly worship at Our Lady of Perpetual Responsibility, then the region's penchant for earnest competence might outshine the Puritans' city on a hill. But the slightly anxious Protestant-Catholic humor inside Garrison Keillor's Lake Wobegon reflects religious complexities and anxieties running across the whole of the Midwest that are critical to understanding religion throughout America as much as in the Midwest.

Of course, Lake Wobegon does what fiction does best, which is to reimagine both others and ourselves. What makes us tick? What makes us wince? What gives us hope?

But fiction also conjures history, leading us beyond stereotypes about midwestern simplicity to probe complexities inside all the Midwest's Lake Wobegones, especially religious complexities obscured by the lime Jell-O salad.

Notes

1. Garrison Keillor, "Clergywomen in Lake Wobegon," *A Prairie Home Companion with Garrison Keillor*, June 1, 2010, accessed May 23, 2015, http://www .publicradio.org/columns/prairiehome/posthost/2010/06/01/clergywomen _in_lake_wobegon.php. A more dyspeptic Keillor emerges in Jon Lauck, "Garrison Keillor: An Interview," *Salmagundi*, no. 184 (2014): 46–67.
2. Anyone interested in varieties of religion in the Midwest should start with Philip Barlow and Mark Silk, eds., *Religion and Public Life in the Midwest: Heartland as Common Denominator* (Walnut Creek CA: AltaMira Press, 2004). Other places to begin might include Michael D. McNally, "Honoring Elders: Practices of Sagacity and Deference in Ojibwe Christianity," in *Practicing Protestants: Histories of Christian Life in America, 1600–1965*, ed. Laurie F. Maffly-Kipp, Leigh E. Schmidt, and Mark Valeri (Baltimore MD:

Johns Hopkins University Press, 2006), 77–99; Christopher Vecsey, *Traditional Ojibwa Religion and Its Historical Changes* (Philadelphia: American Philosophical Society, 1983); Hyman Berman, Bill Holm, and Linda Mack Schloff, *Jews in Minnesota* (St. Paul: Minnesota Historical Society Press, 2002); Allan H. Spear, *Black Chicago: The Making of a Negro Ghetto* (Chicago: University of Chicago Press, 1967); Wallace D. Best, *Passionately Human, No Less Divine: Religion and Culture in Black Chicago, 1915–1952* (Princeton NJ: Princeton University Press, 2005); John W. V. Smith, *The Quest for Holiness and Unity: A Centennial History of the Church of God (Anderson, Indiana)* (Anderson IN: Warner Press, 1980); John T. McGreevy, "Thinking on One's Own: Catholicism in the American Intellectual Imagination, 1928–1960," *Journal of American History* 84 (1997): 97–131; Leonard Joseph Moore, *Citizen Klansmen: The Ku Klux Klan in Indiana, 1921–1928*(Chapel Hill: University of North Carolina Press, 1991); Garbi Schmidt, *Islam in Urban America: Sunni Muslims in Chicago* (Philadelphia: Temple University Press, 2004); Elmer Schwieder and Dorothy Schwieder, *A Peculiar People: Iowa's Old Order Amish* (Ames: Iowa State University Press, 1975); "Police Identify Army Veteran as Wisconsin Temple Shooting Gunman," August 7, 2012, accessed May 26, 2015, http://www.cnn.com/2012/08/06/us/wisconsin-temple-shooting/; Philip L. Cook, *Zion City, Illinois: Twentieth-Century Utopia* (Syracuse NY: Syracuse University Press, 1996); *The History of the "I AM" Activity and Saint Germain Foundation* (Schaumburg IL: Saint Germain Foundation, 2003); Catherine L. Albanese, *A Republic of Mind and Spirit: A Cultural History of American Metaphysical Religion* (New Haven: Yale University Press, 2007), 467–70; Charles C. Muzny, *The Vietnamese in Oklahoma City: A Study in Ethnic Change* (New York: AMS Press, 1989); Chia Youyee Vang, *Hmong in Minnesota* (St. Paul: Minnesota Historical Society Press, 2008); Shannon Prather, "City Council Approves Civil Rights Settlement in Mosque Case," *Star Tribune*, December 24, 2014.

3. Linda M. Clemmons, *Conflicted Mission: Faith, Disputes, and Deception on the Dakota Frontier* (St. Paul: Minnesota Historical Society Press, 2014).

4. Clemmons, *Conflicted Mission*, 217.

5. Michael D. McNally, "The Practice of Native American Christianity," *Church History: Studies in Christianity and Culture* 69, no. 4 (2000): 834–59; Karla Sanders, "A Healthy Balance: Religion, Identity, and Community in Louise Erdrich's *Love Medicine*," *Melus* 23, no. 2 (1998): 129–55.

6. Donald L. Kinzer, *An Episode in Anti-Catholicism: The American Protective Association* (Seattle: University of Washington Press, 1964); John

Higham, *Strangers in the Land: Patterns of American Nativism, 1860–1925* (New Brunswick NJ: Rutgers University Press, 1955); Moore, *Citizen Klansmen*; O. E. Rølvaag, *Their Father's God*, trans. Trygve M. Ager (New York: Harper and Row, 1931), 330–38.

7. Carey McWilliams, "Minneapolis: The Curious Twin," *Common Ground*, Autumn 1946, 61–65, quotation on 61; William Bell Riley quoted in William Vance Trollinger, *God's Empire: William Bell Riley and Midwestern Fundamentalism* (Madison: University of Wisconsin Press, 1990), 70, 71; Stephen J. Keillor, *Hjalmer Petersen of Minnesota: The Politics of Provincial Independence* (St. Paul: Minnesota Historical Society Press, 1987), 154; Hyman Berman, "Political Antisemitism in Minnesota during the Great Depression," *Jewish Social Studies* 38, no. 3/4 (1976): 247–64; Laura E. Weber, "'Gentiles Preferred': Minneapolis Jews and Employment 1920–1950," *Minnesota History* (1991): 167–82, cartoon on 172.

8. Mrs. Clarence Katzenmeyer to Harold Butler, October 31, 1960, in Benjamin J. Butler and Family Papers, Minnesota Historical Society; John Corry, "Malle's 'God's Country' in Minnesota," *New York Times*, December 11, 1985; Doug Belden, "Minnesota Defeats Marriage Amendment," *St. Paul Pioneer Press*, November 7, 2012; Mark Peters and Ana Campoy, "'Religious Freedom' Measures Revamped," *Wall Street Journal*, April 2, 2015.

9. W. Gunther Plaut, *The Jews in Minnesota: The First Seventy-Five Years* (New York: American Jewish Historical Society, 1959); Janet E. Schulte, "'Proving Up and Moving Up': Jewish Homesteading Activity in North Dakota, 1900–1920," *Great Plains Quarterly* 10 (Fall 1990): 228–44; Karen G. Bell and Michael J. Bell, "Iowa Jewish Heritage: An Annotated Bibliography," *Annals of Iowa* 53 (1994): 128–46. Jonathan D. Sarna and Nancy H. Klein, *The Jews of Cincinnati* (Cincinnati OH: Center for Study of the American Jewish Experience Hebrew Union College-Jewish Institute of Religion, 1989); Robert Shelton, *No Direction Home: The Life and Music of Bob Dylan* (New York: William Morrow, 1986), 36; Linda Mack Schloff, "Overcoming Geography: Jewish Religious Life in Four Market Towns," *Minnesota History* 51 (1988): 2–14.

10. Kathleen Neils Conzen, *Immigrant Milwaukee, 1836–1860* (Cambridge MA: Harvard University Press, 1976); Conzen, *Germans in Minnesota* (St. Paul: Minnesota Historical Society Press, 2003); Conzen, quoted in Steven M. Avella, "Roman Catholics," in *The American Midwest: An Interpretive Encyclopedia*, ed. Richard Sisson, Christian K. Zacher, and Andrew R. L. Cayton (Bloomington: Indiana University Press, 2007), 765; Dominic A. Pacyga, *Polish Immigrants and Industrial Chicago: Workers in the South Side, 1880–1922*

(Columbus: Ohio State University Press, 1991); Ann Regan, *Irish in Minnesota* (St. Paul: Minnesota Historical Society Press, 2002); John T. McGreevy, *Parish Boundaries: The Catholic Encounter with Race in the Twentieth-Century Urban North* (Chicago: University of Chicago Press, 1996). For a less optimistic view of relations between immigrants and traditional organized religion, see Rudolph J. Vecoli, "Prelates and Peasants: Italian Immigrants and the Catholic Church," *Journal of Social History* 2 (1969): 217–68.

11. Doug Ohman and Jon Hassler, *Churches of Minnesota* (St. Paul: Minnesota Historical Society Press, 2005); Alan K. Lathrop and Bob Firth, *Churches of Minnesota: An Illustrated Guide* (Minneapolis: University of Minnesota Press, 2003); Peter W. Williams, *Houses of God: Region, Religion, and Architecture in the United States* (Urbana: University of Illinois Press, 1997), 156–208; Dorothy Schwieder, *Growing Up with the Town: Family and Community on the Great Plains* (Iowa City: University of Iowa Press, 2002), 63, 97, 114–15; many state histories discuss religion only peripherally, but Annette Atkins, *Creating Minnesota: A History from the Inside Out* (St. Paul: Minnesota Historical Society Press, 2008), offers more thorough appraisals.

12. Jon Gjerde, *From Peasants to Farmers: The Migration from Balestrand, Norway, to the Upper Middle West* (New York: Cambridge University Press, 1985); Harold P. Simonson, "Angst on the Prairie: Reflections on Immigrants, Rolvaag, and Beret," *Norwegian-American Studies* 29 (1983): 89–110.

13. Ann M. Legreid and David Ward, "Religious Schism and the Development of Rural Immigrant Communities," *Upper Midwest History* 2 (1982): 13–29; Fred W. Meuser, *The Formation of the American Lutheran Church* (Columbus OH: Wartburg Press, 1958); Paul C. Nyholm, *The Americanization of the Danish Lutheran Churches in America* (Minneapolis: Institute for Danish Church History by Augsburg Publishing House, 1963); Leslie Woodcock Tentler, "Who Is the Church? Conflict in a Polish Immigrant Parish in Late Nineteenth-Century Detroit," *Comparative Studies in Society and History* 25 (1983): 241–76.

14. Best, *Passionately Human, No Less Divine*, 147–81; Spear, *Black Chicago*, 174–79; Paul Oliver, *Songsters and Saints: Vocal Traditions on Race Records* (New York: Cambridge University Press, 1984), 186.

15. Irving Cutler, *The Jews of Chicago: From Shtetl to Suburb* (Urbana: University of Illinois Press, 1996); R. B. Williams, "Swaminarayan Hindu Temple of Glen Ellyn, Illinois," in *American Congregations: Portraits of Twelve Religious Communities*, ed. J. P. Wind and J. W. Lewis (Chicago: University of Chicago Press, 1994), 1:612–62; M. Gail Hickey, "Asian Indians in Indiana," *Indiana Magazine of History* 102, no. 2 (2006): 117–40; Delia Fernández, "Becoming Latino: Mexican and Puerto Rican Community Formation in Grand

Rapids, Michigan, 1926–1964," *Michigan Historical Review* 39, no. 1 (2013): 71–100; Eduardo Porter and Elisabeth Malkin, "Way North of the Border," *New York Times*, September 30, 2005; José Ángel N., *Illegal: Reflections of an Undocumented Immigrant* (Urbana: University of Illinois Press, 2014); Leonard G. Ramirez, ed. *Chicanas of 18th Street: Narratives of a Movement from Latino Chicago* (Urbana: University of Illinois Press, 2011); Arlene M. Sánchez Walsh, *Latino Pentecostal Identity: Evangelical Faith, Self, and Society* (New York: Columbia University Press, 2003); Lynne M. Dearborn, "Reconstituting Hmong Culture and Traditions in Milwaukee, Wisconsin," *Traditional Dwellings and Settlements Review* 19, no. 2 (2008): 37–49; Muzny, *The Vietnamese in Oklahoma City*; Vang, *Hmong in Minnesota*; Chao-Hua Li, "Immigrant Religious Experience: The Case of the Vietnamese Buddhist Association in Minnesota," PhD. diss., University of Minnesota, 1997.

16. Marvin Richard O'Connell, *John Ireland and the American Catholic Church* (St. Paul: Minnesota Historical Society Press, 1988); Edward R. Kantowicz, *Corporation Sole: Cardinal Mundelein and Chicago Catholicism* (Notre Dame IN: University of Notre Dame Press, 1983); Fred W. Meuser, *The Formation of the American Lutheran Church* (Columbus OH: Wartburg Press, 1958).

17. Mark Silk, "A Demographic Portrait: America Writ Small?" in *Religion and Public Life in the Midwest*, ed. Barlow and Silk (Lanham MD: AltaMira Press, 2004), 32.

18. Mark Stephen Massa, *Catholics and American Culture: Fulton Sheen, Dorothy Day, and the Notre Dame Football Team* (New York: Crossroad, 1999); Paul M. Bechtel, *Wheaton College: A Heritage Remembered, 1860–1984* (Wheaton IL: Harold Shaw, 1984); Virginia L. Brereton, *Training God's Army: The American Bible School, 1880–1940* (Bloomington: Indiana University Press, 1990).

19. Richard L. Bushman, *Joseph Smith: Rough Stone Rolling* (New York: Knopf, 2005); Michael W. Harris, *The Rise of Gospel Blues: The Music of Thomas Andrew Dorsey in the Urban Church* (New York: Oxford University Press, 1992); James R. Goff Jr., *Fields White Unto Harvest: Charles F. Parham and the Missionary Origins of Pentecostalism* (Fayetteville: University of Arkansas Press, 1988); Thomas A. Kselman and Steven Avella, "Marian Piety and the Cold War in the United States," *Catholic Historical Review* 72 (1986): 403–24.

13

The Development of Midwestern Cities

Jon Teaford

The urban Midwest is a broad, expansive region; eight hundred miles separate Cleveland in the east from Omaha in the west. Its cities are not cookie-cutter entities, indistinguishable one from another. Instead, each has a rich history and supposedly superior qualities that Chamber of Commerce boosters have long been eager to publicize. They are remarkable creations, products of local resources and the ambitions and enterprise of generations of local citizens. Yet this diversity and individuality at least in part veils some common characteristics that distinguish midwestern metropolises and differentiates them from the principal cities in other American regions. Kansas City, Detroit, Omaha, and Cleveland share certain common denominators that define them as midwestern metropolises. A distinctive regional heritage renders them a class apart, and study of this genus *Urbanusmidwesternus* can yield rich findings for historians.

Emergence of Midwestern Urban Hierarchy

Most notably, the chief midwestern cities are all creations of the nineteenth century. The midwestern network of cities developed during the relatively short period from 1830 to 1890. During these six decades the region's urban hierarchy emerged, with some cities rising to first rank both regionally and nationally. Development and growth would continue in later decades, but by 1890 the urban winners had secured their positions and the also-ran communities had to settle for a second- or third-tier existence.

In 1830 Cincinnati was pioneering urban life in the Midwest; it was the only midwestern community to rank among the nation's top ten cities; with twenty-five thousand inhabitants, it was five times as populous as the region's second-place St. Louis. Boasting three thousand residents, Zanesville, Ohio, ranked third in the Midwest with Dayton, Steubenville, and Chillicothe, all in Ohio, holding fourth, fifth and sixth places. By 1840 Detroit, with nine thousand inhabitants, had moved into third position. Zanesville, however, still outranked Chicago in population, the nascent Windy City barely surpassing Steubenville and New Albany, Indiana. In 1850 both Cincinnati and St. Louis ranked among the nation's top ten, and Chicago, Detroit, and Milwaukee were the Midwest's third-, fourth-, and fifth-largest cities. Yet New Albany, Indiana, remained the most populous community in the Hoosier state, followed closely by Indianapolis and Madison.

By the close of the Civil War, such also-rans as New Albany, Madison, and Zanesville had dropped out of contention, permanently consigned to small-time status. Meanwhile west of the Mississippi, Omaha had defeated its early rival Bellevue and had dashed the hopes of boosters in Brownville and Nebraska City for preeminence along the upper Missouri River. To the south, Kansas City was pulling away from Leavenworth and St. Joseph, consolidating its position as the great gateway to the southern plains.

Some midwestern cities would emerge as industrial centers of some importance but still had to resign themselves reluctantly to second-tier status. In 1867 Toledo booster Jesup Scott predicted that his hometown was "the future great city of the world."[1] This was a much-repeated prophecy as Toledoans believed their city's unique and extraordinary advantages destined it to urban supremacy. For a time Toledo endeavored to become the granary of the nation, the center of flour milling and the grain trade. Minneapolis and Chicago, however, handily defeated Toledo for that title. The Ohio city had to console itself with the less lofty distinction of "Clover-Seed Capital of the World."[2] Similarly the port of Toledo hoped to dominate the iron ore trade with the upper Great Lakes and emerge as a preeminent iron and steel manufacturing center. Cleveland, however, surpassed it in this economic endeavor. Eventually Toledo would become the Glass City, but it remained in the shadows of Detroit and Cleveland. It was destined to be a stop along the rail line leading to the region's future great city of Chicago.

Chicago's rise to supremacy was perhaps the most notable development of the formative era of midwestern urbanization. During the years immediately following the Civil War, Chicago pulled ahead of the older hubs of Cincinnati and St. Louis. By 1890, with a population of nearly 1.1 million, it was more than double the size of second-place St. Louis. It was unquestionably the premier midwestern metropolis and the second-largest city in the nation.

By 1890 a permanent urban hierarchy had developed in the Midwest. East of the Mississippi the largest metropolises were Chicago, Cincinnati, Cleveland, Detroit, Milwaukee, Indianapolis, and Columbus. West of the Mississippi the chief metropolitan centers were St. Louis, the Twin Cities, Kansas City, and Omaha. One hundred and twenty years later, in 2010, the same seven metropolitan areas remained the largest east of the Mississippi, and the identical four metropolises retained their place as the largest west of the Mississippi. The urban pattern of the Midwest had jelled between 1830 and 1890. The rank order of the eleven chief metropolitan areas of the Midwest would vary over the decades, with some rising a few notches and others falling. The urban pattern, however, was established.

Moreover, during this same period the Midwest emerged as a major urban region of the nation with more than its proportionate share of major cities. By 1890 the Midwest accounted for twelve of the thirty largest cities in the United States as compared to fourteen for the Northeast and only four for the South and West combined. Six of the midwestern cities had more than two hundred thousand inhabitants; five additional cities could boast of a population of more than one hundred thousand. From 1830 to 1890 the Midwest emerged as a major urban presence, the site of many of the largest cities in America.

The mid-nineteenth-century emergence of the urban Midwest distinguishes it from urban development elsewhere in the nation. The East Coast hierarchy of cities emerged before the nineteenth century. In 1800 the largest cities of the East Coast were Philadelphia, New York City, Boston, and Baltimore, and they would remain the coastal hubs. The urban development of the South and West contrasted even more markedly with that of the Midwest. The urban pattern of these regions is largely a twentieth-century creation and reflects the economic and technological conditions of that century. In 1890 urbanization in the South and West had not reached maturity. Rather, it was at most in a nascent stage; the winners and losers had not yet been determined, and most of the latter-day major metropolises were as yet minor centers. In 1890 Wilmington, with a population of twenty thousand, was the largest city in North Carolina; the state's preeminent late-twentieth-century metropolis of Charlotte had about half Wilmington's population and ranked third among Tar Heel communities. Florida's largest city was Key West with eighteen thousand inhabitants. Miami's Dade County stretched one hundred miles along the state's southeast coast and was home to only 861 people. In Texas, Galveston was the chief port city, exceeding Houston in population. Dallas was a small regional center of thirty-eight thousand people and ranked just above Sioux City, Iowa, among the nation's cities.

Farther west, Virginia City was the metropolis of Nevada; Las Vegas did not exist. Phoenix, Arizona, barely existed with three thousand residents. Los Angeles had fifty thousand inhabitants, trailing Evansville, Indiana, and St. Joseph, Missouri, in population. Sandusky, Ohio; Sheboygan, Wisconsin; and Burlington, Iowa, all surpassed San Diego, California, in size.

The defining urban development of the South and West remained in the future. Those regions were still relatively underdeveloped with only a few major cities such as New Orleans, Denver, and San Francisco. The urban timelines of the Midwest versus the South and West are, then, markedly different. The urban Midwest dates from the decades from 1830 to 1890. In contrast, the urban South and West are primarily products of the twentieth century.

This distinctive timeline is significant. The midwestern urban pattern reflects the economic priorities and the technological realities of the period 1830 to 1890. It was an era during which first water and then rail were all-important to urban development. Most of the great midwestern metropolises developed along the major navigable waterways of the region. Cincinnati was the principal port on the Ohio River, St. Louis dominated the river traffic of the mid-Mississippi, and St. Paul was the head of navigation of the Mississippi. Kansas City and Omaha first developed as ports on the Missouri River, and Cleveland, Detroit, Chicago, and Milwaukee owed much of their early growth and later prosperity to their role in Great Lakes shipping. Cincinnati, Cleveland, and Chicago also benefited from their positions at the terminus of canals constructed by the states of Ohio and Illinois during the antebellum period. As capital cities, the sites of Indianapolis and Columbus were chosen because of their central positions in their states. Yet even those cities were located on rivers that the cities' early promoters hoped would become navigable. Moreover, a branch of Ohio's canal system opened water transportation to Columbus, and Indiana's canal network was also planned to provide water access to Indianapolis.

Beyond navigability, water power was likewise a significant asset that fueled the growth of many midwestern cities. St. Anthony Falls was the lure that drew many entrepreneurs to Minneapolis. A formidable source of water power, it predestined Minneapolis's rise as a great milling center.[3] Lesser midwestern cities such as Akron, South Bend, Grand Rapids, Rockford, and Cedar Rapids similarly benefited from water power. Both as a mode of transportation and source of industrial power, water was a major ingredient in the early development of midwestern cities.

In the second half of the nineteenth century, railroads surpassed waterways as the chief highways of the nation and region and proved vital in the emergence and growth of major midwestern metropolises. The level terrain of much of the Midwest was conducive to rapid rail development. Mountain ranges did not pose engineering challenges to rail builders, and steep grades did not raise the cost of construction and operation. In 1890 mid-sized Illinois boasted the greatest rail mileage of any state. Chicago was the unquestioned rail capital of the nation; myriad rail lines reached out from the city in all directions. Illinois, however, was not an anomaly. A thick web of rail lines overlay the map of each midwestern state, and the major metropolises were all rail hubs. St. Paul was the headquarters of James Hill's Great Northern Railroad empire, earning it distinction as the gateway to the Northwest. Omaha was the hub of operations for the Union Pacific Railroad; that line provided jobs for thousands of workers in the metropolitan area.

Also vital to the emergence of midwestern metropolises were the rich resources of the region. The commerce and manufacturing of the urban

Midwest focused on the distribution and processing of native products, most notably iron ore, timber, meat, and grain. Cleveland, Detroit, Chicago, and Milwaukee became centers for iron and steel goods, exploiting the iron ore shipped via the Great Lakes from the Upper Peninsula of Michigan and northern Minnesota. Chicago was the great meatpacking center, the "Hog Butcher of the World," surpassing once-dominant Cincinnati and rendering the Ohio city's nickname of "Porkopolis" obsolete. Kansas City and Omaha, however, were challenging Chicago as livestock and meatpacking hubs, and local boosters dreamed of consigning the Windy City to the same fate as Cincinnati. Exploiting its water power and the developing spring wheat production of western Minnesota and eastern North Dakota, Minneapolis became the world's preeminent center for flour milling, having surpassed the previous holder of the title, Budapest, as early as 1884.[4] Lumberjacks were felling the vast forests of Michigan, Wisconsin, and Minnesota, providing the raw materials for planing mills, door and sash factories, wagon and buggy builders, and furniture manufacturers. Benefiting initially from Michigan's timber resources, late-nineteenth-century Grand Rapids was establishing its reputation as the "Furniture City."[5]

As steam power increasingly supplanted water power in the late nineteenth century, the Midwest did not suffer. Ample coal supplies in eastern Ohio, southwestern Indiana, southern Illinois, and southern Iowa ensured that the Midwest could generate the steam necessary for industrial advancement. By 1890 Illinois ranked second in the nation in coal production, and Ohio held third place. In the late nineteenth century iron and coal were deemed the basic building blocks for industrial greatness. With the richest iron ore deposits in the nation and a seemingly inexhaustible coal supply, the Midwest was fertile ground for the growing of industrial metropolises.

The industrial profile of midwestern cities contrasted with that of East Coast manufacturing centers. Whereas the economic prosperity of midwestern cities depended primarily on the distribution and processing of the region's resources, East Coast cities were more often distributors and processors of goods imported from other regions or abroad. Far removed from any cotton fields, Massachusetts ranked first in the nation in cotton milling, producing one-third of all the nation's cotton goods at the close of the nineteenth century. It likewise held first place in the manufacture of worsted goods, having initially achieved superiority by importing Ohio merino wool.[6] Though Rhode Island mined neither gold nor silver, Providence led the nation in jewelry manufacturing, accounting for one-fifth of the nation's production in 1890, and the small state similarly dominated the manufacture of silverware with one-half of the country's output.[7] The processing of coffee and spices was a leading industry of Brooklyn, and the borough was the principal center for sugar refining.[8] Sugar was also a major product of Philadelphia's manufacturers; although, as elsewhere along the East Coast, the processing of cotton, silk, and wool textile goods was an industrial mainstay.[9] The East Coast metropolises transformed imported materials; the inland hubs of the Midwest built their success on their region's own bounty.

With the water and rail resources so necessary to nineteenth-century urban development and the mineral, forest, and agricultural output basic to that century's economic growth, the midwestern metropolises thus rose to first rank among the cities of North America. They had what the nineteenth century demanded of cities and accordingly prospered. Their location, growth, and economic development distinguished them as products of the decades from 1830 to 1890, in contrast to the established hubs of the East Coast and the nascent centers of the South and West.

Urban Heyday

By 1890 the principal midwestern metropolises had emerged, and over the following four decades their place among the nation's cities seemed secure. The years 1890 to 1930 were a heyday for the midwestern cities as they built upon their existing advantages and astounded the nation with new manifestations of their greatness. Most notably the rise of the automobile industry accelerated the growth of Detroit and made it the wonder of the industrial world. The gargantuan auto plants of Henry Ford and the Dodge brothers were monuments to the dynamism of midwestern enterprise, and unprecedented job opportunities attracted thousands of newcomers to the Midwest. The number of auto workers in Detroit soared from 2,200 in 1904 to 140,000 fifteen years later.[10]

Equally impressive was the rise of Gary, Indiana, to the south and east of Chicago. When U.S. Steel began development of the city in 1906, its site was a sandy waste, but fourteen years later it housed fifty-five thousand people and was one of the premier steel-producing centers of the world. A local booster proclaimed: "Never before in the history of the material development of the American continent has an industrial enterprise of such gigantic proportions been conceived and put into execution, and carried out, as the marvelous enterprise now building at Gary, Indiana."[11]

Midwestern metropolises also continued to expand their existing enterprises. Flour milling in Minneapolis prospered, reaching peak production in 1915–16.[12] Chicago's stockyards peaked in 1924; the city was as yet unchallenged as the world's premier meat processor. In second place were the still flourishing stockyards and packing plants of Kansas City. Omaha celebrated its continuing place in the meatpacking hierarchy with the completion of the Livestock Exchange Building in 1926. Rising eleven stories in the midst of the stockyards, the new structure was a monument to Omaha's economic success.[13] Cementing Grand Rapids' reputation as the "Furniture City" was the twice-annual Furniture Market, which attracted manufacturers and buyers from throughout the nation in a combination convention and carnival. By the mid-1920s ten furniture exhibition buildings accommodated the displays of 561 manufacturers eager to impress the thousands of representatives of retailers who flocked to Grand Rapids for the famous furniture shows.[14]

Most impressive in advertising the urban Midwest's coming of age were the world's fairs hosted during the 1890s and early twentieth century. Though purportedly intended to celebrate the four-hundredth anniversary of Columbus's landing in America, Chicago's World's Columbian Exposition of 1893 was, in fact, a mammoth celebration of the Midwest's greatest metropolis. Its gargantuan neoclassical exhibition halls and shimmering lagoons bordered by massive sculptural displays announced to millions of fairgoers that Chicago was one of the greatest urban centers in the world. One commentator informed prospective visitors that the fair presented a "sight which . . . has not been paralleled since the Rome of the emperors stood intact."[15] Five years later Omaha advertised its metropolitan status by hosting the Trans-Mississippi and International Exposition. Attracting more than 2.6 million visitors, the Omaha fair, like its Chicago counterpart, was a grandiose neoclassical ensemble including a Venetian lagoon complete with gondoliers.[16] Always sensitive about its failure to keep up with Chicago, St. Louis celebrated itself in the Louisiana Purchase Exposition of 1904. Once again the buildings and layout were imitative of the great Chicago fair, but the St. Louis exposition asserted the Missouri metropolis's status as the gateway to the vast territory of the Louisiana Purchase. As such St. Louis could claim to be equally deserving of notice as its erstwhile Illinois rival.

Deadly race riots in East St. Louis in 1916, and in Chicago and Omaha in 1919, raised doubts as to whether all was well in the midwestern metropolises. Despite these blots on the reputation of the urban heartland, city boosters seemed confident that they were poised to surpass the aging Northeast and had little to fear from potential rivals in the gradually developing South and West. Cynical observers might view world's fairs as lavishly applied cosmetics masking the ugly scars of economic inequality and racial division, but heartland optimists had no interest in looking beneath the makeup at troublesome realities.

Such optimism seemed justified. The midwestern metropolises of the period 1890 to 1930 were literally placing the American public in the driver's seat of new Fords, creating the furniture found in living rooms across the country, putting meat and bread on the world's tables, and offering the greatest world's fair extravaganzas. Midwestern cities had built on their earlier successes and asserted themselves as industrial dynamos and destinations for everyone from furniture buyers to fairgoers.

Age of Readjustment

The late twentieth century was not, however, as favorable to the fortunes of the urban Midwest. The assets contributing to the region's rapid rise in the nineteenth century were no longer so essential to metropolitan growth. Access to water transportation was not a prerequisite for late twentieth-century success. Such fast-growing urban stars as Raleigh, Charlotte, Atlanta, Dallas, Phoenix, and Las Vegas were not on navigable waterways. Railroads still carried much of the nation's freight but were not as significant as they had been a century earlier. Coal and iron were no longer essential ingredients for economic development. The agricultural bounty of the Midwest likewise was not as sure a foundation for urban prosperity as it had been. "Hog Butcher of the World" no longer held the cachet it had in 1890.

In one midwestern city after another, signature industries closed, eliminating jobs and forcing a rebranding of the city's identity. Flour milling declined in Minneapolis; General Mills' giant Washburn A Mill closed in 1965, and Pillsbury's massive facility at St. Anthony Falls ceased operation in 2003, long after Minneapolis had relinquished the title of "Flour Milling Capital of the World." Chicago's Union Stock Yards closed in 1971; the Windy City was no longer "Hog Butcher of the World." Second only to Chicago in meatpacking, Kansas City lost its "Cow Town" distinction with the Armour plant ceasing operations in 1965, Swift radically curtailing production in 1968, and Wilson withdrawing from the city in 1976. Finally in 1991 the city's stockyards closed. Three of the "Big Four" meatpackers left Omaha between 1967 and 1969.[17] The fourth cut production in 1976, and the city's great stockyards followed the example of Chicago and Kansas City, ceasing operations in 1999. Smaller, automated, nonunion packing plants located in small towns were supplanting the antiquated, inefficient, and unionized operations of the midwestern metropolises, destroying an industrial mainstay dating from the nineteenth century.

Other signature industries were also faltering. Milwaukee seemed less worthy of the title of "Brew City" as Blatz Brewing Company closed in 1959, Schlitz left the city in 1981, and Pabst joined the exodus in 1996. Miller remained, but the departures took a toll on the city's employment and identity. Similarly Grand Rapids was finding it increasingly difficult to advertise itself as the "Furniture City." The city continued to produce steel office furniture and stadium and theater seating, but its production of residential furniture, the traditional mainstay, plummeted. With Grand Rapids products accounting for a markedly diminishing share of the furniture in showrooms across the nation, the city's once dominant Furniture Market fell on hard times. Furniture makers in North Carolina had supplanted the

Michigan producers, and the High Point, North Carolina, Furniture Market became the premier exhibition for manufacturers and buyers. Succumbing to this reality, Grand Rapids discontinued its Furniture Market in 1965.[18]

Nowhere was the impact of the decline of a signature industry more evident than in Detroit. The city's name was synonymous with the auto industry; as late as the 1950s no one would deny that Detroit was unquestionably the world's Motor City. Foreign competition from Germany and then Japan, however, weakened Detroit's grip on the industry. Moreover, cheaper, nonunion labor in the South and Mexico spurred a southward flow of auto manufacturers and eroded the employment base of southeastern Michigan. Exacerbating Detroit's ills were well-publicized racial clashes and racial divisions between the city and its suburbs. In the early twenty-first century, Michigan's once invincible General Motors Corporation went bankrupt, followed by the bankruptcy of the city of Detroit itself. Once a symbol of the economic dynamism and ingenuity of the Midwest, Detroit was becoming better known for its ruins and empty fields than for its automobiles.

In both agriculture and manufacturing, the Midwest had been a dynamo of production. It was the region that fed the nation, furnished its homes, and provided its transportation. Automation and mechanization, however, took its toll on employment in both the fields and the factories of the heartland. The new jobs were in service not production, and consequently the many midwestern factory towns suffered disproportionately. Detroit was the largest factory town in the world, and it fell the hardest.

In other cities, the growth in health care, education, and financial and business services mitigated the industrial erosion. As state capitals with substantial government employment—as well as giant, job-generating state universities—the Twin Cities and Columbus both weathered the storm better than many of their fellow midwestern hubs. Indianapolis and Omaha benefited from being the sites of their state university medical schools, ensuring an expanding and lucrative health-care presence. As the preeminent midwestern metropolis, Chicago was a focus of financial and business services that buoyed its economy.

Yet none of the major midwestern metropolises were any longer among the urban boomtowns of the nation. In the early twenty-first century, none ranked in the top quartile of the one hundred largest American metropolitan areas when measured by population growth. Between 2000 and 2010, the metropolitan areas of Raleigh, Charlotte, Fort Myers, Austin, Provo, Las Vegas, and Boise each posted a growth rate of greater than 30 percent; the comparable figures for Chicago, the Twin Cities, St. Louis, Cincinnati, and Kansas City were between 4 and 11 percent whereas the Detroit and Cleveland metropolitan areas lost population.

Moreover, the Midwest's share of the nation's largest metropolises had dropped. The heartland accounted for twelve of the top thirty cities in 1890; in 2010 it was the location of only seven of the thirty largest metropolitan areas. Whereas in 1890 the South and West could claim only four of the thirty largest cities; in 2010 those regions were the site of seventeen of the thirty most populous metropolitan areas.

Other data recorded some troubling realities for the Midwest. Though midwestern cities spent billions on new airports and convention centers, they were not among the nation's leading destinations. The Midwest was literally as well as figuratively the flyover region. In 2013 only four of the nation's thirty busiest airports, ranked according to passenger enplanements, were in the Midwest as compared with eight in the East, eight in the South, and ten in the West. Only Chicago's O'Hare ranked among the top fifteen in passenger boardings.[19] In 2013 and 2014 Chicago likewise was the only midwestern city to make the list of twenty-five top convention and meeting destinations. Detroit, Cleveland, and Milwaukee did not even rank among the top fifty.[20] In an era of air travel and competition for tourist and convention dollars, most midwestern metropolises were not among the winners.

Through decades of changing fortunes, midwestern metropolises have, then, developed in accord with a certain common pattern. They emerged between 1830 and 1890 in an era of water transport, rails, water power, iron ore, and coal. With the great river highways of the Mississippi valley and the largest lake network in the world, the Midwest nurtured a flourishing group of inland ports. Its dense web of rails transported the agricultural produce of its fertile fields to those emerging hubs, and its forests and mineral resources added to the compound so conducive to urban growth and prosperity.

Between 1890 and 1930, cities from Cleveland to Omaha built upon their early successes, and the region led the world in the transportation revolution wrought by the automobile. Whereas Chicago had been the wonder of the late nineteenth century, Detroit was the miracle worker of the early twentieth century.

During the second half of the twentieth century, however, midwestern cities experienced a period of readjustment. Signature industries declined or disappeared. Air travel proved less of an advantage for the heartland hubs than had the rail networks of the nineteenth century. The South and West attracted tourism and convention dollars. The arid mecca of Las Vegas, with no waterways, hog or grain production, coal or iron ore, was the boomtown of a nation devoted increasingly to leisure and consumption rather than production.

Midwestern cities survived with varying degrees of success. Those communities that had been most heavily dependent on manufacturing faced the most difficult readjustment. Metropolises that had developed a more diverse economic base adapted more readily. In the early twenty-first century, as in earlier periods, the heartland hubs differed somewhat in history and fortunes. Yet throughout the decades from 1830 to 2015, they have shared a common trajectory that distinguishes them as midwestern metropolises.

Future urban scholarship might benefit from a recognition of this distinctive midwestern history. A shared pattern of economic development provides a scaffold for scholars of the urban heartland, but patterns of ethnicity, culture, class division, and politics warrant further examination. Regional identity makes a difference, and in coming years a midwestern perspective on metropolitan history could enrich the field of urban studies. There is a midwestern urban story to be told.

Notes

1. Randolph C. Downes, *Industrial Beginnings* (Toledo: Historical Society of Northwestern Ohio, 1954), 2.
2. Downes, *Industrial Beginnings*, 13.

3. See David B. Danbom, "Flour Power: The Significance of Flour Milling at the Falls," *Minnesota History* 58 (2003): 271–85.

4. Danbom, "Flour Power," 273.

5. See Christian G. Carron, *Grand Rapids Furniture: The Story of America's Furniture City* (Grand Rapids MI: Public Museum of Grand Rapids, 1998).

6. *Manufactures, Part II, States and Territories, Twelfth Census of the United States Taken in the Year 1900* (Washington DC: United States Census Office, 1902), 351–52.

7. *Manufactures*, 811.

8. *Manufactures*, 587, 590. Regarding New York, the 1900 *Census of Manufactures* noted that "the news paper products, and cheese, butter, and condensed milk, factory product, are virtually the only ones directly dependent on the state's natural wealth. All the rest of the progressive industries of New York use materials imported from other states" (584).

9. *Manufactures*, 748–49, 751–52.

10. Jon C. Teaford, *Cities of the Heartland: The Rise and Fall of the Industrial Midwest* (Bloomington: Indiana University Press, 1993), 105.

11. Raymond A. Mohl and Neil Betten, "The Future of Industrial City Planning: Gary, Indiana, 1906–1910," *Journal of the American Institute of Planners* 38 (1972): 205.

12. Danbom, "Flour Power," 273.

13. Lawrence H. Larsen, Barbara J. Cottrell, Harl A. Dalstrom, and Kay Calame Dalstrom, *Upstream Metropolis: An Urban Biography of Omaha and Council Bluffs* (Lincoln: University of Nebraska Press, 2007), 185.

14. Carron, *Grand Rapids Furniture*, 71–79.

15. David F. Burg, *Chicago's White City of 1893* (Lexington: University Press of Kentucky, 1976), 115.

16. Larsen et al., *Upstream Metropolis*, 129–32. See also James B. Haynes, *History of the Trans-Mississippi and International Exposition of 1898* (Omaha NE: Exposition Committee on History, 1910).

17. Larsen et al., *Upstream Metropolis*, 339.

18. Carron, *Grand Rapids Furniture*, 79.

19. Federal Aviation Administration, "Commercial Service Airports Based on Calendar Year 2013 Enplanements," accessed March 23, 2015, http://www.faa.gov/airports/planning_capacity/passenger_allcargo_stats/passenger/media/.

20. Charisse Jones, "Top Convention Destinations: Orlando, Chicago, Las Vegas," *USA Today*, August 21, 2013, http://www.usatoday.com/story/travel/destinations/2013/08/21/top-50-destinations-for-meetingplanners; "2014 Top 50 U.S. Meeting Destinations, Event Destination Guide," accessed February 15, 2015, http://www.cvent.com/RFP/DestinationGuide/DGCustomPage.aspx?dgcpstub=06945d34-.

PART 5

The Midwest's Voices

14

Of Murals and Mirrors

MIDWEST REGIONALISM THEN AND NOW

Zachary Michael Jack

It's Friday night in mid-April, and after a day of work in the city I am driving home to Grant Wood Country. To this day some prefer to name my home by its most famous native, and little wonder. It's not just that Grant Wood's childhood school and stomping grounds, Antioch, are a mere dozen miles down the road from my hill farm, but that the rolling land I enter when I cross the Mississippi River are *his* hills, high and buxom and greening just as they are in the maestro's paintings and public murals. To call this place Grant Wood Country is not unlike calling it "Tall Corn Country," or to refer to the larger region in which it resides as the "Corn Belt"; we name ourselves here for the homegrown crops of which we are most proud, whether human or vegetable.

A half-dozen miles down the road from Antioch School, Grant Wood's grave sits on a high hill above his childhood river and mine, the Wapsipinicon. And a few more miles upriver of his grave in Anamosa, Iowa, is the site of Wood's regionally famous art colony at Stone City. There the maestro's personal gravitas and magnetic appeal drew other prominent regionalists in 1932 and 1933, including poet-playwright Jay G. Sigmund, painter Marvin Cone, writer-professor Paul Engle, and muralists John Bloom and Francis Robert White.

The nearness of these important regionalist sites—sacred temples, really, if today's regionalist historian possesses a pilgrim's soul—is not at all accidental. If one includes nearby Cedar Rapids, site of Grant Wood's studio, and Iowa City, where for a time he lived and taught, the near entirety of the painter's too-short life is contained within this thirty-mile radius. Emphatically, the artist lived out his place-based creed, which roughly translates to the old agrarian maxim: dance with the one that brung ya.

"There are . . . two great themes in rural writing," author David Pichaske writes, "the theme of departure and the theme of return."[1] And yet here, too, Grant Wood and the regionalist artist, writers, and thinkers of his Stone City Art Colony stubbornly bucked the trend. In his 1935 manifesto *Revolt Against the City*, Wood reminds us that he belongs to a third category, a hybridity, counting himself among "those of us who have never deserted our own regions for long."[2] For grounded artists like Wood, rural states like Iowa weren't so much "havens of refuge" for artists and intellectuals retreating from the metropolis, but "*continuing* friendly, homely environments [emphasis mine]."[3] And yet in their determined "homeyness" Wood and his fellow Stone City regionalists amounted to conspicuous outliers even in the 1930s, a time when the WPA *Guide to Iowa* opened its chapter "Iowans" with this matter-of-fact statement: "An Iowan is as likely to be found in any of the forty-eight states as in his native one."[4] The guide goes on to cite a National Resources Board survey of 1935 that found that "more than one-third of all the children of Iowa were living elsewhere."[5]

While regionalisms and regionalists have become au courant within a decentered academe, academics are, more often than not, among the worst authorities on nativity, folkways, and "indigenous culture." Academics count themselves lucky to be within the mantric "day's drive of home"—"close enough" to the omphalos as far as they are concerned. Your true regionalist, however, would argue that the displaced and thus spiritually removed scholar, secure in his tenureship and far from home, is merely the sad sack perched precariously in the window, wrapping the antennae in tin foil, hoping against hope to tune in the dying signal from which he once received his most generative and life-giving news.

How far, we might ask ourselves, is "out of range" for a philosophy, regionalism, based on nativeness, if not nativity? In his provocative essay "The Mindset of Agrarianism," editor Maurice Telleen argues that regionalism's close cousin, agrarianism, would be better regarded as a "religion" than a mere "movement," inasmuch as agrarianism puts a "strong emphasis on personal behavior and its consequences."[6] He reminds us that the "religion" of agrarianism, and by implication its cousin regionalism, is a "cultural contract fashioned to work in a specific time and place.... Its job description is to . . . sustain and perpetuate community."[7] Agrarianism, Telleen points out, is rooted in place, and functions as an ecology of proximity stipulating an "inescapable contract that you are stuck with from birth on . . . like it or not."[8]

The agrarian contract, Telleen argues, involves stewardship of the earth and mindfulness of the local, traits most recently, and concretely, manifested in the local foods movement. In their own way a "locavore" is likewise bound by an almost religious obligation to locality, in their case to edibles produced within the local "food shed." The locavore, consuming that which is harvested one hundred miles from home or nearer, acts in sympathy with the regionalist mind.[9] Similarly, those who seek to establish relationships of ontological significance close to home, in person, are regionalists of a sort, too, especially in a digital age where even the most generous of popular dating sites effectively limit the radius of the lovelorn aspirant's search to perhaps sixty miles, it being understood that the real intimacies members seek there become impractical if not impossible beyond certain geographic limits.

Extending the analogy, why is it, then, that so many of today's avowed regionalists presume to date their home region at such frankly impossible distances? We claim, many of us do, to admire the founding regionalists of the 1930s, and yet it's worth asking why we find it so hard to live by their example. How near to where you now live and work, gentle reader, is the locus of your own history—your first school, first date, first kiss, first skinny dip, first poem or paper or painting judged good and worthy? Chances are good that the settings for your life's rites of passage have endured in spite of your restiveness. Your brick-and-mortar elementary school, for instance, likely still stands; the river or lake that first invited you to shed your clothes still beguiles; even the schoolteacher who first gifted you with meaningful and motivating praise still likely lives near the classroom in which they first served as a difference-maker for you. Tellingly, it is we, the supposed scholar-protagonists, who long ago left the scene. And isn't that what protagonist-heroes do in Middle America, almost by definition—leave? Would they in fact qualify for hero status if they stayed? Or is there no story in staying, no press release or newsworthy human interest implicit in the regionalist-friendly headline "Man Stays Home." In eulogizing his fellow regionalist poet Jay G. Sigmund, Paul Engle opined, "He wanted not an ivory tower but simply the water tower of his own village."[10] The same sentiments that in Sigmund's day would have been understood as highest praise, regionalist to regionalist, would today be understood as, at best, backhanded compliment if not passive-aggressive critique of stubborn rootedness and misspent talent.

Chances are good—if you are reading these words—that your headline, unlike Jay Sigmund's, would instead read: "Scholar Leaves Home for Greener Pastures; Returns for Funeral." Frequently cited, perfectly reasonable rationalizations for the ubiquitous ghosting of home among today's educated elites include economic necessity and/or marital compromise. The highly educated, would-be regionalists of the digital age talk a good game, of course, citing economic factors as reasons why they are forced to become transients, economic refugees against their will, migrant-scholars willing to hang out their shingle at whatever college or university would have them, *wherever* it would have them. And yet muralists Wood, White, and Bloom, to name just a few, made their difficult decisions to stay home during the worst of the bread lines of the Great Depression, as did fellow regionalist writers Sigmund and Ruth Suckow, the latter of whom wrote of her region's out-migrating elites: "Many young people forced themselves away and doomed themselves to a kind of rootless exile simply to prove themselves socially or intellectually and artistically enterprising, and to escape the stigma attached to 'just settling down at home.' To say of a bright young man when college was over, 'Oh, he's gone back to Cornville and he's living there,' was to prove him without ambition."[11]

Expect today's deserting regionalist—when confronted with examples of dozens of predecessors who still somehow managed to abide their rural, disadvantaged places throughout the ravages of the Great Depression—to point out that they too might have stayed closer to home with appropriate government support. If only the government would have subsidized them, they claim, to make it economically viable for them to work in their home region, they would gladly have sunk their roots closer to the home place. Here in Grant Wood Country, however, we call theirs a "chicken-and-egg" argument, which is to wonder, openly and rhetorically, about which came first: the determined regionalist's vow to root down such that they might guard their home region with and by their presence, economics be damned, or the subsidy by which it became comfortable for them to do so without so much as a whiff of risk? A farming people, we understand that to act on personal conviction without financial risk is a chimera, a fantasy of the urban.

No matter how one spins it, the decision to stay home, or at least to return to home, defined the regionalist movement, from Thomas Hart Benton, who belatedly jettisoned his New York City life in favor of his native western Missouri, to Grant Wood. Benton, who had been away from his personal and regional omphalos for far longer than Wood, captured his reasons for returning thusly: "This part of the country is going to dominate social change, and I want to be there to see it when it happens."[12] In *Revolt Against the City*, Wood likewise found himself defending his choice to leave the supposed intellectual riches of the metropolis: "Seven years ago my friends had sincerely pitied me for what they called my 'exile' in Iowa. They then had a vision of my going back to an uninteresting region where I could have no contact with culture and no association with kindred spirits."[13]

Then as now, regionalism as a movement brings with it the kinds of slings and arrows postmoderns find uncomfortable if not outright judgmental. As a philosophy as well as an aesthetic it dares ask something of us, namely that we vote with our feet, living in and otherwise helping to sustain the places from which we harvest our inspiration and our scholarship. As Minnesota regionalist Paul Gruchow begs us consider: "What if one's life were not a commodity, not something to be bartered to the highest bidder. . . . What if one's life were governed by needs more fundamental than acceptance or admiration? What if one were simply to stay home and plant some manner of garden?"[14]

I confess that I too find the regionalist standard set by Wood and company difficult to achieve in a digital age; I, like you, fear living in the proverbial glass house. And yet I do strive to make regionalism a lived rather than merely academic enterprise. While I study the movement historically—sometimes hundreds of miles away in dusty repositories and late at night in online archives—such encounters leave me cold *except* when they are coupled with a lived life, and more so with each year that I hang my hat and grind my axe at home in Grant Wood Country. And I do hang my hat and swing my axe here; the language is closer to parable than metaphor or analogy.

On this day, as on far too many others, my professional commute is a long one, taking me into neighboring Illinois. Still I am close enough to home to tune in the hometown radio station in Cedar Rapids, Iowa—WMT—the so-called farmer's radio station, and one of a few remaining to offer the kind of detailed agricultural news real farmers depend on. For a brief moment this April afternoon, temperatures top eighty, and the news director and his good-natured sidekick are agog with the preternatural numbers.

Among the crop of today's other local headlines are these: the University of Iowa Athletic Department has extended tailgating hours for the upcoming football season; a Boys and Girls Club van stolen in Cedar Rapids has been found in Des Moines; the state Economic Development Authority has awarded nearly a million dollars for the development of residential, retail, and office space in New Bohemia in the historic Czech area of Cedar Rapids, not far from Grant Wood's, Paul Engle's, Marvin Cone's, Francis Robert White's, and Jay Sigmund's one-time homes and haunts.[15] In the Cedar Rapids of today, a long-mothballed regionalist heritage is fueling urban redevelopment in New Bohemia, an area of folk life and ethnic richness then as now, with a long period of benign neglect and historical amnesia in between.

But the biggest of the local news stories this balmy afternoon is the slow recovery and re-creation of the 1936 regionalist murals in the former Cedar Rapids Federal Courthouse (now Cedar Rapids City Hall) censored in the fifties for showing a Wild West–style lynching, nudes, and newspaper headlines referencing syphilis.[16] In October 1935 Francis Robert White, director of the Little Gallery in Cedar Rapids and a Grant Wood disciple, was named master artist to design murals by the Works Progress Administration (WPA) for the Cedar Rapids Federal Courthouse Project.[17] Now, eighty-some years later, WMT's Ryan Schlader announces, "Those WPA murals being recovered in City Hall have quite an interesting history. . . . In the fifties there was an upheaval in the way people thought of society."[18] In fact, the murals, painted by a team of artists under White's leadership, had been commissioned specifically by the Treasury Relief Art Project, which employed artists to create paintings and sculptures for federal buildings, like the new courthouse built on First Avenue in Cedar Rapids in 1933.[19] Schlader next plays a sound bite from the man in charge of the restoration, Scott Haskins of Fine Arts Conservation, who's quoted as saying, "In 1951 they [the regionalist murals] were painted out because of what they depicted. And then someone thought of the fact they were an integral part of the building. They were part of the history of the building. Maybe we ought to uncover them."[20]

While stories like these come to us in today's headlines, which is to say in the guise of current events, the story of new/old New Bohemia and the new/old Cedar Rapids City Hall murals are by my definition regionalist *histories*, thens and nows merging in timely simultaneity. Similarly, a homegrown radio station covering the local news of a mural painted by an Iowa muralist who happened to be a product of Wood's Stone City Art Colony in the 1930s, which itself advocated regional artists rendering regional scenery on the ground where they lived, illustrates a remarkable confluence of regionalist thought and deed—the ways history, to paraphrase Twain, *rhymes* rather than merely repeats itself. Wood himself had called for an "honest reliance by the artist upon subject matter which he can best interpret because he knows it best."[21] Localism, the maestro insisted, is more like "patriotism" than "chauvinism" in its spirited appreciation for the artist's own life and immediate surroundings.[22]

The emergence of the mural as perhaps the dominant form of public art in the Midwest during regionalism's apogee in the 1930s makes an intuitive kind of sense. Practically, the artistic commissions offered by massive mural projects served as a means by which FDR and his New Dealers could keep regional artists properly fed and watered at home in hard times. In times of cataclysmic hardship, murals likewise offered federal, state, and county governments a canvas upon which to tell their story of heroic deeds and achievements, and to do so in highly trafficked public places where a citizen's attention could be garnered in person and en masse as nowhere else in those pre-television midlands. The largely patriotic sentiments of the Midwest murals of Wood, Benton, Bloom, and White, for example, served to recall and reinforce dominant Middle American ideologies as well as to offer a visual reminder of their virtues—recording why and wherefore America had once created widespread abundance.

When Francis Robert White completed his controversial courthouse mural in 1936, for example, his home state of Iowa was ninety years removed from admittance into the Union in 1846 and ready to look back nostalgically at providential origins. For the most part, White's, Bloom's, and Wood's WPA-era murals embraced open, optimistic vistas and documentarian perspectives of a region that didn't look too much outward or inward, but naturally and perhaps reflexively at itself in panoramic tableau. In short, if midwestern foodstuffs had helped win wars and stem the tide of hunger, Iowa and its fellow breadbasket states possessed a powerful cultural inheritance worthy of its own epic iconography. The state-sponsored murals were to the Depression-era Midwest what the metopes of the Parthenon were to Ancient Greece: a recitation of past greatness and a hopeful prediction of greatness soon to be renewed.

Despite their universal and even mythic subject matter, the murals of my home state can and *should* mean something different to me as a native Iowan, the true regionalist would argue, than to a scholar studying regionalism from an ivory tower far away. The Hawkeye State murals sponsored by the Federal Art Project of the Works Progress Administration are perhaps the best known, but Iowa also received a disproportionately high number of commissions from a similar program funded by the Treasury Department and administered by Edward Rowan, a former gallery director from Cedar Rapids.[23] Thanks to his efforts, and the network of artists he knew through his friend Grant Wood, artists like John Bloom and Francis Robert White were hired to relay monolithic regional narratives on canvas as they might have been in Rome.

My first real experience with one of my home state's many WPA-era murals came as a know-nothing undergraduate at Iowa State University in 1992. Not surprisingly, I arrived at Iowa's land-grant university afflicted with a high degree of rural-born conscientiousness and a coincident fear of the devilry inherent in idleness. I found myself quite frequently at the university library attempting to stave off the distraction of friends and video games and grunge bands played at ear-splitting volumes in the dormitories. So great was the temptation for my so-called Slacker Generation to affirm in practice its unfortunate sobriquet that merely holing up inside the library proved insufficient for my purposes. After a bit of searching I found in the bowels of the university library an older repository whose original structure had been kept intact, essentially entombed, built over and around as the library grew to accommodate ever-growing collections and rising student enrollments. This perfectly monkish study spot was accessed via the original stairwell that lead to the upper lobby of the "old" library, whose walls were decorated by an eight-paneled mural entitled *Other Arts Follow*.

It says something sad and at the same time true, I think, about the self-centered ignorance of that peculiar species known as the American college student that I surely must have passed under this epic mural hundreds of times before stopping to pay it even the most passing of attention. Though I was then working on a minor in Art History, I am certain I did not then realize that the mural was the work of the great Grant Wood, nor that its creation had been subsidized by the Public Works of Art Project in 1934, and least of all that the eight panels had been created to reflect the divisions of Iowa State College at the time: Veterinary Medicine, Farm Crops, Animal Husbandry, Home Economics, Ceramics and Chemical Engineering, Mechanical Engineering, and Aeronautical and Civil Engineering.[24] In art history classes, after all, we were not learning our uniquely rich heritage of regionalist artists, but were instead learning to identify and recite at a glance the apses and naves and sanctuaries of Old Europe. Little wonder, then, that at the time I gave only superficial consideration to the mural's head-scratching caption, "When tillage begins, the other arts follow." Though I had come straight from an Iowa farm, I had been better trained to recognize and recite a lyric from Nirvana's album *Nevermind* than to attribute the "other arts follow" truism to the agrarian-statesman Daniel Webster.

I recall *Other Arts Follow* as my first real encounter with a large-scale public mural, but in fact I am mistaken. In actuality, the post office in the little county seat town of Tipton, Iowa, where we did our business and banking when I was a boy, boasted a mural by native Iowan John Vincent Bloom, an assistant to Grant Wood for years before he began receiving his own commissions.[25] Perhaps I failed to properly appreciate Bloom's 1940 mural *Cattle* all those years ago, because, like most post-office murals, it loomed above the wall of post boxes, along the ceiling, where a boy in tow on mundane errands would not ordinarily think to look. In their haste to get their letters posted and their packages mailed, my agrarian kin did not stop to cast their eyes upward nor point out to me Bloom's whimsical painting of eight Hereford cattle above the door marked "Postmaster's Quarters."

For me, as a modern-day regionalist, the murals of my home region, once reclaimed, trigger important acts of cultural rediscovery. They were created precisely to remind the viewer to pay attention, to cherish their history, and more than that, to preserve and elevate that history even in its egalitarian plainness and folksiness—its *homeliness*, emphasis on the *home*. These visual representations were, at root, an ideological prod and provocation, not a simple or innocuous or guileless iconography. They served as a canvas upon which public art and public history coalesced, as well as a cautionary tale that a citizenry ignorant of their local and regional histories was a citizenry easily duped, manipulated, or co-opted, their histories, homely and heroic, snowed under, whitewashed, or otherwise silenced.

The reasons why I should have been ignorant of the WPA-vintage mural in the old mothballed Federal Courthouse in Cedar Rapids for the better part of four decades are clear. For most of my young adulthood, the murals were invisible, obscured by five layers of concealing paint, indicative of the strength of the desire to erase them from public memory.[26] The whitewashers did their job so well, in fact, that most of the citizens of that cereal town on the banks of the Cedar River, where Grant Wood and Marvin Cone attended high school and kept their art studios, had long since forgotten the existence of what a Mount Mercy University exhibit deemed "the largest American art project to date."[27]

By the time of the 2013 restoration of the south wall mural, entitled *Inheriting Justice*, the murals had been out of sight, and out of mind, for more than fifty years.

In fact, today's news of the uncovering and restoration of the murals is only the most recent iteration of cover-up followed by rediscovery. The first cover-up occurred in 1951, by most accounts, at which time contractors painted over Robert Francis White's murals, citing the objections of lawyers and federal district court judges such as Henry Graven, who captured his objections thusly in 1956: "Among other things, the jury sits facing a mural portraying a lynching in realistic detail."[28] Photos of the murals, the newspaper reported, were sent to the chief justice of the Eighth Circuit Court of Appeals and the director of the U.S. Courts administrative office who subsequently authorized their removal.

The murals briefly saw the light again ten years later, in 1961 (here again, dates vary), when workers called in to wash the walls detected the ghostly images of faces staring back at them. Consulting artists were called in to determine a reasonable course of action and agreed the murals lacked artistic value and could be painted over permanently. A different judge this time, Judge McManus, ordered the murals to be whitewashed for a second time in their short history. The murals then promptly disappeared from public viewing for another fifty years until 2011, when a federal grant of sixty thousand dollars funded the restoration of the north wall.[29]

The "now and the then" of regionalism, and indeed of historical study more generally, is aptly illustrated by the parable of the Francis Robert White murals. In one sense the modern parable of the Cedar Rapids murals proves the potential worth of the public historian as a sort of public conscience, a keeper of memories whose mere presence serves to discourage those who would attempt to remove or otherwise sanitize unflattering histories. By this analogy the diligent "local" or "regional" historian acts as cultural conservator.

How I or anyone else came to hear the story of the recovery of the lost murals offers an even more compelling manifestation of contemporary regionalism in practice. Hearing this particular story required me to demonstrate sufficient local interest to have tuned in a distant AM radio signal; it required a community with the requisite interest in the history of its homegrown arts and artists, and especially in its painters of public art, to seek the funds necessary for the restoration of a painting whose content many found, and still find, offensive; it demanded a municipality sufficiently mindful of its own history to recall that the murals had been painted over fifty years prior. My knowledge of the once censored, lately recovered murals further depended on a radio station whose news director placed sufficient value on local and regional news to make these "local" murals a story worthy of airing alongside the other dramatic news of the day—a five-thousand-person evacuation of an army armaments center after a possible security breach, for example, and a court-ordered supervision of a Florida postal worker who managed to land a gyrocopter on the White House lawn.

Of course the elevating and upgrading of the local and the regional stories and histories to true parity with more monolithic national narratives is exactly what the comprehensive regionalism of Grant Wood called for, in the same way that it intended scholars, professors, writers, artists, and historians to work from, and on behalf of, their native regions.

Notes

1. David Pichaske, *Late Harvest: Rural American Writing* (New York: Paragon, 1992), xxii.
2. Grant Wood, *Revolt Against the City* (Iowa City: Clio Press, 1935).
3. Wood, *Revolt Against the City.*
4. State Historical Society of Iowa, *The WPA Guide to Iowa*, reprint ed. (Ames: Iowa State University Press, 1986), 26. Citations are from the 1986 edition.
5. *WPA Guide to Iowa*, 26.
6. Maurice Telleen, "The Mindset of Agrarianism Old and New," in *The Essential Agrarian Reader* (Washington DC: Shoemaker and Hoard, 2004), 53.
7. Telleen, "The Mindset of Agrarianism," 53.
8. Telleen, "The Mindset of Agrarianism," 53.
9. For one definition of a "locavore," see locavores.com, last accessed May 9, 2015.
10. Paul Engle, ed., "The Poet and the Man" in *Jay G. Sigmund: Select Poetry and Prose* (Muscatine IA: Prairie Press, 1939), viii.
11. Ruth Suckow, "Iowa," *American Mercury*, September 9, 1926, 39–45.
12. Justin Wolff, *Thomas Hart Benton: A Life* (New York: Macmillan, 2012), 261–62.
13. Wood, *Revolt Against the City.*

14. Paul Gruchow, *Grass Roots: The Universe of Home* (Minneapolis: Milkweed Editions, 1995), 3.

15. "Six Cedar Rapids Projects Receive Tax Incentives through Iowa Economic Development Authority," WMT Radio, April 17, 2005.

16. Rick Smith, "Section of Cedar Rapids City Hall Mural Recreated," *Cedar Rapids Gazette*, April 24, 2015, http://thegazette.com/subject/news/section-of-cedar-rapids-city-hall-mural-recreated-20150424.

17. Busse Library, Mount Mercy University, *When Tillage Begins: The Stone City Art Colony and School* (Cedar Rapids IA: Mount Mercy University), https://projects.mtmercy.edu/stonecity/artists/white.html.

18. Ryan Schlader, "Those WPA Murals . . . ," WMT Headline News, WMT Radio, April 17, 2015.

19. "History of the Cedar Rapids Federal Courthouse Mural," last accessed May 9, 2015, http://www.cedar-rapids.org/things-to-see-do/artsculture/pages/cedar-rapids-federal-courthouse-mural.aspx.

20. Schlader, "Those WPA Murals . . ."

21. Wood, *Revolt Against the City*.

22. Wood, *Revolt Against the City*.

23. Figge Art Museum, "John Bloom: Visions of Iowa," accessed May 9, 2015, http://figgeartmuseum.org/Figge-Art-Museum-%281%29/February-2009/John-Bloom--Visions-of-Iowa.aspx.

24. The Living New Deal, University of California Berkeley, "Iowa State University Library, Murals, Ames IA," accessed May 9, 2015, http://livingnewdeal.org/projects/iowa-state-university-library-murals-ames-ia/.

25. Figge Art Museum, "John Bloom."

26. "History of the Cedar Rapids Federal Courthouse Mural," accessed May 9, 2015, http://www.cedar-rapids.org/things-to-see-do/artsculture/pages/cedar-rapids-federal-courthouse-mural.aspx.

27. Busse Library, Mount Mercy University, *When Tillage Begins*.

28. Diane Langton, "Time Machine: Federal Courtroom Murals," *Cedar Rapids Gazette*, March 23, 2015, http://thegazette.com/subject/news/time-machine-federal-courtroom-murals-20150323.

29. Rick Smith "More of the Depression-Era Mural Is Unveiled," *Cedar Rapids Gazette*, March 29, 2014, http://thegazette.com/2013/07/11/more-of-restored-depression-era-mural-is-unveiled-at-cedar-rapids-city-hall.

15

Midwestern Intellectuals

James Seaton

In a book completed just before his untimely death in 1994, historian and social critic Christopher Lasch noted that "Middle America" had become "a term that has both geographical and social implications."[1] For many shapers of opinion, "Middle America," "flyover country," or simply the Midwest "has come to symbolize everything that stands in the way of progress: 'family values,' mindless patriotism, religious fundamentalism, racism, homophobia, retrograde views of women."[2] More than twenty years later, stereotypes of the Midwest have survived and indeed flourished. Like most stereotypes, these contain a certain measure of truth, misleading though they are. Lasch himself believed that Middle America stood in the way of progress as defined by the elites whose outlook he described and critiqued in his last book, *The Revolt of the Elites and the Betrayal of Democracy*. In his early works a proponent of socialism who used Marx and Freud to demonstrate the limitations of capitalism in general and American society in particular, Lasch in later works such as *The Revolt of the Elites* and *The True and Only Heaven* turned away from the cultural left to reaffirm the significance and value of the "petty bourgeois virtues" derided by postmodernist intellectuals: "hard work, sobriety, self-improvement."[3]

By the end of his life, Christopher Lasch could be seen as a "Midwest intellectual," a thinker whose ideas went against the grain of the progressive consensus dominating the media, academia, and cultural life generally on the coasts. Lasch's journey followed a path taken by other midwestern intellectuals whose works might seem at first to have little or nothing to do with the Midwest. Kenneth Rexroth, poet and critic, gained national attention as one of the leaders of the San Francisco contingent of the Beat Generation in the late fifties and early sixties. Russell Kirk became famous with the publication of *The Conservative Mind* in

1953. The book's emphasis on Edmund Burke and other English thinkers, its near silence about such central American political figures as James Madison and Abraham Lincoln, and its respectful attitude toward the antebellum "Southern conservatism" of John Calhoun suggested to many readers that its author found little worth conserving in twentieth-century America. Deirdre McCloskey, formerly Donald McCloskey, is probably best known to non-economists as the author of *Crossing*, a memoir describing her transition from male to female.

At first glance, there is nothing particularly "midwestern" about any of these figures, at least if one associates the Midwest, for better or worse, with traditional morality, cultural conservatism in art and literature, and a patriotism that, while not uncritical, sees the United States as a force, all things considered, for good. And although it is true that all four were born in the Midwest and all have been shaped to varying degrees by midwestern culture, one must admit that none of the four has consistently embraced traditional morality, cultural conservatism, and American patriotism in a consistent, straightforward way. It is also true, however, that none of the four has entirely rejected what one might call, with only minimal exaggeration, "midwestern values." The Midwest has left its mark on all four, one that is all the more striking because the public images of all four might seem to casual observers at certain times to represent the antithesis of those "midwestern values."

Kenneth Rexroth was certainly one of the leading figures in what has been called the San Francisco Renaissance, but more often the rise of the Beat Generation. Rexroth's essays are filled with declarations condemning almost every aspect of contemporary culture, society, and politics. Rexroth, a poet and critic, saw himself as an outsider, a thorough-going opponent of the literary establishment, whose viewpoint he characterized in 1959 as "a subtle blend of bankrupt, sectarian Bolshevism, the Ku Klux Klan, the provincialism of the subway Neanderthals, and the more blatant propaganda of the State Department."[4] For Rexroth the vices of the literary world were linked to the evils of the world around him. He writes that one "cannot be forgiven for being a parson or a social worker or a professor," because such professions make one part of the "Social Lie" and "a partner in mass murder."[5] The organs of the status quo corrupted would-be Beats by granting them attention and thereby turning them into "simply comical bogies conjured up by the Luce publications . . . trained monkeys, the clowning helots of the Enemy."[6] America of the 1950s was nothing more to Rexroth than "the mindless cacodemon called 'Things As They Are.'"[7] But perhaps the "Enemy" was not so much the United States as capitalism. Rexroth considered Baudelaire "the greatest poet of the capitalist epoch" in large part because Baudelaire's poetry dramatizes the underlying reality of Western society, revealing "the cruel dynamic of an acquisitive and continually disintegrating society, a society which had suddenly abandoned satisfactions which went back to the beginning of human communities in the Neolithic Age."[8]

Yet when Rexroth came to write his autobiography, *An Autobiographical Novel*, he revealed that all along he had been not a revolutionary and certainly not a Marxist, but instead "a conservationist if not a conservative."[9] His values were not formed in Greenwich Village or Haight-Ashbury but instead in the Indiana and Michigan of his youth. The misunderstanding was understandable, since, as Rexroth explained, "in an atomized mass culture a life motivated by inherited standards may well seem eccentric and revolutionary" (ix). It was not only his parents but the diverse cast of midwesterners around whom he grew up in the early 1900s that shaped his character: "Schwenkfelders, Mennonites, German revolutionaries of '48, Abolitionists, suffragists, squaws and Indian traders, octoroons and itinerant horse dealers, farmers in broad hats, full beards and frogged coats, hard-drinking small-town speculators, all have gone to make a personality that has proved highly resistant to digestion by the mass culture and yet, I think, conservative of the characteristic values of American life rather than the reverse."[10]

Rexroth demonstrated his cultural conservatism by celebrating the great works in collections like *Classics Revisited*. While the academic radicals were denouncing "the canon," Rexroth was more than ready to not only argue that some books are really better than others but to rank them in a precise order. In his view, "Gibbon's *Decline* is probably the greatest achievement of eighteenth-century Europe; it is also one of the ten great prose works of all time, ranking just below Thucydides, *Genji*, and *Don Quixote*."[11] Rexroth observes that "the office worker who reads Homer on the subway to work bears little superficial resemblance to either Homer's characters or his audience" and asks "Why should two long poems about the life of barbaric Greece have so great an appeal?"[12] He answers his own question, resoundingly: "Homer has been read for almost three thousand years, and is read today by millions, because he portrays . . . each man to his fellow [as] the only light there is, and all men to one another—as the source of the only principle of order. This, says Homer, is the human condition. Out of it in *The Iliad* he constructed a dramatic architecture of a cogency never to be surpassed."[13]

More than thirty years after his death in 1982, it is Rexroth the cultural conservative, the author of many essays eloquently affirming the permanent value of the great books, who is remembered and read, not Rexroth the supposed godfather of Beat poets like Allen Ginsberg and Gregory Corso.

A reader of the first editions of Russell Kirk's *The Conservative Mind* could be forgiven for suspecting that Kirk's condemnation of the modern world and a fortiori the United States was at least as severe as those issued by radicals on the political left. Kirk's grounds for condemnation were not identical to those offered by the leftists, but they were not entirely different, either. Certainly both were all encompassing. Kirk found himself confronting "a world that damns tradition, exalts equality, and welcomes change; a world that has clutched at Rousseau, swallowed him whole, and demanded prophets yet more radical; a world smudged by industrialism, standardized by the masses, consolidated by government; a world crippled by war, trembling between the colossi of East and West, and peering over a smashed barricade into the gulf of dissolution."[14]

Henry Regnery, the book's publisher, reports that Kirk's first choice for a title was "The Conservative Rout."[15] While the wording was unlikely to attract readers, it reflected Kirk's belief that, from the vantage of the middle of the twentieth century, an honest conservative would have to admit that "by and large, radical thinkers have won the day. For a century and a half, conservatives have yielded ground in a manner which, except for occasionally successful rear-guard actions, must be described as a rout."[16] To be a conservative in America, the book seemed to suggest, was to be doomed to failure. Kirk pays tribute to the southern conservatism of John Randolph and John C. Calhoun but admits that their conservatism was hopelessly entangled with a defense of the indefensible, so that even in the South their philosophical conservatism was ignored: "The great majority of Southern people, indeed, never apprehended much more of the doctrines of Randolph and Calhoun than their apology for slavery and its defense through state powers."[17] Yet Randolph and Calhoun's ideas are given a chapter of their own, while the ideas of the great opponent of slavery and secession, Abraham Lincoln, go unmentioned.

The first readers of *The Conservative Mind* might be pardoned for thinking of its author as a sort of spiritual secessionist. And indeed it is understandable that a half-century that saw two world wars, the triumph of Marxism in Russia and China, and the rise of fascism and Nazism in Europe might well lead a believer in "the permanent things" to leave the struggle behind and secede, if only in thought, from one's country and from the modern world. "We are all at some point or another secessionists," the novelist and shrewd cultural critic Ralph Ellison once observed, even as he warned against such a "retreat in dereliction of our most sacred commitments."[18] Russell Kirk no doubt knew moments of despair, but his long, productive career testifies that, despite temptations, he did not surrender to the seductions of the impulse to secessionism, political, cultural, or spiritual.

Instead, in the years after the publication of the first edition of *The Conservative Mind*, Kirk qualified, altered, and deepened his conservatism and his view of the United States, so much so that in his magisterial study of Western culture from its beginnings in Israel, Greece, and Rome to the present-day United States, *The Roots of American Order*, American society no longer appears as the leading edge of a destructive modernism but instead as a society that has achieved, at the very least, a "tolerable order" that should arouse not indignation and condemnation but appreciation.[19] Abraham Lincoln now receives his due as a conservative in the highest sense, one who upholds not only the political order but also the moral order on which the former depends. Kirk declares that "in Abraham Lincoln, the American democracy would find, at its sternest crisis of disorder, its most capable and self-sacrificing man of order."[20] For Kirk, the example of Lincoln "proved that a democracy of elevation can uphold resolutely the public order and the moral order."[21] The United States that Lincoln did so much to preserve and enrich now seems an exceptional nation, one that has been spared the afflictions, moral and material, that have ravaged so many other nations. Kirk declares that "anyone who appreciates the legacy of moral and social order which he has inherited in America will feel gratitude."[22] Decades after the publication of the first edition of *The Conservative Mind*, Kirk finds reasons to declare that "the American order has been a conspicuous success in the perspective of human history. Under God, a large measure of justice has been achieved; the state is strong and energetic; personal freedom is protected by laws and customs; and a sense of community endures."[23] Kirk speaks here with the voice of a midwestern patriotism that acknowledges American failings but also recognizes the ways in which this nation is truly exceptional. In *The Roots of American Order*, his true magnum opus, Russell Kirk returned to his midwestern roots.

Christopher Lasch would have disputed such a positive appraisal, in his earlier books because the country was perversely unwilling to welcome a socialist revolution, but in his later works because of the dominance in America of "a liberalism obsessed . . . with the need for regulations against offensive speech, and with curricular reforms designed to end the cultural hegemony of 'dead white European males.'"[24]

Lasch was always a critic of liberalism, but in his earlier works he critiqued it from the left, while in the later he spoke on behalf of a "tradition or sensibility . . . populist or petty-bourgeois" that resisted the cultural radicalism of what Lasch calls "their self-appointed spokesmen and would-be liberators" among the elites.[25] Cultural conservatism, Lasch observes, is the world view not of the rich and famous but of the classes for which the left claims to speak: "It is the working and lower middle classes, after all, that favor limits on abortion, cling to the two-parent family as a source of stability in a turbulent world, resist experiments with 'alternative lifestyles,' and harbor deep reservations about affirmative action and other ventures in large-scale social engineering."[26] In his last work before his death in 1994, Lasch became an unabashed spokesman for the real "Middle America." Lasch declared that "they understand, as their betters do not, that there are inherent limits on human control over the course of social development, over nature and the body, over the tragic elements in human history in life."[27] For Lasch the caricature spread by the media and the academy reveals more about the worldview of academic and corporate elites than about the people it allegedly describes: "Middle Americans, as they appear to the makers of educated opinion, are hopelessly shabby, unfashionable, and provincial, ill-informed about changes in taste or intellectual trends, addicted to trashy novels of romance and adventure, all stupefied by prolonged exposure to television."[28]

In his earlier works, Lasch had asserted that the only real answer to America's problems was socialist revolution. In *The Agony of the American Left* Lasch offered devastating critiques of radicalism on all fronts but nevertheless concluded that "radicalism—socialism—is the only long-term hope."[29] Even in *The Culture of Narcissism*, with its emphasis on culture rather than class, on Freudian psychoanalysis rather than Marxist economics, Lasch affirmed his belief that "a thoroughgoing transformation of our social arrangements remains a possibility," a transformation that he specifically identified as "socialist revolution."[30] Lasch's journey from the far left to a defense of Middle America was reluctant and slow. On the way he lost favor with the academic and cultural elites whose worldview was expressed by the *New York Review of Books*, where he, once a frequent contributor, found himself no longer welcome. Yet Lasch's true legacy, the cultural, political, and moral critique carried out in books like *The True and Only Heaven*, *Haven in a Heartless World*, *The Minimal Self*, and *The Revolt of the Elites*, remains valuable decades after the notion that "socialist revolution" as the solution to America's problems had been exploded.

Deirdre McCloskey, formerly Donald McCloskey, is best known to the general public as the author of *Crossing: A Memoir*, which describes her transition in middle age from man to woman. In a 2015 column in the *Des Moines Register*, McCloskey described the typical reaction of fellow Iowans to her change from man to woman, while she was teaching at the University of Iowa, as "Iowa calm."[31] The person who turns out to be the most antagonistic and causes the most trouble for McCloskey is her sister, "a professor of psychology . . . a liberal woman with liberal views on gay rights and South Africa."[32] Although she taught at a state university in the Southwest, the sister was spending a sabbatical "in Boston, visiting without academic appointment at the Harvard School of Public Health," when Donald McCloskey told her he was determined to become a woman.[33] The sister was certain that her brother must be insane and must be treated, if necessary against his will. Her tenuous connection to Harvard became important because at least some midwestern judges and psychologists gave what seemed to McCloskey undue deference to her sister's arguments because they were imbued with the authority of Harvard. At one hearing a doctor in Iowa City seemed "cowed by her [the sister's] self-confident presentation as a 'Harvard' professor of psychology."[34] Later two psychiatrists at a Chicago hospital seemed "frightened by his [Donald's] sister's letters on Harvard stationery."[35]

Almost always discussions of those who change their sex are linked to the movement for radical cultural and political change on behalf of the LGBT community. Those who speak on behalf of the movement often condemn capitalism and especially bourgeois morality as patriarchal and bigoted. Deirdre McCloskey, however, while adamantly defending her decision to "cross," to use her word, has written a series of magisterial works defending capitalism and bourgeois culture on both economic and moral grounds. In *The Bourgeois Virtues* she persuasively argues that capitalist society, to a greater extent than any alternative, fosters the seven traditional virtues of prudence, temperance, justice, courage, love, faith, hope, and love. Capitalism encourages and often rewards

the prudence to trade rather than to invade . . . the temperance to educate oneself in business and in life, to listen to the customer humbly, to resist the temptations to cheat, to ask quietly whether there might be a compromise here . . . the justice to play willingly for good work, to honor labor, to break down privilege, to value people for what they can do rather than for what they are, to view success without envy . . . the courage to overcome the fear of change, to bear defeat unto bankruptcy, to be courteous to new ideas, to wake up next morning and face fresh work with cheer . . . love to care for employees and partners and colleagues and customers and fellow citizens, to wish well of human kind . . . faith to build monuments to the glorious past, to sustain traditions of commerce, of learning, of religion . . . hope to see the future as something other than stagnation or eternal recurrence, to infuse the day's work with a purpose, seeing one's labor as a glorious calling.[36]

To leftists of all stripes, avant-garde artists, neo-Confederates, and those wishing to return to the Middle Ages, "bourgeois" is a dirty word. Deirdre McCloskey thinks otherwise: In *Bourgeois Dignity* she argues:

The dual ethical change of dignity and of liberty for ordinary bourgeois life led to a reign of sense and sensibility from which we are all still benefitting. Its virtues are commercial prudence and family love, combined in the self-defined middle class with an almost insane inventive courage fueled by hope, protected in its politics by faith and temperance, and by a just if often unintended improvement in the condition of the other, working classes . . . who themselves at last by the competition among the innovative bourgeoisie and their purchased politicians came to partake of the citizenly, bourgeois dignity of a vote, a house, a car, an education, and became themselves "gentlemanly" middle class.[37]

In studying the culture of the Midwest it is important to take account of figures who, like the four discussed in this essay, may refer to the Midwest rarely or not at all but whose attitudes and ideas nevertheless reveal its influence. Kenneth Rexroth, Russell Kirk, Christopher Lasch, and Deirdre McCloskey may be described as Midwest intellectuals not because they are regional chauvinists and not because they have been unwilling to search for the true, the good, and the beautiful wherever in the world they may be found. They are midwestern intellectuals because all four, despite sometimes long detours sampling attitudes hostile to the values of what Lasch called "Middle America," came to affirm, deepen, and enrich attitudes and ideas too often caricatured by those to whom the Midwest is just flyover country.

Notes

1. Christopher Lasch, *The Revolt of the Elites and the Betrayal of Democracy* (New York: W. W. Norton, 1995), 29.
2. Lasch, *Revolt of the Elites.*
3. Lasch, *Revolt of the Elites,* 83.
4. Kenneth Rexroth, *Bird in the Bush: Obvious Essays* (New York: New Directions, 1959), vii.
5. Rexroth, *Bird in the Bush,* viii.
6. Rexroth, *Bird in the Bush,* ix.
7. Rexroth, *Bird in the Bush,* x.
8. Kenneth Rexroth, "Unacknowledged Legislators and 'Art Pour Art,'" in *Bird in the Bush,* 14.
9. Kenneth Rexroth, *An Autobiographical Novel* (New York: Doubleday, 1966), x.
10. Rexroth, *An Autobiographical Novel,* vii.
11. Kenneth Rexroth, "Science and Civilization in China," in *Assays* (New York: Ross Erikson, 1961), 83.
12. Kenneth Rexroth, "Homer, *The Iliad,*" in *Classics Revisited* (Chicago: Quadrangle Books, 1968), 8.
13. Rexroth, "Homer, *The Iliad,*" 11.
14. Russell Kirk, *The Conservative Mind: From Burke to Santayana* (Chicago: H. Regnery, 1953), 4.
15. Henry Regnery, "The Making of *The Conservative Mind,*" in *The Conservative Mind: From Burke to Eliot,* ed. Russell Kirk, 7th rev. ed. (Washington DC: Gateway, 2001), iv.
16. Kirk, *Conservative Mind,* 4.
17. Kirk, *Conservative Mind,* 158.
18. Ralph Ellison, "Presentation to Bernard Malamud," in *The Collected Essays of Ralph Ellison,* ed. John F. Callahan (New York: Modern Library, 1995), 465.
19. Russell Kirk, *The Roots of American Order,* 4th ed. (Wilmington: Intercollegiate Studies Institute, 2001), 474.
20. Kirk, *Roots of American Order,* 449.
21. Kirk, *Roots of American Order,* 457.
22. Kirk, *Roots of American Order,* 475.
23. Kirk, *Roots of American Order,* 470.
24. Lasch, *Revolt of the Elites,* 208–9.

25. Christopher Lasch, *The True and Only Heaven: Progress and Its Critics* (New York: W. W. Norton, 1991), 530; Lasch, *Revolt of the Elites*, 27.

26. Lasch, *Revolt of the Elites*, 27.

27. Lasch, *Revolt of the Elites*, 28.

28. Lasch, *Revolt of the Elites*, 28–29.

29. Christopher Lasch, *The Agony of the American Left* (New York: Vintage Books, 1968), 210.

30. Christopher Lasch, *The Culture of Narcissism: American Life in an Age of Diminishing Expectations* (New York: W.W. Norton, 1979), 349.

31. Deirdre McCloskey, "Before Caitlyn Jenner: When I Went from Donald to Deirdre," *Des Moines Register,* June 4, 2015, http://www.desmoinesregister.com/story/opinion/columnists/2015/05/04/jenner-sex-change-professor-iowa/26897519/.

32. Deirdre McCloskey, *Crossing: A Memoir* (Chicago: University of Chicago Press, 1999), 43.

33. McCloskey, *Crossing*, 43.

34. McCloskey, *Crossing*, 97.

35. McCloskey, *Crossing*, 125.

36. Deirdre McCloskey, *The Bourgeois Virtues: Ethics for an Age of Commerce* (Chicago: University of Chicago Press, 2006), 507–8.

37. Deirdre McCloskey, *Bourgeois Dignity: Why Economics Can't Explain the Modern World* (Chicago: University of Chicago Press, 2010), 403–4.

16

Midwestern Musicians

James P. Leary

Midwestern musicians—performers of the real homegrown, grassroots, folk, vernacular stuff—were no mystery to me as a kid growing up in northwestern Wisconsin in the 1950s. They were evident in Hamms Beer commercials broadcast on Twin Cities' television and in Scandihoovian dialect songs spun seasonally on local radio.

Hamms ads featured a prominent rhythm inspired by Woodland Indian powwow drumming, vocals that leapt from bass register to an echoing yodel-like falsetto, a cartoon bear alternately birling like a lumberjack on a beaver-gnawed timber or bowling on ice like a stout Dutchman, and environmentally evocative lyrics:

> From the Land of Sky Blue Waters,
> From the land of pines, lofty balsams,
> Comes the beer refreshing,
> Hamms the beer refreshing.

The "beer refreshing" refrain resonated with other familiar regional slogans—Schmidt's "Brew That Grew with the Great Northwest" and Schlitz's "Beer That Made Milwaukee Famous"—and with a pair of the era's most popular polka songs, "Roll Out the Barrel" and "In Heaven There Is No Beer." Meanwhile comic Scandihoovian dialect ditties, performed theatrically to approximate the broken English of immigrant Norwegians and Swedes, were winter standards through which Ernest "Slim Jim" Iverson lamented the "Vistling Drifting Snow" and Harry Skarbo, aka "Yogi Yorgesson," rendered "Jingle Bells" as "Yingle Bells" to convey the tribulations of "da coldest Svede in da whole darn Middle Vest."[1]

"Yingling" Scandihoovian songs and Hamms cartoon jingles, considered together, condensed key elements of my regional reality more than any other music. My community, Rice Lake, had been the home of Dakota and, subsequently, Ojibwe peoples. The Knapp Stout company that flooded Native wild rice beds in 1860 to make a holding pond for its sawmill attracted lumberjacks aplenty, including French Canadians, Irish, Slavs, Germans, and Scandinavians. My childhood home was between a woods, a swamp, and two lakes where pines swayed, waters sparkled, and bears sometimes roamed. Winters were long, dark, snowy affairs requiring sociability, and there were scores of local bars and a few bowling alleys. My dad enjoyed friendly gatherings over a brew, especially Leinenkugels from Chippewa Falls and the local elixir, Breunig's Lager.

Each site, season, and scene had discrete local performers. Venturing north to Lac Court Oreilles reservation or at occasional community events, I heard Ojibwe dance drums. Rindlisbacher's "Friendly Buckhorn" bar/café, its wall festooned with "The World's Largest Collection of Odd Lumberjack Musical Instruments," was a hangout for wool-clad former "timber beasts." From a hill west of town, wjmc radio broadcast live performances by local Bohemian, German, and Scandinavian polka bands, a Polish Barn Dance, and occasional Sunday afternoon interludes with Swiss yodelers. These musicians all contributed to a collective upper midwestern soundscape as inescapable as wind through the pines and waves against the shore.

Yet my retrospective, regionally grounded familiarity with roots musicians, while likely resonating with other upper midwesterners, surely differs from the experiences of those raised in the region's central and lower realms. In 1939, folksong scholar Mary O. Eddy—focusing on Ohio but sketching a pattern roughly prevailing across the central Midwest—argued that settlement by Christianized Indians, Pennsylvania Dutch, Germans from Europe, Virginians, New Englanders, New Yorkers, and "an immigration of all sorts of people attracted by the industries of the larger cities" fostered folk/roots musicians in a prevailing Anglo-American vein, with polyglot pockets in urban areas. Elsewhere African American, German, Irish, and upland southern musicians intermingled in the region's southern realm, along the Ohio and Upper Mississippi River valleys especially, producing a rich amalgam of fiddle tunes, ballads, minstrelsy, singing games, and sacred songs.[2]

In the twenty-first century, in my seventh decade, I now regard the concept of "midwestern musicians" as amorphous, elusive. Still we can encounter quintessential regional performers by focusing on Chicago—an urban place, an agricultural marketplace, a destination, and a crossroads at the Midwest's center—during a crucial formative period extending from the late nineteenth through the mid-twentieth centuries. Chicago as the nexus for midwestern musicians is most evident in key historical moments, movements, and infrastructures featuring the sometimes contested public performance, staging, publishing, recording, broadcasting, and dissemination of regionally grounded, evolving, and intermingling folk and vernacular genres: powwow drum songs; polka music, yodeling, and broken-English dialect ditties; the songs of lumberjacks and laborers; African American blues, jazz, and gospel; old time fiddling and polkabilly fusions.

Halls, Taverns, Fairs, Tours, Contests, Festivals

Musicians aplenty—once locally known, now largely forgotten—established Chicago as a regional site of sonic ferment in the latter decades of the nineteenth century. Hull House, founded in 1889 as a settlement house by social reformer Jane Addams to benefit Chicago's immense foreign-born working class, countered wholesale assimilation by fostering genteel evening culture shows featuring the "ethnic food, dancing, music" of "Italian, Greek, German, Polish," and other newcomers.[3] Surveying "Enterprises of Chicago Clubs" in 1901, Mrs. Alfred Bayless lauded a particular settlement house—"in a neighborhood inhabited by Irish, Germans, Poles, Bohemians, Lithuanians, Scandinavians, Hungarians, Finns, Welsh, and Scotch"—that celebrated the presence of each through singing gatherings.[4]

Culturally diverse settlement-house musicians overlapped with and were complemented by performers in ethnic halls and working-class taverns. Sometimes mannered, formal, ethnocentric, insular, or conservatively oriented toward respective old-world ways, these institutions likewise sponsored rowdier informal occasions for singers, musicians, and dancers that crossed or blurred generational and cultural boundaries.[5] "The old people," among five thousand Bohemians turning out en masse for a "Monster Picnic at Pregler's Grove" in 1891, for example, "would only appear on the dance floor when their old-time dances were played," yet the picnic's two bands otherwise "kept the young folks busy dancing" by playing "everything from a Bohemian polka to the latest" dance tunes.[6] A few weeks earlier, fortified by "the flow of beer all the time," Chicago's Danes, Norwegians, and Swedes held a decidedly pan-Scandinavian and American Fourth of July celebration at Kuhn's Park, "dancing by daylight and electric light."[7] Germania Hall had opened its doors the previous December to all comers for dancing classes and a grand ball.[8]

Like settlement houses and open-door ethnic halls, Chicago's labor unions, working-class coalitions, and sympathetic tavern keepers welcomed diverse musicians whose repertoires intermingled regularly. Alarmist stories concerning gatherings of "REDS," "ANARCHISTS," and "SOCIALISTS" from the xenophobic, antilabor, temperance-minded *Chicago Tribune* preceding and in the aftermath of the 1886 Haymarket Affair repeatedly mentioned beer, singing, instrumental music, and dancing, with occasional derisive attention to specifics, as in this 1885 account: "Every variety of step might have been witnessed yesterday. The 'Bohemian dip,' the 'German lunge,' the 'Austrian kick,' the 'Polish romp,' the 'Scandinavian trot.'"[9]

Suspicious of musicians associated with the foreign born, the working class, their taverns, and the labor movement, Chicago's late nineteenth-century "powers that be" paradoxically invigorated the city's grassroots polyglot performance traditions by hosting the World's Columbian Exposition of 1893—a sprawling world's fair juxtaposing emerging technocratic modernity with supposedly disappearing exotic rusticity. Thanks to "exhibits sponsored by different ethnic and national groups of the city," the exposition's "Midway sustained serious counter-sacralized and counter-imperial music programming."[10] Performers in Chicago's small Swiss community enjoyed vigorous song swaps with visiting yodelers and alphorn blowers.[11] The German Village "was one of the most popular concessions on the Midway," drawing more than one million people, for whom "the greatest attraction" was a "band composed of the best musicians in the German army."[12] Influencing and performing with Chicagoans, these musicians drew customers for Otto Georgi. A native of Saxony, Georgi had settled in Chicago around 1890, joining other newcomers to import, play, teach, publish music for, and promote the Chemnitzer or "German" concertina. Ensconced in the German Village, allied especially with Chicagoans of German, Czech, and Polish origins, Georgi not only helped found concertina clubs whose members launched the distinctive ethnic-American "Dutchman" and Chicago-style Polish polka genres, but also teamed with the Czech immigrant entrepreneur Louis Vitak to form what became the leading regional polka music publisher.[13]

The Irish Village likewise sparked trans-Atlantic musical mixing, as chronicled by Chicago's police captain, Irish-born Francis O'Neill, whose fieldwork with fellow immigrants resulted in a collection of Irish traditional tunes that remains the standard work. Through O'Neill we know that visiting Donegal piper Charles McSweeney exchanged jigs, reels, and slow airs with Chicago's legendary Irish pipers Patsy Touhy and "Blind" Murphy.[14] Perhaps these musical interludes also attracted denizens of the exposition's Michigan Logging Camp, a contingent from the "dense pineries of the almost unexplored north section of Michigan."[15] Subsequently documenting upper midwestern lumber-camp music and song, folklorist Franz Rickaby found "the Irish were dominant" as fiddlers and ballad singers.[16]

The Indian Village, significantly, was occupied by Potawatomi and Ho-Chunk (Winnebago) peoples whose ancestors' territory had included Chicago. Snidely heralding their "RETURN AS FREAKS," the *Chicago Tribune* observed that "the young men of the village have a band among their instruments being an old bass drum. . . . They will play, and the braves and squaws will give daily presentations of the famous ghost and war dances."[17] Combining dramatic elements of the era's Wild West Shows, venerable and recent dance songs, and the newly adopted "big drum" spreading from Plains to Woodland peoples especially in the wake of the December 1890 Wounded Knee massacre, these performances helped launch the intertribal powwow phenomenon that persists to the present.[18]

The public presence of Chicago's Indigenous and foreign-born folk/roots musicians was not, however, shared by the city's African Americans, who were excluded from settlement-house affairs.[19] They were offered only a token Colored Folks Day at the Columbian Exposition that was opposed by African American leaders as "an exhibition of the unabashed official rejection of the principle of racial equality."[20] Undaunted, black musicians, especially vocal quartets and ragtime exponents, were active in Chicago theaters and cabarets.[21] In 1905 Robert T. Motts converted a beer hall into the Pekin Theater, Chicago's first successful black-owned musical venue. Featuring black entertainers and open to black and white audiences, it also served as a base and a way station for an emerging black vaudeville circuit extending throughout the Midwest.[22]

Chicago's European ethnic musicians likewise toured the region, performing in opera houses and tent shows. From 1905 to 1925, for example, the singing dialect humorists Eleonora and Ethel Olson, daughters of Norwegian immigrants to Chicago, entertained crowds in both their hometown and on the Midwest's chautauqua and lyceum circuits.[23] In 1917 Bohumir Kryl's Chicago-based Bohemian Band played for a Big Chautauqua Special in Suttons Bay, Michigan, attracting "lumbermen, fishermen, storekeepers, farmers, teachers; Norwegians and Swedes and Bohemians, a few Frenchies and Chippeway Indians—two hundred in all."[24] In turn, traveling musicians from the hinterlands, especially old-time fiddlers, found appreciative Chicago audiences and newspapers publicizing their prowess.

In 1926 the *Chicago Herald and Examiner* held a competition for the Midwest's best old-time fiddler. This regional event coincided with a series of local contests sponsored that year by Henry Ford's car dealerships. The Michigan industrialist perversely regarded fiddling as a wholesome antidote to jazz, which he deemed the musical bastard of blacks and Jews. Although hardly sharing Ford's ideology, old-time fiddlers contests were nonetheless imbued with agrarian nostalgia.[25] First emerging in the South, they arrived in the Lower Midwest by the 1890s. In 1899 the Travelers Protective Association touted their old-time fiddlers contest in Indianapolis's Tomlinson Hall as "the grandest aggregation of homespun musicians ever congregated in the world."[26] On the contrary, early newspaper accounts reveal mostly Anglo-American men sawing out tunes shared with southern fiddlers: "Leather Breeches," "Rye Straw,"

"Devil's Dream," "Girl I Left Behind Me," and "Arkansas Traveler."[27] By the 1920s, however, as contests spread to the Upper Midwest, French Canadian, German, Irish, Scandinavian, Slavic, and Woodland Indian fiddlers interjected their particular repertoires. The winner of the *Herald and Examiner's* 1926 contest was Leizime Brusoe, a French Canadian from Rhinelander, Wisconsin.[28] A dray-line operator and an avid hunter and fisherman who hobnobbed with vacationing Chicagoans in Wisconsin's Northwoods, Brusoe took a Chicago and Northwestern train south to beat all comers.[29]

In the 1930s Chicago hosted two landmark events paradoxically situating Indigenous, immigrant, and rural old-time musicians in a contemporary cosmopolitan setting: the 1933 Chicago World's Fair and the 1937 National Folk Festival. Both involved Chicago-based musicians, active participation and organizational support from the city's ethnic communities, performers from afar whose locales relied on Chicago tourists, and genres reminiscent of the 1893 Columbian Exposition: Woodland Indian drum groups, Swiss yodelers, German concertina players and brass bands, Irish pipers and fiddlers, and lumberjack musicians.

Ho-Chunks (Winnebagos), prominent within Chicago's Native citizenry, were also well known through the *Chicago Tribune's* ads for Wisconsin Dells where tourists might see "annual Indian ceremonial dances every evening, July 1st through Labor Day. Two hundred Winnebago Indians in full native dress in tribal songs and dances given in their own outdoor, natural outdoor Amphitheatre in the heart of The Dells."[30] In the 1930s Chicagoan Whirling Thunder, a Wisconsin-born Ho-Chunk veteran of the Redpath Chautauqua circuit, was sought after by sportsmen and civic clubs, schools, Boy and Girl Scout troops, and such downtown department stores as Marshall Field and Carson Pirie Scott for educational programs of songs, dances, and Woodland flute playing.[31] Under his leadership the 1933 World's Fair featured the big drum, "emblematic of the heartbeat," accompanying *haylushka* or warriors' dances, "the Swan dance by Winnebago women," and "Green Corn and Snake dances by Winnebagos from Wisconsin."[32]

Echoing the Columbian Exposition, the 1933 World's Fair included Swiss and German Villages. The former featured the Moser Brothers, virtuoso musicians and yodelers from Bern whose tours had included Chicago since the mid-1920s. Rudy Burkhalter, a button accordionist who barnstormed with the Mosers from 1928 to 1934, recalled the Swiss Village: "Very pretty . . . beautiful [painted] mountains, beautiful restaurants. We performed every hour. . . . We had an Italian man there that was taking pictures—snap a postcard of people right then and there." Burkhalter met his wife, a Minnesota schoolteacher, at the world's fair, and soon after, they settled in Madison, Wisconsin, where he was a mainstay of local old-time polka and Swiss music until the early 1990s.[33]

The German Village, benefitting from Prohibition's repeal, drew immense crowds to its Old Heidelberg Inn, complete with a biergarten and rathskeller where singing servers from the city's German-speaking citizenry, togged in lederhosen and dirndls, held forth along with button accordion, concertina, and zither players. The rathskeller's star attraction was Henry Moeller, the son of Bavarian immigrants to Davenport, Iowa, who assumed the persona of "Herr Louie" to spout broken-English wisecracks as the leader of a classic Little German Band, the "Hungry Five."[34] When the fair ended, the inn moved to downtown Chicago and advertised regularly in regional newspapers: "Delightful, unique entertainment . . . Rathskeller: Herr Louie . . . Original Hungry Five."[35]

The chairman of the Irish Village's musical events was Captain Francis O'Neill, the renowned Irish piping devotee who had been active in the Columbian Exposition. Chicago's pipe band, the Shannon Rovers, was a fixture along with the Harp and Shamrock Orchestra, organized by the immigrant step dancer Pat Roche. Propelled by Chicagoan Eleanor Kane's dazzling piano renditions of Irish reels, the band included immigrant newcomers from Tipperary, Limerick, Mayo, and Roscommon.[36]

Unlike the Columbian Exposition, the 1933 World's Fair lacked a lumber camp, perhaps because the Chicago Coliseum had been hosting annual Outdoor Life expositions since 1923. Promoting the Northwoods tourist industries of Michigan and Wisconsin, these events featured imported "tall spruces and pines," assorted wild game, Ojibwe dancers "in full regalia," and lumberjack birlers and carvers.[37] Lumberjack musicians were in force at the National Folk Festival held May 22–28, 1937, in

Chicago's Orchestra Hall. The Michigan Lumberjacks troupe asserted the extension of Irish traditions into upper midwestern lumber camps with "Miss McLeod's Reel," the doleful ballad "Jack Haggerty," and the comic "Never Take the Horseshoe from the Door" by Irish American music-hall composer Edward Harrigan. Meanwhile the Wisconsin Lumberjacks, led by Rice Lake's Otto Rindlisbacher, offered an upper midwestern mixture of French Canadian, Irish, Scandinavian, and Swiss songs and tunes.[38]

Chicago's 1937 National Folk Festival involved several veterans of the 1933 World's Fair, including Pat Roche and Whirling Thunder, respectively organizing Irish and Ho-Chunk performers. French, German, Lithuanian, Polish, Scottish, and Swedish musicians from the Chicago area also participated. Southern and western migrants to the Windy City—including Kentucky-born Floyd "Salty" Holmes of the Prairie Ramblers and Arizona cowboy Romaine Lowdermilk—entertained, in turn, for "Dances, Music, and Ballads" and "Cowboy Ballads" segments. And Chicago's African American singers—a forceful presence in South Side neighborhoods since the Great Migration commenced in 1916—were appropriately abundant and prominent. Indeed the festival concluded with a star-studded "Negro Spiritual Chorus" alternately led by Thomas A. Dorsey, a former hokum artist whose fusion of jazz and blues rhythms with Christian hymns earned the accolade "father of gospel music"; Sallie Martin, a fiery Holiness singer dubbed the "mother of gospel music"; and Roberta Martin, who emerged from Dorsey's Ebenezer Baptist Church choir to found the revered Roberta Martin Singers.

Records and Radio

The early twentieth century's new media of audio recordings and radio cast the sounds of midwestern musicians far beyond the earshot of halls, taverns, fairs, tours, contests, and festivals. Few at first, folk/roots musicians' commercial recordings in Chicago accelerated in the 1920s when, as performers on newly launched Windy City radio stations, their music blanketed the region. Indeed many of the aforementioned musicians made records or performed on radio. Their collective media-aided music fostered widespread familiarity, ensured barnstorming opportunities, lured hinterland musicians to Chicago studios and stations, and inspired musical acolytes.

Columbia and Victor, America's major record labels, relied initially on musicians nearby their respective studios in New York City and Camden, New Jersey. In 1908 Columbia launched an "E" (European) series for foreign-born Americans, with 1912 Victor introducing discrete ethnic catalogs in 1912.[39] By the early 1920s the labels' "foreign" series were augmented by a "hillbilly" series featuring rural white, mostly southern, performers and a "race" series comprised of African Americans' blues and gospel music. Midwestern musicians' presence in these series was facilitated by local musical entrepreneurs.

In 1897 Wladylslaw Sajewski opened a general store, the Columbia Supply House, named for the Columbian Exposition, in his Polish neighborhood on Chicago's North Side. "By 1910 the store had turned almost exclusively to music, supplying phonographs, records, and printed music" to Chicago Poles, and Sajewski hired a songwriter, arranger, and musician, Frank Przybylski, to develop new material.[40] On January 8, 1915, thanks to Sajewski's efforts, Columbia made its first foreign-series recordings in Chicago when the Przybylski-led "Orkiestra Columbia" recorded a kujawiak, a polka mazurka, and two marches issued in the Polish and Lithuanian catalogs.[41] The Czech immigrant store owners and music publishers Joseph Jiran and Louis Vitak were likewise talent scouts and recruiters, and in August 1915 a Czech band and chorus recorded in Chicago for Columbia.[42]

Chicago's Polish and Czech musicians continued actively recording in the 1920s. By the decade's end musicians had also made Finnish, German, Greek, Irish, Italian, Jewish, Lithuanian, Mexican, Norwegian, Serbo-Croatian, Slovak, Slovenian, Swedish, Swiss, and Ukrainian foreign-series records for Brunswick, Columbia, Okeh, Victor and Vocalion labels.[43] During this period influential ethnic performers throughout the region sought Chicago studios: Cleveland's Hoyer Brothers, whose Slovenian sound paved the way for polka star Frankie Yankovic; New Ulm, Minnesota's Whoopee John Wilfahrt, progenitor of the "Dutchman" polka sound; Milwaukee's Sosnowski Trio, a prototypical Polish

concertina combo; Romy Gosz of Manitowoc, Wisconsin, the quintessential Bohemian trumpeter; Gunleik Smedal, champion Norwegian
Hardanger fiddler from Albert Lea, Minnesota; and Minneapolis-based
Swedish comic singer Olle i Skratthult. Besides recording for Victor,
Skratthult appeared on Wallin's Svenska Records, the earliest Chicago-
based European ethnic label, which issued songs, hymns, and old-time
dance tunes by midwestern Swedish performers from 1923 to 1925, thanks
to "the technical resources of Paramount."[44]

Paramount Records, a subsidiary of the Wisconsin Chair Company of
Port Washington, Wisconsin, stumbled into the "race" market in the early
1920s when its cheaply priced record-pressing services were contracted
by Harlem's African American label, Black Swan. Fortuitously enlisting
the Chicago-based African American producer and talent scout J. Mayo
Williams, who founded his own Black Patti record label in 1922, Paramount issued classic performances by blues and jazz performers, many
of whom recorded in Chicago's Marsh Laboratory studios. Although
notable black musicians like Blind Lemon Jefferson traveled from afar
to record in Chicago, others were based there in the 1920s, including
Jelly Roll Morton and King Oliver's Creole Jazz Band, featuring trumpeter Louis Armstrong.[45]

In 1933, as Paramount fell victim to the Great Depression, Lester
Melrose, a Chicago music-store entrepreneur who had worked with
Jelly Roll Morton, assisted RCA Victor as a scout and producer for the
budget Bluebird label. Favoring blues and relying on "a regular pool of
Chicago musicians including Big Bill Broonzy, Roosevelt Sykes, Tampa
Red, Washboard Sam, and Sonny Boy Williamson," Bluebird developed
a distinctive small-band style, which, once amplified, became a major
influence on early rock and roll, as well as the "Chicago blues" sound
that Muddy Waters, Howlin' Wolf, and Little Walter established on the
post–World War II Chicago label Chess Records.[46]

The Depression and the aging of Chicago's foreign-born community
affected record sales, and the interest of major labels in recording the
area's ethnic musicians declined markedly. In the post–World War II era,
however, small independent Chicago labels emerged to serve various
constituencies, including Atticon (Greek), Balkan (Slovenian, Serbo-

Croatian), Jay Jay (Polish), Quality (Swedish), and several (Radiant, Rondo, Royal) devoted to polka music in various ethnic styles.[47] Notably, Walter "Li'l Wally" Jagiello, like the neighboring Bluebird and Chess blues artists who were his contemporaries, combined "down home" style and memory with amplified instrumentation and urban experiences to create a new regionally forged peasant-in-the-city Polish sound that became known as "Chicago Style" polka.[48]

"Hillbilly" musicians from the Midwest, the South, and the West also recorded steadily in Chicago beginning in the late 1920s, initially for Paramount but soon after for Brunswick, Columbia, Decca, Vocalion, and Victor.[49] Most combined recording with radio appearances, especially on Chicago's WLS, owned in turn by the rural-oriented Sears Department Store and the *Prairie Farmer* newspaper.[50]

Live radio broadcasts of midwestern musicians commenced in 1924 when the WLS Barn Dance featured fiddler Tommy Dandurant of Kankakee, Illinois. Resembling Nashville's subsequent Grand Ole Opry, WLS nonetheless offered distinctively midwestern musicians: a yodeling Little Swiss Miss, a Little German Band, the dialect comedian Olaf the Swede, and such influential polkabilly stringband/accordion fusions as the guitar-strumming Texas cowboy crooner Gene Autry paired with the Wisconsin Polish accordionist Frank Kusczynski, aka Pee Wee King. WLS Barn Dance musicians played throughout the region, stimulating local "home talent" barn dances, as well as similar programs like the Polish Barn Dance (Illinois), Hoosier State Barn Dance, Iowa Barn Dance Frolic, Keweenaw Barn Dance (Michigan), Sunset Valley Barn Dance (Minnesota), Hayloft Jamboree (North Dakota), and Badger State Barn Dance that sometimes combined hillbilly music with Croatian, Czech, Finnish, German, Italian, and Polish polka sounds.

Chicago radio stations also sold air time in the mid-1920s to immigrant entrepreneurs hosting German, Irish, Lithuanian, Polish, and other "ethnic hours" in their respective languages.[51] In 1926, for example, the touring Moser Brothers offered an "Alpine Interlude" on WGN, supplemented by local Swiss yodelers Bertha Allbisser and Wilhelmina "Minnie" Freitag.[52] Meanwhile ethnic humor and song in broken English were delivered to the general public by Herr Louie and his sidekick,

Weasel, who began an extended radio career in 1928 on WGN.[53] In 1935 Katherine Avery appeared similarly on WGN, writing and producing the *Sentimental Selma* show, joined by dialect-singing sidekicks Elmer the Swede and Lutefisk Ole.[54]

Ironically the blackface comedy show *Amos n' Andy* debuted on Chicago's WMAQ in February 1928, a year and a half before an African American, Jack L. Cooper, launched the All-Negro Hour on Chicago's WSBC. Mindful of racist characterizations of blacks, Cooper not only introduced a mixture of live and recorded musicians in faultlessly executed Standard English, but also favored gospel and sophisticated jazz to the exclusion of blues and hokum. Those "low down" genres were absent from Chicago airwaves until Al Benson, a Mississippi-born DJ with a down-home dialect, began spinning the city's urban blues records in 1945 on WGES.

The foregoing sketch of Chicago-centered yet regionally significant midwestern musicians from the late nineteenth through mid-twentieth centuries does not testify to a unified homogenous sound. Rather the Midwest's bedrock folk/vernacular musicians are culturally plural, polyglot, and multifaceted. Indeed they have been and continue to be rooted in the region but attentive to musical strains in contingent regions, the nation, and hearth or old-world nations; extensions of Anglo- and African American traditions, and their intersections, but also bound up with the sounds of Woodland Indians and European immigrants, especially Germanic, Irish, Scandinavian, and Slavic peoples; and evident in powwow drum songs, in polka music, yodeling, and broken-English dialect ditties, in the songs of workers from the woods and factories, in old-time country music, in African American blues, jazz, and gospel, and in assorted fusions, bygone, ongoing, and to come.

Notes

1. The Hamms Beer jingle borrows from Charles Wakefield Cadman's 1909 composition, "From the Land of the Sky-Blue Water," invoking the Dakota name for Minnesota and inspired by cylinder recordings of Omaha and Ho-Chunk (Winnebago) singers. Ernest "Slim Jim" Iverson, son of Norwegian immigrants to North Dakota, was a popular Scandinavian dialect and cowboy singer on Minneapolis radio stations from the 1930s to the 1950s. "Yogi Yorgesson," likewise born to Norwegian immigrants, was raised in

Seattle and based in Los Angeles, but was very popular in the Upper Midwest, where he toured in the early 1950s.

2. Howard L. Sacks and Judith Rose Sacks, *Way Up North in Dixie: A Black Family's Claim to the Confederate Anthem* (Urbana: University of Illinois Press, 2003).

3. Barbara Garland Polikoff, *With One Bold Act: The Story of Jane Addams* (New York: Boswell, 1999), 76; Derek Valliant, *Sounds of Reform: Progressivism and Music in Chicago, 1873–1935* (Chapel Hill: University of North Carolina Press, 2003), 107–9.

4. *Chicago Tribune*, November 17, 1901. Newspapers were accessed through the search engines ProQuest Historical Newspapers: Chicago Tribune and NewspaperArchive.com.

5. Perry R. Duis, *The Saloon: Public Drinking in Chicago and Boston, 1880–1920* (Urbana: University of Illinois Press, 1983), chapter 5.

6. *Chicago Tribune*, July 27, 1891.

7. *Chicago Tribune*, July 5, 1891.

8. *Chicago Tribune*, December 13, 1890.

9. Bruce C. Nelson, "Dancing and Picnicking Anarchists? The Movement Below the Martyred Leadership," in *Haymarket Scrapbook*, ed. David Roediger and Franklin Rosemont (Chicago: Charles Kerr, 1986), 76–79.

10. Valliant, *Sounds of Reform*, 53–54.

11. *Chicago Tribune*, August 15 and November 1, 1893.

12. *Chicago Tribune*, November 11, 1893.

13. James P. Leary, "The German Concertina in the Upper Midwest," in *Land without Nightingales: Music in the Making of German-America*, ed. Philip V. Bohlman and Otto Holzapfel (Madison WI: Max Kade Institute for German American Studies, 2002), 196–97; Victor Greene, *A Passion for Polkas: Old-Time Ethnic Music in America* (Berkeley: University of California Press, 1992), 54–55.

14. Francis O'Neill, *Irish Folk Music: A Fascinating Hobby* (Chicago: Regan Printing House, 1910), 211–15; *Chicago Tribune*, May 4, 11, and 27, 1893.

15. J. W. Buel, *The Magic City* (St. Louis and Philadelphia: Historical Publishing Company, 1894).

16. Franz Rickaby, *Ballads and Songs of the Shanty-Boy* (Cambridge MA: Harvard University Press, 1926), 25.

17. *Chicago Tribune*, July 1, 1893.

18. Thomas Vennum Jr., *The Ojibwe Dance Drum: Its History and Construction* (Washington DC: Smithsonian Institution, 1982), 44–75.

19. Valliant, *Sounds of Reform*, 95.

20. Lynn Abbott and Doug Seroff, *Out of Sight: The Rise of African American Popular Music, 1889–1895* (Jackson: University of Mississippi Press, 2002), 296.

21. Tim Brooks, *Lost Sounds: Blacks and the Birth of the Recording Industry, 1890–1919* (Urbana: University of Illinois Press, 2004), 92, 253, 268, 329.

22. Thomas Bauman, *The Pekin: The Rise and Fall of Chicago's First Black-Owned Theater* (Urbana: University of Illinois Press, 2014).

23. Paul F. Anderson, preface to *Yust for Fun: Norwegian-American Dialect Monologues*, by Eleonora and Ethel Olson (1925; repr., Minneapolis: Eggs Press, 1979).

24. James P. Leary, *Polkabilly: How the Goose Island Ramblers Redefined American Folk Music* (New York: Oxford University Press, 2006), 22–23.

25. Michael T. Bertrand, "Race and Rural Identity," in *The Hayloft Gang: The Story of the National Barn Dance*, ed. Chad Berry (Urbana: University of Illinois Press, 2008), 130–52, 134–35.

26. *Indianapolis Journal*, September 30, 1899.

27. *Akron Daily Democrat*, June 16, 1899.

28. Paul L. Tyler, "Hillbilly Music Re-imagined: Folk and Country Music in the Midwest," *Journal of American Folklore* 127, no. 504 (2014): 173.

29. James P. Leary, *Folksongs of Another America: Field Recordings from the Upper Midwest, 1937–1946* (Madison: University of Wisconsin Press, 2015), 21–23.

30. *Chicago Tribune*, July 15, 1928.

31. *Chicago Tribune*, September 8, 1929; Whirling Thunder, *Chief Whirling Thunder: Winnebago Indian* (Chicago: Grand Council Fire of American Indians, 1931).

32. *Chicago Tribune*, July 30, 1933.

33. James P. Leary, *Yodeling in Dairyland: A History of Swiss Music in Wisconsin* (Mount Horeb: Wisconsin Folk Museum, 1991), 48–49.

34. James P. Leary, "Herr Louie, the Weasel, and the Hungry Five: German American Performers on Midwestern Radio," *Jährbuch, Deutsches Volksliedarchiv 2010*, Freiburg, Germany, 101–33.

35. *Mason City Globe-Gazette, Wisconsin State Journal*, both March 20, 1935; *Vidette-Messenger* [Valparaiso IN], April 10, 1935; and *Oshkosh Daily Northwestern*, May 15, 1935.

36. Kathleen M. Flanagan, "'Dance and Song of the Gael': Pat Roche and Irish Dance in Chicago, 1933–1953," *New Hibernia Review / Iris Éireannach Nua* 4, no. 4 (2000): 9–28.

37. *Chicago Tribune*, May 8, 1928; May 5, 1930; May 8, 1932.

38. National Folk Festival Program (Chicago: Adult Education Council of Chicago, 1937); Leary, *Folksongs of Another America*, 74–98.

39. Pekka Gronow, "Ethnic Recordings: An Introduction," in *Ethnic Recordings in America: A Neglected Heritage* (Washington DC: American Folklife Center, 1982), 34, 36.

40. Richard K. Spottswood, "The Sajewski Story: Eighty Years of Polish Music in Chicago," in *Ethnic Recordings in America: A Neglected Heritage* (Washington DC: American Folklife Center, 1982), 133–35.

41. Richard K. Spottswood, *Ethnic Music on Records: A Discography of Ethnic Recordings Produced in the United States, 1893–1942* (Urbana: University of Illinois Press, 1990), 691.

42. Greene, *A Passion for Polkas*, 72; Spottswood, *Ethnic Music on Records*, 609.

43. Spottswood, *Ethnic Music on Records*.

44. Gronow, "Ethnic Recordings," 7.

45. Alex van der Tuuk, *Paramount's Rise and Fall: The Roots and History of Paramount Records*, 2nd ed. (Denver CO: Mainspring Press, 2012).

46. Mike Rowe, *Chicago Blues: The City & the Music* (New York: Da Capo Press, 1975), 17–25.

47. Gronow, "Ethnic Recordings," 46–48.

48. Charles Keil, Angeliki V. Keil, and Dick Blau, *Polka Happiness* (Philadelphia: Temple University Press, 1992), 46–60.

49. Tony Russell, *Country Music Records: A Discography, 1921–1942* (New York: Oxford University Press, 2004).

50. James F. Evans, *Prairie Farmer and WLS* (Urbana: University of Illinois Press, 1969).

51. Lizabeth Cohen, *Making a New Deal: Industrial Workers in Chicago, 1919–1939* (Cambridge UK: Cambridge University Press, 1990), 138; Valliant, *Sounds of Reform*, 236.

52. *Chicago Tribune*, March 23, 1926.

53. Leary, "Herr Louie, the Weasel, and the Hungry Five."

54. *Chicago Tribune*, September 24, 1935.

17

Midwestern Writers

THE FOURTH WAVE

David Pichaske

One rule of life is that we rarely know what's happening when it's happening. Only after the fact can we look back and say, "The roots of sixties protest may lie in the Beat Generation, which emerged in the late 1940s," or conversely, "Protest against The System bubbled up again around 2011 with Occupy Wall Street, but it quickly disappeared." Which cultural (or biological) "innovations" shape the future, and which experiments are mere curiosities? Only hindsight tells us.

We can, however, sometimes use common sense to think ahead: "If global warming raises the ocean level, what becomes of New York and Los Angeles?" Not that this always works. Some ideas, recognizably stupid even when proposed, get implemented anyway, only to prove just as lame-brained as we predicted. "Let's cut the interstate speed limit to 55 mph to conserve gasoline, because cars get better mileage at 55 than at 65." Or, "I know: we'll build a wall between East and West Berlin . . ."

We can also look to history for patterns that might be repeated if and when we pursue whatever we're considering pursuing. Depending on our proclivities, we can chart history as a line slanted irregularly upward; a pendulum, swinging back and forth; a circle, or maybe a spiral. Where are we now on that line? Where are we headed?

To address the matter under consideration, where are we now with regard to Midwest writing in terms of content and audience? Where might Midwest writing be headed in the near future?

America has had "Midwest writers" continuously since before the Civil War; our "Lost Region" has never been entirely lost . . . except in the national consciousness, and in our own consciousness to the extent that we subscribe to the current national agenda. In the national consciousness, Midwest literature has come and gone several times, attractive for different reasons—reasons which suggest approaches we can take to resurrect it from its present marginality.

Early on, our region proved marketable nationally as a frontier Other, full of mystery, danger, adventure, potential. Cooper's Natty Bumpo out on the prairie; Huck and Jim floating down the Mississippi River; Caroline Kirkland's Michigan in *A New Home—Who'll Follow?* Decades later, Willa Cather was still writing about *O Pioneers!*, Ole Rølvaag about *Giants in the Earth*, Laura Ingalls Wilder about *Little House on the Prairie*. Ralph Leslie Rusk's study of *The Literature of the Middle Western Frontier*, published in 1925, runs to two volumes.

Then came a wave of Midwest writers depicting our region as the quintessence of early twentieth-century America—industrial-capitalist America in the writings of Carl "Chicago" Sandburg, Frank *The Pit* Norris, Upton *The Jungle* Sinclair; and small-town America, a settled community romanticized by some and critiqued by others in the realism ascendant before the Great Depression: Zona Gale's Friendship Village, Edgar Lee Masters's Spoon River, Sherwood Anderson's Winesburg, Vachel Lindsay's Springfield, Illinois. "Draw a circle of two hundred miles radius around Chicago, and you will enclose four-fifths of the real literature of America, particularly four-fifths of the literature of tomorrow," wrote H. L. Mencken in a 1920 editorial for *The Smart Set*.[1] Sinclair Lewis's *Main Street* focused national attention on Gopher Prairie, Minnesota.

The age of literary realism, promoted by midwestern writers like Hamlin Garland, coincided with this resurgence of Midwest as subject, but modernism turned the attention of writers and readers from *what* gets said to *how* it gets said, and—despite Faulkner and Joyce—separated writing from place, especially Midwest place. Postmodernism exaggerated this trend, and as Annie Dillard notes, "It throws out the baby and proclaims the bath."[2] As postmodernism—a literature of surfaces over substance—came to dominate in academia and in the public consciousness, the Midwest lost currency in the years following World War II.

Many good writers continued to write about midwestern people and places: Fred Manfred, Paul Corey, Tillie Olson, Harry Petrakis, Mari Sandoz, Meridel LeSueur, Herbert Krause. But while Northern Illinois University Press could, in 1967, publish Lucien Stryk's *Heartland: Poets of* the Midwest, of all the poets in his collection, only Jim Wright made the 1967 *Norton Anthology of American Literature*. With a few exceptions—Gwendolyn Brooks, Saul Bellow, Joyce Carol Oates—young midwesterners were not part of the American literature canon of the 1950s. Chicago was no longer the literary capital of America. The Midwest was just flyover country. Looking back in 1976, Harrison Salsibury wrote, "New Yorkers didn't seem to understand the difference between Minneapolis and Indianapolis. And even when I explained they didn't seem to think it really made a difference."[3] Clarence Andrews ended his 1974 Midwest bibliography with a heartfelt request: "The writer will appreciate receiving information on any middle western writer writing now—who he is, where he lives, what he is up to."[4]

National interest in the Midwest revived in the 1970s and '80s as Americans, weary of postmodern dislocations and pepped up by John Denver's "Country Roads, take me home to the place I belong," retreated to the (in many ways retrospective) rural visions of Garrison Keillor, Robert Bly, Louise Erdrich, Jane Smiley, and other writers I tracked in *Late Harvest* and *Rooted: Seven Midwest Writers of Place*. Meridel LeSueur, blacklisted in the fifties as much for her place as for her politics, was back in the limelight. Poet Robert Bly (Madison, Minnesota) made the Norton anthology; one of his wife Carol's *Letters from the Country* was taught to freshmen, including my son, at the U.S. Naval Academy. William Maxwell, fiction editor for the *New Yorker* and mentor to a passel of modernists and postmodernists, published his memoir *So Long, See You Tomorrow*, set in Lincoln, Illinois. In 1985, Garrison Keillor made Lake Wobegon, Minnesota, the center of American literary consciousness. In advertisements sponsored by Pushcart Foundation, Raymond Carver called Dave Etter's *Alliance, Illinois* "hands down the most impressive long work of poetry I've read in years."

I recall a whirlwind of literary activity at this time throughout the Midwest: writers, writers groups, reading circuits, workshops, conferences, magazines, journals. The Society of Midland Authors, founded in 1915, reasserted itself. The Society for the Study of Midwestern Literature (SSML), founded in 1971, was publishing *MidAmerica* and *Midwestern Miscellany*. The shelves of my own publications from this time contain issues of *The Great River Review, Illinois Quarterly, Rhino, Western Illinois Regional Studies, Ohioana Quarterly, Illinois Writers Review, Old Northwest, Mississippi Valley Review, Midwest Quarterly*. On another shelf I see *Sou'wester, Great Lakes Review, Dacotah Territory, North Dakota Quarterly, Cincinnati Poetry Review, North Country Anvil, Karamu, Voyages to the Inland Sea, Midwestern Miscellany*. In addition to the university presses, hundreds of smaller operations published Midwest literature: Clarence Andrews's own Midwest Heritage Publishing Company, Jim Haining's Salt Lick Press, John Judson's Juniper Press, Jim Perlman's Holy Cow! Press, Robert Sutherland's Pikestaff Press, Don Olson's Ox Head Press, and my own Spoon River Poetry Press/Ellis Press, which published Dave Etter, Linda Hasselstrom, Bill Holm, Norbert Blei, William Kloefkorn, John Knoepfle, and Leo Dangel. Initial print runs on some of their books were five thousand copies. Publishers and writers gathered at celebrations like the Great Midwestern Book Fair, and Marshall Festival: A Celebration of Rural Writing. The Minnesota Independent Publishers Association distributed small-press books in Minnesota; Illinois had Illinois Literary Publishers Association (ILPA did not run a "book bus" as did MIPA). Grant support was plentiful, and applications were simple (we did not need a 401c3): private foundations, state arts boards, even state humanities commissions funded writing projects, writers' festivals, book and journal publishing, distribution, conferences tied to place. Regional literature was part of the grant agencies' social agenda.

Seymour Yesner published his *25 Minnesota Writers* in 1980; Gerald Nemanic published his *Bibliographical Guide to Midwestern Literature* in 1981; Robert Bray published his *Rediscoveries: Literature and Place in Illinois* in 1982. Momentum carried us through a good deal of valuable scholarship on the Midwest: Clayton and Onuf's *The Midwest and the Nation* (1990), Franklin and Steiner's *Mapping American Culture* (1992), Cheryl Temple Herr's *Critical Regionalism and Cultural Studies* (1996), and the SSML's 666-page *Dictionary of Midwestern Literature* (2001). But the nineties and new millennium brought a decline in both midwestern literature and scholarship, as America went global and culturally diverse (the triumph, in a way, of social postmodernism), steered in that direction by media in New York and Los Angeles—those places Americans change airplanes en route to Europe or Asia. America's turn to what James Howard Kunstler in 1993 termed *The Geography of Nowhere* hurt the Midwest. Keillor survived, but other writers either adjusted to the new agenda or dropped below even our radar. Even in the Midwest, academia followed the national trends. Literature anthologies changed their focus dramatically: Garland out, Bly out, Hemingway down, Anderson surviving only with his story "Queer." At my own university, Rural and Regional Studies closed and Global Studies opened. My own *Spoon River Quarterly*, passed in 1987 to new editors, went for "innovative voices/ forms"; *Mid-American Review* became an *international* magazine disconnected from place. Illinois Writers, Inc. died around 1986. The Great Midwestern Book Fair folded tent around 1990. *Illinois Quarterly*: gone. *Western Illinois Regional Studies*: gone. *The Old Northwest*: RIP. My 2006 article for *The Midwest Quarterly* titled "Where Now 'Midwestern Literature'?" was originally titled "Is Anything Left of 'Midwestern Literature'?" "Bioregionalism" proved to be a late twentieth-century bubble, not the wave of the future. When I asked several author/publisher friends for names, titles, and ideas for this essay, most admitted to being hard pressed. "Sadly, most of the talented young writers I know are not much interested in our region," wrote Bart Sutter in an email. When I asked my former student Angela Arvidson, who has reviewed new juveniles for over a decade, how many of the books she sees are set in the Midwest, she answered, "I cannot remember any of them."

On the other hand, there are writers alive and well in the Midwest, and some small magazines survive: *MidAmerica* and *Midwestern Miscellany*, *Great River Review*, *Midwest Quarterly*, *Ohioana Quarterly*, even *Rhino*. We are inventing new journals like *Middle West Review*, Jim Reese's *Paddlefish*, Judy Wilson's *Yellow Medicine Review*, and Rob Zoschke's *The Lowdown*. SSML still hosts an annual conference, and volume two of the *Dictionary of Midwestern Literature* was published in May 2016. The "8th Annual Great Midwest Book Fest" took place in Milwaukee, 2016, a three-hour event presented by UrbanReviewsOnline. The South Dakota Festival of the Books (not online and lots more than three hours) continues annually. Jim Perlman at Holy Cow! Press has kept the faith, and Scott King's Red Dragonfly Press publishes Midwest writers. So do new small presses like Brighthorse Books, Truman State University Press, and Hastings College Press.

Midwestern university presses tell the Midwestern History Association that they are interested in regional books—and I'd say Iowa, Nebraska, and Wisconsin are—but many publish regional material only when it overlaps the current agenda. Just two of the 2016 Minnesota Books Award winners were set in Minnesota; one was set in the deserts of the Southwest, and another involved a group of LGBTQ teens in New York City.

Although I'm largely out of the picture these days—and especially oblivious to what's going on east of the Mississippi—I see what might become a new wave of Midwest writers, some of whom receive occasional national attention. Since 1998, William Kent Krueger has made a career out of Pocket Book mystery novels set in Minnesota: *Iron Lake*, *Boundary Waters*, *Purgatory Ridge*, *Ordinary Grace*, *Tamarack County*. Likewise Joanne Fluke's Hannah Swensen novels, most recently *Wedding Cake Murders*, set in Lake Eden, Minnesota. Leif Enger received significant attention for his 2001 novel *Peace Like a River*, about a family named Land, and which is grounded in rural Minnesota: barley fields, geese, tornadoes, churches, snow. Through a new project at the Marshall, Minnesota, Public Library, called "Read Local," I have met authors of novels and books of poetry set in our region: Forrest Peterson, Steve Linstrom, Scott Thoma, Ronald Mackendaz. I note with some satisfaction that the current editors of *Spoon River Poetry Review* have changed the journal's preference for new, innovative, cutting-edge poetry to what they call poetry of "emplacement." Joshua Preston, a young poet from Illinois now on a writing fellowship at Stanford, emails, telling me that all the fellows in his cohort are, with one exception, "connected to a place." And I found very thought-provoking Charles Baxter's recent comment: "In the shadow of people like Donald Barthelme . . . I wrote a number of failed novels, which had nothing to do with the areas of the country I grew up in. [Then] I thought, well, I'll try writing about the areas and the sorts of people that I actually know."

Perhaps we have passed postmodernism—in America and in the Midwest. The paradigm, after all, is that you go out—in this case move away from place and into postmodernism—*and then you return* to what Dana Yost calls in his book *The Right Place*. Are the signs I see of a new wave of Midwest writing an indication of things to come, or just a bubble? Only time will tell. Meanwhile, what strategies can we adopt for reclaiming the lost region of Midwest writing in our own and the national consciousness? Can we model our pitch on those used previously?

The two overarching problems are (a) teaching students to read books and (b) reclaiming our region's history and literature in the curricula of our schools (Paul Theobald, author of *Teaching the Commons* and director of RuralLitR.A.L.L.Y., says the roadblock is large corporations who have seized control of the national standards and testing program, and do not include local literatures on those standardized tests). Beyond them, I see four key matters: content, promotion, finances, and media. Let me address all four.

First, content. "Midwest writing" is not just writing by people who happen to live in and collect their salaries from places in the Midwest but writing in the Midwest tradition. Creative writing programs—more popular these days than literature programs—have brought to the Midwest a flock of foreigners who take the job and the money, but are unwilling to adjust their writing to the values of the region that pays their salaries. I once called them "Pigeons of Buchenau" (now the title of my book *Pigeons of Buchenau and Other Stories*) swooping in from god-knows-where to gobble up the prairie grain, giving little in return except pigeon shit. Midwest writers understand the region and write about the region using accurate markers of place, the language of the Midwest, and the thought, values, and behavior of the Midwest. They are not—to reference Garrison Keillor's *Lake Wobegon Days*—a University of Minnesota professor from "somewhere east of East" who pronounces "Minnesota" to sound like "Moose turds."[5]

The Midwest belief system is partly historical (settlers struggling for survival on the frontier, battling with friends and neighbors against nature and eastern bankers) and partly environmental (fighting grasshoppers, digging out after blizzards). The Midwest is about values as well as a landscape, but the abstract values are in synch with the physical environment. Lisel Mueller called our region an "experiment in grassroots democracy," which makes "experience the touchstone of knowledge" and creates a society characterized by "a distrust of 'impractical,' abstract thinking."[6] Cheryl Temple Herr goes into more detail, calling the Midwest mindset

> a metaphor accentuating an amorphous traditionalism deployed in the "family"; a largely unreflective patriotism; an ethic of hard work and democratic-socialist egalitarianism; community spirit of the action-oriented, "barn-raising" sort; a commitment to "basic values"; moral, spiritual, and educational fair-dealing and loyalty to one's employer; a parsimony on principle; a verbal commitment to the myth of the family farm even in a period of agribusiness takeover; an international export-ethic and aspiration to multinational prowess; a healthy local skepticism about all such claims; and the social practices surrounding American rural and small-town life, particularly those of the community potluck supper, the church social, and the county fair.[7]

So how can we write about the region in the spirit of the region? And how can we market that writing to the national audience?

One way might be to make the Midwest what it was in the first wave: a new frontier. The West is probably better positioned for this pitch, but these days we are a mystery to most Americans: collapsing barns, abandoned houses and towns, and amplitudes that can be as interesting to modern Americans as was the Mississippi River to Huck and Jim. Elizabeth Oness's *Leaving Milan* (Ohio), winner of the 2014 Brighthorse Prize, is, in a colleague's words, "a novel about getting the hell OUT" and having adventures.

Or we might emulate writers of the second wave and pitch the Midwest as what America thinks it is—not, today, small towns or industrial centers, but whackos and curmudgeons. We can sell them our eccentrics. David Rhodes did this in the 1970s; Jim Heynen did this in the 1980s. The *Minneapolis Star-Tribune* review of Ann Bauer's *Forgiveness 4 You* was headlined "Sex Trafficking and Murder in Minnesota." "Foulmouthed, skinny, death-head-looking, oxy-addled, thieving Maggie Boylan" in Michael Henson's *The Way the World Is* comes from Appalachian

Ohio. This would be Kent Krueger's approach to selling the Midwest to today's American mentality.

We could pitch the Midwest not to America's popular enthusiasm for whackos, but to the ascendant PC agenda: multiculturalism, feminism, cultural and sexual diversity, the green movement, self-esteem. In a personal letter, *Great River Review* editor Robert Hedin nominates as significant younger Midwest writers half a dozen people, "representing the growing literary and multiculturalism in the state [of Minnesota]." Jim Heynen brought cultural diversity to Dutch Center, Iowa, in his 2012 novel *The Fall of Alice K*. The 2015 winner of the Minnesota Book Awards in the "Minnesota" category was *Her Honor: Rosalie Wahl and the Minnesota Women's Movement*. Nicole Lea Helget is getting a lot of attention these days for her "memoir," *The Summer of Ordinary Ways*, which critiques "homophobia" in the town of Sleepy Eye, Minnesota. Forrest Peterson's novel *Buffalo Ridge* addresses conventional versus organic agriculture. Gene Stark, whose collection of poems is titled *Flyover Seasons*, recently published an autobiography titled *Accidentally Green: Building an Organic Livelihood*.

Will this accommodation work? Can Herr's Midwest accommodate the new politically correct and culturally diverse worldview? Yes and no. Minnesota author Paul Gruchow was fond of noting that species not suited to the local environment disappear quickly . . . and social constructs not in harmony with the local environment also die off quickly. Historically the Midwest has been an ethnic patchwork and thus a battle zone (Catholic-Protestant, Polish-Icelandic, farmer-banker), but midwesterners did open the door in a manner PC folks would appreciate. However, the Midwest also poses a test—environmental or social—which not everyone passes. What do you bring to the table beyond attitude and appetite? There is none of the Dodo's "Everyone has won and all must have prizes." I do not think that we can sell the Midwest as what PC America is today.

But unless we pitch ourselves as diverse—which we pretty much are these days—we don't have to accommodate the national agenda. On his jacket blurb for Connie Wanek's *Bonfire*, Louis Jenkins wrote, "Wanek's poems . . . are not about current hot topics, say, alcoholism or domestic abuse. There is no sensationalism . . . the poems never shout or whine."

Other new-wave works and authors take a seventies approach and pitch our Midwest as an escape from McAmerikkka. Coming to terms with chaos has always been a prominent theme in novels, poems, stories, so this might work. Thomas Maltman's murder mystery *Little Wolves* finds resolution for problems in the Minnesota prairie. Ditto J. J. Luepke's *Rich by Accident*: get out of the cities, settle into a farm place near Cottonwood, Minnesota, and breathe again.

In a sense, options one and three reassert the Midwest nationally by recovering our past. Some evidence suggests that the pendulum is swinging from postmodern abstract apocalypse to hard-nosed history. Dennis Clausen's "creative nonfiction" book *Prairie Son* is described on the jacket as a "faithfully researched and vividly retold" piece of "fascinating history informed with a suspenseful narrative." The news in Sara DeLuca's *The Crops Look Good: News from a Midwestern Farm Family* is recovered history from 1923 to 1955. Marty Seifert's *Sundown at Sunrise* recounts with remarkable accuracy an axe murder, which took place in southwestern Minnesota a century ago. Karen Jones Schutt retired from teaching to a farmstead near Sioux Falls and set to writing memoir-stories and essays: *Knee High by the Fourth of July*, *Make Hay While the Sun Shines*, *The Callie Stories*. Linda Hasselstrom and Twyla Hansen take the same approach in *Dirt Songs: A Plains Duet*. Dana Yost's book on Minneota, Minnesota, 1940, is in the design stages as I write.

These books rarely receive national attention, but let's forget the *New York Times* best-seller list and address the local audience. Many Midwestern writers past started out doing just that. Some made the big time; others did not. In an age of print on demand, we can produce perfect-bound books targeted at a fairly small audience, and sell locally. And there is nothing wrong with saddle-stapled chapbooks like *The Good Hard Times*, a booklet of interviews with local farmers published by the Minnesota Machinery Museum in Hanley Falls, which I printed on a photocopier, then folded, stapled, and trimmed myself. The seventies abounded in saddle-stapled seventies "magazines" like the *Iris* out of Bloomington, Illinois.

Photos help. Increasingly people look for and appreciate graphics with text. I first noticed the attraction of graphics while working on Vachel Lindsay, Norbert Blei, and Ken Patchen, and with my 1979 book

A Generation in Motion. People flipped through its pages, reading not a word I wrote but looking at the photos, and nodding appreciatively: "Cool book." I began carrying a camera, shooting photos as well as taking notes, and integrating graphics with the text: *Jubilee Diary, Poland in Transition, Here I Stand,* and *Crying in the Wilderness.*

Distribution is today a serious problem, and the 1980s strategies will not work today: book stores are few, direct orders to at least the Ellis-Spoon River Poetry Press website are almost nonexistent (I remember the days of a post-office box filled to capacity twice a day!), tweets and posts do not seem to replace reviews (which are now limited and late), and competition from internet white noise is enormous. We can resurrect writers' groups and perhaps even journals and magazines, but very few copies of a new book get sold these days, including books published or distributed by university and commercial presses. Libraries do not buy books the way they did, and people do not buy books. When Garrison Keillor read Leo Dangel poems on two July 2016 broadcasts of *Writers' Almanac,* the results were zero book sales . . . and one inquiry from a poet looking for a publisher. Or people buy online, from amazon.com, which orders one book at a time, takes a 55 percent discount, publisher to pay shipping. Often people buy used copies, probably review copies that generated no reviews. Certainly a small-press book distribution system is not going to work, but a book bus might. Readings and conferences sell books. We're back to being door-to-door salesmen.

So write local, print local, sell local. When I take books to a local event—Ole and Lena Days in Granite Falls, Dylan Days in Duluth, the South Dakota Festival of Books—I unload about one hundred dollars' worth of books, including *The Good Hard Times;* my book on southwestern Minnesota summer festivals, *Hallelujah Anyway;* and the coffee-table book *Southwest Minnesota: The Land and the People.* I've sold more copies of *Southwest Minnesota* than Continuum Press (New York and London) reports selling of *Song of the North Country: A Midwest Framework to the Songs of Bob Dylan.* Even poetry can find a local audience. Recently a farmer from Montevideo, Minnesota, ordered eighteen copies of Leo Dangel's *Home from the Field* as Christmas presents for his farmer friends. Imagine that: farmers read poetry!

What about online publication? In my mind, posts and blogs are not literature, but my writer friend Hugh Curtler has an international audience for his blogs, and writer friend Adrian C. Louis spends hours each day reading online. Schools and libraries are very much online these days. I personally distrust electronic books, and I react more to a printed flier than to an email announcing a new book, but I'm atypical. I seek permanence. Will those electrons stay put? Will today's digital files, unlike those on my old floppy discs, be readable in ten, twenty, fifty years, or are we setting up—as Vint Cerf, an internet founder, warned in a speech to the American Association for the Advancement of Science—"a digital Dark Ages"? Many printed books began as ebooks and even blogs. I understand that after the 2011 Chicago mayoral election, San Sinker combined his tweets into a printed book, *The F***ing Epic Twitter Quest of @MayorEmanuel*. Maybe we can open our windows a little. My daughter Kristin, a producer of documentary films, says this is the future. We can do that.

Or *you* do that (I don't even have a Facebook page). Balance digital and print. Resurrect the local writers' circuits on campus and in the community. Settle at times for local audiences and topics. Print books as chapbooks or in short runs. Maybe some of it enters into the larger world, maybe not. But keep the faith. *Ave, frater, atque vale.*

Notes

1. H. L. Mencken, *Smart Set Criticism*, ed. William Nolte (Ithaca NY: Cornell University Press, 1968), 12.
2. Annie Dillard, *Living by Fiction* (New York: Harper and Row, 1982), 63.
3. Harrison Salisbury, "The Victorian City in the Midwest," in *Growing Up in Minnesota*, ed. Chester Anderson (Minneapolis: University of Minnesota Press, 1976), 71.
4. Clarence Andrews, "The Literature of the Middle West: A Beginning Bibliography," *Great Lakes Review* 1, no. 1 (1974): 36.
5. Garrison Keillor, *Lake Wobegon Days* (New York: Viking, 1985), 19.
6. Lisel Mueller, "Midwestern Poetry: Goodbye to All That" in *Three Essays on Midwestern Poetry in Midcentury* (LaCrosse WI: Center for Contemporary Poetry, 1971), 3.
7. Cheryl Temple Herr, *Critical Regionalism and Cultural Studies* (Gainesville: University of Florida Press, 1996), 106.

PART 6

The Midwestern Experience

18

The Upper Midwest as the
Second Promised Land

Gleaves Whitney

Americans associate the founders of the nation with developments along the East Coast. But these same founders wrote frequently and fervently of what would become the Midwest. They thought a lot about the strategic importance of places like the Upper Mississippi Valley, Great Lakes, and Detroit. After winning independence from Britain, George Washington attached world-historic significance to the "Western Lands" stretching beyond the Appalachian Mountains north of the Ohio River.[1] Settling the territory in the Northwest would provide a suitable stage on which Americans could flourish. Shortly after securing the Northwest Territory from the British, Washington dispatched a 1783 circular to the states in which he wrote, "The Citizens of America, placed in the most enviable condition, as the sole Lords and Proprietors of a vast Tract of Continent, comprehending all the various soils and climates of the World, and abounding with all the necessaries and conveniences of life, are . . . to be considered as the Actors in a most conspicuous Theatre, which seems to be peculiarly designated by Providence for the display of human greatness and felicity."[2]

As Washington's words suggest, the new nation was to become more than just another empire. A 1785 letter of his runs thick with biblical allusions and anticipates the sonnet by Emma Lazarus associated with the Statue of Liberty: "Let the poor, the needy and oppressed of the Earth, and those who want Land, resort to the fertile plains of our western country, the *second land of Promise*, and there dwell in peace, fulfilling the first and great commandment."[3]

In another letter and with a dash of humor Washington continued the thought: "I wish to see the sons and daughters of the world in Peace and busily employed [not in war but] in the more agreeable amusement of fulfilling the first and great commandment, *Increase and Multiply*: as an encouragement to which we have opened the fertile plains of the Ohio to the poor, the needy and the oppressed of the Earth; any one therefore who is heavy laden, or who wants land to cultivate, may repair thither and abound, as in the land of promise, with milk and honey; the ways are preparing, and the roads will be made easy."[4]

Clearly, to Washington, securing the Northwest was not just another real estate transaction. As his letters in the summer of 1785 suggest, opening up "our western country" to pioneers almost rose to the level of Moses leading the Hebrews to the Promised Land some three thousand years earlier.[5] This audacious vision of the Northwest as a "second land of Promise" was cultivated not just by Washington but by other founders as well. The Northwest would become their field of dreams, a new republic where pioneers would transform America's wilderness frontier into an empire of liberty.[6]

In terms of the impact on the Upper Midwest's historic geography, three founders especially would influence our future heartland. Thomas Jefferson, Alexander Hamilton, and John Adams all developed ideas for the new republic's western lands that were both overlapping and competing. We see traces of their impact in the West from the 1780s to the 1820s and beyond.[7] This chapter focuses on how those ideas manifested in the Upper Midwest.[8] It joins intellectual history to historical geography to answer the question: How did ideas impact the American landscape in the Upper Midwest between the nation's founding and the age of Jackson? To answer that question, we look at the Jeffersonian vision of establishing an *agrarian* republic; the Hamiltonian vision of establishing a *commercial* republic; and the Adamsian vision of establishing a *virtuous* republic. The ideas associated with these three species of republic were translated into corresponding landscape features in the Upper Midwest. While the conventional use of these adjectives—Jeffersonian, Hamiltonian, Adamsian; agrarian, commercial, virtuous—simplifies as well as overstates the differences among the three visions, it also provides useful analytic categories to understand at least some of the development of the United States from the 1780s to the Jacksonian era, when the three visions coexisted and would make their mark in the Upper Midwest.[9] After the mid-1820s, these three republican visions would undergo considerable alteration, even obliteration, due to the rise of the market revolution in the age of Jackson, the acceleration of the Industrial Revolution in the wake of the Civil War, the urban revolution, and the closing of the frontier.

Excellent Statecraft: The Northwest Ordinances

Before delving into the specifics of the three republican visions, it would be useful to review the legal and cultural framework provided by the Northwest Ordinances. In the 1780s, the Confederation Congress faced severe challenges in the territory. Besides ridding the region of both pacific and hostile Indians—"Canaanites" in the second promised land— the Congress wrestled with numerous challenges before the Northwest Territory could deliver on its arcadian promise.[10] Not the least of these challenges was to bring administrative order to the frontier. Peter Onuf describes the threats: "The West that policy makers imagined—peopled by orderly, industrious settlers, connected to the old states by common interests and loyalties, and busily contributing to the national wealth and welfare—was nothing like the West that already existed. Speculators, squatters, and other adventurers infested the new settlements, promoting their private interests, defying state and national authority, and entertaining overtures from foreign powers."[11]

To address both immediate practical as well as long-term civilizational concerns, northern and southern delegates to the Confederation Congress drew up three Northwest Ordinances between 1784 and 1787. It was a time when representatives from diverse regions of the country could still find common ground for the common good. Considered as a whole, the three Northwest Ordinances not only accommodated the founders' various visions of the nation's republican future; they exhibit some of the finest statecraft ever produced by a U.S. Congress. We see this in how the delegates decided early in their deliberations to reject the ambitions of eastern states to keep enlarging themselves or to establish colonies in the West. Rather, under the influence of Montesquieu's *The Spirit of the Laws*, Congress decided that the new states should be independent and scaled to manageable governing units consistent with traditional republican models.

Next, the ordinances spelled out enlightened rules for surveying the land, assuring immigrants and investors of orderly settlement, and administering the territory.

Beyond the mechanics of governing, the ordinances made a powerful cultural statement. This Northwest frontier would be a land of freedom; traditional Anglo-American rights—religious freedom, habeas corpus, trial by jury, and representation—would here be observed. This Northwest frontier would be a land of opportunity; free markets and the right to make contracts would here be honored. This Northwest frontier would not look like the Tidewater of the Cavaliers.[12] Nor would it resemble the plantations of the inland South; slavery and indentured servitude would here be prohibited. This Northwest frontier would be alive to Washington's vision of the second promised land; thus a bold statement was written into the Ordinance of 1787—a statement not found even in the Declaration of Independence, Articles of Confederation, or emerging Constitution—that good government was impossible where religion, morality, and knowledge were lacking. This Northwestern frontier would be home to the institutions of ordered freedom; hence the pioneers would here establish houses of worship, mutual aid societies, and schools near the center of every township.[13]

Delving deeper, we can better appreciate the cultural impact of the ordinances. For example, the drafters' concerns for the happiness of humankind and for those institutions and habits that conduce to happiness—religion, morality, knowledge, and public education; ancient rights, free markets, and good government—give us a case study of the best republican thinking in the world in the 1780s. Leading thinkers in Anglo-America drew on a broad understanding of republican principles to forge common ground among the various factions in Congress. Recall that even the slave-owning Jefferson was eager to prohibit the peculiar institution from taking root in the Northwest (which was considered part of Virginia until 1783–84).[14]

The abolition clause in the Ordinance of 1787 had no parallel in the U.S. Constitution, composed at the same time. That clause would prove significant to the course of U.S. history. It would keep much if not all of the heartland of the United States—especially in the Upper Midwest—

free of slavery. There are other considerations that played a role in discouraging slavery from moving into the Old Northwest—for example, the Wheat Belt of the Upper Midwest entailed short harvests and relatively little (thus relatively cheap) labor on family farms.[15] Nevertheless, the heartland started out trying to be true to the principle in the Declaration that "all men are created equal." More than forty years later, Alexis de Tocqueville, touring the Ohio River country, would observe stark differences between the slave culture to the south of the Ohio and the free culture to the north.[16] Two decades after Tocqueville's visit, Abraham Lincoln famously observed that the ordinance led to many great differences between those states north of the Ohio and those south of it.[17] During the Civil War, the heartland gave the Union the Iron Brigade and other fighters to wash, with blood, the stain of slavery out of American life.

The three Northwest Ordinances also provided an orderly framework for spreading democratic institutions and cultivating knowledgeable citizens. The "lot number sixteen" provisions of the 1785 ordinance called "for the maintenance of public schools." This commitment to public education reflected the lobbying of New England delegates for public schools and adequate public funding for those schools. Jeffersonian republicans had no problem with the provision and in fact enthusiastically supported the measure. From the standpoint of historical geography, it is important to recognize that lot, or section, sixteen was near the center of each township. Thus, where topographic conditions allowed, communities were meant to form around public schools near the center of each township. Even if a school could not be physically located near the center of a given township, "lot sixteen" sales would be set aside "for the maintenance of public schools." This vision arises from a New England tradition going back to the seventeenth century. Yankees provided for public education in their land grants in order that citizens could read their Bibles, build their communities, and spread republican ideals among the rising generation. Thus the township-and-range grid with its vast web of "lot sixteen" schools was not just about surveying and purchasing land. It was also about building a moral, civically integrated, republican culture.[18] Again, this measure represented the common ground shared by New England Yankees and southern Jeffersonians, who were in agreement that education was foundational to the future of the republic (whether imagined as an empire for liberty or the second promised land).

The systematic way the new republic was to grow—with hundreds of local communities spread through the western lands, each in its own township with its own local government and its own "intellectual common" dedicated to public education—represented a remarkable experiment in ordered freedom.[19]

The Jeffersonian Landscape

Let's now explore how Jeffersonian ideas got etched into the American landscape during the formative years of the nation. At the center of Jefferson's political philosophy, which was influenced both by Lockean liberal and classical republican traditions, was the ideal of an agrarian or pastoral republic.[20] Republics in the ancient world often faltered over the lack of available land for an expanding population of yeomen farmers. With abundant new lands and a rational land policy, the American republic had a chance to succeed where earlier republics had failed. The American West was meant to attract independent, enlightened farmers who were not in thrall to the big banks and moneymen back east. The states were to be the primary instruments of republican principle; thus the national government would be strictly contained within its constitutional limits, and the resulting federal budget was to be small. So compelling was this vision that generations of Jeffersonian arcadians would advance this ideal—arguably with the passage of the Homestead Act of 1862, up through the presidency of Grover Cleveland at the end of the nineteenth century, and even the presidency of Calvin Coolidge in the 1920s.[21]

The Jeffersonians contributed to the historical geography of the Upper Midwest by leaving four distinctive marks on its landscapes. First is the rectangular-grid survey by which the land was measured and sold to eastern investors and hardscrabble settlers.[22] Township-and-range surveying comes straight out of the instructions in the Land Ordinance of 1785 and gives the region its long, straight roads. The resulting landscape has frequently been described as a "checkerboard" or "quilt" of seemingly endless one-mile squares and rectangles of various dimensions. This grid makes up the Public Land Survey System (PLSS) in use to this day, and it is what one sees when flying over the Midwest in clear weather.[23] Jefferson's seemingly infinite township-and-range lines cut indiscriminately across watersheds, hilltops, lakeshores, and wetlands, irrespective of topography. His vision represented the triumph of Enlightenment utility over Romantic nature. It also represented unimaginable toil: the early surveyors in the Old Northwest and their families are the unsung heroes of the early republic.[24] The rectangular grid stipulated by the Land Ordinance of 1785 contrasts markedly with the colonial British metes-and-bound system on the East Coast and compares more subtly with the colonial Spanish Laws of the Indies on the West Coast.[25]

The rectangular grid reflected utility as well as reason. Jefferson, a man of the Enlightenment, argued for the Cartesian grid to keep order in lands that would be rapidly settled and invested in. With the grid, every sale could be identified by its township number, range number, section, subsection, and lot—the system that is used in land purchases to this day. The concept was borrowed from the military engineers Jefferson knew, men like the first geographer of the United States, Thomas Hutchins, who in turn had borrowed the grid from Roman and Crusader military colonies.

A second distinctive mark of the Jeffersonian landscape is mile after mile of isolated farmsteads built by "yeomen farmers" with the aid of neighbors. This is the reason the midwestern hinterland so little resembles the European hinterland. In feudal Europe, many peasants traced their settlements to medieval times when they lived in village workshops outside castle walls. The reason for compact villages was that the lower orders could be more easily controlled by the landed gentry when corralled into a confined space. Jefferson found these crowded European settlements not only unhealthy, but also undignified for a free people. In theory, Americans were not to be the vassals of anyone, certainly not the moneymen.[26] He did not want to see crowded towns and cities mar either the American character or the American landscape. So he went in the opposite direction. In the United States, each farmhouse was to be the castle of its own lot of land and set a little back from the nearby baseline or meridian road.

A third feature of the Jeffersonian landscape was the iconic, one-room schoolhouse either located in, or supported by, every township's section sixteen. This provision of the Land Ordinance of 1785 provided a focus for the yeomen households scattered throughout a township. These schoolhouses were also meant to be the backbone of a powerful republican institution, a network of public schools that instilled economic independence, political community, and a sense of civic duty and leadership.

Like the Land Ordinance of 1785, the Northwest Ordinance of 1787 made public education a cultural centerpiece. Article 3 reads as follows: "Religion, morality and knowledge, being necessary to good government and the happiness of mankind, schools and the means of education shall forever be encouraged." This remarkable provision anticipated not only the spectacular growth of publicly supported schools throughout the United States but also, later, a number of distinguished land-grant universities. The ordinances promoted at once a liberal and a practical education. Speaking of the American farmer, Jefferson was proud that "ours are the only farmers that can read Homer."[27] He further championed education—his "crusade against ignorance"—when he wrote, "If a nation expects to be ignorant & free, in a state of civilization, it expects what never was & never will be."[28] The sage of Monticello famously argued, "I know of no safe depository of the ultimate powers of the society but the people themselves, and if we think them not enlightened enough to exercise their control with a wholesome discretion, the remedy is not to take it from them, but to inform their discretion by education."

A fourth Jeffersonian feature on upper midwestern landscapes is its architectural heritage. Because of Jefferson's own classical education, he approached the Northwest with an ancient ideal in view, that of the agrarian or pastoral republic. Pastoral societies had long been at the root of Western civilization—among the ancient Hebrews, Greeks, and Romans especially—and Jean-Jacques Rousseau was their indefatigable modern champion. So pastoralism was an ideal that Jefferson hoped to continue in some form. His hope was that the American frontier would live up to its arcadian potential by being transformed into a republican society of freedom-loving farmers. For that reason, the architect of Monticello was an advocate of Greek revival and Roman republican architecture to give the young nation the visual vocabulary of yeomen virtue grafted onto ordered freedom.

To sum up, because the ordinances reflect Jefferson's debt to John Locke and the Enlightenment, the Jeffersonian vision is optimistic, bullish on human nature. It believes in the efficacy of education in the pursuit of happiness, in the possibilities of educating citizens for independence, and in the development of an empire of liberty. Democracy and relative equality of holdings would foster the growth of a large middling class of farmers, as opposed to the corrupt moneymen in their corrupt cities. Freedom and individualism would cultivate a yeoman class of homesteaders who could not be herded into crowded settlements. The heart of the Jefferson's agrarian republic was to be found in the vast spaces settled by the "common man," each a New World lord on his 40 acres.

The Hamiltonian Landscape

We now come to the second member of the troika whose republican ideas influenced the historical geography of the Upper Midwest. Alexander Hamilton's heft in U.S. intellectual history hardly needs to be rehearsed here. His most incisive writings include a number of *The Federalist Papers* and the *Report on Manufactures*, which reflected his admiration of Adam Smith and other thinkers of the Scottish Enlightenment and telegraphed his vision of a commercial republic that would spur the growth of great cities and global centers of manufacturing. The wealth generated by a powerful national economy would provide reliable sources of revenue for a strong federal government, world-class military, and growing commercial empire.

Hamilton's ideas to shape the territory into the heartland of a commercial republic may have been slower to unfold than Jefferson's agrarian republicanism—we see a hint of it in the founding of Marietta, Ohio. Yet the effects were increasingly dramatic as the young nation passed through the market revolution, ordeal of civil war, and Industrial Revolution.

Hamilton's ideas shaped the historical geography of the United States by leaving four distinctive marks on the nation's landscapes, including those in the Upper Midwest. The first concerns a place name. The first secretary of the U.S. Treasury made such an impression on early settlers in the Northwest that they named the second organized county in the territory after him. It was no insignificant gesture. For a period in the 1790s, Hamilton County stretched from the Ohio River to the Straits of Mackinac—a jurisdiction larger than nearly half the original thirteen states combined.[29]

Besides the symbolic weight of his namesake county, Hamilton left a second, more significant mark on the landscape of the Upper Midwest. Because the New Yorker abhorred slavery, he did everything within his power to insure that the Northwest would not be like the Tidewater of the Cavaliers or the Kentucky of slave-owning pioneers. These western lands would be settled by a free, not a slave-owning, population.

Common ground between Hamiltonians and Jeffersonians existed when it came to education, a third way that the ideas of the New Yorker impacted the landscape. Hamilton was a student of Adam Smith. Consistent with the thought of Smith and the Scottish Enlightenment, Hamiltonians assume that human beings will act with enlightened self-interest—if they have access to knowledge and the open marketplace of ideas. The "lot sixteen" provision of the 1785 ordinance, guaranteeing public support for public education, as well as article 3 of the 1787 ordinance, declaring that a happy, well-governed people are also an educated people, were items of faith to Hamilton. His own dreary childhood—the suffering caused by the lack of a stable family in his youth—no doubt contributed to his belief in the pivotal role of education in social advancement, the training up of leaders, and the pursuit of happiness.

In addition to schools, a prosperous republic needs a well-developed infrastructure to produce wealth, and this led to the fourth and perhaps most dramatic way that Hamilton and his ideas and followers would shape the landscapes of the Upper Midwest (much to the consternation of Jeffersonians). A wealth-generating society needed free markets, stable financial institutions, transportation improvements, and a sufficiently powerful central government to guarantee rights conducive to innovative, hard work. Article 2 of the 1787 ordinance protected the right of workers to make contracts in a free market.

Hamiltonians had faith that free-market capitalism was the fastest, most efficient way to increase the wealth of nations, bring prosperity to increasing numbers of people, and create an economic powerhouse in the global marketplace. Hamilton's commercial republic required a strong central government that had the ability to negotiate favorable treaties with tough competitors, legislate for robust trade, and promote (even with protectionist measures) strong commercial and industrial growth. Not insignificantly, Hamiltonians also supported a strong military to protect commercial interests at home and abroad.

The landscape of the Upper Midwest developed, decade after decade, into the commercial republic Hamilton envisioned. To the dismay of Jeffersonians, the dominant feature of that landscape is the city—or better, a network of large cities. The most prevalent expression of the Hamiltonian republic is the modern cityscape that began dominating the hinterlands in the second half of the nineteenth century. You can see its progress in the way America's urban skylines have changed. Where once it was a church or county courthouse or grain elevator or water tower that rose over the neighborhoods and corn and wheat fields of the Upper Midwest, now it is skyscrapers. The downtown skylines of the larger cities in the Upper Midwest reflect Hamilton's vision of the commercial republic. Towering over all the rest and uniting these cities in a vast economic web is Chicagoland. The Chicago skyline, rising dramatically above Lake Michigan, is an international symbol of the power of the free market in a commercial republic. Its economic power, its global reach, make downtown Chicago the crown jewel of Hamilton's vision in the Northwest.

Other manifestations of the commercial republic in the landscapes of the Upper Midwest can be seen in institutions ranging from military bases to malls. In the early days of the republic, for example, Fort Detroit, Fort Dearborn (Chicago), and the military road that connected them—basically today's U.S. 12 across the southern Lower Peninsula of Michigan—attest to the early strategic importance of the Upper Midwest. In the postwar United States, commercial malls sprouted in fast-growing suburbs and showcased the Hamiltonian dream of a thriving commercial republic. Arguably the first mall built in America, Southdale, was created in a Minneapolis suburb.

The Adamsian Landscape

Since many migrants move as families and clans, transplanting their culture to new locales, it is not surprising that the Upper Midwest was initially populated by Anglo-Americans who uprooted themselves from homes back east. The Erie Canal, which opened in 1825 to take advantage of trade with postwar Europe, sparked one of the great migrations in U.S. history and led to one of the engendering cultural experiences of the Upper Midwest. Settlers from New England and Upstate New York migrated latitudinally to the new Northwest Territory. This explains why New England place names correspond to place names throughout the Upper Midwest. More than that, Adams, according to David Hackett Fisher, "attempted to force Yankee cultural and political values" on the West and other regions of the country—hence his central place in this study.[30]

This "quintessential Yankee" contributed prodigiously to the intellectual foundations of the new republic, including its new western territory. His copious writing on constitutions would influence the crafting of the Northwest Ordinance of 1787.[31] Likewise, numerous state constitutions drafted throughout Yankeedom in the nineteenth century reflected his erudition and expertise in this area.[32]

For pedagogical purposes, Adams is sometimes characterized as the advocate of the "virtuous republic." His values originated in a rather dim view of "fallen" humankind. While no orthodox Christian, the dour New Englander did assent to the classical view of man's tragic nature grafted onto the Augustinian view of the radical evil within. In contrast to Jefferson's optimism and Hamilton's realism, Adams's pessimism led him seriously to question whether the American republic could long endure. He dismissed the rational plans that men of the Enlightenment put confidence in. He warned against the corrupting luxury that a commercial republic would inevitably generate. He abhorred the acid radicalism of the French revolutionaries.

How did the conservative ideas of John Adams express themselves in the landscapes of the Upper Midwest? First, as we saw above, he was honored by migrants from New England and Upstate New York carrying the names of their former homes to the frontier. Yankees paid the founder homage by naming transplanted communities after him.

Second, like Jefferson and Hamilton, Adams rued the existence of slavery on American soil and did everything in his power to halt its spread; thus the Northwest would not have the aristocracy of the Lower South or the plantations of the Upper South.

Third—and in this matter, too, he resembled Jefferson and Hamilton—Adams and his New England compatriots in Congress supported the section-sixteen school near the center of each township to equip citizens to read, spread republican values, and participate in local government. Because of the Protestant origin of early New England settlements, grammar schools were built so that children from an early age could read and search sacred scripture to discern God's message. As the generations passed, and as New England society and schools became more secular, the emphasis on reading remained, not just for religious and moral lessons but also for political and commercial uses.

This support for public education leads to an additional point, one that sharply distinguishes Adams from the other members of the troika. His New England allies in Congress not only supported section-sixteen schools near the center of each township, they also sought to encourage the development of Yankee-style ordinance societies in the proximity of the school. The New Englanders were drawing on 150 years of custom.[33] The transference of some rudimentary principles of New England town planning to the townships of the Upper Midwest made perfect sense to them. Near the school of these nucleated towns would be the village gathering place—a common, green, or square—sometimes used for pasturage and other times for meeting to air communal concerns. Other buildings near or around this central space might include a meetinghouse, tavern, merchant, storehouse, magazine, and church or two. This arrangement made the Adamsian landscape qualitatively different from either the Jeffersonian landscape with its independent farmers in spread out homesteads or the Hamiltonian landscape with its entrepreneurs and merchants in a great network of dense cities. The focus on tight village communities originated in a different view of a republic—to wit, a virtuous republic that would be sustained by close-knit neighborhoods in the vicinity of the section-sixteen school.

Because Adams thought that a good constitution was one bulwark to keep religious and cultural decline at bay, it is instructive to see how his constitutional thought informed the cultural and social articles of the Land Ordinance of 1785 and the Northwest Ordinance of 1787. This latter document was drafted mainly by New Englanders. More than a few Yankee delegates argued, like Adams, that the recently acquired territory should reflect not just their region's political heritage, but also its cultural traditions. It is instructive to compare what Adams drafted in article 3 of the Massachusetts Constitution of 1780, with "Article the Third" of the Northwest Ordinance of 1787. Let's look first at the Massachusetts Constitution: "The happiness of a people, and the good order and preservation of civil government, essentially depend upon piety, religion and morality; . . . these cannot be generally diffused through a community, but by . . . the support and maintenance of public protestant teachers of piety, religion and morality."[34]

Compare this Massachusetts provision with article 3 of the Northwest Ordinance of 1787: "Religion, morality and knowledge, being necessary to good government and the happiness of mankind, schools and the means of education shall forever be encouraged."[35]

By these words, the Massachusetts Constitution and Northwest Ordinance of 1787 were making powerful *cultural* statements about the nature of republics. New England delegates admonished the Congress that cultural formation in the new republic should not be left to chance. Frontier society needed "religion, morality and knowledge." Indeed, it was an article of faith to Adamsians that good government was impossible in the absence of religion, morality, and knowledge. Moreover, self-government was less likely to succeed in the absence of "schools and the means of education." Thus the literal and geographic centrality of the section-sixteen school made a powerful cultural argument for how the virtuous republic could be sustained.[36]

What made this ordinance society different was that it sought to attract not lone individuals who lacked social bonds (stereotypical of what would later be called "rugged individualism") so much as families and clans, the salt of the earth who would bring their Bible, their church, and their Blue Back speller to the second promised land. Because these migrants would also bring the habits of an observational shame society along, as a check against the evil that always lurked, they would tend to settle in close, inward-looking communities such as those back in New England. In this way, communal values could be more easily enforced, in contrast to the Jeffersonian vision of a dispersed yeomanry, and in contrast to the Hamiltonian vision of a mobile entrepreneurial class that perhaps looked for values more in the marketplace than in church or a civic republican tradition.[37]

Today the ideals of Adams's virtuous republic and its ordinance society survive in the murals, sculpture, classical architecture, and inscriptions in state capitols and county courthouses—from Columbus, Ohio, to St. Paul, Minnesota; from Lansing, Michigan, to Springfield, Illinois.

Why did the authors of the Northwest Ordinances care so much about the culture of the Northwest? Why did they write and ratify article 3 in 1787? It is a striking proposition, standing alone among the best-known passages of the Declaration, Articles of Confederation, U.S. Constitution, and Bill of Rights, in that it explicitly extols the links among "religion, morality, and knowledge." The evidence suggests that New Englanders and other Americans were afraid that stable communities might not form in the Northwest Territory if left to chance. Without the stipulations of article 3 and other provisions of the 1787 ordinance, it was believed that a large class of shiftless pioneers would be constantly on the move and thus prone to falling out of a civilized state.[38]

Thus the influence of John Adams is all over, under, and through the Northwest Ordinances and especially article 3 of the 1787 document. As Adams would later observe, in a statement that bridges what happened in the Confederation Congress in New York City and the Constitutional Convention in Philadelphia—both meeting during that hot summer of 1787—"Our Constitution was made only for a moral and religious people. It is wholly inadequate to the government of any other."

Ideas Have Consequences

In this chapter that joins intellectual history to historical geography, we can see how the ideas of three American founders had material bearing on the landscapes of the Upper Midwest. Thomas Jefferson's optimistic ideal of an agrarian republic is spatially expressed to this day in isolated farmsteads that are connected to each other by long straight roads. Alexander Hamilton's realistic ideal of a commercial republic is spatially expressed to this day in cities that are linked by considerable internal improvements (highways, railroads, airports, and harbors), integrated into the global economy, and surrounded withal by malls and military bases. John Adams's more tenuous ideal of a virtuous republic is spatially expressed to this day in villages and suburbs that center around schools, churches, and other institutions that reinforce civic responsibility and traditional moral precepts.

All three founders knew that the early decades of the United States would be a drama whose main stage was the Northwest frontier. To all three, there was something compelling about George Washington's audacious vision of the Northwest as a second promised land. But certain conditions had to be met for the potential to be realized. Thus, all three founders accepted that good government in a republic is impossible where "religion, morality, and knowledge" are lacking. All three committed to expand an empire of liberty that would suppress the spread of—and eventually stamp out—slavery. All three recognized the literal and geographic centrality of public schools to ready the rising generation for the marketplace and civic square. All three acknowledged that preserving the right of sovereign workers to make contracts in the open marketplace was inexorably tied to the pursuit of happiness. All three accepted what I call the "Burkean synthesis"—the liberal use of eclectic architectural styles and humanistic learning that draw prodigally from ancient Jerusalem, classical Greece and Rome, medieval Europe, and the Renaissance to give symbolic expression to America's cultural values.[39]

These are the important similarities among the three visions. There are also key differences. Where Jefferson's landscape is a Cartesian masterpiece that balances the axis of freedom with the axis of equality on behalf of the common citizen (in an agrarian republic); and where Hamilton's cityscape is a rapidly expanding capitalist dynamo that generates opportunity and wealth for the energetic entrepreneur (in a commercial republic); so Adams's landscape derives from the experience of New England villages, where close-knit communities of "fallen" men and women need the cultural legacy of Western civilization to keep the republic alive at the same time they need to keep evil at bay (in a virtuous republic).

Despite their apparent differences, all three republican visions coexisted in the early nineteenth century in creative tension—cohabiting the land in ways that the nation's founders could not have anticipated. Of course, they nowhere existed on the landscape of the Upper Midwest in some idealized Platonic form. Their intellectual power diminished with time. In a nod to Frederick Jackson Turner, we would be wise to ponder the extent to which the West's successive frontiers would blend and "Americanize" the various republican ideals at the same time that they would attenuate the Burkean synthesis of old.[40]

That such intellectual forces continue to engage us demonstrates that ideas do indeed have consequences, even in the shaping of our landscapes.

Notes

1. George Washington to William Grayson, June 22, 1785, in *George Washington: A Collection*, ed. W. B. Allen (Indianapolis: Liberty Fund, 1988), 300.
2. George Washington, Circular to the States, June 8, 1783, at http://press-pubs.uchicago.edu/founders/documents/v1ch7s5.html.
3. George Washington to David Humphreys, July 25, 1785, in Allen, *George Washington*, 301; Washington's emphasis. Regarding Washington's allusion to the first and greatest commandment, see his letter to the Marquis de Lafayette, July 25, 1785, in Allen, *George Washington*, 304. The reference is to the Old Testament book of Genesis 1:28, where God commands all living things to increase and multiply.
4. George Washington to the Marquis de Lafayette, July 25, 1785, in Allen, *George Washington*, 304.
5. See David D. Anderson, "New England, Ohio's Western Reserve, and the New Jerusalem in the West," in *MidAmerica*, vol. 18 (East Lansing: Midwestern Press, Center for the Study of Midwestern Literature, Michigan State University, 1991).

6. The optimism of the project was reflected in the great seal of the Northwest Territory, which contained the Latin phrase *Meliorem lapsa locavit*—"He has planted one better than the one fallen"—meaning that Anglo civilization was superior to either the wilderness or to Native American cultures.

7. See Darren Staloff, *Hamilton, Adams, Jefferson: The Politics of Enlightenment and the American Founding* (New York: Hill and Wang, 2005).

8. Since the geographic and historical terms in this chapter overlap, definitions are in order. In brief, this chapter focuses on the Upper Midwest, which is a subsection of the Old Northwest, which is a subsection of the Midwest. These terms are scaled and defined as follows: (1) The smallest geographic and cultural unit of this chapter is the "Upper Midwest" and "western Yankeedom," both of which refer to the Great Lakes Basin and Upper Mississippi and Upper Illinois River valleys; they are the primary focus of this chapter. (2) The next largest geographic unit discussed in this chapter is variously called the "Northwest," "Old Northwest," "Northwest Territory," "western country," "western lands," "lands north of the Ohio," and "Second Land of Promise"—historic terms for some 260,000 square miles surrendered by Britain to the U.S. in 1783, and bounded by the Ohio River on the south, Pennsylvania on the east, the Upper Mississippi River and Lake of the Woods on the west, and the approximate centerline of Lakes Erie, Huron, and Superior on the north. The Northwest Territory, as a legal unit, existed from 1787 to 1803, when Ohio was incorporated into the Union. Much of the Great Lakes Megalopolis—Chipitts, as defined by the French geographer Jean Gottman—is in the Old Northwest. (3) "Midwest" and "heartland" refer to the largest geographic unit discussed in the chapter and include the Upper Midwest and Old Northwest, and are by convention defined as the twelve-state region stretching from Ohio, Indiana, and Illinois; across Michigan, Wisconsin, and Minnesota; to the Dakotas; then south through Iowa, Nebraska, Missouri, and Kansas. Note that while scholars are turning their attention to actual and imagined interior borderlands between the Midwest and Great Plains, this chapter does not self-consciously reference the Great Plains west of the hundredth meridian.

9. Again, as defined in this chapter, the Upper Midwest is physiographically identified with the Great Lakes Basin and Upper Mississippi and Upper Illinois River valleys. Culturally it encompasses the area west of the Appalachian Mountains that author Colin Woodard, in his book *American Nations* (New York: Penguin, 2012), calls "Yankeedom." It does not include the Great Plains west of the hundredth meridian.

10. See Daniel P. Barr, ed., *The Boundaries between Us: Natives and Newcomers along the Frontiers of the Old Northwest Territory, 1750–1850* (Kent OH: Kent State University Press, 2006).

11. Peter S. Onuf, *Statehood and Union: A History of the Northwest Ordinance* (Bloomington: Indiana University Press, 1987), xiii.

12. Refer to the classic work of intellectual history by William R. Taylor, *Cavalier and Yankee: The Old South and American National Character* (New York: Braziller, 1961; republished by Oxford University Press, 1993).

13. The most powerful cultural statement in the 1787 ordinance is arguably made in article 3: "Religion, morality and knowledge, being necessary to good government and the happiness of mankind, schools and the means of education shall forever be encouraged."

14. It turns out that article 6, the antislavery provision in the 1787 ordinance, was only inserted between the July 11 reading of the document and its July 13 passage. See Paul Finkelman, "Slavery and Bondage in the 'Empire of Liberty,'" in *The Northwest Ordinance: Essays on Its Formulation, Provisions, and Legacy*, ed. Frederick L. Williams (East Lansing: Michigan State University Press, 1989), 61–95.

15. Carville Earle, "Beyond the Appalachians, 1850–1860," in *The Historical Geography of a Changing Continent*, 2nd ed., ed. Thomas F. McIlwraith and Edward K. Muller (Lanham MD: Rowman and Littlefield, 2001), 166–67.

16. Alexis de Tocqueville, *Democracy in America*, part 2, chapter 10 (1835).

17. "Abraham Lincoln, Speech at Cincinnati, Ohio," September 1859, in *The Collected Works of Abraham Lincoln*, 9 vols., ed. Roy P. Basler (New Brunswick: Rutgers University Press, 1953–55), 3:454–57.

18. See paragraphs 11 and 14 of the Land Ordinance of 1785 at http://www.in.gov/history/2478.htm; and article 3 of the Northwest Ordinance of 1787 at http://avalon.law.yale.edu/18th_century/nworder.asp.

19. Alexandra Usher, "Public Schools in the Original Federal Land Grant Program," Center on Education Policy (Washington DC, April 2011), 8, at http://www.eric.ed.gov/ERICWebPortal/search/detailmini.jsp?_nfpb=true&_&ERICExtSearch_SearchValue_0=ED518388&ERICExtSearch_SearchType_0=no&accno=ED518388.

20. For the ongoing debate over whether Jefferson was more of a Lockean liberal or a classical republican, see Garrett Ward Sheldon, *The Political Philosophy of Thomas Jefferson* (Baltimore: Johns Hopkins University Press, 1991 and 1993); Lance Banning, *The Jeffersonian Persuasion: Evolution of a Party Ideology* (Ithaca: Cornell University Press, 1978 and 1980); also see

John Locke, *Some Thoughts Concerning Education* at http://legacy.fordham
.edu/halsall/mod/1692locke-education.asp.

21. Paul W. Gates, "The Homestead Act: Free Land Policy in Operation, 1862–
1935," in *The Jeffersonian Dream: Studies in the History of American Land
Policy and Development*, ed. Allan G. Bogue and Margaret Beattie Bogue
(Albuquerque: University of New Mexico Press, 1996), 40ff.; Ryan S. Wal-
ters, *The Last Jeffersonian: Grover Cleveland and the Path to Restoring the
Republic* (Bloomington IN: Thomas Nelson/WestBow Press, 2012); Amity
Shlaes, *Coolidge* (New York: HarperCollins, 2013) and Calvin Coolidge,
"Great Virginians," in *The Price of Freedom: Speeches and Addresses* (New
York: Scribner's, 1924), 173–82.

22. For a fun article about the impact of the Jeffersonian grid on an American
city, see http://www.kcet.org/socal/departures/columns/laws-that-shaped
-la/how-thomas-jefferson-made-the-streets-of-la.html.

23. For the federal government's webpage that explains and maps out the PLSS,
see http://nationalmap.gov/small_scale/a_plss.html.

24. See, for example, Andro Linklater, *Measuring America: How the United
States Was Shaped by the Greatest Land Sale in History* (New York: Pen-
guin/Plume, 2003).

25. The rectangular-grid survey stipulated by the Land Ordinance of 1785 was
laid out on a due north-south and due east-west grid, in contrast to the
Laws of the Indies that dominated Spanish colonial settlements in North
America. The Spanish oriented the plaza and rectangular grid according to
prevailing winds and river courses.

26. In theory, at least. The work of Cornell University historian Paul W. Gates
explored the many political and policy erosions of the Jeffersonian ideal at
the hands of eastern politicians and moneymen. His research into the dis-
posal of public lands in the West exposed how the "scandalous" management of public lands "perverted the development of democratic institutions" in the U.S. See, for example, Allan G. Bogue and Margaret Beattie
Bogue, "Introduction [to] Paul Wallace Gates," in Bogue and Bogue, eds.,
Jeffersonian Dream, x.

27. Thomas Jefferson to J. Hector St. John de Crèvecœur, January 15, 1787.

28. Thomas Jefferson to George Wythe, August 13, 1786; Thomas Jefferson to
Charles Yancey, January 6, 1816.

29. Hamilton County is in southwestern Ohio. Its seat is Cincinnati. See
http://www.ohiohistorycentral.org/w/Hamilton_County and http://
www.historykat.com/TNWRO/territory-northwest-river-ohio-territory
-hamilton-county.html. In the mid-1790s, Hamilton County, Ohio, was

about the size of South Carolina and larger than six of the original thirteen states—Connecticut, Delaware, Maryland, Massachusetts, New Hampshire, and Rhode Island.

30. Colin Woodard, *American Nations: A History of the Eleven Rival Regional Cultures of North America* (New York: Penguin, 2011), 162.

31. To see the development of the constitutional thought of Adams, New England's most brilliant political philosopher, consult five of his major works on the subject: the *Novanglus* essays (1774–75), which define the constitutional struggle between England and the thirteen colonies: *Thoughts on Government* (1776), which circulated throughout the colonies as the major guidebook for drafting new state constitutions; the Massachusetts Constitution (1780), which Adams coauthored and which became the model for later state constitutions and influential as well when the U.S. Constitution was drafted; *A Defence of the Constitutions of Government of the United States of America* (1787), which provided arguments for the new federal framework; and *Discourses on Davila* (1790–91) which, as Jonathan Allen Green has noted at http://presidentialfellows.wordpress.com /2012/03/20/john-adams-discourses-on-davila/, defended mixed government and Burkean traditionalism over against Condorcet, Turgot, and other radical French revolutionaries who were leaders of the Continental Enlightenment. Taken together, these five works imagined a framework of government that had eluded the major European powers for centuries. None—not one—had devised a constitution that could provide the fundamental law for a stable, sustainable republic. Adams's thought would exercise an estimable influence on Yankee constitution-making during the first half of the nineteenth century—up to the outbreak of the Civil War—when the Northwest Territory was giving birth to new states in the new republic.

32. Ultimately, all or part of six states—including all of Ohio (1803), Indiana (1816), Illinois (1818), Michigan (1837), Wisconsin (1848), and a good portion of Minnesota (1858)—would be organized out of the Northwest Territory.

33. John D. Cushing, "Town Commons of New England, 1640–1840," *Old-Time New England* 51, no. 3 (Winter 1961): 86–94, at http://www .historicnewengland.org/preservation/your-older-or-historic-home /articles/pdf86.pdf.

34. The Massachusetts Constitution can be found at http://press-pubs .uchicago.edu/founders/print_documents/v1ch1s6.html.

35. For a photographic image of the original in the National Archives, see http://www.ourdocuments.gov/doc_large_image.php?doc=8.

36. For an article that broaches how New England institutions that were situated around a central square were transplanted to the West, see the discussion of Bronson Park in Joel J. Orosz, "Lincoln Comes to Kalamazoo," *Chronicle: The Magazine of the Historical Society of Michigan* 14 (Summer 1978): 12–18.

37. Steven J. Keillor, *Shaping Minnesota's Identity: 150 Years of State History* (Lakeville MN: Pogo Press, 2008).

38. The testimony of Dwight and others is quoted in John Mack Faragher, *Sugar Creek: Life on the Illinois Prairie* (New Haven: Yale University Press, 1986), 51.

39. For historical background behind the coinage "Burkean synthesis" that I am developing, see Russell Kirk, *The Roots of American Order* (Wilmington DE: ISI Books, 2003).

40. For the historical argument against Kirk, see Frederick Jackson Turner, *The Significance of the Frontier in American History* (New York: Dover, 2012), 22–25.

19

Growing Up Midwestern

Pamela Riney-Kehrberg

After setting myself the task of writing a paper on "growing up midwestern," otherwise known as "midwestern childhood," I realized I had made a horrible mistake. The harder I thought about the topic, the muddier my thoughts became. The truth is that we know a great deal about *individual* midwestern childhoods, but what we know about midwestern childhood, writ large, is considerable less clear. What does it mean to "grow up midwestern?" If a historian takes her cues from economist John Ise's autobiographical account of growing up in the late nineteenth century in north central Kansas, it means to work hard on a family's land, experience drought, grasshoppers, and near economic ruin, and decide in one's adult years to make a life somewhere other than the farm. To grow up midwestern, in Ise's experience, and that of his many brothers and sisters, was to be born in the country, but live one's adult days in cities and towns. Drawing inspiration from John Miller's recent book, *Small Town Dreams: Stories of Midwestern Boys Who Shaped America*, growing up midwestern might mean coming from a small place, but embodying great ambition, and using that ambition to propel oneself to fame and fortune, often beyond one's midwestern origins. This was the story of Henry Ford, Meredith Willson, and Lawrence Welk. Equally, a historian could draw inspiration from a later period of history, and Beth Bailey's *Sex in the Heartland*, which chronicled the sexual revolution on the campus of the University of Kansas. To be young and midwestern in that account was to escape the stifling conformity of the nation's midsection and experiment with all of the joys that freedom from parental restraints had to offer.[1] The growing up midwestern of the late nineteenth century was not that of the early twentieth century, nor was it that of the 1960s. Place, space, and time all changed the contours and meaning of childhood and youth.

As is true of other types of history, place, space, and time have considerable roles in the history of childhood. As a result, many histories of childhood and youth have a strong connection to a particular region of the United States. Histories of Puritan childhood, of course, are placed within the context of New England. The rough conditions of early settlement shaped lives and expectations, in contrast to that of others left behind on English soil. Discussions of nineteenth-century American slave childhood are written within the context of the larger geographic South and are shaped by the environmental and social conditions of that place. Place, of course, matters, and that story could not be written within any other spatial context. Place and space also informed Elliott West's masterful narrative *Growing Up with the Country: Childhood on the Far Western Frontier*. West's discussions of western childhood were bounded on two sides. On the one side was place, to the west of the Missouri River. The other boundary was a more elusive concept, the frontier. The children West described were living in new places, recently opened to settlement by Euro-American peoples. These two features of their lives strongly shaped their prospects. Being west of the Missouri River brought them, and their parents, into contact with environments with which they had no previous experience. Being among the early settlers of these locations also meant that the conditions in which they lived were rough and often unforgiving. This gave youngsters developmental experiences that were far different than those of their parents, and an identity that was also different from that of their mothers and fathers, who were often far more intimidated by these wild western lands than their children. As West wrote, "The westering experience meant one thing to older pioneers and quite another to the younger. The youngest emigrants had little of the East to remember, and those born in the new country had none whatsoever. For the young, in a sense, this was not a frontier at all—not, that is, a line between the familiar and the new. Rather, it was the original measure for the rest of their lives, and that measure was not the one their parents had known."[2] As West so carefully delineated, being raised in a particular place and time mattered.

In each of these cases, multiple conditions bounded children's lives. It was possible to define their experiences because researchers could see the edges of those children's universes. Puritan children lived in New England, and within a particular religious culture. Slave children lived in the South, and under the economic and social constraints created by bondage. West's frontier children lived in a broad region, but in situations in which their communities were just being settled. When I wrote about midwestern farm childhood, in *Childhood on the Farm: Work, Play, and Coming of Age in the Midwest*, I also was careful to rough out the edges of my topic; I researched the lives of children and youth who lived in a particular set of states, between 1870 and 1920, and whose parents engaged in a certain type of activity in order to earn their daily bread. Because I drew the lines in that way, I could come to relatively confident conclusions about those children's lives. In general, work defined their days. School, for the vast majority, had to take a back seat to work, and play came in a distant third. Usefulness was the most important expectation imposed upon them by parents, and that fact changed little between the end of the Civil War and the end of the First World War. I found very few variations in this expectation between the children of middling parents and those of the poor. For these young farmers, middle-class urban expectations of a relatively leisurely childhood, defined by school and play, were as yet in the distance. Only in the post–World War II period would the lives of the Midwest's farm children come to resemble those of their urban peers.[3]

Historical surveys of family history and the history of childhood are not without discussions of place, but there is little consideration given to the Midwest. Steve Mintz and Susan Kellogg published *Domestic Revolutions: A Social History of American Family Life* in 1988, and it is one of the standard texts on American family history. In it, we find the predictable geographic markers: Puritan New England and colonists at Jamestown. In fact, the early period is fairly well signposted in regional terms, with discussions of the variety of experiences imposed by varying terrain, climates, and natural resources. Slavery, too, is located in the South. Industrialization, somewhat problematically, is placed in the large cities of the Northeast. The rest of the book is largely without the nation's midsection, although Chicago does merit the occasional mention.[4] Place, for the most part, was not central to the authors' discussions of children's lives in the period following the Civil War.

Joseph Illick's 2002 book, *American Childhoods*, takes a different approach. He categorizes childhood experiences based on race, class, and broad categories of residence, such as suburban, inner city, and rural. In places where a discussion of region would have substantially enhanced the discussion, such as the very short section on rural childhoods, he remains silent. The result is rather unsatisfactory, given the enormous ways in which rural childhood was, and is, shaped by regional considerations.[5]

Even Steven Mintz, in his tour de force on childhood, *Huck's Raft*, spends little time on the meaning of region in children's lives. The enormity of his task lends itself to "bucket" discussions of the experiences of childhood and youth. While the use of examples occasionally leads to examinations of child life that could be construed as regional, that is not the usual way in which Mintz organizes his material. Much of the discussion of World War II, for example, focuses upon Japanese-American youth and relocation, and ethnic tensions in places like Los Angeles. There is, however, no discussion of larger regional variations in the experience of children and youth in the midst of World War II.[6] Region is simply not a significant part of Mintz's story, and the Midwest as a place does not figure strongly.

If the standard texts on the history of childhood have little to tell us about the midwestern experience, there are a plethora of other accounts that do provide us with snapshots of childhood in the heartland. While there probably is no such thing as a "representative story" or a representative midwestern childhood, there are many useful narratives of growing up in the nation's midsection. I am going to use three of those stories as examples. Each of the stories I have chosen is from a best-selling book. I have done this for several reasons. Each of these stories, to some degree, will be familiar to those of us interested in the Midwest. They are also known to a host of other Americans who read for pleasure and who are captivated by a good story. These stories sometimes tell us something we want to hear about this region we have chosen to study. They tell us about a life that in some way represented an ideal. But sometimes these stories tell us about something we ought to do better—something that needs improving because it so flies in the face of societal perceptions of what a childhood in the nation's heartland *should have been.*

One of the best known of my chosen stories is that of Mildred Armstrong Kalish, who grew up in rural Iowa, and recounted her childhood in the best-selling book *Little Heathens: Hard Times and High Spirits on an Iowa Farm During the Great Depression.* Unlike the usual late 1920s and early 1930s script, Kalish's grandfather banished her father from their lives, and her father and mother divorced, something that was rather unusual in that era. From then on, Kalish's father was dead to them. Her grandparents took in the now-fatherless family of five and settled them on one of the family's properties, a farm near Garrison, Iowa. Although she and her siblings lived in town during the winter in order to attend school, Kalish's story is largely one of farm life in hard times.

Although Kalish's childhood story began with a somewhat unusual and largely unexplained family breakdown, what followed was a tale of what many midwesterners would like to believe was a typical, farm-based childhood. It almost reads like a stereotype. Kalish's stern grandfather was definitely in charge of the household, and he believed in rules, rigid and unyielding. The children did chores, and the adults insisted upon thrift. Although their mother was somewhat unconventional, she enforced upon her brood serious attention to education. When describing her mother, Kalish wrote, "She was a tyrant when it came to learning, or anything else pertaining to school. She encouraged, nay, demanded, that we do our homework, that we do more in school than was asked of us, and that we participate in spelling, dramatic, and music . . . competitions."[7] True to stereotype, Kalish's rural Iowa was a place where parents cared about their children's education.

Kalish's narrative includes all the homey and important elements of their lives such as domestic and wild pets, farm work, and cooperation, topped off by the kind of food your grandmother would have taken to a midwestern potluck supper. The reader, in fact, learns how to make such midwestern farm favorites as wilted lettuce salad, scalloped corn, buttermilk pancakes, and homemade marshmallows. There is also a strong note of earthiness about her story, as well there should be, given its location in the heart of Iowa's farm country. It is the tale of lives lived within a framework of hard labor, thrift, and caring. What resulted was a love story about growing up in the rural Midwest. As the book reviewer for the *New York Times* commented about Kalish's writing, "She reports quite convincingly that she had a flat-out ball growing up ('It was quite a romp') and her terrifically soaring love for those childhood memories saturates this book with pure charm, while coaxing the reader into the most unexpected series of sensations: joy, affection, wonder and even envy."[8] Mildred Armstrong Kalish lived a midwestern childhood well within the parameters of what we would expect of such a set of experiences, and she conveyed her experiences in such a way that most of us with the tiniest bit of nostalgia would want to share a piece of it, even if just in the form of a piece of her grand-mother's pumpkin pie.

Move forward a generation and, in *The Life and Times of the Thun-derbolt Kid*, the interested reader can take a stroll through Bill Bryson's childhood in the Des Moines of the 1950s and 1960s. Clearly, this was a different place and a different kind of childhood than Mildred Kalish's, but nonetheless, one that inspires a bit of the same sort of awe and envy. Bryson was the child of two working parents, growing up in the midst of postwar prosperity. Bryson wrote, "No wonder people were happy. Suddenly they were able to have things they had never dreamed of having, and they couldn't believe their luck. . . . It was the last time that people would be thrilled to own a toaster or a waffle iron."[9] Bryson spent this time of prosperity in Des Moines, which he described as a "safe, wholesome city. . . . It was a nice city—a comfortable city."[10] It was also a city with which its young inhabitants were incredibly familiar. The kids, in this urban, midwestern world, wrote Bryson, "were always outdoors—I knew kids who were pushed out the door at eight in the morning and not allowed back in until five unless they were on fire or actively bleeding—and they were always looking for something to do. If you stood on any corner with a bike—any corner anywhere—more than a hundred children, many of whom you had never seen before, would appear and ask you where you were going."[11] It was a world where chil-dren could easily and happily play in the park, on their street corner, or in the buildings downtown, all places that Bryson frequented regularly, and without adult supervision. The only real terrors in this world were poison sumac and neighborhood bullies.[12]

Bryson also remembered his summer visits to his grandparents in rural Iowa with a sense of awe and great satisfaction. His description of the state's vast agricultural lands is telling: "Stride across an Iowa farm field and you feel as if you could sink in up to your waist. You will certainly sink in up to your ankles. It is like walking around on a very large pan of brownies."[13] His warm and fragrant memories encompassed the small town of Winfield, a place he dearly loved. It was an Iowa of walks downtown, cold bottles of Nehi, jiggling bowls of Jell-O, and tornadoes looming on the horizon. The rural and urban worlds Bryson described have largely vanished in the intervening years, but in the meantime, it was a heady experience. As the book reviewer in the *New York Times* remarked, almost with a sense of wonder, "At the heart of the manifold exaggerations is a much larger truth, a shocking revelation that few memoirists have been so brave to admit: he had a happy childhood."[14] A joyous engagement with place sits front and center in Bryson's memories of his early years in Des Moines.

The last set of midwestern childhoods I want to discuss is unrecognizable in relation to those of Mildred Armstrong Kalish and Bill Bryson. This set of midwestern childhoods is that of Pharoah and Lafeyette Rivers, with whom journalist Alex Kotlowitz became acquainted in 1985, just a generation beyond the Des Moines childhood described by Bill Bryson. Again, the boys' experiences became the subject of a bestselling book, this one titled *There Are No Children Here: The Story of Two Boys Growing Up in the Other America*. As the title might suggest, this is no story of hard-working but happy rural families. It is also no story of heartwarming high jinks playing out against the background of a wholesome and comfortable city. Instead, it is the story of the failures of the midwestern family system in a particular time and place. It is the story of a mother who cared, but had no support from an absent partner. It was the story of a place that was not conducive to the needs of children, and an urban environment that was completely unhealthy in a way that the Des Moines of the 1950s was not.[15]

Pharoah and Lafeyette Rivers grew up in Chicago's infamous Henry Horner Homes. As historian D. Bradford Hunt has explained, Chicago's housing projects were anything but conducive to healthy child life. There were many problems in the high-rise housing projects, including cheap construction, inadequate and badly designed elevators, and poor placement of the buildings relative to the needs of the residents. And one of the most significant problems was that there were so many children, relative to the number of playgrounds and schools, and relative to the number of adults available to supervise their time. The children in these housing projects overwhelmed the resources of their surroundings and their caregivers.[16] Over time, the Henry Horner Homes and places like it became high-rise ghettoes, no better, and in many ways worse, than the low-rise ghettoes they replaced.

There was no golden glow surrounding the Rivers boys' childhood story. Nobody comes away from that book wanting to visit their childhoods, as readers might with Kalish or Bryson. These boys lived with unrelenting struggle. There was never enough money. There was never enough parental support, with an overwhelmed mother and a largely absent father. And the physical environment in which they lived was hardly conducive to a happy childhood. Because of the physical and human dangers out of doors, some mothers in the projects constantly kept their children indoors. And if children played outdoors, the thirteen-story, high-rise construction made it difficult for parents to supervise their activities.[17] When Pharoah and Lafeyette wanted to experience anything like the outdoors available to other children in earlier generations, they had to make their way to a railroad track some distance from the Henry Horner Homes. There, bushes and trees grew wild, and the boys might find butterflies and wildflowers, and dig for snakes. It was a very small taste of the wonders of nature that were, for Kalish and Bryson, so easily available.[18] That little patch of dirt, however, was unable to compensate for inadequate economic, social, and educational resources. They were children without what most midwesterners thought of as a "real" childhood, and children largely without hope, hence the title "there are no children here." As Kotlowitz wrote in his epilogue, "Both Lafeyette and Pharoah want to move to a safe and quieter neighborhood. Lafeyette talks about it on occasion. So does Pharoah, who sat on his bed one day and cried because he worried that he might never get out of the projects."[19] Unfortunately, it was not to be, and neither of the boys got the happy ending that we want for the heartland's children. Their story, in myriad ways, is at odds with so much that we would like to believe about the collective history of the region's young.

These crazily juxtaposed stories leave the historian in a quandary. If we are going to write the history of midwestern childhood, how should we do it? I am back to the sense of panic I felt upon contemplation of the vastness of the topic, "growing up midwestern." A fellow midwestern historian to whom I expressed my concerns, commented, "That's so midwestern of you to say there's no such thing [as a midwestern childhood]. That's EXACTLY what it's like to grow up midwestern—basically to not know where you're from or why it matters. White midwesterners believe we are so generically American that we assume people with regional identities are somehow misguided."[20] But how do we go about writing about a regional history of childhood, when the individual stories that make up that collective whole are so at odds with each other?

We are, I believe, stuck with the challenge of boundaries. When the historians of the 1970s and 1980s began the monumental task of creating a social history of the American people, they soon discovered that everyday life in the American past was more complicated, and fragmented, than anyone might initially have thought. The experience of men was not that of women. Ethnicity and race added on additional layers of complication, as did class. Communities in their first stages of development, too, were not the same as they would become, once they had matured and gained a certain degree of stability. A community in decline was different, as well. Then historians added on another layer, discovering that the North was not the South, and the West was another creature altogether. Rural was not urban, and rural/non-farm, was not the same as farm. Farm tenants and farm owners might, or might not, share a common history, depending on the vagaries of place and time. One of the more recent discoveries has been that child life is significantly different than that of adults. We are, it seems, a people of layers, and which one of these layers was more important in any one place and time is entirely dependent upon the point of view of the person doing the looking.

So, can we write a history of growing up midwestern? It is probably best, from the very beginning, to take a cue from Joseph Illick's work (*American Childhoods*) and to title it "The History of Midwestern Childhoods," instead of "A History of Midwestern Childhood." It is a story composed of many layers. Some of those layers are going to look remarkably like those embodied in larger histories of American childhoods, while others will not. Was midwestern farm childhood in the immediate post–Civil War period similar to that of their peers in the South? There were certainly some similarities, but the differences had to have been significant. Was midwestern youth culture during World War II more similar to, or different from, the youth culture of Los Angeles in the same time period? I would err on the side of difference, but the truth is, we don't really know. Would Pharoah and Lafeyette's childhoods have borne a greater resemblance to that of children with the same economic and social background in New York City, or those in Dubuque? Here, other factors might very well trump geography. The history of childhood is still enough of an unknown country that we are a very long way from comfortably being able to answer these and host of other questions, but being willing to ask the questions is certainly the best place to start.

Notes

1. John Ise, *Sod and Stubble: The Story of a Kansas Farm* (Lawrence: University Press of Kansas, 1996); John E. Miller, *Small Town Dreams: Stories of Midwestern Boys Who Shaped America* (Lawrence: University Press of Kansas, 2105); Beth Bailey, *Sex in the Heartland* (Cambridge MA: Harvard University Press, 1999).
2. Elliott West, *Growing Up with the Country: Childhood on the Far Western Frontier* (Albuquerque: University of New Mexico Press, 1989), 21.
3. See Pamela Riney-Kehrberg, *Childhood on the Farm: Work, Play and Coming of Age in the Midwest* (Lawrence: University Press of Kansas, 2005).
4. Steven Mintz and Susan Kellogg, *Domestic Revolutions: A Social History of American Family Life* (New York: Free Press, 1988).
5. Joseph E. Illick, *American Childhoods* (Philadelphia: University of Pennsylvania Press, 2002).

6. Steven Mintz, *Huck's Raft: A History of American Childhood* (Cambridge MA: Belknap Press, 2004), 269–72.

7. Mildred Armstrong Kalish, *Little Heathens: Hard Times and High Spirits on an Iowa Farm During the Great Depression* (New York: Bantam, 2007), 20.

8. Elizabeth Gilbert, "The Home Place," *New York Times Sunday Book Review*, July 1, 2007, accessed April 2, 2015, from http://www.nytimes.com/2007/07/01/books/review/Gilbert-t.html?ref=review%20&_r=0.

9. Bill Bryson, *The Life and Times of the Thunderbolt Kid* (New York: Broadway Books, 2006), 6.

10. Bryson, *Life and Times of the Thunderbolt Kid*, 34, 35.

11. Bryson, *Life and Times of the Thunderbolt Kid*, 36.

12. Bryson, *Life and Times of the Thunderbolt Kid*, 41–43.

13. Bryson, *Life and Times of the Thunderbolt Kid*, 172.

14. Jay Jennings, "Happy Days," *New York Times Sunday Book Review*, October 15, 2006, accessed April 2, 2015, at http://www.nytimes.com/2006/10/15/books/review/Jennings.t.html.

15. Alex Kotlowitz, *There Are No Children Here: The Story of Two Boys Growing Up in the Other America* (New York: Anchor Books, 1992).

16. See D. Bradford Hunt's *Blueprint for Disaster*, chapter 6, which details the problems posed by a very high child-to-adult ratio in Chicago's high-rise housing projects. D. Bradford Hunt, *Blueprint for Disaster: The Unraveling of Chicago Public Housing* (Chicago: University of Chicago Press, 2009), 145–81.

17. Kotlowitz, *There Are No Children Here*, 25–26, 72.

18. Kotlowitz, *There Are No Children Here*, 4–6.

19. Kotlowitz, *There Are No Children Here*, 303.

20. Jenny Barker Devine, email communication with the author, March 24, 2015.

20

The Best of Babbitt

THE MIDWESTERN VISION
OF ARTHUR VANDENBERG

Hank Meijer

The stereotypes and contradictions inherent in what it means to be a midwesterner may be nowhere better exemplified than in the unlikely odyssey of Arthur Vandenberg.

The senator who dominated the American delegation at the founding of the United Nations, engineered passage of the Marshall Plan, created the Federal Deposit Insurance Corporation, and wrote the resolution enabling the North Atlantic Treaty Organization—who embodied bipartisan foreign policy at the outset of the Cold War—was born in Grand Rapids, Michigan, in 1884. Within months, another notable midwesterner, author Sinclair Lewis, was born in Sauk Center, Minnesota. In the intersection of their lives lies one of the great tensions that define this region. Half a century later, a daughter of a friend of Senator Vandenberg's was married in Grand Rapids to the son of another prominent midwesterner—and fellow senator—Robert Taft of Ohio. In the intersection of their lives lies what is perhaps the other defining tension of the heartland.

The first contrast was cultural: the ongoing disconnect between coastal arbiters of art and society and inhabitants of the land between the mountain ranges. The second was political: what role America should play in the world—a debate that continues today, although one in which geography looks increasingly irrelevant. In Vandenberg's case, the first was personal, the second civic.

Arthur Vandenberg was, like his New Deal nemesis Harry Hopkins of Iowa, the son of a harness maker. He dropped out of the University of Michigan to work as a reporter for the *Grand Rapids Herald*. A frustrated writer, he published half a dozen stories in the vein of Horatio

Alger or O. Henry before turning to a more ambitious project, a study of his hero, Alexander Hamilton, entitled *The Greatest American*.[1]

In 1922, as Vandenberg pecked out a second book on Hamilton, Sinclair Lewis published, to rather greater acclaim, his second novel. Coming on the heels of *Main Street*, his sensational debut, *Babbitt* was another biting critique of midwestern life, the story of a middle-aged, middle-brow striver.[2]

George Babbitt was a booster, a progressive-enough Republican, a proud and somewhat vainglorious resident of a middle-sized midwestern city. Lewis called the place Zenith. He could have called it Grand Rapids. Arthur Vandenberg bristled at the description of Mr. Babbitt, mocked by Lewis for so much that Vandenberg cherished in his midwestern hometown and its inhabitants. In Grand Rapids, Vandenberg had become editor and publisher of the town's Republican newspaper, the *Herald*. He refused to accept backwater status. Why, Colonel McCormick of the *Chicago Tribune*, waging his decades-long war with Washington, even suggested that the nation's capital move to Grand Rapids, as a more representative American locale.[3]

Vandenberg was ambitious and restless, no longer the wunderkind of midwestern journalism that he was when he became editor in 1906, at the age of twenty-one. He was a middle-aged, middle-brow burgher with pretensions to literature, in demand as an after-dinner speaker for the service clubs. In Republican circles he was making his influence felt. He had supplied phrasing—"unshared idealism is a menace"—employed by Henry Cabot Lodge in arguing for reservations to the League of Nations Covenant. He wrote Warren Harding's key speech on foreign policy. He even appears to have coined the Harding campaign slogan that has always grated on the ears of grammarians: "Let's Return to Normalcy."[4]

When he looked in the mirror, what he wanted to see was not George Babbitt, but another Alexander Hamilton, the dashing prodigy from a remote corner of the continent who helped create a country. The Lewis character tapped a fund of intellectual contempt for the pieties of the middleclass. For H. L. Mencken and other social critics, he provided a shared reference and easy target for all that was boring and banal in American culture. The name itself entered the language as shorthand for midwestern mediocrity, Mencken's new term of opprobrium for the booboisie.

What Arthur Vandenberg wanted to see in the mirror was a prominent young editor, a Republican power broker, an eloquent spokesman for a rugged nationalism that could easily be confused with isolationism. He saw a speechwriter for presidents, a thoughtful author, a future U.S. senator.

But what he saw might also have reminded him, in darker moments, of George Babbitt, of a character with, as Lewis wrote, "some genius of authentic love for his neighborhood, his city, his clan." Babbitt, like Vandenberg, was a cigar-smoking man of the service-club luncheon, "given to high oratory and high principles." As Lewis put it, "he enjoyed the sound of his own vocabulary and the warmth of his own virtue."

Lewis had the gall to name Babbitt's supercilious son "Theodore Roosevelt Babbitt." To Vandenberg, TR was a beacon of vigorous "Americanism," whose bunting-draped portrait hung behind the editor's desk. Yet despite that hero worship, Vandenberg was, as Lewis described Babbitt, "an organization Republican," who had refused, back in 1912, to bolt with the Bull Moose, and instead supported William Howard Taft.

Vandenberg used his editorials to promote modestly progressive civic initiatives such as those the "Good Citizens' League" strove for in Babbitt's Zenith. Grand Rapids: the name itself was Zenith-like in its hyperbole. Vandenberg began to worry, as Babbitt did, that he could never be anything but what he was then.[5]

In 1925 H. L. Mencken reviewed the memoir of Vandenberg's friend Milton McRae, head of the Scripps-Howard newspaper chain. Just the year before, Vandenberg had proposed that the University of Michigan award an honorary degree to McRae, who he described as "one of the leading figures in American journalism." McRae, a Detroit native, had just published his life story, which Vandenberg judged to be a "tremendously fascinating chronicle."[6]

Mencken had not seen fit to review Vandenberg's Hamilton books. Perhaps that was just as well, for he observed of McRae, "He is, as he depicts himself, Babbitt to the life . . . the perfect Rotarian. . . . Most of his sheets are published in small towns, and . . . those that are not still bear a small-town air." Not only that, Mencken wrote, but McRae had adorned his memoir with letters from presidents of the United States. This cut close to the bone for the *Herald* editor, whose hagiography of Hamilton opened with an endorsement from another one-time, small-town midwestern editor, Warren Harding.

In October 1925, the author of *Babbitt* led off Mencken's *American Mercury* magazine with an essay on "Self-conscious America." Had Vandenberg read it closely, he might have discerned in "Red" Lewis a closet conservative. But it was a conservatism born of reaction to any facile notion of human improvement, not just to the boosterism of Zenith and Grand Rapids. Hence, Lewis declared, "To the question of all Sunday newspapers and teachers' associations, 'What is the matter with America and how shall we do something about it?' there is one final answer: There are too many people who ask, 'What is the matter with America?' and then dash out and try to do something about it."[7]

Another writer in the same issue of *American Mercury* was more provocative. Arthur O'Dane saw George Babbitt motivated by "a conviction that it is humanly possible—nay, easily feasible—for a man to be somewhat other than he is."

Arthur Vandenberg believed in self-improvement. Why, look at the great Hamilton! Vandenberg tried to syndicate a weekly column he wrote for the *Herald* called "What Makes a Man." He walked to his office with his eyes fixed straight ahead, working up a passage of verse in his memory.[8]

O'Dane scoffed. Of Babbitt he wrote, "The God he affected to admire had been exceeding generous toward the nation of which Zenith was a conspicuous adornment. . . . Mr. Babbitt at 45 saw himself not least among business captains and kings of Zenith." The Babbitt-baiters laughed at his pretension. "He thought," concluded O'Dane, "he became automatically a gentleman when he dressed like one, a scholar by reading *Literary Digest*." George Babbitt's small-city delusions were fostered everywhere "by a concerted and continuous gas attack from press, pulpit, rostrum and blackboard."

Vandenberg could not abide the contempt. He was only forty-one, yet far from the least among the captains and kings of his midwestern city.

"Let Us Save the Best of Babbitt," was the title of his editorial rejoinder. He decried the way "a lot of intellectual snobs"—Mencken among them—"have been preening their own rarified wisdom at the expense of this poor yokel. . . . Babbitt has been buried beneath the scornful contempt of these metropolitan sophisticates who pity his confinement to the lesser realities of life."

He wrote of Rotarians in New York who spoke out for their maligned midwestern brethren, of a former Michigan governor addressing Kiwanians on the virtues of the "noonday luncheon club movement . . . tying together the social structure of America with ideals of unity and justice." (And perhaps community, as the sociologist Robert Putnam, an Ohio native, might have alluded to eighty years later in "Bowling Alone," his celebrated study of the loss of community.)[9]

The very expressions of uplift that characterized Vandenberg's editorials—his notions of "What Makes a Man," borrowing quotes from Emerson to Edison—were to Mencken, who scorned newspapermen as eagerly as he did preachers and salesmen—objects of ridicule.

"Babbitt has a right to strike back," Vandenberg wrote. "Without him this would be a sodden land. . . . He is happy and satisfied to be a part of his own 'home town'—and to strive, with his neighbors, to make the old 'home town' a little better and a little cleaner and a little healthier. . . . He is worth a thousand of his supercilious detractors who puff themselves horrendously on the winds of their own vanity."

"Save us," he continued, "from a land that is all 'New York.' Save us from a society that is all 'Mencken' and 'Sinclair Lewis.' Give us 'Babbitt' at his best—interested in his home—living with his own wife—striving to educate his children—helping along his church—still believing in a just God—loving his country and his flag." Arthur Vandenberg was all for the "Zip" that George Babbitt prized. Where it would take him was highly uncertain, but for another decade he was spared the society of that "inky charlatan," Sinclair Lewis.

Vandenberg's strident defense was an attempt to show in George Babbitt more than a caricature. Behind his knee-jerk reaction, the *Herald* editor was himself a more complex figure, all the more sensitive to stereotyping, and hardly representative of the "noonday luncheon club movement."[10]

This was Vandenberg at a cultural crossroads. The writer of short stories, the would-be senator, was fighting a rearguard action in defense of his home and readers and presumptive constituents—in defense of his life so far.

This was the editor whose morning shave had been interrupted by a ringing telephone. "Mr. Vandenberg," the caller began, "I happened into the *Herald* office last night and I saw something you should know about." The man refused to give his name as he continued, "I represent a one hundred per cent American organization and we don't like certain kinds of people." (Perhaps this was the Ku Klux Klan, which flourished in the Midwest, in the 1920s?) "I discovered you have working for you in your news room a man who is of a religion we don't like."

"That's enough," Vandenberg grumbled into the mouthpiece. "If you don't have the guts to tell me your name I have only this to say: That fellow you mention has worked for us for a long time. I don't care what his race or religion is or the color of his skin as long as he continues to do a good job. Good day to you, sir, and please don't bother me again."[11]

Ultimately, Vandenberg would be spared the company of neither H. L. Mencken nor Sinclair Lewis. In the meantime, however, his notions of civil liberty had advanced beyond the days of Great War jingoism, even when the liberty in question was that of Babbitt's chief antagonist, Mencken himself.

In 1926 Mencken challenged a Boston censor by publishing an issue of *American Mercury* that featured the story of a small-town prostitute. The censor appealed to the United States Post Office, which barred the magazine from the mails. The Hat Rack Case, as it was known, became a national sensation.

Mencken assumed that supporters of the First Amendment would rally to his cause. Students and socialists and Sinclair Lewis made vigorous protests, but no groundswell followed. Mencken could understand the politicians' hostility, and that of the clergy and other bluestockings he had managed to offend. But what about his colleagues in the press?

The *New York Times* and *New York World* (whose influential late editor, Frank Cobb, had started as a young reporter at the *Herald*) voiced support, but others had little sympathy or suspected a publicity stunt—magazine sales did soar, after all. Mencken sent a mimeographed appeal to editors across the country explaining the gravity of the issue and denying any attempt to capitalize on the publicity. Yet only two more newspapers came to his defense. One was Arthur Vandenberg's *Grand Rapids Herald*.[12]

In 1928 Vandenberg was appointed to the United States Senate. A year later the stock market crashed and the Midwest felt the onset of the Great Depression. The new senator became one of Franklin Roosevelt's chief antagonists in legislative battles over the New Deal. He also reflected a public consensus that the country must steer clear of the foreign intrigues that drew the United States into World War I. He had been a full-throated backer of President Wilson's war to make the world safe for democracy, only to see a cynical peace sow the seeds of future conflict. Washington's farewell address, written by Hamilton and warning against foreign entanglements, was Vandenberg's lodestar.

The distinguished senator and his wife, Hazel, counted among their friends in Washington Dorothy Thompson, noted columnist and the most influential female journalist of the day. In a union that would grow beyond tumultuous, Dorothy married Sinclair Lewis.

And in 1935 Lewis would publish *It Can't Happen Here*, the novel in which he anticipates the 1936 election as a contest in which a populist demagogue Democrat—read Huey Long, but Lewis makes him a New Englander!—supplants Franklin Roosevelt and defeats a midwestern Republican senator to become president. The Republican is fictional, although on page one Lewis mentions Vandenberg as well as Roosevelt and Hoover as one of the unsuccessful contenders for the office.

The populist regime becomes a fascist one, jailing dissidents and suppressing freedoms. A revolution breaks out—in Michigan of all places—led by the bulky senator Walter Trowbridge, who was said by Thompson to have been based in large part on Arthur Vandenberg.

On the eve of the publication of *It Can't Happen Here*, in the fall of 1935, Thompson and Lewis and the Vandenbergs all sailed to England.

Thompson was en route to Germany for an exclusive interview with Adolph Hitler, after which she became an ardent interventionist, sounding an alarm over the Nazi menace. The Vandenbergs were met in London by Milton McRae's daughter, who had married an Englishman. Theirs was no provincial tour. They visited H. G. Wells and dined with Lord Beaverbrook, a fellow publisher.

Settling into their stateroom for the voyage home, they received an invitation to cocktails from a fellow passenger, Sinclair Lewis. The note expressed the novelist's admiration for the senator. Hazel was more curious than her wary husband to meet the Nobel Prize winner. From *Main Street* to *Elmer Gantry* with *Babbitt* in the middle, Vandenberg saw in Lewis a jaded view of American life.

Lewis had lingered in England after Thompson left for New York. He met the Vandenbergs in the ship's lounge. "S. L. tight," Hazel wrote. But the surprise was that the two nearly exact contemporaries, the ponderous senator and the acerbic novelist, found much in common. Each was in his way a sentimentalist about their shared midwestern world. Each looked at the unfolding drama of European politics with a jaundiced eye and a worry for America's future.[13]

It Can't Happen Here was soon to arrive in American bookstores as martinis were shaken in the first-class lounge. Over several days the Vandenbergs and Lewis, wrote Hazel, had "just a hilarious happy time."

Upon their return, the Vandenbergs departed for Michigan. Red Lewis was so drunk he had to be hospitalized. But their unlikely friendship continued.[14]

In the 1940 election, Vandenberg had been among the early favorites for the Republican presidential nomination. Other aspirants included a young prosecutor from New York by way of Owosso, Michigan, named Thomas Dewey and a freshman senator from Ohio with a famous name, Robert Taft. With the outbreak of war in Europe and a growing clamor for American support of Great Britain, however, yet another midwesterner, the charismatic Wendell Willkie—a New York lawyer by way of Elwood, Indiana—outflanked the others and swept to the nomination.

Vandenberg had come of age when Teddy Roosevelt had picked Taft's father, William Howard Taft, as his successor. It was in Grand Rapids at a Lincoln Day dinner in 1908 that William Howard Taft declared his candidacy for president. The editor stuck by the party's choice four years later, when the restless Roosevelt came out of retirement to challenge the incumbent.

When Bob Taft arrived in the Senate in 1939, he and Arthur Vandenberg were aligned in their opposition to both the New Deal and to American intervention in the looming European war. By intellect and hard work Taft quickly established himself as a formidable force on the Hill.

Arthur Vandenberg succeeded William Borah as the party's leading isolationist. Robert Taft set his sights on the domestic agenda, bringing new energy to the fight against Roosevelt's expansion of federal power.

World War II changed the political landscape for both men, as it did for the rest of the country. With Roosevelt moving from Professor New Deal to Dr. Win-the-War, and the country uniting in its mission to defeat the Axis, debate was muted.

To have a chance at winning the presidency in 1944, Republicans needed to patch up their 1940 rupture. Over Labor Day in 1943, party leaders took ferries to Michigan's Mackinac Island and commandeered its famous Grand Hotel to plan their platform for the next election. Their goal was to paper over the schism between interventionists and isolationists, between Willkie and Taft, which could split the party down the middle.

In what looked like a nod to the isolationists, Vandenberg led the foreign policy committee. The group met behind locked doors. After grueling hours of deliberation, Taft sent out for a bottle of scotch and a bottle of bourbon. They were having some trouble reaching agreement, the dour Ohioan hinted, and maybe some lubrication would help. The result was a compromise that Taft and Willkie could both live with, calling for American participation in a postwar organization of nations.

In two days, the party that had torpedoed the League of Nations charted a new course. "When I succeeded in putting forty-nine prima donnas together at Mackinaw," Vandenberg crowed to Henry Luce, "I discovered the necessary formula."[15] Taft would not have shared the observation of Liz Carpenter, a young reporter covering the conference who literally eavesdropped on Vandenberg as he buttonholed other

Republicans to engineer the compromise. Carpenter recalled Vandenberg's tactic of strolling with another conferee to the far end of what was said to be the world's longest porch. There, she said, where the terrace ended with a view of the straits of Mackinac, was where American isolationism ended as well.

In 1945, with victory on the horizon, Taft and Vandenberg found their paths diverging. Taft had never shaken his conviction that the greatest threat to the country was the centralization of power in Washington. Vandenberg, also vocal in his hostility to the New Deal and federal power, came to see the Soviet regime in Moscow as a greater threat than the Roosevelt regime in Washington.

Taft was, in a sense, more conservative than his father, who had been an advocate for American engagement in the world. Former President Taft had supported Wilson's campaign for the League of Nations—until then-editor Vandenberg challenged him, on the occasion of a speech in Grand Rapids, to seek reservations that would protect American interests and insure passage by the Senate.[16]

Vandenberg and Taft were emerging, though neither had even ranking status on prominent committees, as the twin poles of power among Senate Republicans. Taft set the party's domestic agenda. Vandenberg was its voice in foreign policy.

Taft may have sensed a growing distance between them when Vandenberg, on the eve of FDR's journey to Yalta for a summit with Stalin and Churchill, gave what some called the speech heard round the world. The erstwhile isolationist Vandenberg called for a first-ever peacetime treaty among the Allies that centered on the demilitarization of Germany. His intent was to guarantee security for the Soviet Union and other victims of German aggression. This was an entangling alliance for sure. Taft, along with the *Chicago Tribune*, may have been taken aback, but this was a prescription for future peace that war-weary Americans hungered for.[17]

Then Roosevelt, rather reluctantly, but wishing not to repeat Wilson's mistake in trying to ram through the League of Nations with insufficient Senate support, appointed Vandenberg as a delegate to the United Nations organizing conference in San Francisco.

Then Roosevelt died, and another midwestern contemporary, Harry Truman, knew he needed Arthur Vandenberg.

In San Francisco, the delegates experienced, firsthand, Soviet intransigence. But they brought back to Washington a charter that won overwhelming approval. Taft went along as well when President Truman asserted American intentions to succeed Great Britain in providing aid to pro-Western Greek and Turkish governments when the British could no longer afford to. Truman then went further. In the Truman Doctrine, he urged support for peoples anywhere resisting totalitarian aggression.

But when Truman's secretary of state, George Marshall, proposed a massive aid program to rebuild Western Europe, many Republicans blanched. Even as Vandenberg took pains to pare down the package and vet its particulars in one of the most long-lasting, far-reaching efforts in Senate history, Taft went along reluctantly, challenging appropriations at every turn.

Even as Vandenberg felt a growing confidence in his own convictions, the fragile Republican consensus was fraying. Was the party's foreign-policy leader getting just a little too cozy with an administration that depended on GOP support? The president was asking Congress to approve vast sums for foreign aid.

Republicans had recaptured Congress in 1946. Taft and Vandenberg ran the Senate. For Vandenberg, who had negotiated with the Soviets in San Francisco, and then at peace conferences in London and Paris, the Cold War was up close and personal. For Taft it could appear an excuse to divert attention from the domestic agenda.

For Vandenberg, it also became clear that economic aid alone was not enough to counter the Soviet threat in Europe. Working with State Department Undersecretary Robert Lovett, he typed out in his apartment what became the Vandenberg Resolution, enabling American participation in a permanently entangling new alliance, the North Atlantic Treaty Organization. This, for Taft, was a bridge too far. As Vandenberg acknowledged to his wife, "Evidently I am to have some degree of trouble with Bob Taft. So be it!"[18]

Meanwhile, Vandenberg was lionized in the press. In May 1948, Richard Rovere, in a *Harper's* story entitled "The Unassailable Vandenberg," suggested that Republicans in 1948 call off their primary season and nominate Van as the surest candidate for "President of the World." No American politician, he argued, stood higher: "His prestige is global. The press of the world, that of Russia excepted, hurries to report everything he says. Here at home he is beyond reproach from his friends and, by the magic of bipartisanship, beyond judgment by his enemies." His worst enemies were the communists, although the McCormick press, unrepentantly isolationist, sometimes contended for the honor.

On the eve of the 1948 convention, Vandenberg feared an effort by Taft and others to challenge a platform that reflected Vandenberg's bid for consensus. They might try, he wrote, "to upset any sort of enlightened foreign policy and return to the 'good old days' when it took two weeks to cross the ocean."[19]

Dewey, the frontrunner for the nomination, fended off a challenge from Taft. Clare Luce begged Van to get into the fight. He was also the favorite of an old friend, Sinclair Lewis. But Vandenberg replied to Lewis that such encouragement was more a tribute to his heart than to his head. And Taft losing to Dewey was not the worst thing that could happen, Colonel McCormick said later, "It could have been Vandenberg."[20]

After Dewey won the nomination, Vandenberg urged him not to appease Taft by picking an isolationist for vice president. Instead, Dewey chose Earl Warren, governor of California, to form a ticket that reflected Vandenberg's views.

After Truman upset Dewey and Democrats regained control of Congress, supporters of Vandenberg proposed to oust Taft from his chairmanship of the Republican Policy Committee. But Vandenberg wanted no open breach with his colleague—even as Taftites bedeviled him over the Marshall Plan and NATO.

Though Taft and Vandenberg found themselves at odds, a survey of Washington correspondents in 1949 judged Taft the "most conscientious" of senators and Van as the "most statesmanlike." They were the giants. As the Senate took up the NATO treaty, Vandenberg wrote his wife, "The Taft speech will lengthen the battle because it lends a certain respectability to the opposition."[21]

Vandenberg was fighting for NATO while seeking renewed funding for the Marshall Plan. Of the battle for the latter he wrote, "I get so damned sick of that little band of GOP isolationists who are always in the way that I could scream." There was no little irony here and he knew it.[22]

As the debate to fund military aid for NATO allies dragged on through the summer of 1949, a spot was detected on Vandenberg's left lung. He postponed surgery until the fall, working to pass the aid bill. "This is the last of my really big efforts," he wrote, and it involved defeating the forces of Robert Taft.

Taft came to see him in 1950, when Vandenberg was in Georgetown Hospital recuperating from cancer surgery. The old warhorses found broad agreement in their frustration with Truman's executive action in Korea. That fall, as Van fought for his life, Republicans were once again diverging on foreign policy.

Taft told Vandenberg he did not want a rift. "Please do not be 'upset' (your word) by anything that appears in the papers involving our relationships," Vandenberg replied. "We have lived through several years of press efforts to put us at odds."[23]

As the senator lay on his deathbed, a one-time supporter of his, the junior senator from Wisconsin, began to throw around charges of communists in high places in the government. Although Taft had no brief for Joseph McCarthy, there was a sense in the party that he was tolerating his offensive against the Truman administration. But Tail Gunner Joe was attacking not just Democrats with false and reckless charges. He even went after George Marshall.

As journalist Herbert Agar wrote later, "The complaisance of the Senate . . . cannot be explained. . . . The whole of this privileged body of powerful and experienced men seemed to be hypnotized by McCarthy's atrocious talk—or even worse, they seemed to be afraid." He noted the absence of "the great Vandenberg," who "did not scare easily."[24]

In 1951, Vandenberg consoled himself with the hope that a general from Kansas named Eisenhower would wrest the Republican Party from Robert Taft. When this appeared likely, the dying Senator told a reporter, "I feel as though a great load has been lifted from my back."[25]

All these other midwesterners had something in common beyond their native region. Each came to rely on the leadership of Arthur Vandenberg, whose journey from booster of Zenith to would-be president of the world began and ended in Grand Rapids, a city squarely in the heart of the country.

Notes

Some portions of this chapter are adapted from the author's book Arthur Vandenberg: The Man in the Middle of the American Century (Chicago: University of Chicago, 2017). Used by permission.

1. Arthur Hendrick Vandenberg, "The Shrewdness of Hawkins," *Lippincott's Monthly*, February 1905, 203–11; Arthur Hendrick Vandenberg, *The Greatest American, Alexander Hamilton* (New York: G. P. Putnam's Sons, 1921).
2. Arthur Hendrick Vandenberg, *If Hamilton Were Here Today: American Fundamentals Applied to Modern Problems* (New York: G. P. Putnam's Sons, 1923).
3. Lynn Olsen, *Those Angry Days: Roosevelt, Lindbergh, and America's Fight Over World War II, 1939–1941* (New York: Random House, 2013), 230.
4. Henry Cabot Lodge to Arthur Vandenberg, July 15 1919.
5. *Grand Rapids Herald*, June 10, 1919.
6. Arthur Vandenberg to University of Michigan president, October 31, 1924, University of Michigan Bentley Historical Library.
7. H. L. Menken, *American Mercury*, January 1925, 123.
8. First in the series published in *Grand Rapids Herald*, June 30, 1920.
9. *Grand Rapids Press*, April 2, 1928.
10. *Grand Rapids Press*, April 2, 1928.
11. John Kelly, "The Day the KKK Was Here," undated, Vandenberg Scrapbooks, University of Michigan Bentley Historical Library.
12. See H. L. Mencken, *Thirty-five Years of Newspaper Work* (Baltimore: Johns Hopkins University Press, 2004), 161; *The Diary of H. L. Mencken* (New York: Vintage Books, 1989), 357, 375.
13. Hazel Vandenberg Diaries, October 9, 1935, University of Michigan Bentley Historical Library.
14. Hazel Vandenberg Diaries, October 15, 1935, University of Michigan Bentley Historical Library.
15. *The Private Papers of Senator Vandenberg* (Boston: Houghton Mifflin, 1952), 59–60.
16. *Grand Rapids Herald*, May 28, 1920.

17. *Private Papers of Senator Vandenberg*, 126–45.
18. *Private Papers of Senator Vandenberg*, 378–79.
19. *Private Papers of Senator Vandenberg*, 427–28.
20. Richard Norton-Smith, *Thomas E. Dewey and His Times* (New York: Simon and Schuster, 1982), 498–99.
21. Hazel Vandenberg Diaries, July 11, 1949, University of Michigan Bentley Historical Library; *Private Papers of Senator Vandenberg*, 498.
22. *Private Papers of Senator Vandenberg*, 500.
23. *Private Papers of Senator Vandenberg*, 515, 565.
24. Herbert Agar, *The Unquiet Years: U.S.A. 1945–1955* (London: Hart-Davis, 1957), 107.
25. *Private Papers of Senator Vandenberg*, 575.

21

Of Conformity and Cosmopolitanism

MIDWESTERN IDENTITY SINCE WORLD WAR II

J. L. Anderson

In 1969 historian Laurence Lafore resigned his post at Swarthmore College and accepted a teaching position at the University of Iowa. Lafore grew up in relative wealth and privilege in the East, made the Midwest home, and lived in Iowa City until his death in 1985. Predictably, his journey in the Midwest began with expressions of surprise and contempt on the part of fellow easterners that he would choose to live "in the sticks."

Lafore's journey was as much about culture as it was about geography. In a provocatively titled essay "In the Sticks," published in *Harper's Magazine* just two years after arriving in Iowa, Lafore observed that "everything Easterners take for granted about Iowa (including the assumption that it is a variant spelling of Ohio and Idaho) is wrong, and it follows that the assumptions I have grown up with about the definition and location of civilization are also probably wrong."[1] In his words, adapting to Iowa was "like taking off tight shoes; after the first elation of comfort has faded, you forget how great the discomfort was."[2] Having lived in Pennsylvania and France, Lafore's provinciality was unmasked in the Midwest, even as he affectionately described Iowa provinciality.

Most midwesterners would not have been surprised to find that there were many things to like in Iowa City or any number of midwestern locales, just as people from countless villages, farmsteads, and cities around the world admired things about the places they called home. Like Lafore, I left home and began a journey of discovery about my identity; in my case as a displaced midwesterner. At this point an apology to readers is in order for self-referential writing. It goes without saying that readers (excepting my family members) do not and should not care about my biography. But, having lived in the Midwest from 1973 to 2006, the position of "participant-observer" (to borrow a concept from cultural anthropology) is appropriate in this instance. Coming to adulthood in the Midwest, my sense of what it meant to be midwestern was mostly unspoken and unexamined, just as Lafore's eastern-ness was unexamined before he came to Iowa. When I left the region in 2006 for a job in the American South, many aspects of that midwestern identity that had previously been hidden were exposed. I gained a new awareness of what it is to be midwestern.

There were surprises in the South, despite having studied the region's history. One particularly striking physical example was the state of decay of houses in middle-class neighborhoods. Decaying soffits, copious algae growth on siding, and blistered or cracked shingles were common. Equally surprising was the extreme height of the grass in lawns of these middling neighborhoods. The *Atlanta-Journal Constitution* even ran a story about lawn care: posing the age-old question of how tall grass should be before it is cut. When I brought the article to the office to discuss it over lunch with a colleague (an eighth-generation southerner), his reaction was, "My God, the conformity!" My response was "Yes, please!"

In one sense, our differing reactions were hard to explain. We were born in the mid-1960s, grew up in two-parent, middle-class households without fear of homelessness or missing a meal. We were both confirmed in Protestant denominations and joined the Boy Scouts, earned PhDs in American history, married, and had children. Yet there was a regional chasm that helped explain our varying standards of maintaining the lawn; an important middle-class cultural artifact. The disconnect was all the more striking given that during my previous years in Iowa we associated with many friends and neighbors who were our opposites on just about every political issue. Regardless of political differences, we all agreed on when the grass should be cut. Without making too much of lawn care or making too much of my limited experience, the fact remains that my midwestern self was challenged by my southern brother from another mother. What was going on?

This essay is an exploration of the ways in which midwesterners have presented themselves to the world. Of course this brief essay cannot deal with all aspects of midwestern identity or all of its incarnations. There is no single midwestern identity, as discussed below. Even so, there are several salient characteristics of a mostly white, midwestern, middle-class identity that gained currency in American life after World War II. The focus here is on conformity as well as a sense of belonging in the wider world. These seeming opposite traits allowed midwesterners to belong within the region even as they saw possibilities in the wider world.

It is important to note that there is much diversity in the Midwest and, consequently, it is impossible to claim that a single identity can reflect such diversity. Just as there are many Souths (Appalachian, coastal, pied-mont, Bluegrass, Delta, etc.), there are many Midwests (cutover, Corn Belt, Upper Peninsula, etc.). Even Americans who live in the twelve mid-western states never fully agree about where they are and which states comprise the region. Cultural geographer James Shortridge demon-strated the fluidity of the label "midwestern" in his research conducted in the 1980s.[3] This lack of consensus persists today. Historian Drew Cay-ton explained this phenomenon in 2008. Cayton observed that "people who live in Nebraska do not necessarily think Ohio is in the Midwest" and "people in Ohio do not necessarily think Minnesota is in the Mid-west."[4] Walt Hickey of fivethirtyeight.com conducted a survey in 2014 of self-identified midwesterners in which he asked them to name the states that they located as midwestern. The results were ambiguous, with 70 percent of respondents identifying Illinois, Indiana, and Iowa as midwestern and Michigan, Minnesota, and Wisconsin, each polling over 60 percent. Kansas, Missouri, and Ohio, each polled over 50 per-cent. More surprisingly, but reminiscent of the phenomenon that Shor-tridge documented, over 10 percent of respondents identified the states of Montana, Wyoming, Colorado, Pennsylvania, and West Virginia as belonging in the Midwest.[5]

While confusion over geographic boundaries prevails, it is much eas-ier to recognize that there are a multitude of social Midwests. Chicago, Illinois, and Defiance, Ohio, are both midwestern, but they occupy dif-ferent economic, political, and social spaces in addition to their geo-graphic distance. Multiple identities exist, including urban and rural, rural non-farm and rural farm, not to mention socioeconomic, racial, and ethnic identities. African Americans who came to the region's cities of Cleveland, Chicago, and Detroit after World War II may not have shared an identity with Hispanic immigrants who came to midwestern small towns, even though both groups wanted a share of the American Dream, as historians Debra Reid and Jim Norris have noted.[6] Similarly, small-town elites in Minnesota who saw themselves as "self-made" were suspicious of those community members who lost farms through foreclosure, framing the issue of debt and dispossession as a moral failing that set the economic and social "losers" apart from elites.[7]

While many scholars have emphasized the variation in geographic and social identities, Drew Cayton suggested that changing demographics and economic conditions contributed to regional identity. Specifically, during the postwar period the West and Sunbelt grew in population and power while the Midwest became more peripheral in American life, exposing the physical and cultural boundaries of the Midwest. As Cayton explained in an interview, "People did not use the term Midwest in a widespread way until they began to think of the Midwest as being peculiar or out of the mainstream."[8] Historian David Danbom arrived at a similar conclusion when he claimed that rural midwesterners still cling to cultural forms and expressions that formerly defined them but no longer matter. This is a useful insight that bears restating. The importance of midwestern identity has increased as the pace of economic and political marginalization accelerated in relation to other regions.

In 1949 Kansan Kenneth S. Davis provided an opening to explore the subject of midwestern identity. He addressed readers of the *New York Times* about his home region, explaining that regional differences persisted despite the increasing standardization of American life. Among the midwestern traits Davis highlighted was middle-class conformity, echoing Sinclair Lewis's critique in *Babbitt* (1922). Midwesterners even conformed to a knee-jerk praise of rugged individualism. The irony did not escape Davis: "It is precisely because the Midwest holds the individual person in such esteem and lays such stress on individual rights and obligations that pressures develop which tend to crush individualism of mind and spirit into a dead level of conformity."[9] He noted a relentless, numbing, midwestern boosterism and booster-speak of the type espoused by the fictional George Babbitt.

Yet Davis also saw praiseworthy traits. He singled out his fellow midwesterners for a high degree of gregariousness when compared to "easterners." More importantly, he asserted that midwesterners shared a sense of the wider world that was often lacking in people from other regions. Davis described a cosmopolitanism that made easterners look provincial by comparison. He illustrated this by recounting that during World War II, soldiers at Fort Riley, Kansas, who called Manhattan Island home were surprised to learn that residents of Manhattan, Kansas, had indoor plumbing. Davis balanced criticism and praise in his depiction of midwesterners as friendly and engaged, if overly conforming strivers.

There is no evidence that Davis revisited regionalism in later life. He moved on to more profitable subjects, most famously a multivolume biography of FDR. But if Davis was right and conformity and cosmopolitanism were dominant midwestern traits, how and where would we see these traits on display?

Film depictions of the Midwest by midwesterners have conveyed multiple images of the region. Allowing for the influence of directors and producers that were part of the Hollywood machine, the stories these insiders tell allow a glimpse of regional identity. In a presentation given over fifteen years ago at a regional Organization of American Historians meeting, Alan Marcus described the trajectory of cinematic representations of the Midwest from an all-American utopia during the 1930s to a dystopian wasteland by the 1980s. Musicals of the 1940s and '50s depicted the region favorably, even while recognizing midwestern eccentricities.[10] In the 1945 film version of *State Fair*, Iowan Phil Strong depicted his fellow Iowans sympathetically, even as he exposed their naiveté.[11] In *The Music Man*, released as a film in 1962, Meredith Willson depicted his fellow Iowans as suspicious of outsiders, although admittedly for good reason, as the foibles and schemes of the lead character and outsider Professor Harold Hill demonstrated.

A generation later, film depictions were far less favorable. In *What's Eating Gilbert Grape?* (1993), viewers see a fictional Iowa family and community in crisis. The screenwriter, Iowan Peter Hedges, provided resolution and relief from midwestern dysfunction for his protagonist by leaving. The film adaptation of Jane Smiley's Pulitzer Prize–winning

A Thousand Acres (1997) depicted midwesterners behaving badly in her riff on *King Lear*.

These film representations, both positive and negative, contributed to an understanding of the Midwest as flyover country, a conformist place where very little happens and what does happen either does not matter or is too bleak to endure. Drew Cayton observed that many depictions of the region show that "its residents are distorted by conformity and repression," reinforcing the declension narrative of the Midwest that many journalists articulated.[12] For Cayton, the particular location of many films set in the Midwest did not matter, which made the Midwest an ideal setting.[13]

The film *The Bridges of Madison County* (1995) is a good example of how the Midwest served as a blank slate. Based on the novel of the same title by Iowan Robert James Waller, *The Bridges of Madison County* was a story of an Italian war bride in Iowa who conducted an extramarital affair with another outsider, a photographer on assignment for *National Geographic*. For fictional Francesca and Robert Kincaid (played by Meryl Streep and Clint Eastwood, respectively) the rolling hills of the southern Iowa drift plain and the picturesque covered bridges could have been anywhere, so long as they brought Meryl and Clint together. The passionate affair was a brief one, taking place while the family was away at the state fair. At the end of the film, the protagonists parted, allowing Francesca to conform to marital and family obligations and Robert Kincaid to move on to presumably new encounters with other lonely women.

It is no small irony that the state fair, the only Iowa landmark in the film other than the bridges, was the pretext for the liaison in Waller's novel and film. The fair remains a venerable regional institution that reinforces midwestern conformity, agrarianism, and boosterism. Nothing says conformity like meeting prescribed physical confirmation standards for livestock or floriculture and competing for the best set of human twins, triplets, or multiples at the Iowa State Fair. (Full disclosure: the twin competition is for "most alike" *and* "least alike.") The fair lionizes agriculture and rurality, reflecting both contemporary commercial agriculture as well as a link to the mid-nineteenth century past when many of the state fairs were founded. The booster ethos of rural life and agrarianism is built into the fair. The demonstration of the products of field, farmyard, and home that meet community and organizational standards embody the ethos of "good farming, clear thinking, and right living" that occupied the masthead of another Iowa institution, *Wallaces Farmer*, until the mid-twentieth century.

Of course, many states outside the Midwest have large fairs. The state fairs in Oklahoma, New York, and Washington rival Iowa's and attendance at the Texas fair surpasses that of most midwestern fairs. Furthermore, some midwestern fairs have not been successful. Michigan ceased state funding in 2009 but the fair continues, now as a private corporation. The Midwest has the most and some of the largest fairs in the nation, with the Minnesota fair attracting approximately two million visits over the twelve days of the fair. State fairs in Illinois, Indiana, Iowa, Ohio, and Wisconsin are robust events that regularly attracted large crowds throughout the postwar period.

So what is different about the midwestern state fair? "The Midwest is State Fair Central," Minnesota's famous son Garrison Keillor claimed, because industrious and abstemious midwesterners could liberate themselves from their conformity and engage in an uncharacteristic holiday of overindulgence. Just as the youth depicted in Phil Strong's *State Fair* were liberated from parental oversight during the fair, so too are parents liberated from farm and small-town conformity and social control, albeit to a lesser extent. Keillor playfully noted that the fair reinforced an image of the Midwest as the "breadbasket of America, Hog Butcher, Stacker of Particleboard, Player with Chainsaws, [and] Land of Big Haunches."[14]

The agricultural production and rurality that are embodied in state fairs remain important to every American region, but perhaps no more so than in the Midwest. California agriculture is the most profitable in the nation, but we also know that agricultural wealth there is concentrated in the Central Valley. Large swaths of the state are mountainous, forested, or desert. Driving the length and breadth of California, one is not confronted with an agricultural landscape that stretches to the horizon. Colorado is heavily agricultural, but the mountains shape the identity of many residents. What about the Southeast, which has been heavily agricultural in the postwar period? The difference here is one of relative prosperity. In the old Cotton Belt, tenancy and wage labor conspired to shape an identity that juxtaposed poverty and subordination with wealth and social, economic, and political control. In the Southwest and West, irrigated farmland of the river valleys is juxtaposed with mountain, desert, and sagebrush. The dominant midwestern farm story has been somewhat different from these other regions. With the exception of the Northwoods of Michigan, Wisconsin, and Minnesota, the Midwest is relentlessly agricultural. Here, the image of the farm owner-operator has attained mythic status; thanks in part to the prominence of the midwestern regionalist painters of the 1930s and 1940s. Grant Wood, John Steuart Curry, and Thomas Hart Benton provided Americans with memorable images of the Midwest, notably those of the red barn–white farmhouse–picket fence variety that typified midwestern farms. When the 1980s farm crisis struck, Americans purchased tickets to the first Farm Aid benefit concert in 1985 to benefit "family farmers"; in other words, worthy, independent producers who used their physical, mental, and emotional strength to feed the nation while enduring natural hazards as well as man-made issues of capricious markets and changing government policies.

Farmers themselves participated in an identity-making exercise that reflects the conformity and boosterism that Kenneth Davis observed in 1949. The Wallace family of Iowa took over the editorship of the farm publication *Iowa Homestead* and remade it as *Wallace's Farmer and Iowa Homestead* (later shortened to *Wallaces Farmer*). The family eschewed a one-size-fits-all approach to farming, but the previously noted motto of "good farming, clear thinking, and right living" reinforced middle-class ideals of conformity to commercial farming that encouraged improvement through investment in education and technology. So, too, did the editors of *Successful Farming*, another Des Moines institution, established in 1902 and still family-owned. A study of the images of success embodied in these publications argued that the emphasis was on "conventional values of production, efficiency, specialization, and concentration." Both publications featured farmers as protagonists in news stories and features, using the experiences of farm people to structure a narrative of success and innovation that excluded alternate images and values, simultaneously reflecting and producing an identity of the "conventional, market-oriented, and individualistic" farmer. In this telling, agrarianism is embodied in the farmer as "skillful problem solver and user of technology, both as a steward of the land and as a highly productive provisioner for a hungry world."[15]

Midwestern rurality and agrarianism has been reinforced many times and in many ways since 1945. At the end of the war, one booster claimed that the Midwest produced "more benefits for humanity today than any region on earth." These benefits were tied to agricultural and industrial power, not cultural, artistic, or spiritual dimensions of the region. The purely material nature of these contributions was partially offset in the same article by another commentator who highlighted the fact that the Midwest led the nation in voter turnout in the 1944 election and in educational attainment. But it was the fact that midwesterners embodied a producer-oriented, agrarian ideology that made these claims resonate. Midwesterners have conformed to an agrarian image so much so that *urban* residents, not just rural people, frequently claimed that farming was superior to urban life. The pervasive agrarian ideology is what has made the region unique.

This is not to suggest that other regions fail to successfully sell their rural heritage or lack numerous rural and agricultural museums and attractions. It is easy to make a list of sites from across the United States that recall a rural past or evoke agrarian imagery. But every other region has something else that drives the tourist enterprise. When the South sells agricultural heritage it is more often the plantation than the yeoman farm, tenant farm, or sharecropper experience that receives the attention. Nostalgic visitors have often favored the Old South moonlight and magnolia plantation story that obscures racial hierarchy and oppression.[16] Even more important to Southern tourism is the American Civil War and, increasingly, sites and museums related to the civil rights movement. The West has the largest number of iconic national parks such as Yellowstone, Bryce Canyon, and Yosemite. Along with New England, the West led the nation in selling nature and nature parks to Americans. New England, the Mid-Atlantic, and Virginia trade heavily in the Revolutionary era (think Boston, Philadelphia, and Colonial Williamsburg), while both New England and the Mid-Atlantic have promoted industrial history as part of their past, including Lowell, Slater's Mill, Hopewell and Cornwall Furnaces, and Paterson's Great Falls. Mention New York and the first images that come to mind are of New York City.

Of course, the Midwest has its share of sites that pertain to all of these stories and time periods. John Deere's shop in Grand Detour, Illinois, and Watkins Mill near Liberty, Missouri, depict nineteenth-century industrial history, while Silos and Smokestacks National Heritage Area in Iowa shows the significance and interdependence of agriculture and industry. George Rogers Clark National Historic Park in Indiana commemorates the Revolutionary War. Important sites in the history of the transportation revolution can be seen in Ohio, Indiana, and Illinois. St. Charles, Missouri, was the departure point for the Corps of Discovery, while Missouri and Kansas boast numerous important sites relating to the rise of sectional tension and the American Civil War. These midwestern places, however, are not likely be the first on the list for tourists from outside the region for visiting sites relating to those topics. Sites like the Amana Colonies, while depicting both industrial and agricultural history, however, resonate at a deeper level for tourists due to the agrarian nature of the society that thrived there.

We can only wonder how Kansan Kenneth Davis would have assessed the changes in the Midwest and the nation twenty or thirty years on. Fortunately, we have the well-documented views of another native son and midwestern icon, Garrison Keillor. It is difficult to deny the important role Keillor played in explaining the Midwest to Americans (even midwesterners) through his fictional, now mythical, Lake Wobegon. Almost a decade ago, Sam Anderson of *Slate* wrote that since the first broadcast of *A Prairie Home Companion* in 1974, Keillor "turned himself into a kind of EveryMidwesterner."[17]

Most importantly for this essay, Keillor confronted regional conformity and cosmopolitanism. The heart of Keillor's midwestern sensibility is this: "Don't think too much of yourself because you are no better than anyone else." Work hard and do your best and do not draw attention to yourself. Implicit in this notion of egalitarian conformity, however, is a cosmopolitan world view. For all of our attention on the conversation at the Chatterbox Café or to Pastor Inqvist's sermons, listeners and read-ers were made aware of how these things are simultaneously banal and important to us. Here is the echo of Davis. Midwesterners have been self-effacing enough to be aware of the world beyond. Keillor himself claimed that he had to leave his roots before he could know those roots.[18]

There is an important corollary to Keillor's version of midwestern conformity. He shows that it is acceptable to laugh (or at least smile) at it. Part of the message is that we are in on the joke. Again, *Slate*'s Sam Anderson saw this gentle mocking as Keillor's way of honoring his home and his people, "an approach that ingeniously echoed the region's ethic of self-deprecating pride."[19]

Non-midwesterners sometimes have a difficult time getting this. When midwesterner Emily Langer moved to Washington DC to attend uni-versity she endured the kinds of jokes and quips that many people who leave the Midwest hear. According to Langer, several students specu-lated that she must have been so glad to "get out of there"; there pre-sumably being a "drab territory where everyone lives off the land and [works at] pollution spewing factories." This view was so pervasive that Langer wanted to lobby the university international education office "to supplement its programs in Paris, Cairo, and Beijing with a junior year abroad in Columbus, Ohio's capital." Without reducing or elevating the Midwest into some romanticized idyll, the author argued that midwest-erners are more than stereotypes. "My own parents," Langer opined, "are sophisticated enough to know that children have been venturing out on their own since the beginning of time, sometimes to look for someplace more exciting, other times because that's just how life unfolds, hardly ever to turn their backs on their families and almost always to make them proud. I hit pay dirt the day I was born in Ohio, and if I ever move back, I'll hit pay dirt again."[20]

For midwesterners at home and abroad in the world, then, Keillor's comforting tales of midwestern conformity have served as a balm. Blog-ger Abe Sauer recalled how *A Prairie Home Companion* was a midwest-ern touchstone as he lived and traveled around the world. While fellow expats were excited to receive VHS recordings of popular American tele-vision shows, Sauer confessed that his "secret glee" was bootleg *Prairie*

Home Companion recordings sent by his brother. Keillor's voice, Sauer observed, "reminded me, and still does, that home was still an actual place to which I could go back, even if the years had faded the memories too [much] to any longer proffer proper nostalgia."[21] For many midwesterners, Keillor's Midwest was home.

Despite all this, iconic midwesterner Garrison Keillor does not formally embrace regionalism. In a 2013 interview by historian Jon Lauck, Keillor was downright cagey; hesitant to even recognize the value of region as a lens of analysis. He conceded that claiming the Midwest was a "useful disguise," but would go no further.[22] Whether Keillor accepts the term or not, however, it is the identity that he projects, as Lauck observed in his 2014 essay in *Belt Magazine* titled "The Death of the Midwest: Garrison Keillor's Impending Retirement as a Wake for Midwestern Regionalism."

As Lauck suggests, the post-Keillor Midwest may exist without regionalism. Indeed, for Keillor the Midwest is fading. Contrast his comments of 1985 with those of the twenty-first century. In 1985 he described how residents of Lake Wobegon would rather purchase hideous eye glasses at a local retailer than designer frames from the boutique in the city. This made sense to people because, as Keillor stated, "Calvin Klein isn't going to come with the Rescue Squad and he isn't going to teach your children about redemption by grace. You couldn't find Calvin Klein to save your life."[23] Being local mattered to these people. Yet twenty-plus years later, Keillor noted, "The question, 'Where are you from?' doesn't lead to anything odd or interesting. They live somewhere near a Gap store, and what else do you need to know."[24] Even for Keillor, then, the standardization that Kenneth Davis feared in 1949 had come to pass, erasing traces of midwestern culture.

All of which brings us back to where we started. Is the creation of this identity a response to the fact that what was once the "most American" of regions is losing that which made it the standard by which all other regions were judged? This is historian David Danbom's view of the rural Midwest; that whatever traits made midwesterners and their region distinct existed before World War II and probably began to fade around World War I.[25] The conformity that Kenneth Davis witnessed in 1949 still exists, but in Danbom and Keillor's view it is conformity to mass culture and that is what is killing or, perhaps, has already killed the Midwest.

This is a persuasive telling of the story, but it does not fully reflect midwestern identity. The standardization of culture, including the ever-present tyranny of chain restaurants, media and cable companies, and celebrity culture has eroded regionalism. But if midwesterners still doubt whether or not their regional identity is real, they simply need to leave the Midwest to find it.

Notes

The author is grateful for the opportunity to have participated in the conference "Finding the Lost Region: Rediscovering the Midwest, America's Most Common Ground," hosted by the Hauenstein Center for Presidential Leadership at Grand Valley State University, Grand Rapids, Michigan.

1. Laurence Lafore, "In the Sticks," *Harper's Magazine*, October 1971, http://www.lib.uiowa.edu/scua/archives/guides/rg99.0100.sticks.html.
2. Lafore, "In the Sticks."
3. James R. Shortridge, *The Middle West: Its Meaning in American Culture* (Lawrence: University Press of Kansas, 1989).
4. George Bullard, "The Meaning of the Midwest," *Hour Detroit Magazine*, September 2008, http://www.hourdetroit.com/Hour-Detroit/September-2008/The-Meaning-of-Midwest/.
5. Walt Hickey, "Which States Are in the Midwest," fivethirtyeight.com, April 29, 2014, http://fivethirtyeight.com/datalab/what-states-are-in-the-midwest/.
6. Debra A. Reid, "'The Whitest of Occupations': African Americans in the Rural Midwest, 1940–2010," in *The Rural Midwest since World War II*, ed. J. L. Anderson (DeKalb: Northern Illinois University Press, 2014); Jim Norris, "Hispanics in the Midwest since World War II," in *The Rural Midwest since World War II*.
7. Kathryn Marie Dudley, *Debt and Dispossession: Farm Loss in America's Heartland* (Chicago: University of Chicago Press, 2010), cited in J. L. Anderson, ed., introduction to *The Rural Midwest since World War II*, 5.
8. Bullard, "Meaning of the Midwest."
9. Kenneth S. Davis, "East Is East and Midwest Is Midwest," *New York Times*, November 20, 1949.
10. Edward Recchia, "There's No Place Like Home: The Midwest in American Film Musicals," *Midwest Quarterly* 39 no. 2 (Winter 1998): 202–14.

11. Cara Leanne Wood, "Representing the Midwest in American Stage and Film Musicals, 1943–1962," (PhD diss., Princeton University, 2010), 39–43.

12. Drew Cayton, "Movies," in *The American Midwest: An Interpretive Encyclopedia*, ed. Richard Sisson, Christian Zacher, and Andrew Cayton (Bloomington and Indianapolis: Indiana University Press, 2007), 74.

13. Cayton, "Movies," 73.

14. Garrison Keillor, "Take in the Fair with Garrison Keillor," *National Geographic*, June 2009, http://ngm.nationalgeographic.com/2009/07/state-fairs/keillor-text.

15. Gerry Walter, "A 'Curious Blend': The Successful Farmer in American Farm Magazines, 1984–1991," *Agriculture and Human Values* (Summer 1995): 57, 65–67.

16. Jennifer L. Eichstedt and Stephen Small, eds., *Representations of Slavery: Race and Ideology in Southern Plantation Museums* (Washington DC: Smithsonian Institution Press, 2002).

17. Sam Anderson, "A Prairie Home Conundrum: The Mysterious Appeal of Garrison Keillor," *Slate*, June 16, 2006, http://www.slate.com/articles/news_and_politics/assessment/2006/06/a_prairie_home_conundrum.html.

18. "Inside Garrison Keillor's Fabled World of 'A Prairie Home Companion,'" *PBS NewsHour*, July 26, 2014, http://www.pbs.org/newshour/bb/inside-garrison-keillors-fabled-world-prairie-home-companion/.

19. Anderson, "A Prairie Home Conundrum."

20. Emily Langer, "Excuse Me, But I'm from Ohio," *Washington Post*, August 31, 2008, http://www.washingtonpost.com/wp-dyn/content/article/2008/08/29/AR2008082902338.html.

21. Abe Sauer, "Real America, with Abe Sauer: Garrison Keillor Will Die," *The Awl*, December 16, 2009, http://www.theawl.com/2009/12/real-america-with-abe-sauer-garrison-keillor-will-die.

22. Jon Lauck, "Garrison Keillor: An Interview," *Salmagundi Magazine* 184 (Fall 2014): 58.

23. Beverly Beyette, "Fishing for Meaning in Lake Wobegon Waters: Garrison Keillor Reflects on the Success of His Semi-Autobiographical Best Seller," *Los Angeles Times*, September 18, 1985, http://articles.latimes.com/1985–09–18/news/vw-6254_1_wobegonians.

24. Sauer, "Garrison Keillor Will Die."

25. David Danbom, "The Indistinct Distinctiveness of Rural Midwestern Culture," in *The Rural Midwest since World War II*, ed. J. L. Anderson (DeKalb: Northern Illinois University Press, 2014).

Contributors

Michael Allen, professor of history at the University of Washington, Tacoma, was born and raised in Ellensburg, Washington. He served as a U.S. Marine artilleryman in Vietnam and worked as a towboat deckhand, oil tankerman, and cook on the Mississippi River and its tributaries. He has written six books, including the prizewinning *Western Rivermen, 1763–1861: Ohio and Mississippi Boatmen and the Myth of the Alligator Horse* (1990), *Rodeo Cowboys in the North American Imagination* (1998), *Congress and the West: Trans-Appalachian Settlement Policy, 1783–1787* (2007) He is author of the *New York Times* and Amazon best seller *A Patriot's History of the United States* (2004) with Larry Schweikart. Michael Allen lives in Ellensburg and has three children, Jim, Davy, and Caroline.

J. L. Anderson is associate professor of history at Mount Royal University, Calgary, Alberta. He earned his PhD at Iowa State University and is the author of *Industrializing the Corn Belt: Agriculture, Technology, and Environment, 1945–1972* (2009). Anderson is editor of *The Rural Midwest since World War II* (2014) and coeditor with Ginette Aley of *Union Heartland: The Midwestern Home Front during the Civil War* (2013).

Jon Butler is Howard R. Lamar Professor Emeritus of American Studies, History, and Religious Studies at Yale University. He attended the Hector, Minnesota, public schools and the University of Minnesota, where he received his BA in 1964 and his PhD in 1972. He is the author of numerous books and articles about religion in America from the colonial period to the twentieth century. He lives in Minneapolis.

James E. Davis, after teaching in the Dearborn Public School System from 1963 to 1971, earned his PhD in 1971 from the University of Michigan in history, with a cognate in geography. From 1971 to 2011, he taught history and geography at Illinois College, where he was the first faculty member to earn twice (1981 and 1993) the college's top teaching award. He reviews for various journals, including the *American Historical Review* and the *Journal of American History*. His most recent book is *Frontier Illinois* (1998).

Nicole Etcheson is the Alexander M. Bracken Professor of History at Ball State University. She is the author of *A Generation at War: The Civil War Era in a Northern Community* (2011), which won the Avery O. Craven Award from the Organization of American Historians and Best Nonfiction Book of Indiana from the Indiana Center for the Book at the Indiana State Library. She has also published *Bleeding Kansas* (2004) and *The Emerging Midwest* (1996) as well as numerous articles on Civil War and midwestern history.

Susan E. Gray is associate professor of history at Arizona State University. She is the author of *The Yankee West: Community Life on the Michigan Frontier* (1996) and coeditor of *The Identity of the Midwest: Essays on Regional History* (2007) and *Contingent Maps: Rethinking Western Women's History and the North American West* (2014). From 2003 to 2012, Gray was coeditor of *Frontiers: A Journal of Women Studies*. At present she is coordinator of the ASU Public History Program.

Jeffrey Helgeson is associate professor of history at Texas State University. His book *Crucibles of Black Empowerment: Chicago's Neighborhood Politics from the New Deal to Harold Washington* (2014) examines how black Chicagoans developed a unique political culture through the everyday struggle to access housing, job opportunities, and political power in a city that was both "the capital of black America" and one of the most segregated and unequal places in the nation. He is currently researching the history of public-private collaboration in housing development and education policy in Boston during the second half of the twentieth century.

Joseph Hogan is the host of *Common Ground*, the podcast of the Hauenstein Center at Grand Valley State University. He received his MA in English and American Literature at New York University, where was a Charles Wickham Moore fellow. His work has been published in *Middle West Review* and elsewhere.

Zachary Michael Jack is a board member of the Midwestern History Association and a seventh-generation, rural midwesterner. The author of many award-winning books on the region and its history, Jack's most recent work on the Midwest appears in his Shambaugh Award–

nominated book *The Midwest Farmer's Daughter: In Search of an American Icon* and in articles in the *Middle West Review*, the *Daily Yonder*, and *Front Porch Republic*, among many others.

Christopher R. Laingen is associate professor of geography at Eastern Illinois University in Charleston, Illinois. He grew up on a family farm in southern Minnesota near the town of Odin, where much of his interest in the rural landscape and regional geography began. His research focuses on changes in farming and the landscapes of the rural Midwest and Great Plains, which has been published in *Great Plains Research, Focus on Geography, The Geographical Review*, and *The Professional Geographer*. He is also the coauthor of the book *American Farms, American Food: A Geography of Agriculture and Food Production in the United States* (2016).

Jon Lauck is the founding president of the Midwestern History Association, the associate editor and book editor of *Middle West Review*, and adjunct professor of history and political science at the University of South Dakota. He is the author of *Prairie Republic: The Political Culture of Dakota Territory, 1879–1889* (2010), *Daschle vs. Thune: Anatomy of a High Plains Senate Race* (2007), *American Agriculture and the Problem of Monopoly: The Political Economy of Grain Belt Farming, 1953–1980* (2000), *The Lost Region: Toward a Revival of Midwestern History* (2013), *The Midwestern Moment: The Forgotten World of Early Twentieth-Century Midwestern Regionalism, 1880–1940* (2017), and *From Warm Center to Ragged Edge: The Erosion of Midwestern Literary and Historical Regionalism, 1920–1965* (2017).

James P. Leary is emeritus professor of folklore and Scandinavian studies at the University of Wisconsin–Madison, where he co-founded the Center for the Study of Upper Midwestern Cultures. Formerly coeditor of the *Journal of American Folklore*, he has done field and archival research since the 1970s on regional music, resulting in books that include *Yodeling in Dairyland; Polkabilly: How the Goose Island Ramblers Redefined American Folk Music; Folksongs of Another America: Field Recordings from the Upper Midwest, 1937–1946;* and *Pinery Boys: Songs and Songcatching in the Lumberjack Era.*

David R. McMahon is professor of history and campus coordinator for the Democracy Commitment at Kirkwood Community College, Iowa City campus. An accomplished public historian, McMahon's work has appeared in numerous publications, including *Sport and Memory in North America* (2001) and *Outside In: African-American History in Iowa, 1828–2000* (2001), as well as public history exhibits. A former city councilor in Lone Tree, Iowa, he has served on the Historic Preservation Commission in Iowa City and on the Herbert Hoover Presidential Library's Travel Grant Committee. As campus coordinator for the Democracy Commitment, he has facilitated numerous discussions in the community on current issues and coordinated Constitution Day activities. In 2008 he was named a National Institute for Staff and Organizational Development Excellence Award recipient. A popular and innovative instructor, he is a native of Manilla, Iowa, and a longtime resident of Iowa City.

Hendrik G. Meijer is cochair and CEO of Meijer, Inc. He is vice chair of the Gerald R. Ford Presidential Foundation, serves on the boards of Fifth Third Bank, the Kettering Foundation, the Food Marketing Institute, and the National Constitution Center. A graduate of the University of Michigan with a degree in English and significant graduate work in history, Meijer is a biographer of Senator Arthur Vandenberg, one of the great bipartisan political leaders of the Midwest. He is the executive director of the documentary film *America's Senator: The Unexpected Odyssey of Arthur Vandenberg* and has published numerous articles on the topic.

John E. Miller grew up in six small towns and one large-city suburb in the Midwest, graduating from the University of Missouri in 1966. He received his MA and PhD in history from the University of Wisconsin in 1968 and 1973, punctuated by a tour as an army court reporter in Vietnam. He taught mostly twentieth-century American history courses for a year at the University of Tulsa and then for twenty-nine years at South Dakota State University before becoming a full-time writer in 2003. Among his eight books are *Looking for History on Highway 14*; a political biography of Wisconsin governor Philip F. LaFollette; and a biography of and two books of essays on children's author Laura Ingalls Wilder. His latest books, *Small-Town Dreams: Stories of Midwestern Boys Who Shaped America* and *First We Imagine: 22 Creative South Dakotans Speak on the Subject of Creativity*, were released in 2014. In addition to his work on small towns and on state and midwestern history, Miller has maintained a continuing interest in political history, having been coeditor of two volumes and currently working on a third volume of *The Plains Political Tradition: Essays on South Dakota Political Culture*. He is also researching a political biography of U.S. senator and 1972 presidential candidate George McGovern.

Paula M. Nelson is the author of three books on South Dakota, as well as articles and essays on the Dakotas and other grassland places. Her research interests include rural life and culture in the Upper Midwest and northern Great Plains, agriculture, Scandinavian immigrants, and small towns. Nelson is professor of history emeritus, University of Wisconsin–Platteville.

David Pichaske, professor of English at Southwest Minnesota State University and editor-publisher of Spoon River Poetry Press/Ellis Press, also spent four years of Senior Fulbright Fellowship teaching American Studies in Poland, Latvia, and Mongolia. He is author-editor of two dozen books, including: *Beowulf to Beatles, A Generation in Motion, Writing Sense, Chaucer's Literary Pilgrimage, The Jubilee Diary, Late Harvest: Rural American Writing, A Place Called Home, Southwest Minnesota: A Place of Many Places, Poland in Transition, UB03, The Father Poems, Rooted: Seven Midwest Writers of Place, Song of the North Country: A Midwest Framework to the Songs of Bob Dylan, Ghosts of Abandoned Capacity*, and most recently the memoir *Here I Stand*.

Pamela Riney-Kehrberg is professor of history at Iowa State University and a faculty member in the department's Rural, Agricultural, Technological and Environmental History Program. She is the author of a number of books and articles, including *Childhood on the Farm: Work, Play and Coming of Age in the Midwest*; and *The Nature of Childhood: An Environmental History of Growing Up in America since 1865*; and *Rooted in Dust: Surviving Drought and Depression in Southwestern Kansas* (1994).

Gregory Rose has been dean and director for Ohio State–Marion since 2004, having started his career there as a faculty member in 1982. He received his undergraduate degree from Valparaiso University, with a double major in history and geography, and his master's and PhD (focused on historical geography) from Michigan State University. His research focuses on the birthplaces and previous residences of various nineteenth-century populations in the Midwest and their distribution within those states. He has presented papers and published work on the early settlement of Indian, Michigan, Ohio, and the Old Northwest region.

James Seaton was professor of English at Michigan State University. His books include *Literary Criticism from Plato to Postmodernism: The Humanistic Alternative* (2014), the scholarly edition of *The Genteel Tradition in American Philosophy and Character and Opinion in the United States* (2009), and *Political Liberalism: From Criticism to Cultural Studies* (1996). His essays and reviews have appeared in such publications as the *Weekly Standard*, the *Wall Street Journal*, the *American Scholar*, the *Claremont Review of Books*, *Society*, the *Hudson Review*, *MidAmerica*, *Midwest Miscellany*, *Yale Journal of Law & the Humanities*, the *University Bookman*, *First Things*, and *Modern Age*.

Michael C. Steiner is professor emeritus of American studies at California State, Fullerton. He earned his PhD in American Studies from the University of Minnesota in 1978 and during his forty years at CSU–Fullerton, Steiner taught courses on environmental history, folk culture, the built environment, regionalism, California, and the West. He won a national teaching and advising award from the American Studies Association in 2006 and was twice a Distinguished Fulbright chair (in Hungary in 1998–99 and in Poland in 2004). Steiner has published prize-winning essays on Frederick Jackson Turner's sectional thesis and Walt Disney's Frontierland. He is author or editor of four books, including most recently, *Regionalists on the Left: Radical Voices from the American West* (2013) and is currently writing a book on the intellectual and grass roots history of the idea of the Midwest.

A lifelong midwesterner, **Jon Teaford** was born and raised in Columbus, Ohio. He received his PhD from the University of Wisconsin and is professor emeritus at Purdue University. A specialist in urban history, he is the author of *Cities of the Heartland*.

Gleaves Whitney has been director of the Hauenstein Center for Presidential Studies at Grand Valley State University since 2003. A member of Phi Beta Kappa and a Fulbright Scholar to (then) West Germany in 1984–85, he received his graduate education at the University of Michigan, Ann Arbor, and is the editor or author of fifteen books and numerous articles and chapters on American history, the presidency, and leadership.

Index

Page numbers in italic indicate illustrations.

Dandurant, Tommy, 262
Dangel, Leo, 270, 277
Davis, James, xiii
Davis, Jeff, 42
Davis, John Givan, 41
Davis, Kenneth S., 332, 333, 336, 338, 340
Dawes General Allotment Act (1887),
    63–64
Dayton OH, 212
"The Death of the Midwest" (Lauck), 340
DeLuca, Sara, 276
Democratic Party, 41, 43
Denver, John, 269
Denver CO, 214
Des Moines Register, 169, 170, 246
Detroit, Treaty of (1855), 63
Detroit MI: decline of, 221; industrial
    development of, 212, 217; popula-
    tion of, 212
Dewey, John, 10
Dewey, Thomas, 321, 325
Dillard, Annie, 268
Dirt Songs (Hasselstrom and Han-
    sen), 276
Disunion blog, 39
Dixieland Jazz, 190
Dodge brothers, 217
Domestic Revolutions (Mintz and Kel-
    logg), 305
Dorsey, Thomas A., 205, 259
Douglas, Stephen A., 41
Dowie, John Alexander, 197
Doyle, Don Harrison, 98, 102
Drake, St. Clair, 47
Dreiser, Theodore, 10
Dylan, Bob, 191

early settlements in the Middle West:
    at confluence of rivers, 30; at cross-

ing of railroads with rivers, 29–30;
emergence of towns, 26–27; "fall
line" connecting, 26; flooding of,
29; guiding principles of, 25, 34, 35,
36; head-of-navigation sites, 25–26;
houses in, 35; industrial develop-
ment and, 27; regional differences
of, 34–35; on river bends, 28–29;
roads and bridges as connectors of,
27, 34; as territorial and state capi-
tals, 30. *See also* farmsteads
Eddy, Mary O., 252
Edmunds, R. David, 59
Eisenhower, Dwight David, 326
Ellison, Ralph, 123, 244
Emancipation Proclamation, 43, 44, 47
Enduring Nations, 59, 60
Enger, Leif, 272
Engle, Paul, 227, 230
Episcopal Church, 204
Erdrich, Louise, 269; *Love Medicine,* 199
Erie Canal, 392
Etcheson, Nicole, xiv
Etter, Dave, 269, 270
Evans, Robin, 167
Evansville IN, 214

The Fall of Alice K (Heynen), 275
farming: cash-grain, 144, 151; geogra-
    phy of, 147–48; as source of income,
    151, 153; transformation of, xvii
farmsteads: dwellings, 33; gardens, 33;
    guiding principles of, 30–31; hen
    houses in, 32; houses' design and
    location of, 31–32, 34, 38n7; mills
    in, 37nn3–4, 38n9; plants, 32–33, 34;
    prevailing winds and, 31, 33; smoke-
    houses in, 32, 37–38n6; soil condition
    and, 31; wells in, 32; windbreaks, 34

after, 290; support for public education, 290; writings of, 289
Hamms Beer commercial broadcasts, 251
Hanna, John, 41
Hansen, Twyla, 276
Harding, Warren, 315
Harmon, Ronnie, 170
Harrigan, Edward, 259
Harris, Paul, 106
Harrison, William Henry, 181, 186
Hartford, John, 191
Haskins, Scott, 233
Hasselstrom, Linda, 270, 276
Hat Rack Case, 319–20
Haven in a Heartless World (Lasch), 246
Hawthorne, Nathaniel: *The Scarlet Letter*, 196
Heartland: Poets of the Midwest (Stryk), 268–69
Hebrew Union College, 205
Hedges, Peter, 333
Hedin, Robert, 275
Helgeson, Jeffrey, xvi
Helget, Nicole Lea, 275
Hemingway, Ernest, 271
Henry Horner Homes, 310
Henson, Michael, 274
Herr, Cheryl Temple, 270, 274, 275
Heynen, Jim, 274, 275
Hickey, Walt, 331
Highway 61 Revisited (music album), 191
Hill, James, 215
Hirsch, Arnold, 118
Hitler, Adolph, 321
Ho-Chunk (Winnebago) peoples, 255, 257
Holm, Beret, 202
Holm, Bill, 270
Home from the Field (Dangel), 277

Homestead Act (1862), 286
Home Town (Anderson), 131
Hoosiers (film), 166
Hopewell Indians, 178–79
Hopkins, Harry, 314
Houston TX, 214
Huck's Raft (Mintz), 306
Hunt, D. Bradford, 310
Hunt, Myron, 12
Hutchins, Thomas, 287

identity. *See* midwestern identity
Illick, Joseph, 312; *American Childhoods*, 306
immigration, 74, 75, 88–89, 202, 203–4
Indiana Constitutional Convention, 186
Indianapolis IN, 212, 213, 215
Indiana "Religious Freedom Restoration Act," 201
Indian Fish and Wildlife Commission (GLIFWC), 68
Indian Removal Acts, xv, 56, 180
Indigenous peoples. *See* Native Americans
industrial development: decline of, 220–21; materials used for, 224n8. *See also individual industries*
"In the Sticks" (Lafore), 329
Iowa: mural projects, 232–37; press, 336; provinciality of, 329; sports, 166–67; State Fair, 334
Iowa Girls Basketball Academy, 168
Iowa Girls High School Athletic Union, 168
Iowa Homestead (magazine), 336
Ise, John, 303
It Can't Happen Here (Lewis), 320, 321
Iverson, Ernest "Slim Jim," 251, 263n1
Iverson, Peter, 56

Lee, Robert E., 185
Lerner, Max, 129
LeSueur, Meridel, 268
Lesy, Michael, 131
Letters from the Country (Bly), 269
Lewis, Meriwether, 181
Lewis, Sinclair, xxii, 132, 133, 140, 268, 314, 315, 316, 317, 320–21, 325, 332
Lewis and Clark Expedition, 181
The Life and Times of the Thunderbolt Kid (Bryson), 308
Life on the Mississippi (Twain), 185
Lincoln, Abraham, 7, 42, 184, 186, 187, 241, 244–45
Lindsay, Vachel, 10, 268, 276
Linstrom, Steve, 272
literature: anthology of American, 269; challenges of modern, 273; content of, 273; decline of interest to, 270–71, 272; depiction of Midwest in, 268; distribution of, 270, 277; fairs and festivals, 271, 277; financial support of, 270; graphics integrated in, 276–77; journals and magazines, 269–70, 271; locality of, 277; national consciousness and, 267–68; online publications of, 278; postmodernism in, 268, 272–73; promotion of, 275–76; realism in, 268; scholarly, 270; in school curricula, 273. *See also* book fairs; publishers; writers
The Literature of the Middle Western Frontier (Rusk), 268
Little Heathens (Kalish), 307
Little House on the Prairie (Wilder), 268
Little Wolves (Maltman), 276
Lodge, Henry Cabot, 315

Los Angeles CA, 214
Louisiana Purchase, 181
Lovejoy, Elijah P., 186
Lovell, James, 168
Lovett, Robert, 324
Luce, Clare, 325
Luce, Henry, 322
Luepke, Ditto J. J., 276
Lutheran church: decline of, 107–8; internal division, 203
lynching, 48
Lynd, Helen, 139
Lynd, Robert, 139

Mackendaz, Ronald, 272
Madison, James, 48, 241
Madison IN, 212
Main Street (Lewis), 132–33, 268, 315
Main-Travelled Roads, 12
Make Hay While the Sun Shines (Schutt), 276
Malle, Louis, 201
Maltman, Thomas, 276
Manfred, Fred, 268
Manilla Times (Iowa), 169
Marcus, Alan, 333
Marquette, Jacques, 180
Marshall, George, 324, 326
Marsh Laboratory studios (record studio), 261
Martin, Roberta, 259
Martin, Sallie, 259
Masonic lodges, 102–3, 104, 105
Massachusetts Constitution, 294
Masters, Edgar Lee, 268; *Spoon River Anthology*, 189
Maxwell, William, 269
May, Henry F., 131
McCarthy, Joseph, 326

McCloskey, Deirdre (b. Donald), xix, 241, 246, 247–48
McCormick, Robert, 325
McElwain, Max, 168
McIlvain, W. H., 44
McMahon, David, xvii, xviii
McMurtry, Larry: *Lonesome Dove*, 196
McRae, Milton, 316–17
McSweeney, Charles, 255
McWilliams, Carey, 199
meat processing, 216, 218
Mecklenburg, Rev. George, 199
Meet Me in St. Louis (film), 189, 190
Meijer, Hank, xxi
Meinig, D. W., 121
Melrose, Lester, 261
Memminger, Christopher G., 46
Mencken, H. L., 268, 315–16, 319–20
Methodist movement, 204
Methodists, 204
metropolises, 211, 213, 215–16, 217, 218–19, 222–23. *See also* cities
"Middle Border" label, 7
Middle West: agriculture of, xvii, 335, 336–37; art of, xix; civic life in, xvi; cultural values of, 240, 241, 273–74; culture-geography interplay in, xiii–xiv; definition of, 177; during economic depression, 57; exploration of, 57, 180–82; in films, depiction of, 333–34; first use of term, 6, 7–8; founding fathers' vision of, xxi; geography of, 3, 25, 27–28, 57, 331; historic sites, 337–38; immigration, xv, 74, 75, 202, 203–4; impact of Civil War on, xiv; Indigenous peoples in, 4–5; intellectual life in, xix–xx; landscape of, xviii; in national consciousness, xiii;

national parks in, 337–38; Native names for, 3; natural resources of, 215–16; population of, 40; prominent intellectuals of, 9–10, 240–48; public images of, 57–58; racial attitudes in, 40–41; regional consciousness, 5; regional histories, 58; religious diversity of, xviii–xix; segregation in, 47; sports, xvii–xviii; state fairs, 334–36; stereotypes of, xxi–xxii, 240; strategic importance of, xxi; ties with Upper South, xiv; urban development, xix, 213–14
midwestern history, xi, xii, xiii, xiv–xv, xxii–xxiii
Midwestern History Association, xii
midwestern identity: agrarianism of, 337; architects of, 10–19; comparison to eastern identity, 333; conformity of, 331, 332, 338–39, 340–41; cosmopolitanism of, 333, 338; farmers' participation in making, 336–37; formation of, xix, 8; provinciality of, 329; regionalism and, 340; rural heritage and, 337; variations of, 331–32
Mille Lacs Band et al. v. State of Minnesota, 66
Miller, John, xvi, xvii, 303
Milwaukee WI, 212, 213, 215, 220
The Minimal Self (Lasch), 246
Minnesota constitution, 201
Minneapolis MN, 213, 214, 216, 218
Minnesota v. Mille Lacs, 67
Mintz, Steve, 305, 306
Mississippian people, 178, 179
Mississippi River, 185–86, 188, 191
Mississippi Valley explorers, 180
Mistral, Frederic, 13
Mitchell, Ellis, 40

Mitchell, Frosty, 166
Moeller, Henry, 258
Monroe, Harriet, 10
"Monster Picnic at Pregler's Grove" (music performance), 254
Montesquieu, Charles de Secondat, 283
Moody Bible Institute in Chicago, 205
Morrison, Toni, 119, 120
Morton, Jelly Roll, 261
Morton, Oliver P., 43
Moser Brothers (virtuoso musicians), 257–58, 262
Mueller, Lisel, 273
Muir, John, 9
Mumford, Lewis, 14
Mundelein, Cardinal George, 204
mural projects in Iowa: *Cattle*, 236; in Cedar Rapids City Hall, 232–33; in Cedar Rapids Courthouse, 236; *Inheriting Justice*, 237; *Other Art Follows*, 235, 236; restoration of, 236–38; sponsors of, 234, 235; at State University, 234–35; themes of, 233–34, 236
music: commercial broadcasts, 251; festivals, 254, 258–59; styles, 251, 261; traditions, 259; venues, 254, 256
musicians: at 1933 World's Fair, 257–58; African American, 255–56, 259, 261; audio recordings, 259–60, 260–62; Chicago-based, 253–54; concept of "midwestern," 253; contests, 256; cultural diversity of, 251, 252–53, 256, 260–61, 263; foreign-born, 254–55, 256, 257–58, 260; Great Depression and, 261–62; Hamms Beer commercials, 251, 263n1; "hillbilly," 262; Indigenous, 255, 257, 259; old-time fiddler competition, 256–57; radio broadcasts, 259, 262–63;

repertoires, 254; settlement-house, 253; suspicions about political affiliation of, 254; at World's Columbian Exposition, 254–56
The Music Man (film), 189, 190
The Music Man (film), 333

Naison, Mark, 161
Nash, Newman C., 100, 104, 105, 107
Nathan, Daniel, 163
National Folk Festival (1937), 257, 258–59
National Indian Youth Council (NIYC), 66
Nation of Islam, 205
Native Americans: American government's treaties with, 61–62, 63, 66; areas inhabited by, 4–5, 55, 59, 61; economic conditions of, 55, 65; environmental degradation and, 64; federal policy toward, 63; fight for treaty rights, 66–67; on historic maps, 60–61; historiography of, 56, 58–60; intertribal organizations of, 67–68; legal cases involved, 66–67; in midwestern narrative, 56–57; military conquest of, 58; music of, 251, 252; off-reserve living, 65; population of, 5, 59; poverty relief programs, 65; relations with the whites, 60, 67–68; religious practices of, 197, 198–99; relocation of, 56, 59–60, 62–63; reservations, 63; rural-to-urban migration of, 65–66; settlements founded by, 178–79; social movements of, 66, 67; territory ceded by, 61–62; Waabanong Run, 67; westward movement of, 55; women's status, 55; during World War II, 65. *See also individual tribes*

Nebraska City NE, 212
Nelson, Paula, xvi
Nemanic, Gerald, 270
New Albany IN, 212
New Deal programs, 188
A New Home—Who'll Follow? (Kirkland), 268
New Orleans LA, 214
Nicholson, Meredith, 39, 132
Nienstedt, John, 201
Norris, Frank, 268
Norris, Jim, 332
Northwest Ordinances: abolition clause, 284–85, 299n14; Adams' influence on, 292, 294, 295; cultural impact of, 284; cultural statement in, 294, 295, 299n13; introduction of, 283; land surveying rules, 284; provisions on public education, 285–86, 288, 290
Northwest Territories. *See* Upper Midwest
nostalgia: historical perspective on, 165
Notre Dame University, 205

Oates, Joyce Carol, 269
Obama, Barack, 113
O'Connor, Flannery: *The Violent Bear It Away*, 196
O'Dane, Arthur, 317
Odawa (Ottawa) people, 55, 61
Ohio River, 184, 186
Ohio Valley Indians, 181
Ojibwe (Chippewa) people, 55, 61, 62–63, 252
O'Keefe, Georgia, 9
Old Northwest, 73, 74. *See also* Middle West; Upper Midwest
Oliver, King, 261
Olivet Baptist Church, 203

Olson, Don, 270
Olson, Eleonora, 256
Olson, Ethel, 256
Olson, Tillie, 268
Omaha NE, 212, 213, 214, 215, 216, 218, 219
O'Neill, Francis, 255, 258
Oness, Elizabeth, 274
Onuf, Peter, 270, 283
O Pioneers! (Cather), 268
Our Town (Wilder), 131

Page, Walter Hines, 13, 16, 17
The Pajama Game (film), 189, 190
Paramount Records (record studio), 261
Parham, Charles, 205
Paris, Treaty of, 180
Parkman, Francis, 180
Patchen, Ken, 276
Pentecostal movement, 205
Perkins, Dwight, 12
Perlman, Jim, 270, 271
Peterson, Forrest, 272, 275
Petrakis, Harry, 268
Phagan, Mary, 48
Phillips, Christopher, 7
Phoenix AZ, 214
Pichaske, David, xx, 228
Pigeons of Buchenau and Other Stories (Pichaske), 273
Pine Tree Treaty, 62
The Pit (Norris), 268
Pittsburgh, 178, 180, 185
place-names: as linguistic symbols, 7
population (mid-nineteenth-century): accuracy of data about, 74–75; African Americans, 83–84; Canadian-born immigrants, 88; concentrations of U.S.-born settlers, 77, 79; Connecticut natives, 78, 80; cultural

community in, 140–41; similarity of, 132, 137; social structure of, 138–39; spirit of, 129–30; studies of, xvi–xvii; tourism in, 137, 138; urban design, 134; vertical dimension of, 132; voluntary organizations in, 139; women's occupations in, 139; zoning restrictions, 134. *See also* cities

Smiley, Jane, 269, 333

Smith, Abe, 48

Smith, Adam, 289, 290

Smith, Elder Lucy, 203

Smith, Henry Nash, 6, 7

Smith, Joseph, Jr., 184, 205

Smith, William, 41

The Social Order of a Frontier Community (Doyle), 98

So Long, See You Tomorrow (Maxwell), 269

Song of the North Country (Pichaske), 277

Soto, Hernando de, 180

South Bend IN, 215

South Dakota: civic society in, 98; voluntary associations in, 97

Southwest Minnesota (Pichaske), 277

Spencer, Robert, 12

The Spirit of the Laws (Montesquieu), 283

sports: academic studies of, xvii–xviii, 165, 171; in American history, role of, 161–62; collective identity and, 161, 164–65, 167; in colleges, 162, 163–64; critical nostalgia and, 165–69, 171; discrimination in, 162; girls in, 166–68, 167–68, 173n19; in high schools, 166–67, 168–69, 173n18; historiography of, 162–64; media coverage of, 169–70, 173n14; social relations and, 162–63; television network, 163; Title IX legislation on, 166, 168

sports writing, 169–70

Stalin, Joseph, 323

Stark, Gene, 275

State Fair (film), 189, 190, 333, 335

state fairs, 334–36

steel production, 218

Steiner, Michael C., xiii, 270

Steubenville OH, 212

St. Joseph MO, 214

St. Louis MO: industrial development of, 214; Louisiana Purchase Exposition in, 219; population of, 211, 213; race riots in, 219; in urban hierarchy, 212

Stone, Henry Lane, 42

Stone City Art Colony, 228, 233

Strong, Phil, 333, 335

Stryk, Lucien, 268

Stuntz, William J., 121

Successful Farming (magazine), 336

Suckow, Ruth, 230

Sullivan, Louis, 8, 10

The Summer of Ordinary Ways (Helget), 275

Sundown at Sunrise (Seifert), 276

Sutherland, Robert, 270

Sutter, Bart, 271

Sykes, Roosevelt, 261

Taft, Robert, xxii, 314, 321, 322, 323, 324, 325, 326

Taft, William Howard, 321–22

Tampa Red. *See* Whittaker, Hudson

Tanner, Helen, 60

Teaching the Commons (Theobald), 273

Teaford, Jon, xix, 121

Telleen, Maurice, 228–29

Terrell, W. H. H., 43

Their Father's God (Rølvaag), 199

Theobald, Paul, 273